THE
KITCHEN
ANSWER BOOK

ALSO BY HANK RUBIN

Spain's Cause Was Mine:
A Memoir of an American Medic in the Spanish Civil War

THE
KITCHEN
ANSWERBOOK

Answers to All of Your Kitchen and Cooking Questions

HANK RUBIN

CAPITAL
BOOKS, INC.
Sterling, Virginia

Capital Books, Inc.
P.O. Box 605
Herndon, Virginia 20172-0605

Library of Congress Cataloging-in-Publication Data
Rubin, Hank.
    The kitchen answer book: answers to all of your kitchen and cooking questions
    Hank Rubin.– 1st ed.
        p.cm.
    ISBN 1-892123-74-6
    1. Cookery. 2. Kitchens. I. Title.
    TX651 R68 2002
    641.5–dc21   2001055985

Printed in the United States of America on acid-free paper that meets the American National Standards Institute Z39-48 Standard.

First Edition

10 9 8 7 6 5 4 3 2 1

For Lillian, without whom I couldn't have completed this book.

CONTENTS

ACKNOWLEDGMENTS

After some years at Washington High I moved to John O'Connell Trade School where I worked with Chef Peggy Goodell, a teacher to whom I am indebted for the knowledge she shared with me. I also owe thanks to Richard Lucchesi of Quilici Meats in San Francisco who taught me more than I ever thought I wanted to know about meat.

I owe a special debt to my students, who researched the questions I put to them and kept asking for more. Without them, I wouldn't have compiled page after page of questions, which after a while seemed to beg to be compiled into this book.

INTRODUCTION

This book had its origin some ten years ago when I began volunteer teaching at Washington High School in the San Francisco School District. The class, Advanced Food Preparation, was designed to teach students every aspect of the hotel and restaurant business, but its main focus was on cooking. At the beginning of each day I would pose a question about food and ask that the students research it and bring the answer back at our next session. These questions ranged from fun ones such as, "If you put an egg in a glass of water and it floats, what does it tell you?" to more serious ones such as, "What should you look for when you buy asparagus?" or "What is a good way to cook garlic and avoid mushiness while retaining flavor?"

My own experience—five years as a food technologist and technical director for food processing companies, fifteen years as restaurateur and executive chef, and some seven decades cooking at home—made it relatively easy at first to come up with questions. The thirty-plus years that I have been a professional wine writer and had to pay attention to how food and wine could complement each other also helped. But the class was voracious, and I needed more and more questions. I began searching food magazines and books, focusing during my regular visits, and examining the food served when eating out.

The questions piled up—the answers too, a bit more slowly, but they did come, and five thousand were there before I expected. To put them in book form and make them more accessible, I worked them into thirteen chapters: Baking; Chocolate, Coffee and Tea; Dairy; Eggs; Fruits and Nuts; Grains, Beans and Pasta; Meat; Poultry; Seasoning and Oils; Stocks, Sauces and Soups; Vegetables; and Utensils.

CHAPTER ONE

BAKING

MEASURING

What is the biggest source of failure in baking?

Inaccurate measurement causes most failures.

What is the most accurate way to measure?

Doing it by weight is the simplest and most accurate.

Why isn't measuring by volume as accurate as measuring by weight?

When measuring by volume, one baker dips the measuring cup directly into the bag of flour, then levels it off with a finger; another spoons the flour into the measuring cup, taps it on the counter, then levels it off with a metal spatula. These methods generate two different amounts even though the cup size is the same.

Does this variation apply when measuring sugar?

This difference is true for sugar, particularly for brown sugar. For example: 1 cup powdered sugar equals two grams, while 1 cup brown sugar equals 100 grams (even though they are comparable in sweetness).

Why aren't eggs accurate when chosen by size and number?

The designation of "large" for eggs varies in different parts of the country. It may not be very important in making a pastry cream but can make or break the results in baking. "Large" eggs should equal two ounces each. But in a dozen some may be lighter, some heavier.

When is a weighing scale especially useful?

1. When doubling or halving a recipe.
2. It can also be used to determine whether the division of batter for separate pans is equal.

How should you proceed if no scale is available?

Scoop enough of the sifted flour in the dry measuring cup until it mounds slightly over the top. Then level with a flat metal spatula. Scooping and leveling without sifting can add more flour than the recipe calls for.

What is the second most problematic baking measurement?

The other *mis*-measurement is of the baking temperature, because the temperature dials of the oven frequently may be off as much as twenty-five to fifty degrees.

How do professional bakers measure their ingredients?

By weighing.

Can recipes be halved or doubled?

Only some are fail-safe, such as dips, spreads, uncomplicated soups, stir-fries, salads, simple salad dressings, sherbets and ice creams. Seasoning must be tasted in any case, so start with less and add as necessary.

Should the original amounts be changed exactly when recipes are halved or doubled?

Halved: Reduce the amount of liquid by one-third instead of one-half of the liquid.

Doubled: Multiply the liquid by one and a half, not twice the amount, to avoid a soupy result.

Can recipes for baking be doubled?

Don't double; rather, make two batches.

Can recipes for baking be halved?

Halving can usually be done, but it may be necessary to halve an egg, which is not easy.

How can an uncooked egg be halved?

Break the egg into a measuring cup, *lightly* whip it into a liquid and then measure.

What volume should be expected from large eggs?

5 large eggs	= 1 cup
5 large yolks	= ⅓ cup
5 large whites	= ⅔ cup

Is price an indicator of accuracy in measuring cups?

Cost is not necessarily an indicator of accuracy of the cup.

What kind of cup should be chosen for measuring?

A metal cup is good for dry ingredients, a glass (Pyrex) one for liquid.

How should the measuring glass be held?

For liquids, view at eye level.

How can you measure fat without a scale?

1. A stick of butter equals eight tablespoons, which are usually marked on the paper wrapping.
2. Oil should be measured in a Pyrex measuring cup.
3. Pack solid shortening into a dry measuring cup.

DEFINITIONS & FUNCTIONS

What is a lean dough?

A lean dough can be formed with only flour, yeast and water.

What kind of dough is needed for crusty breads?

The formula for a French baguette contains only small amounts of sugar and fat, if any. Breads made this way tend to have a chewier texture, more bite and a crisp crust.

Which breads are considered lean?

Hard rolls, French and Italian style breads, whole wheat, rye and pumpernickel breads.

What is a rich dough?

A rich dough is produced by the addition of shortening or tenderizing ingredients such as sugars, syrups, butter, oil, whole eggs, egg yolks, milk or cream. It should have a cake-like texture. It may be golden in color and have a crust that is very soft.

What is it used for?

Challah (egg bread) and egg rolls are examples.

Which is more difficult to work with?

The lean dough is usually softer and a little more difficult to work during kneading and shaping.

What is the function of fat in baking?

Fat makes baked goods tender by coating the proteins in flour and preventing them from joining together to form tough strands of gluten. Fat also contributes to moistness.

What is the role of fat in flaky pastry?

To keep the thin dough layers separate.

What happens when fat is creamed with sugar?

It helps to lighten and aerate the dough and carries flavor.

What can be done to make a creamy shortening mix more easily with a sugary substance?

Add a few drops of water to the mixture.

What are the effects of butter in baking?

Its 80–84% milk fat gives flavor.

What is the downside of butter?

It has a low melting point and can burn easily.

What is a croustade?

An edible container of a shaped, fried pastry or a toasted, hollowed loaf of bread that is filled with creamed meat or vegetables or other ingredients. Small croustades may be used as hors d'oeuvres.

Which is better for baking, salted or unsalted butter?

Unsalted is best. Salted butters vary too much in salt content, and if there is too much salt it could provide more gluten development than wanted.

Does margarine differ from butter in baking?

Margarine is made from either vegetable or animal fats combined with milk or cream, but some are 100% vegetal. It has a higher melting point than butter but doesn't contribute the same texture or taste as butter. Use unsalted margarine.

What does a solid vegetable shortening contribute?

It is 100% fat and produces tenderness because of its malleable consistency. Its lack of liquids gives it more shortening power than butter.

What is solid vegetable fat good for?

Very high, tender, flaky-textured pastry such as pie crust.

What is lard?

It is a shortening rendered from pig fat, 100% animal fat.

What is lard best for?

For savory meat pies.

What are lard's negatives?

It is not good for desserts because of its flavor, and it is not as plastic as vegetable shortening.

Is vegetable oil good for baking?

Adding vegetable oil together with solid fat helps to coat the flour particles and thus reduce the strength of the flour protein. As a result, the gluten is less likely to develop a strong, continuous network.

Should oil be used for flaky pastry?

No. It contributes to tenderness but not flakiness.

What are the functions of salt in baking?

1. Primarily, it gives flavor.
2. In yeast dough and breads it helps strengthen the gluten to bond in a tighter fashion and thus traps the gases from the yeast better, resulting in a higher rise.

What is acidulated water?

Water to which a little vinegar, lemon or lime juice or wine has been added.

What is bottled water?

Water that meets all federal and state standards, is sold for human consumption, is sealed in a sanitary container, cannot have any sweetener or chemical additives and must be calory and sugar free. If any additions are more than 1% by weight the water must be labeled soda water.

What are the various bottled waters?

Artesian: bottled from a well that has a water-bearing layer with a rock basis.

Mineral: one with not less that two hundred ppm (parts per million) of total dissolved solids. No minerals added.

Purified: by distillation, deionization or reverse osmosis or other process that has removed the dissolved minerals.

Sparkling: has the same amount of carbon dioxide gas as when it emerged from its source.

Spring: from an underground formation and collected only at the source and has all the physical properties as when it came to the surface.

Deionized, distilled, reverse osmosis can be labeled so if one of the processes was used to purify the water.

What should be done routinely when taking water from the tap?

In the morning let the water run for a few minutes to get rid of any accumulated minerals.

What acidic products are used in pastries or in marinades?

Vinegar, lemon juice, wine, yogurt, buttermilk, sour cream or lemon juice.

What is the purpose of the acidic product?

1. To prevent discoloration of cut fruits and vegetables (apples, pears, mushrooms, potatoes—two tablespoons per pint).
2. To set eggs quickly and keep the white snowy white (one-quarter cup lemon juice or vinegar per quart).

What are the functions of sugar in baking?

1. Sweetens.
2. Adds to the volume.
3. Affects the grain and texture.
4. Rubbing the sugar against the fat helps to trap air cells in the fat.
5. During baking the sugar caramelizes, coloring the crust.
6. Since it traps moisture it contributes to a cake's freshness.
7. Aids in the functioning of yeast.

What is a leavener?

An agent that causes dough or batter to rise through the release of carbon dioxide gas.

What are some leaveners?

Examples are baking powder, baking soda and yeast.

What are some examples of unleavened bread?

Flat matzos, Indian naan, grilled pizza and Scandinavian crisps.

What is yeast?

A living organism that is packaged in suspended animation.

What is active dry yeast?

Sold as a granular powder and dated for freshness, it feeds on the sugars in the dough and releases carbon dioxide.

What is cooking en papillote?

It means baking in sealed parchment paper or foil.

What are the advantages of cooking en papillote?

1. No loss of nutrients.
2. No loss of flavor.
3. No addition of fat is necessary.
4. The food keeps its moisture.
5. Flavoring agents such as fruit juice concentrate, miso paste or fresh basil can be added in the preparation without losing their character.

What is meant by creaming?

Beating the sugar and fat together at room temperature to incorporate air and mix thoroughly before adding the other ingredients. This ensures that a cake will be light and fluffy.

How is creaming done?

Mix a solid fat, usually at room temperature, with sugar until light and fluffy, then add the rest of the ingredients in a specific order until the batter is formed. This can be done by machine and will yield a fine-grained texture and a velvety cake.

How warm should the ingredients be?

The optimal temperature for the ingredients is 70 °F.

What kind of butter should be used?

Use unsalted butter that, when it is at the right temperature, is waxy, smooth and pliable. Use one with the highest butter fat content.

Should the egg yolks and whites be added separately after creaming?

It's not necessary, but using whole eggs produces a firm, moist texture, and the extra step of separating produces no noticeable increase in volume. Then the rest of the liquid ingredients can be added after the eggs.

How should eggs be added when machine whipping a mixture?

It's best if eggs are added by hand one at a time, which gives better control and keeps the batter creamy and smooth without disturbing its airy volume.

Why is hand-whipping good?

Doing it this way the fat actually surrounds the flour and the suspended air bubbles are held in place, resulting in maximum volume.

Why does vegetable shortening possess good creaming properties?

It is 100% fat, so it is able to trap more air and produce a lighter texture than butter, which is 80–85% milk fat.

What is docking?

Putting small holes in dough or a crust to allow steam to escape.

What can happen if salted butter is used to grease baking pans?

Baked goods may stick to the pan.

Can baking be done in a convection oven?

Yes for muffins, cookies and some cakes.

What is the advantage of a convection oven in baking?

Large batches can be done at once, because two levels of oven racks can be filled.

What is a cobbler?

A fruit dessert that is oven baked for about ten minutes, with a layer of fruit topped with a cake batter or biscuit-like topping. It should not be over-baked; bake only until it is golden brown all over and the fruit juice is bubbling up around the edges, becoming shiny and slightly thickened.

What is a grunt?

A fruit stew baked in a casserole with a steamed topping.

What is the function of water in making a grunt?

Water is added to create steam during the baking to cook the dumplings that are dripped on top. The dish is then covered and returned to the oven to steam.

What is a galette?

A round, flat cake of flaky dough topped with fruit, jam, nuts or cheese.

What is bruschetta?

Thick slices of crusty, Italian-style bread grilled or baked with toppings of olive oil, vegetables, creamy cheese or herbs.

What is a frangipane?

A pastry of egg yolk, butter, milk and flours flavored with ground almonds; it is used as a topping or filling.

BAKING AIDS

What should you consider when substituting ingredients in a recipe?

1. Will the substitute be compatible in flavor?
2. Will it fulfill the same functions, such as binding or leavening?
3. Finally, will it give the desired texture?

What can be used for a quick substitute for a pastry bag?

Cut a small hole in the corner of a Ziplock bag.

Why should the salt not be sprinkled into the dough in baking?

If dissolved in a little liquid it will be distributed more evenly.

What can you do when the available butter crumbles or is granular, or when tiny water droplets form around it, indicating poor plasticity?

Blend one-half butter with one-half solid shortening.

Why must the eggs and liquids be at 70 °F?

Only at this temperature can they combine and penetrate one another to give a smooth, homogeneous batter.

What happens if the ingredients are too cold?

If an ingredient is too cold, such as an egg refrigerated at 42 °F, it can solidify the finely dispersed butter that is holding the millions of bubbles. These bubbles then become rigid, pop open and collapse, letting the air escape.

What happens if ingredients are too warm?

The same results as described above for ingredients that are too cold also occur when the temperature is too warm.

What happens if eggs are warmer than 70 °F?

If eggs are warmer than 70 °F, the batter will suddenly become wet and lumpy.

Why do some recipes call for soaking raisins or currants before adding them to a batter?

Called plumping, it is done to overcome dryness and also to keep dried fruits plump when they are baked.

Why are cakes and cookies often cooled on a rack?

To cool faster and more evenly, by allowing air to circulate around them.

Why is this necessary?

This prevents condensation and thus protects crispness.

How can pans be prepared for baking so that the dough won't stick?

1. Grease them evenly with shortening, butter or oil.
2. Make sure that no spots are left uncovered.
3. Dust lightly with flour.
4. Chill the greased pan in the freezer for five to ten minutes before adding the dough.

What will over-greasing a baking pan do?

It will result in under-browning.

Why is parchment paper better than waxed paper for lining a baking pan?

Pros: 1. It is paraffin coated on both sides and is moisture proof and grease proof.
2. It stays flat and smooth when wet.
3. It is good for candying and gooey foods.

Con: It is more expensive.

What can be used if sufficient cooling racks are not available?

Try using inverted muffin tins. Just place the pies and cakes on the upside-down tins.

When mixing batter, how can the batter be prevented from climbing up the beaters?

Spray the beaters with Pam or similar nonstick cooking spray.

How can dried fruits and/or nuts added to the batter be prevented from settling to the bottom during baking?

Before adding them, coat the fruits or nuts with a little of the flour that is being used in the recipe.

How can a moist cake or cookies be achieved?

Cake: Add 2 tablespoons corn oil honey to the mixture.
Cookies: Add a teaspoon of jelly to the batter.

How can good rising of dough be achieved in a cold, drafty room?

Set a heating pad on medium heat and then put the pan with the dough on the pad. Or turn on the oven for a few minutes, turn it off again, set the pan inside the slightly warmed oven.

How can a glaze be put on rolls and cakes?

Brush before baking with:

Rolls: One egg white beaten lightly with one tablespoon milk.

Cake: A small amount of brown sugar dissolved in one tablespoon milk.

What is a good way to avoid dark spots (overbaking) on the bottom of cookies, pastry cases, etc.?

Halfway through the baking, loosen the cookies from the baking sheet by sliding a metal spatula under them.

Why does loosening them help?

Loosening allows heat to be distributed evenly top and bottom.

Is it possible to over-mix dough?

Yes. What happens if mixed too long is that the gluten polymers will begin to break down; then the dough becomes sticky and yields a dense, coarse crumb.

How can you keep dough from sticking to the dough hook or clogging the beater?

1.   Spray the hook with a little oil.
2.   Divide the dough and do the mixing in halves or thirds.

What effect does a glass pan have on baking?

Food cooks faster in glass than it does in metal, so reduce the oven setting by 25°.

What will a shiny pan do to pie crusts?

Pie crusts will not brown properly if you use a shiny pan.

What pans should be used to yield browned crusts?

To brown a crust use glass or dull-finished pans because unlike the shiny variety they do not reflect the heat.

How is heavy, translucent parchment paper used?

1.   To line baking pans and sheets to prevent sticking, making removal easier.
2.   For cooking en papillote.

BAKING SODA, BAKING POWDER AND CREAM OF TARTAR

What is baking soda?

It is an alkaline chemical (sodium bicarbonate), a leavener, derived from a naturally occurring mineral called toona that was left behind after the evaporation of salt lakes.

What is its function in baking?

When exposed to moisture and acid, such as buttermilk, yogurt, cream of tartar or fruit juice, it produces carbon dioxide. This is the expanding gas that stretches the dough.

What does the baking soda do when used with baking powder?

In recipes calling for both baking soda and baking powder, the soda neutralizes the acidity of the other ingredients.

Can baking soda be used alone?

If an acidic agent such as buttermilk, yogurt or molasses is also present, baking soda can be used alone.

What happens when too much baking soda is used?

1. It can cause loss of volume at the end of baking.
2. It can give a bitter taste.
3. The dough might collapse at the end of baking.

What effect will too little baking soda have?

This results in loss of leavening, therefore heaviness of texture.

Will baking soda deteriorate with age?

Soda doesn't deteriorate with age.

How does baking soda react to acidic components?

It reacts as soon as it comes into contact with most acids, such as buttermilk, honey and cream of tartar, so that once baking soda is added the batter should be baked immediately, before its action is lost.

What is baking powder?

A mixture of baking soda, a moisture absorber such as cornstarch and an acidic agent such as cream of tartar. Together they act as a leavener.

What do its components do?

The soda prevents the mixture from caking, and some acidic agent (such as cream of tartar) counterbalances the alkalinity.

Is baking powder equally stable?

It will deteriorate. To test for its effectiveness, add a teaspoon to half a cup of hot water. It should bubble immediately if still effective.

What are cautions for using baking powder?

1. Check the date on the bottom of the can to make sure it isn't too old.
2. Store in a cool, dry place.
3. Remove the powder from the container only with a dry spoon.

Why is double-action baking powder good for making cakes?

It contains two different acids that are designed to create carbon dioxide gas slowly and over a long period of time so that a cake, for instance, will have time to bake and set before all the bubbles are dissipated.

Why is double-acting baking powder not good for making waffles?

Waffles, on the other hand, are baked quickly, so the rise is desired at room temperature.

What can be substituted for baking power?

Use baking soda plus an acidic ingredient (such as buttermilk) to form a quick-action baking powder.

What is cream of tartar, and how is it used?

It is a common, solid salt of tartaric acid, a natural by-product of wine making. It acts as a stabilizer when beaten with egg whites.

What is its effect?

It makes a higher, lighter cake. It also acts as a bleach to make the cake whiter.

How does cream of tartar work?

Chemically it adds hydrogen ions to create a more stable molecular structure. It works as a coagulant. It is a component of baking powder in which its acidity reacts with the alkali of the powder to set loose the bubbles of gas that cause the dough to rise.

FLOUR

Do ingredient lists from different producers or different locations have the same meaning?

Flour labeled "all-purpose" will vary in protein content; in the southern United States it will usually be low in protein, while in the North it could be medium in protein, and in Canada, high.

What is gluten?

A plastic and elastic compound. Under pressure it will change its shape, such as in kneading. It tends to resume its original shape when the pressure is removed. Because of its delicate balance of gluten, wheat dough can expand to incorporate carbon dioxide from the yeast and yet put up enough resistance so that it doesn't thin to the breaking point.

What would happen if the dough were entirely elastic?

The gas would migrate to the surface and escape, or it would accumulate in a few pressurized pockets and the bread would come out heavy and coarse.

Why is the gluten in flour important?

Gluten is the "glue" that holds dough together and imparts texture. It is related to the protein content of the flour. Proteins are the building blocks of gluten, which comes into being when the flour is moistened and then mixed or kneaded. It then forms an elastic and stretchable or rubbery product.

Where is the presence of gluten particularly essential?

1. Light, airy breads or a chewy pasta get their texture from the presence of gluten.
2. Flaky, crisp pie crusts or tender cakes owe their texture to the absence of gluten or low gluten content.

What is high-gluten flour?

One milled from a high protein wheat and has 14% gluten. It is used by commercial bakers.

What are tips for developing gluten properly?

1. Moisten the flour just enough to form a cohesive mixture. Too little and the dough will fall apart and more gluten than desired will develop.
2. Without some manipulation, gluten can't develop. The more manipulation the more the gluten will be activated.
3. Use correct temperature of liquid, rolling surface and resting surface, as cold retards development, heat promotes it.
4. Rest puff pastry when it shows signs of resistance to rolling.

How does the percentage of protein affect the gluten formation?

The higher the percentage of protein in the flour, the more gluten will be developed, and the gluten formed will be stronger.

Which are high-protein flours?

Durum flours are high in protein.

Which are low-protein?

Cake flours are low in protein.

Which are in-between?

All-purpose flours are in-between.

What is the function of the flour?

It not only provides protein but is also important in the absorption of water. The more protein, the more water absorbed.

What is the effect of sugar on gluten formation?

Since sugar molecules are in intense competition with flour molecules for the small amount of liquid, higher sugar content slows gluten formation.

What happens if you over-knead dough in a mixer?

The dough will overheat and the gluten will break down.

What should be done if the dough becomes warmer than room temperature?

Stop and let it rest for 5–10 minutes until it cools.

Why must flour be aged?

It needs a few months of maturing for the gluten to develop, the factor that gives the flour its strength, but the manufacturer of the flour usually takes care of this.

Why is wheat the main source of flour?

Wheat is the only grain whose proteins form a gluten strong enough to produce raised breads.

Is wheat flour consistent from brand to brand?

Only relatively so, and the same brand can vary from crop to crop and the market the miller wants to cater to.

What is hard wheat?

Planted in the spring and harvested in the fall, it is grown in climates with short, hot summers. The flour is low in starch and high in protein, causing good gluten development. These are known as *strong* or *bread* flours. Durham is the particular variety for producing semolina, a high-gluten flour also used in pasta making.

How is soft wheat different?

It is planted in winter and harvested the following summer, usually in southern climates where there is a long growing season. Its flour is lower in protein, higher in starch. It is also known as *weak* flour and includes cake and pastry flours, which are used for cakes, biscuits and some pastry dough such as pie crust.

What is the advantage of stone grinding in making flour?

The slow milling, using a granite stone mill, disperses the wheat bran evenly throughout the flour. This allows the flour to stay cooler than when ground with steel rollers. It has more nutrition and flavor.

How do the large, commercial flour mills grind wheat?

They use moisture and huge steel rollers for grinding grain.

What is pastry flour?

It is made from soft wheat, and it has a protein content of about 8%, which makes it unsuitable for bread making but good for cookies, pies and galettes.

How does cake flour differ?

It is finer still, with 6–8% protein content. Bleached, made from soft wheat, it has weak strength. Use for cakes and cookies. Its acidic balance helps set eggs in baking and results in a smooth-textured cake.

What happens when cake flour is used with baking powder?

When used with baking powder, cake flour can result in a metallic aftertaste if the batter is not enriched with fat or eggs.

What is whole wheat flour?

Flour made from whole grain that contains bran and the wheat germ. The flour often includes corn and rye.

Is it stable?

Wheat flour needs refrigeration to keep.

How does graham flour differ?

This is a flour named after Sylvester Graham that can be used interchangeably with whole wheat but is milled very coarsely with some flecks of bran, which gives it a rich, sweet flavor.

What is rye flour?

A strong grain from the rye plant, which contains some gluten.

How is rye flour used?

For bread making and, in Poland, for making vodka.

What is medium rye?

Medium rye is a mixture of light and dark flour and is best for all-purpose rye bread. It is the one found in the supermarkets.

How does pumpernickel differ from rye flour?

Pumpernickel is a coarse, dark rye flour with much of the bran left in, and it yields a very dense bread.

What is barley flour?

Flour ground from pearl barley (the whole barley with the outer husk removed).

How is self-rising flour different?

It has baking powder and salt added at the mill, and it is used for biscuits and sometimes for cakes and pastry. It is cheaper to make your own.

What is bread flour?

Made from hard wheat with 12–13% protein, it is strong, unbleached, and thought to have more flavor.

What happens with bread flour that has been refrigerated a day or more?

Dough made with unbleached flour turns gray after refrigerator storage of a day or two, but this color change doesn't otherwise affect the dough.

What is all-purpose flour?

This bleached flour is a mixture of soft and hard wheat, of medium strength, about 10.5% protein, and has a dough conditioner that makes the dough more acidic and the gluten more extendable when rolled. Used for cakes, cookies, bread and pastries.

Is all-purpose flour used by professional bakers?

No, professional bakers use flours specific to each task.

Why is it impossible to give exact flour measurement for yeast dough?

Flours vary in their abilities to absorb moisture and develop gluten and, as well, yeasts vary in strength by brand, age and storage conditions.

What is the difference between using whole wheat and white flours?

Whole wheat: More nutritious, more fiber, more interesting texture.

White: Will rise to greater height; more delicate flavor, which is particularly useful in making cakes.

If you don't measure flour by weighing what is the next best way?

Stir the flour in the container and then lightly spoon it into the measuring cup, finally level the top level with a knife.

How accurate is the term "pre-sifted" on the label of flour?

Not very. Disregard. While it might have been triple sifted, it no longer can be considered sifted after being packaged and stacked on the grocery shelf.

How should flour be sifted?

A single sift will not eliminate all lumps, even though flour appears smooth. Either use a triple sifter or use a single sifter and repeat three times.

Should modern dry flour be sifted?

Not unless the recipe specifies it.

When a recipe calls for sifted flour should it be sifted before or after measuring?

If the recipe says: One cup sifted flour, measure after sifting.

One cup flour sifted, measure before sifting.

Should the leavening and salt be added before or after sifting?

Before, for a better distribution.

How should white flour be stored?

It is best stored in a tightly sealed glass jar or metal canister to protect against its three enemies: moisture, air and pests.

Is storage for whole wheat any different?

Whole wheat (including other whole grain flours such as rye) become rancid quickly, so store them in an airtight container in the refrigerator.

What must be done when using a yeast-leavened recipe?

First bring the flour back to room temperature so as not to inhibit growth of the yeast.

How should roller-ground meal be stored?

Store roller-ground meal in an airtight container in a cool, dark place. Store water-ground meal in the refrigerator to prevent rancidity.

What is the difference between bleached and unbleached flour?

Bleaching removes the light yellow color in flour caused by the same carotenoid pigments that are also found in potatoes and onions. Chlorine dioxide is used to speed the bleaching process, but the chemical residue that remains in the flour is well below the FDA levels allowed.

Is the color difference significant?

The color has no significance in a practical or nutritional way. Freshly ground white flour is naturally yellowish.

How much of flour is starch, how much protein?

Starch is 70–75% of the flour, protein 6–20%.

How can you tell the protein content?

When buying flour, check the label for the protein content. Sometimes the same brand's proportions may vary from large to small packages with the assumption that small bags will be used for pastry or gravies and sauces while the larger are used primarily for bread.

YEAST

What is the function of yeast?

Yeasts are living organisms that become active when they feed on starch or sugar and then give off carbon dioxide gas as they convert their food to energy. The gas is what is trapped in a gluten mesh and causes the dough to rise.

How much live yeast remains after baking?

Eventually the oven heat kills all the yeasts.

What is instant yeast?

Yeast that is dried at a much lower temperature so that almost all of the yeast cells are active. This makes for a vigorous, fast action.

How does instant yeast vary from regular yeast?

1. Instant yeast is a different strain that is more vigorous.
2. Both are dried in a manner so that live yeast cells are encapsulated inside of dead cells. Adding warm water releases the live cells.

3. The drying process for instant yeast is done at a lower temperature and thus has only about 5% dead cells (as opposed to 25% dead cells in a regular), and, therefore, the warm water is absorbed more quickly.
4. Instant yeast has a shorter shelf life than regular yeast.

What is the difference in usage?

Instant yeast does not need to be soaked in water to be proofed but can be added directly to the flour.

Does using instant yeast mean changing the amount called for in the recipe?

When using instant yeast, decrease the quantity of yeast by one-quarter (a packet of active dry yeast is replaced by two teaspoons of instant).

How does cake yeast work?

The choice depends on the needs of the baker. Fresh yeast, available in cake form, must be dissolved in water but remains fairly inactive until mixed with sugar or flour.

How should yeast be stored?

Store in a cool, dry place, paying attention to its expiration date.

Why is granular yeast the choice of most home bakers?

Granular is by far the most popular because it has a long shelf life and is sold in pre-measured packets. It requires very warm water, between 105–110 °F, to become active.

Is there a difference in taste between the two?

The difference in taste is virtually imperceptible.

Which yeast has the longer life?

Compressed. Even if refrigerated, however, it can only be expected to last a few weeks.

How is yeast examined?

1. If it's blotched or brown it is over the hill.
2. A sour odor is a negative indicator.
3. When crumbled it should break into jagged-edged pieces.

Is dry yeast fragile?

Dry yeast is much more stable and need not be refrigerated. Store the packets in a sealed jar in a cool, dark place, and it should last up to a year. Check the expiration date.

What are the necessary conditions for yeast to multiply and be active?

Warmth, moisture, food and oxygen.

How should yeast be prepared?

Add each packet of dry, granular type or cube of the fresh type to ¼ cup lukewarm (about 110°) water in a measuring cup. Give the yeast more nourishment by adding one-quarter teaspoon sugar (subtract this amount of sugar from the recipe). Blend the yeast, sugar and water and let stand for 10 minutes.

What is meant by "proofing" the yeast?

This is the activation of the yeast.

How can you tell if the yeast has lost its power?

If it has not actively bubbled when put into warm water, the yeast is impotent and should be discarded.

How long will active fresh yeast last?

In the refrigerator, about a year.

What happens if you use too much yeast?

Your bread has a strong yeasty flavor and can have a distorted form.

What is the effect of sugar on yeast dough?

It feeds the yeast, but also slows the rising.

Why use less yeast when baking at high altitudes?

At, say, 5,000 feet, there is less atmospheric pressure, therefore the carbon dioxide formed expands with greater force and more quickly. So, unless the amount is cut back, a very rough texture in the bread will result.

In hot weather what should be done?

1. Bake in the cool part of the day or in the evening.
2. Use chilled liquids in recipes.

What happens in cold weather?

1. If below 50 °F use lukewarm liquids (100–110 °F).
2. Use a candy or yeast thermometer to make sure the temperature is right.

Where is a good place to put the dough for rising?

Allow dough to rise in the oven. Turn on the oven to the lowest setting for a few minutes, then turn it off. Place the covered bowl on the oven rack and close the door.

What does it mean if a baked item tastes strongly of yeast?

It is an indication that the dough was not allowed sufficient time to proof before baking OR that too much yeast was used.

BISCUITS, ROLLS, SCONES AND DUMPLINGS

How do you prepare soft, fluffy biscuits?

1. Use a soft flour such as White Lilly or Gold Medal mixed with cake flour, which is soft.
2. Use butter for shortening.
3. Gently make balls of dough with lightly floured hands.
4. Work on well-floured surfaces.

What do you do for flaky biscuits?

1. Use a soft flour such as Hicks, King Arthur or Gold Medal flour combined with bread flour, which is strong.
2. Use two parts of butter for flavor, one part shortening or lard for texture, and make sure the shortening is cold.
3. Dough must be rolled out and cut, but use a light touch with the rolling pin.
4. Flatten the pieces of cold butter before adding to the dough.

How is a drop biscuit made?

More liquid in the batter results in a lighter consistency, so it can therefore be dropped by the spoonful onto the sheet. This eliminates the need for rolling and cutting the dough.

What happens if the biscuit dough is overworked?

The biscuits will be tough.

How can you prevent biscuits from becoming lopsided when baked?

1. Roll or pat the dough to an even thickness.
2. When cutting the biscuit, dip the cutter in flour, press firmly into the dough and remove without twisting, since the twisting distorts the dough and prevents the biscuit from rising evenly.

What might happen if dough scraps are used?

1. Biscuits made from gathered scraps are more likely to be uneven.
2. Avoid overworking the scraps to get an even thickness, as this causes toughness.

How can biscuits be reheated?

Put in a well-dampened paper bag, seal tightly and heat in the oven at a low temperature.

Why should biscuit pans not have sides like muffin tins?

So the heat will circulate more easily.

What will prevent biscuits from rising?

1. Over-kneading the dough. Limit it to ten to twelve strokes.

2. Over-worked scraps that are being put together.

3. The baking powder is not effective, perhaps too old.

What happens if a teaspoon of granulated sugar is added to the dry biscuit ingredients?

The biscuits will brown to a rich golden color.

Why do biscuits or scones made with honey or molasses keep better than those made with granulated sugar?

Both honey and molasses are hygroscopic (water-attracting), and thus they keep baked goods moist longer.

How do scones differ from biscuits?

Scones are rolled and cut, are usually enriched with eggs or cream and are sweeter than biscuits.

Why is it important to be very quick and limit the handling of dough when making scones?

The longer the handling, the tougher the scones will be.

What are shortcakes?

Small, tender, sweetened biscuits (although some are made larger and cut as for a pie). They should be light and airy and just barely brown.

What does "short" in shortcakes refer to?

The "short" refers to the crumble-in-the-mouth texture, which is achieved by working the fat into the flour until small granules are formed.

Why is a little sugar added to the fruit in making fruit shortcake?

The sugar draws out the natural juices, which are a good moistener for the shortcake biscuits.

Which is better for making dinner rolls—a short time, high temperature bake or a long, slow bake at low temperature?

Fast: Encourages tenderness in the finished product because the interior retains moisture that migrates to the surface.

Slow: This bake will provide a thick, heavy crust.

What can be done to prevent rolls from drying out too quickly?

Change half of the whole eggs called for by the recipe to yolks only.

What is necessary to produce a hard crust on rolls?

1. Commercially it is done with an oven that generates steam.

2. At home it is necessary to brush the surface of the roll with a wash or to spray mist over the surface.

What are dumplings?

A variety of soft dough or batter items. They may be steamed, poached, simmered, or deep fried and may be filled or not. This category includes Chinese dim sum.

What are cooking rules for dumplings?

1. Poach in boiling water or broth.
2. Drain and sauce.
3. Don't freeze them, as freezing toughens them and reduces the flavor.
4. They can be prepared ahead of time, then cooked when needed.

When dumplings are simmered what should the cooking procedure be?

The simmering should be gentle, lightly bubbly and without interruption.

BREADS

What are things to look for when buying bread?

1. Check the date and also see that the wrapper, if any, is tightly sealed (except for crusty baguette types).
2. Whole wheat breads are generally more interesting than white breads, and they are also more nutritious.

Are breads labeled "wheat breads" necessarily made exclusively with whole wheat flour?

Not necessarily. They could also contain white flour.

What are the guiding label indicators of whole wheat bread?

"Whole wheat" and "100% whole wheat."

Are today's white breads more nutritious than formerly?

While white breads have been less nutritious than whole wheat ones, in recent years the white flour used has been enriched with thiamin, riboflavin, iron and niacin in amounts equal to those of wheat breads.

How about fiber content?

Some white breads have more fiber than wheat breads.

What does the term "enriched" mean on a loaf of bread or a sack of flour?

It means that some eight nutrients have been added. However, since the miller originally took out about twenty-two nutrients it is like a thief robbing you of twenty-two dollars and then returning eight dollars.

What besides slices of bread can be used to make sandwiches?

Pita, tortillas, lettuce leaves, bagels, rolls, buns (hamburger).

Do breads made with oils and fats have a longer shelf life?

Breads made with oils and fats have a longer shelf life than those made strictly with flour and water, because the oils and fats hinder moisture loss.

What if there is too much oil used?

If there is too much oil or fat, the bread will be highly susceptible to rancidity.

What precautions must be taken if buttermilk is added to a bread batter in which baking powder has been used?

To maintain the proper level of alkalinity, add one-half teaspoon of baking soda per cup of buttermilk.

How do you give a bread a hard crust?

Brush with water during baking.

What should be used to make a golden brown crust?

If you want it to be golden brown, too, use beaten egg yolk instead of water.

For a softer crust?

Brush with an oil or fat such as melted butter.

How can cutouts of bread slices be cut with clean, sharp edges?

Freeze the bread first.

How can breads be flavored?

1. Use garlic or onion salt instead of regular salt.
2. Add chopped herbs, nuts or olives to the dough.
3. Add chopped dried fruit.

Is a crack down the middle of a fruit bread a sign of over-baking?

No, this often happens, especially if there are considerable nuts or fruits or, especially, moist fruits.

What does excess flour do to bread?

Creates dryness and denseness.

What does scalding milk mean?

Scalding has various definitions:

1. Heating to 180 °F.
2. Heating to just below 200 °F.
3. Heating until a thin skin appears on the milk surface.
4. Heating until tiny bubbles form around the edge of the pan.

Need you scald if the recipe calls for scalding and the milk has been pasteurized?

Until early this century milk was often scalded to kill bacteria that interfered with thickening of dishes such as custard or a béchamel sauce. Modern pasteurization does this but if you are pleased with a recipe calling for scalding, then don't change.

What must be watched for in scalding?

The modern function of scalding is to help bring up all the ingredients, such as flour or butter, to proper temperature. Low temperature will slow the rising process. However, very hot milk will kill the action of the yeast cells if the milk is not combined with other ingredients first to cool it down.

How should a bowl in which dough has been mixed be cleaned?

Use cold water, not hot.

What is the basic ratio of liquid to flour in making breads?

Use one-third cup liquid to one cup flour, but if the result is too dry, add a teaspoon of water; if the dough is too sloppy, add a tablespoon of flour.

What is a brioche?

A rich, light yeast bread made with butter and eggs, or a cake made from yeast dough. It is baked in a long, narrow pan or a special, fluted pan. It is traditionally used for sweet dishes.

What is a modern way to use brioche?

Stuff it with sausage and/or cheese.

When making a filled brioche what can be done to prevent the dough from pulling away from the stuffing?

1. Coat the stuffing material with flour.
2. Use fewer egg whites.
3. Chill the cheese just before adding so it is cold when put into the oven.

If sugar is used in the dough, what should be done to compensate for the reduced yeast activity that results?

Add extra yeast.

How does buttermilk affect bread dough?

1. Adds a tang to the flavor.
2. Produces a soft, light texture.
3. The bread will be sweeter.

What results from over-kneading?

Elasticity is lost as water is released.

What are the standards for corn bread as to thickness, sweetness and color?

It varies from one part of the United States to another.

How can you make cornbread more flavorful?

To get better flavor and better texture use water-ground or stone-ground meal instead of that ground with steel rollers.

Which type of cornmeal is more nutritious?

Water-ground is more nutritious, because it still contains the germ (embryo).

How should cornbread be made?

1. Add a little sugar to bring out the natural sweetness of the corn.
2. Stir the dry ingredients well.
3. Use buttermilk as the liquid.
4. Then stir minimally, just to moisten.
5. Pour the batter into a hot skillet in which the butter is sizzling.

How can you get a crisp crust for cornbread?

Preheat the greased pan before adding the dough and have the batter thin enough to pour into the pan.

Can oatmeal be used for making bread?

Since oatmeal is low in gluten it can only be used in combination with flour, about one-third oatmeal and two-thirds flour.

What is pumpernickel made from?

White and rye flours colored with caramel.

Does the term "rye bread" on the label mean 100% rye flour was used?

No. Usually rye bread is made with mostly white flour. Look for a label saying "Whole Rye Flour."

What are the effects of sugar in baking bread?

1. If the yeast dough contains more than two tablespoons of sugar per cup of flour the bread will be heavy, because the gluten-forming proteins of the flour combine with the sugar instead of with each other, preventing the formation of a good network in which the carbon dioxide gas from the yeast action can be caught to lighten the finished product.
2. Sugar added to cakes or pie crust makes them more tender.

What is challah? (also hallah, challa)

A traditional Jewish yeast bread (white) enriched with eggs, sweetened with honey and usually in braided form.

What is the effect of salt in bread dough?

1. It strengthens the gluten, which strengthens the dough.
2. It enhances flavor.

What does egg yolk accomplish?

Helps the gluten to develop and results in a better shelf life.

What do different liquids do in making bread?

Water:	Makes crisp crust, brings out wheat flavor.
Milk products (milk, buttermilk, cream):	Gives a soft brown crust, fine texture.
Fruit juices:	Add flavor and body.
Meat stock:	Add flavor, crisp crust.
Potato water:	Results in a moist, velvety bread
Beer:	Gives a strong flavor; the darker the beer, the stronger the flavor.

If beer for bread making has stood open long enough to lose its carbonation, will that make a difference?

No. The bubbles, or their lack, have little effect.

What are good flavoring ingredients for breads?

Cheese, seeds, nuts, lemon or orange zest, fruit, and liqueurs.

Which are better for flavoring, fresh or dried fruits?

Dried, as they are more intense, but they need to be moistened before adding.

What is the effect of honey in bread dough?

1. Helps to retain moisture and thus makes the bread last longer.
2. It destroys gluten and therefore must be used in limited amounts.
3. Some honeys destroy yeasts.

How can the protein value of bread be increased?

Remove one-half tablespoon of wheat flour and replace it with an equal amount of soy flour.

What is the difference between yeast breads and quick breads?

Quick breads use a chemical leavener rather than an organic one and thus do not require a rising period. Muffins, biscuits and scones are examples of quick breads.

Sponge

What is a bread sponge?

A mixture of sugar (optional), yeast, flour and liquid beaten smooth and allowed to rise a half hour to two days until it is light and spongy. It is then elastic (streaky gluten strands have formed), which makes for a fine texture and a light loaf.

Why the long resting period?

The resting time gives the flour enough time to absorb the liquid and thus less flour is needed.

Is the sponge used universally?

A sponge is often needed to produce a good texture when using low-gluten flour, such as rye or oat. Once the sponge is formed, the dough is prepared using same methods and materials as yeast bread.

When is the sponge omitted?

The sponge method is omitted in most bread recipes, particularly for sweet, more delicate breads, but the yeast gets started easily in the absence of salt (which inhibits it) and in the presence of plenty of oxygen. Gluten is formed when the sponge stretches in rising, which would otherwise come from kneading. This added elasticity makes the remaining ingredients more easily incorporated and kneading more easily accomplished.

Why are any salts and fats added after a sponge for bread has risen?

Because both salt and fat tend to inhibit yeast growth.

What does allowing the sponge to set overnight at room temperature or in the refrigerator up to four days accomplish?

This creates a dough that is finely textured with a tangy flavor, such as in Italian peasant bread.

Sourdough Starter

Will a sourdough starter made in the San Francisco Bay area produce a bread that tastes the same as one made with identical ingredients in Kansas City?

No, apparently a starter will be more pungent when kept near the sea.

What is important about the water used in making a sourdough starter?

It should not be chlorinated; use bottled spring water if necessary.

What kind of flour should be used for a sourdough starter?

Flour is not always necessary. Cornmeal gives the strongest flavor, mashed potatoes the mellowest.

What flours should be avoided?

Avoid bleached flour, because the bromates or other chemicals used in bleaching shorten the gluten strands that are necessary for good texture.

What liquid should be used for starters?

Bottled water (one with a zero or very low salt content) is probably best, because using it makes the starter less likely to spoil.

Which liquids should be avoided?

1. A milk starter will sometimes spoil.
2. Avoid tap water because of the chemicals it might contain.

How can a sourdough starter be made?

1. Soften the yeast with warm water.
2. Add flour to the mixture.
3. Stir well but don't overdo it and don't worry about some lumps in the mixture.
4. Cover the bowl loosely with plastic wrap that has been pricked a few times so air can enter.
5. Leave at room temperature (65–80 °F) for 3 days.
6. It will rise and fall one or more times.

How can you tell when the starter is ready to use?

When ready to use, the starter will smell slightly sour, be bubbly and look runny.

How can you ensure a crunchy crust for sourdough bread?

Spray with water to put a light, moist cover over the surface just before baking.

What is a dough relaxer?

A compound to make the gluten ingredients relax and make dough easier to roll. This is useful for items such as a thin pizza crust, croissants, light dinner rolls and more tender pancakes.

Baking

How can you tell when bread is fully baked?

Use an instant thermometer to check for a temperature of 190–205 °F.

How can egg wash be made so it doesn't streak?

Add a pinch of salt to 1 whole egg beaten with 1 tablespoon of water. The salt breaks down the egg white protein so that the wash is fluid and will give baked bread an even color without streaks.

How can the oven be used as a proofing box?

Heat the oven for 10 minutes at 200 °F and then turn off the heat.

How can you tell when a dough has risen sufficiently?

When it no longer springs back when poked lightly in the center with two fingers, that is, when it holds the indentations.

What will help create a big puffy loaf?

Use ceramic tiles or a pizza stone in the oven.

What size should the baking stone be?

At least four or five inches narrower than the oven, so it can be moved easily.

How can too-hard crusts be avoided in bread making?

Put a pan of water in the oven while baking.

Why should freshly baked breads be cooled on a rack?

So air can circulate around it as the bread cools, keeping the bread from becoming soggy.

How can a chewy crust be obtained?

Bake the bread at a lower temperature.

What does steam, when baking bread, accomplish?

1. Slows down the formation of the crust if steam is in the oven from the beginning (a pan of water in the oven), allowing the loaf to rise fully.
2. Introduced at the end of baking (spraying), it produces a hard crust by drying the surface.

What is the purpose of slashing the tops of loaves of bread that are to be baked?

1. Permits even dough expansion.
2. Allows steam in the loaf to escape.
3. Creates an attractive appearance.

When should the loaves be slashed?

Early in the rising.

What is focaccia?

A flat, round, usually large Italian bread that is brushed with olive oil and sprinkled with salt before baking.

How is focaccia made?

1. Roll or push the dough into a large round about ¾" thick.
2. Make shallow indentations in the dough with your fingertips.
3. Brush the surface with olive oil (plain or garlic-flavored).
4. Sprinkle with coarse salt.
5. Optional slits that are stuffed with rosemary or other herbs are made on the surface.
6. Bake at 450 °F until golden.

Storage

How should bread be stored?

1. If you plan to consume it within one day, store in a cool, dark spot, wrapped snugly to minimize loss of moisture.
2. If leftover bread has dried out but otherwise is still fresh, wrap it in a damp towel and refrigerate for six hours.

How can leftover bread be resuscitated?

Unwrap and heat the bread in a preheated 300° oven for 5–10 minutes, depending on thickness.

How should bread be frozen?

For longer storage freeze it, tightly wrapped, so that it doesn't absorb freezer odors.

How should frozen bread be used?

Without thawing, slice off what you will need and return the unused portion to the freezer. The less time exposed to air, the longer its storage life.

How should newly baked bread be stored?

1. Completely cool before wrapping to prevent the loaf from becoming soggy from excess moisture.
2. If the loaf is sliced, then refrigerate or freeze in a plastic bag with the air squeezed out of the bag.

How can bread be kept fresh when frozen?

Tuck a paper towel into the bag with the bread or rolls to absorb the moisture that the breads give off.

How should frozen bread be thawed?

There are four different methods:

1. Thaw in a microwave.
2. Defrost overnight in the refrigerator, then reheat in the oven at 400 °F for about 10 minutes.
3. Thaw at room temperature.
4. Take directly out of the freezer and toast.

How can soft bread be reheated in a microwave oven without become tough?

Wrap in paper toweling and heat for only five to ten seconds per roll or slice of bread. The towel will keep the moisture in without causing it to condense on the outside as will happen if wrapped in plastic. The bread will be barely warm when removed but in a few minutes the heat will have distributed evenly. Don't overheat.

What kind of bread should be reheated by this method?

This is good only for soft breads, *not* for hard or stale products.

What does freezing do to the nutritional value of bread?

Freezing may diminish the vitamin level somewhat but it protects the fatty ingredients such as nuts, wheat germ and cheese.

How can you prevent staleness or moldiness in a loaf of bread?

Refrigerated bread won't mold but it will get stale in about a day because the starch molecules change and cause the bread to harden. Freezing inhibits mold and also keeps the starch from setting.

If a slice of bread is moldy, is the rest of the loaf ok?

Probably not. Throw out the whole loaf.

How can moisture be reintroduced into French or Italian type hard breads?

Sprinkle the crust with cold water and place in a 350 °F oven for about 10 minutes.

How about regular breads?

Wrap in a damp cloth or towel for about 1 to 2 minutes and then place in a preheated 350° oven for about 10 minutes.

How should you make dry bread crumbs?

With dried or slightly stale bread (crust removal is optional) lightly pulverize in the food processor. If not sufficiently dry, first toast in a preheated 225 °F degree oven and then crumb in processor or blender.

How can you make soft crumbs?

Cube day-old bread and pulse into fine crumbs. If you need crumbs in a hurry, chop unsugared breakfast cereal, such as Shredded Wheat, in the blender or food processor.

How should you buy soft crumbs?

Select crumbs sold in a metal container, because those in plastic or paper containers will absorb moisture on the shelf.

How can bread crumbs be seasoned?

Add dried herbs, finely ground cheese, salt, pepper and then lightly bake.

Bagels

How is a bagel different from bread?

1. It is a round, yeast bread with a hole in the center.
2. It is boiled or steamed before baking.
3. The water reduces the starch and results in a chewy crust.
4. Many bagels are made with a variety of seeds on the surface, some are flavored and some on today's market are sweet.
5. Some bagels are made with eggs.

Are bagels freezable?

Yes. They can be sliced in half before freezing.

When making bagels, how long should they be boiled?

A minute at the most.

Bread Sticks

How can bread sticks be flavored?

1. Add seasoning such as seeds, garlic, or cheese (Parmesan or Roquefort) to the dough.
2. As they come out of the oven, sprinkle with a fruity olive oil and sprinkle with salt.
3. Roll the baked sticks in caraway or poppy seeds.

Can bread sticks be frozen?

Yes, but they need to be heated in a hot oven for about 5 minutes before use.

CAKES

How do you evaluate quality in a cake?

1. It should rise evenly.
2. It will just have begun to shrink away from the pan's side when it is done.
3. When cut there should be no large tunnels or air pockets.
4. Even though there is a large proportion of eggs in foamed cakes (such as angel food) there should not be a marked egg flavor.

Why must the mixing of cake batter be done carefully?

1. Excessive speed or friction from the mixer will damage the air bubbles. The butter will melt and thus cause a reduction in volume, resulting in a cake that is too dense.
2. The gas from the baking powder or soda makes for a lighter texture, but excessive beating breaks the gas bubbles apart.
3. The rough edges of the sugar crystals poke holes in the fat that then become air bubbles that give a lighter texture. Too much beating defeats this.

What is cake flour, and what are its cooking properties?

Finely milled, soft, winter wheat that is high in starch and low in gluten-forming protein. It has a lower acid level (pH), which results in a sweeter flavor and more velvety, finer crumbs. It supports more butter, sugar or chocolate in the recipe. It gives cookies a somewhat fragile texture.

How can you make cake flour?

Mix three parts all-purpose flour with one part corn or potato starch.

What must you guard against if you make your own cake flour?

Avoid too much corn or potato starch, as it will affect the structure of the cake as well as its flavor.

What are the advantages of cake flours?

Cake flours are made with flour-starch blends in varying proportions. They are generally more expensive than other flours. They produce lighter cakes in recipes using baking powder. They make little difference in cakes leavened with beaten eggs.

How should you grease a cake pan?

Brush melted, unsalted butter over the bottom of the pan with a pastry brush. Then lightly dust it with flour to prevent sticking.

Why shouldn't the sides of the pan be greased?

Most cakes rises more evenly when they can cling to the ungreased sides while baking.

Why is the size of the baking pan important?

Too large: Won't rise properly.

Too small: Not baked through, poor appearance.

How can the cake at the sides of the pan be loosened?

Loosen edges with a thin knife before removing cake from pan.

What can be used instead of greasing?

Greasing is not necessary if a baking pan lining paper is used.

What should you look out for in cake baking pans?

If the baking pan is too thin, the cake sides will likely scorch before the center is done.

What can be done if there are large bubbles in the batter?

If a few, oversized bubbles form in the batter when poured into the pan, rap the bottom of the pan a couple of times with your knuckles.

How can you tell if the cake is done?

Near the end of the estimated baking time, stick a toothpick or thin skewer into the middle of the cake. If it comes out moist, the cake needs more baking time.

How can a dome on the cake be prevented?

If the cake develops a dome when baked, try lowering the oven temperature the next time you make the recipe. This will mean that you will have to extend the baking time to compensate.

What is indicated if one side of the cake rises higher then the other.

If one side of the cake rises higher than the other side, the chances are that one edge of the pan was placed too close to an oven wall. Otherwise the oven is not level.

How can this be avoided?

Compensate by turning the pans 180 degrees halfway through the baking.

What causes a cake to fall?

1. Too much sugar, fat, liquid or baking powder.
2. Under mixing.
3. Under baking from too low a temperature setting.
4. Moving the cake during baking before it has a chance to set.

What causes excessive shrinkage?

1. Excess liquid or fat.
2. The baking pan is filled too high.
3. Overgreasing the pan.
4. Wrong oven temperature.

When rolling a cake, what is the best surface to work on?

Foil is better than plastic wrap or parchment paper because of its strength and flexibility.

What is the result of using liquid fat?

1. The cake tends to be denser and less high because the liquid fat disperses completely through the batter during mixing.
2. The texture is always moist and tender.

How can a cake be prevented from falling after the batter is in the baking pan?

Raise the pan, drop it suddenly onto the counter to raise the air bubbles.

How can icing be prevented from slipping off a cake as it is being applied?

Sprinkle the cake first with a little powdered sugar or flour.

Should frosted cakes be frozen?

It is better to frost them after they have thawed.

What is a good way to cut a cake while it is still hot?

Use unwaxed dental floss instead of a knife.

Why are shiny pans best for cake making?

They reflect the heat better, thus giving a tender crust.

What adjustments should be made if cocoa powder is to be added to a cake mixture?

1. Decrease the amount of flour (for two tablespoons cocoa, decrease flour one tablespoon).
2. Add a little sugar to counterbalance the cocoa's bitterness (about equal sugar to the amount of the cocoa).

What should be done to prevent the bottom of a cake from sticking to a plate?

Lightly sprinkle the plate with sugar.

How can the cut edges of a cake be prevented from drying?

Cover the cut edges with pieces of bread and attach them with toothpicks.

What should be done before removing the cake from the pan?

With mitts on, rotate the pan slightly and gently tap on the counter to see if the cake is released from the metal sides. If not, run a metal spatula or knife blade around the edges so that air can get under the cake.

How should a cake that is to be glazed be handled after baking?

1. Place on a rack to cool for five to seven minutes.
2. While it is cooling, heat the jam (glaze) just to simmering (cook two to three minutes) and then cool to evaporate some of the liquid and thicken it.

What precaution should be taken in making a glaze?

Do not overcook.

How hot should the glaze be?

Cool, but the consistency should not be as chewy as caramel candy.

How can the glaze be tested?

Put a drop of glaze that has been simmering on an ice cube. Then rub the glaze between your thumb and forefinger to feel the consistency.

How should you accomplish the glazing?

1. Cover the counter space with a sheet of foil to catch the drippings of the glaze.
2. Place a rack over the cake pan, invert it onto the rack and carefully lift off the pan.
3. Coat the surface with the glaze using a pastry brush.
4. Let it wait five minutes before adding the final translucent sugar glaze, using another pastry brush. If this coating is too thick, appearing opaque rather than translucent, stir in a few drops of water at a time until translucent. Then cover the entire cake.
5. Do not move the glazed cake to a serving plate for several hours.

How can nut meats be prevented from falling off the top of a cake after baking?

Soak the nuts in cold water six to eight minutes, drain well, and then add to top of the cake.

How should the cake be moved?

To move the cake, slip two long metal icing spatulas under it, cross them and lift.

How should the glazed cake be stored?

Store at room temperature, as no refrigeration is necessary.

How should an ice cream cake be handled before serving?

1. Unmold it onto the chilled serving platter and refreeze.
2. About twenty to twenty-five minutes before serving, transfer to the refrigerator.
3. Cut in wedges to serve.

At what temperature should chocolate cake be baked?

At about twenty-five degrees lower than a plain cake, to avoid changing the flavor of the chocolate.

Angel Food Cake

What are the ingredients of an angel food cake?

Egg whites, sugar, flour, cream of tartar and flavorings.

Why shouldn't confectioners sugar be used in making an angel food cake?

It comes with a small amount of cornstarch and its texture is too dense for angel food.

Why should you avoid superfine sugar?

Superfine, made from granulated sugar in a food processor, is too fine and produces a soft cake with little substance.

Which sugar is best?

Ordinary granulated sugar is best, but be sure to sift it to break down clumps and remove any unusually large granules.

How can cake flour be substituted?

Flour is the starch that sets the cake batter, but since it adds weight, the flour should be as light and as airy as possible. Start with cake flour, which is finer and lighter than all-purpose.

What can be substituted for cake flour?

Cake flour generally produces more delicate baked products. If a recipe calls for all-purpose flour you can substitute cake flour at the rate of $\frac{7}{8}$ of a cup for each cup of all-purpose. Then sift the cake flour twice before adding to the batter. The result will be a light, white, tender cake.

Can you make angel food cake in a microwave?

No! The exterior will be pure white, the egg proteins will toughen and the texture will be gluey because the flour absorbs liquid quickly in the microwave. The result is a cake that has a damp, uneven texture, is dense and treacly in spots, lighter in others and almost lacking in taste.

What is the purpose of cream of tartar in angel food cake?

It acts as a bleach to make the cake snowy white. (Lemon juice does the same.) Cream of tartar also does not increase the volume.

What are the results of over-beating egg whites when making an angel or sponge cake?

The cake won't rise high enough, and it will probably fall after baking.

How should the egg whites be whipped?

Under-whip for more volume.

How and when should the flour and sugar be added when mixing the batter of angel food cake?

1. The whites should be shiny and form soft peaks.
2. Add when large bubbles stop appearing around the edge.
3. Then add the sugar one tablespoon at a time, slowly, until all is incorporated.
4. The mass should still flow slightly when the bowl is tipped. Do not beat until the peaks are stiff, to make sure the sugar is dissolved and fully incorporated.

What happens if the whites are too stiff?

If the whites are too stiff, it is difficult to fold in the flour, which, if not done properly, will deflate the whites and reduce the volume.

How should the cake flour be handled?

Using cake flour, sift twice before measuring and once again after measuring.

What flavorings can safely be added to angel food cake batter?

Salt and/or extract of vanilla or almonds. These don't change the chemistry of the batter.

What shouldn't be added?

Avoid fat flavorings such as chocolate and nuts because they can greatly alter the texture of the cake.

In what kind of pan should a chocolate angel food cake be baked?

In a tubed pan to compensate for the weight of the cocoa. The tube distributes the heat more evenly and sets the batter more quickly.

How should an angel food cake be baked to achieve moistness?

Bake on the bottom rack of the oven at 350 °F.

Why is it necessary to allow a just-baked angel food cake to cool, suspended upside down in the pan?

It must be cooled completely. Inversion and suspension allows the cake to stretch and prevents it from settling. Removing from the pan before completely cool or letting it cool in the pan upright can result in a very soggy cake.

Butter Cake

What are the requirements for making a perfect butter cake?

1. A large proportion of fat to eggs.
2. The liquids (eggs, milk, etc.) are well combined.
3. The batter is well aerated so it will rise to its fullest during baking.

Can you make substitutions in the recipe for butter cakes?

Yes. Milk can be replaced with yogurt, buttermilk, sour milk, coffee, orange juice, applesauce, burnt sugar syrup or a combination of these.

What will happen as a result of these substitutions?

Each substitution will vary the taste and texture.

Cheesecake

What happens if cheesecake is baked at too hot a temperature?

The cake will toughen.

Why are some cheesecakes baked in a water bath?

Those that are custard-like, and thus very delicate, need the mixture of cream and cheese to set and not separate.

How can you tell when a cheesecake is done?

It should be firm and golden around the edges but still slightly moist in the center.

What happens if it is over-baked?

Cracks will develop.

What should be done if the cake has finished baking but the center is still somewhat soft and wiggly?

Don't worry, the center should firm as the cake cools.

How can a spring-form aluminum pan be kept from discoloring when used for making a cheesecake?

1. Line the bottom of the pan with a circle of parchment paper.
2. Coat the paper with nonstick spray.
3. Once the cake is baked be sure to loosen the springform sides once it has cooled to room temperature.

What can you do if the surface of a cheesecake cracks?

Cover the surface with a little sour cream.

How do you prevent a cheesecake from cracking?

1. Bake in a humid oven. Set a water bath under the pan and don't open the oven door until the end of the baking time.
2. Cool in a turned-off oven by reducing the cooking time by a minute or two.
3. Leave the oven door open during the first 10 minutes of the cooling period.

How should cheesecake be handled when removed from the oven?

1. Run a knife around the edge of the cake.
2. Set the cake on a wire rack away from drafts.
3. Let it cool thoroughly for about 2 hours.

Why is the pan containing a cheesecake mixture frequently dropped onto the counter before baking?

To get rid of any bubbles.

How should cheesecake be cut?

Dip the knife into hot water and then dry it before cutting.

Fruitcake

What is fruitcake?

There is no one recipe or definition, other than it is a cake with some fruit in or on it. The cakes are generally rich, spicy and moist. The fruit is often dried, candied or crystallized.

How is fruitcake baked?

Slowly, for an extended time in a pan. When finished baking, it should be left standing for about 10 minutes before removing.

Pound Cake

What happens if the butter/sugar mixture for a pound cake is over-beaten?

The air cells will rupture and the batter becomes heavy. This is especially true in a warm room.

How should pound cakes be handled when the baking is finished?

1. Leave them in their pans for 15 to 20 minutes, then turn them onto a cake rack to finish cooling.
2. Don't slice for at least 24 hours.

COOKIES

What is gingerbread?

1. A full-bodied, ginger-spiced hard cookie.
2. A moist cake with molasses and ginger.

What sweetener should be used for gingerbread?

Dark molasses, which is less sweet than sugar and has a smoky flavor, is slightly acidic and therefore needs to be countered with baking soda.

What is the difference between butter and oil in making cookies?

Cookies made with butter are crunchier, while those made with oil are more tender and soft.

What are the steps necessary to prevent cookies from burning or sticking to the pan?

1. Use a heavy-gauged steel baking sheet rather than the common, thin aluminum ones. Shiny, heavy aluminum sheets are good heat conductors and work well.
2. If there is ample butter or shortening in the dough you don't have to grease the sheet.

What cautions should be taken when working with cookie dough?

1. The dough must not be too soft.
2. Don't add too much flour, for while the dough will be easier to handle, the cookies will be practically inedible.
3. If the dough is overworked, the gluten level from the flour will be too high and the cookies will be tough.
4. If the dough is first chilled and then rolled out on a floured cloth or between sheets of waxed paper, there is no need for excess flour.

How should a cookie cutter be used?

Cut cookies as close to each other as possible.

Does the cutter need flouring?

Unless the dough is very soft and sticky, the cutter need not be floured.

Can the dough scraps be used?

If you have been careful not to get the dough too floury it is all right to reroll the scraps.

Should rolled cookies be frozen before or after baking?

Rolled cookies can be frozen either before or after baking.

How can a crunchy texture be achieved with oatmeal cookies?

Lightly toast the oatmeal before mixing into the batter by sprinkling the oatmeal flakes in a thin layer on a cookie sheet and heating to 180 °F for 10 to 15 minutes or until the flakes are brown.

How can stiffness and toughness in sugar cookies be avoided?

Roll the cookies in sugar instead of flour.

What can be substituted for grated coconut?

An equal amount of quick cooking oats.

What can be done to prevent chilled cookie dough from crumbling when sliced?

Warm the knife first in hot water, wipe dry and slice. When the blade cools, reheat it.

What should be done if cookies are not browning properly?

Move the sheet to a higher oven shelf.

How should a recipe be altered so that cookie dough won't spread too much?

1. Refrigerate the dough.
2. Decrease the amount of sugar.
3. Use shortening for some of the butter.

How should cookies be handled upon removing from the oven?

Cool on a wire rack.

How should they be stored?

Store in a covered container.

Are ice-box cookies "baked" in the refrigerator?

No, but the dough must be chilled first before baking.

How can brownies be cut and removed from the pan without creating rough edges?

1. Butter and flour the pan before adding the batter.
2. Let the brownies cool completely before cutting.
3. Use a very sharp knife, wiping it clean after each cut.

What kind of knife should be used for cutting brownies containing nuts or chocolate chips?

A serrated knife.

How can over-baking of cookies be avoided?

Take the pan out of the oven a few minutes before they are done, since the hot pan will continue to bake them.

How should a plastic cookie cutter be used?

Dip in warm vegetable oil periodically while cutting.

How should crisp cookies be stored?

In a can with a loose cover.

How should soft cookies be kept?

Put in a well-sealed can with half an apple or a slice of bread, changing the bread or the apple regularly.

How should the pan be handled when baking cookies in several batches?

Run the pan bottom under cold water between baking sessions, but don't get the cookie surface wet. This will reduce the risk of burned bottoms.

CUSTARD

What is a custard?

A sweetened or unsweetened mixture of eggs, sugar and milk that is heated. All types require slow cooking and gentle heat, or they will curdle. Custards can have various flavorings added.

What are the two types of custard?

Baked: Firm enough to hold its shape.

Stirred: Creamy, stirred on the stove and pourable.

What are timbales?

Individual custards, most often made with cheese.

Why should only a wooden spoon, not a whisk, be used when cooking a custard?

A whisk will stir up bubbles that will prevent accurate judging of the custard's thickness.

How should a custard be stirred?

Use an exaggerated figure eight pattern in a light motion to stir.

What cautions should be taken when making a mixed custard?

1. Drain vegetables, after cooking, until very dry.
2. Chop finely or coarsely grind any meat.

Why use a thermometer when making custard?

Custard must be heated to 170 °F to thicken and kill salmonella bacteria. A thermometer will help ensure that the proper temperature is maintained, therefore avoiding overheating.

How can a custard be tested for doneness?

Insert a knife blade into the center of the mold. If it comes out completely clean and the custard looks fairly solid, remove the custard from the oven and put it on a rack to cool.

Will the custard continue to cook after being removed from the heat?

Yes, so the "done point" will be if the center of the custard quivers when jiggled, and is still a little loose.

What can cause a baked custard to be watery?

1. It was baked too long.
2. It was baked at too high a temperature.
3. It was served warm.

How long should a custard bake?

Large custards will take thirty to forty minutes at 350 °F, individual servings, less time.

What should be done when a stirred custard has finished cooking?

When it reaches 175 °F to 180 °F immediately remove the pan from the heat and pour the mixture into another mixing bowl. Set the new bowl in ice water, continuing to stir a minute or two to cool quickly.

What will too long or too high a temperature cooking do?

The custard will curdle, or separate.

What happens if the water bath for a custard begins to boil?

The custard won't set properly.

What should be done if the custard starts to curdle?

1. Put it into a blender, starting at a slow speed and then increasing and continuing until the mixture is smooth. Don't over-blend.
2. Turn it into a clean pan and begin cooking again.

How does Bavarian cream differ from a custard?

It is a variation of a soft custard to which gelatin and whipped cream are added after the mixture has cooled.

How should it be served?

Served chilled.

What must be done if unpasteurized milk is used to make the custard?

Unpasteurized milk must be scalded to destroy enzymes that will block thickening.

When are extra eggs needed to make a good custard?

When sugar or acid is added to the mixture.

How do flan and crème caramel, both a mixture of sugar, flavorings and a milk product, differ?

Flan is Spanish in origin and is made with sweetened condensed milk.

Crème caramel is French and is made with whole milk or cream.

DONUTS

What are the two types of donuts (or doughnuts)?

Raised: Leavened with yeast.

Cake: Leavened with baking powder.

How can the absorption of grease be minimized when frying donuts?

1. Let them stand 15 to 20 minutes before frying. This will allow air to escape and the donuts to firm.
2. Place the donuts in boiling water for an instant and then remove. The hot water will keep the excess grease from sticking to the donut.
3. Chill the donuts before frying.
4. Increase the amount of eggs in the dough.
5. Make sure that the oil temperature is correct.
6. Cook only a few at a time.

What flour should be used for tender donuts?

Cake flour.

When should donuts be coated?

Coat (sugar) donuts while they are still warm.

How can donuts be sugarcoated?

1. Shake donuts gently in a paper bag containing sugar.
2. Make a sugar glaze by bringing to a boil sugar (two cups) and water (one and one-half cups).
3. Make a confectioner's sugar glaze by mixing one cup confectioner's sugar with a little liquid (milk, orange juice), enough to make a smooth, creamy glaze.

MACAROONS

Should blanched or unblanched almonds be used for making macaroons?

Unblanched.

What is the advantage of flourless macaroons?

They have greater intensity of flavor.

How must macaroons be handled?

1. They are more fragile than other cookies and must be handled with care.
2. They will stay fresh longer when stored in plastic or in tin and will keep for a week with just a gradual shift in texture to more crisp and less chewy.

MARZIPAN

What is marzipan?

A smooth almond mixture, sweeter than almond puree, that can be rolled into thin sheets or strings for decoration.

How can it be made?

It is made by adding sugar syrup to almond paste while the paste is in the firm ball stage (250 °F).

Can it be shaped?

It can readily be colored and shaped into small flowers.

What is the difference between almond paste and marzipan?

Both are made from the ground, blanched almonds. The paste has less sugar, is the base for marzipan and has a more distinct almond flavor.

What is almond paste used for?

Pastries and other baked goods.

What is marzipan used for?

Confections and decorations. The higher sugar content makes it more malleable than almond paste.

Can marzipan and almond paste be used interchangeably?

No.

What can be done to an almond paste that is not workable at room temperature?

Process for a few second in a food processor with a plastic blade.

MUFFINS

How can you get high-cap muffins?

1. Work with room temperature eggs, fats and liquid, since a cold batter entering a hot oven has to work hard to boost itself up.
2. Scoop the batter generously almost to the top of the tin.
3. Allow muffins five minutes of rest before removing from the pan and then put them on a wire rack to cool.

How can muffins be made lighter?

1. Separate the egg whites, beating them stiff and folding them in as the last step.
2. Substitute buttermilk for milk in the recipe and add ½ teaspoon baking soda per cup of buttermilk.
3. Cream the sugar and butter and then alternately beat in the dry and sweet ingredients; or mix the dry ingredients, then add the melted butter and eggs. When the flour is coated, stir in yogurt or an other moisturizing agent.

What is the best way to mix the dry ingredients?

Instead of sifting, use a wire whip which will aerate the mixture.

What will result if lumps are left in the muffin batter?

The lumps will disappear during baking, so *don't* over-mix.

What happens when muffin dough is beaten rather than folded?

The muffins will be tough.

How can you minimize the fat content when making muffins?

1. Use apple butter instead of butter.
2. Sprinkle the top of the muffin with rolled oats before baking to accentuate the nutty flavor. By doing so you can cut down on the nuts.

How can you decrease the amount of pecans or walnuts used without decreasing flavor?

Toast the nuts in the oven before adding the butter.

How can muffins and rolls be removed from the pan more easily?

Place the muffin tin directly from the oven onto a wet towel for about 30 seconds.

PANCAKES

What is a way to make better pancakes?

Refrigerate the batter thirty minutes or more before using.

How can pancakes be made lighter?

1. Substitute club soda for milk.
2. Use fruit juice instead of milk.
3. Mix the batter only until the dry ingredients are moistened. Don't over-beat.
4. Add the egg whites last, stiffly beaten.
5. Don't press down on the pancakes with a spatula while cooking.
6. Don't turn more than once.

How can pancakes be prevented from sticking to the griddle?

Fill a small piece of cheesecloth with salt. Just before pouring in the batter rub the cloth over the surface of the hot griddle.

What can be added to batter to improve flavor?

A tablespoon of maple syrup.

What is an easy way to make chocolate flavored pancakes?

Substitute two teaspoons of cocoa powder for an equal amount of flour.

How can pancakes be frozen?

Put a piece of waxed paper between cakes, then wrap the stack in plastic and freeze.

PASTRY

What kind of flour is most commonly used in pastry making?

White wheat flour, which is milled from the wheat kernel for its fine texture, mild flavor and ability to form gluten.

Why is white wheat flour best?

When liquid is added to the flour and the dough is manipulated, the flour protein develops into gluten, which allows the dough to stretch and expand in the oven and thus gives shape and structure. It forms an elastic network.

Why does cake flour make a more tender product?

It contains less protein.

How should the pastry dough be handled?

1. Work the dough as little as possible.
2. The larger the fat flakes before the liquid is added, the larger the flakes in the baked dough.

What happens if the dough is overworked?

The crust will have small flakes and be mealy.

What fat can be used?

Shortening, butter or lard.

What is the role of fat in flaky pastry?

To keep the thin layers of dough separate.

What characteristics should the fat have?

It should be cold but still plastic.

Is this also true when making cake-like items?

For cake-like items such as cookies, it might be desirable to have fat at room temperature so that it can be easily creamed together with the sugar.

What sort of fat is best for pastry?

Butter is much better than oil for both texture and flavor.

What liquid should be used?

The liquid is customarily water, but milk or cream can be used.

What adjustment is necessary if milk or cream is used?

The amount of fat should be decreased because of the fat content of the milk or cream.

How should the salt be handled?

It is a good idea to completely dissolve salt in the liquid before adding to the dough to ensure that it is evenly distributed.

Should the liquid be added a little at a time?

No. Add the cold liquid all at once and mix quickly into the flour and fat mixture and keep mixing until a shaggy mass forms.

What is the function of fat in pastry making?

1. Adds richness and flavor.
2. Lubricates and tenderizes.
3. Contributes to flakiness.
4. Assists in leavening the dough.

How do you keep butter cool for pastry?

1. Work in a cool kitchen.
2. Handle the dough as little as possible.
3. Chill the pastry board and roller beforehand in refrigerator or freezer.
4. Marble slabs are ideal for working with butter-rich pastry dough, because they stay cool.

How can you tell if the butter is starting to melt?

The dough begins to develop a greasy sheen.

What should be done if the dough is too warm?

Wrap it in plastic wrap or place in a covered bowl, then refrigerate 20–30 minutes before proceeding with the recipe.

What is a caution to be taken for pastries with a high egg content?

They should not be eaten within a few hours after coming out of the oven.

What should be done to ensure maximum pastry flavor?

Bring a refrigerated pastry to room temperature before serving.

What is the effect of salt in pastry making?

1. Strengthens glutens.
2. Enhances the flavor of other ingredients.

What is puff pastry?

A rich, many-layered, delicate pastry.

How is puff pastry made?

By placing a small amount of chilled butter between layers of the dough, rolling it out and allowing it to rest. This process is repeated many times.

What gives the flakiness to puff pastry?

During baking, the heat acts on the fat to release steam, which separates the layers.

Should salt be used for sweet desserts?

Very little should be used for sweet desserts.

Why is pastry dough easier to roll after it has rested?

The flour contains an enzyme, protease, that changes some of the insoluble proteins in the dough to soluble form. It mellows and softens the gluten, making it extendable during rolling, but this takes time, hence the resting periods.

What purpose does egg wash serve when used in pastry making?

Egg wash (egg beaten with water or milk), when brushed over the dough before baking, helps the crust to brown.

Phyllo Dough

What is phyllo dough?

Paper-thin pastry sheets made of flour and water that originated in the Mediterranean region.

How long should phyllo be kept?

Frozen, 1 year; refrigerated, 1 month.

How should phyllo be handled?

Handle slowly and gently, because rough handling causes it to break.

What are some ways to make working with phyllo dough easier?

1. Thaw the frozen dough in the refrigerator for at least 8 hours or overnight. This will prevent damp spots from forming that could cause the sheets to stick together.
2. Remove from the refrigerator and leave unopened at room temperature for one to two hours.
3. Clear a large work space before removing the dough from the box.
4. Carefully unroll a sheet onto a dry surface.
5. Keep the remaining sheets covered with plastic or waxed paper or a towel until ready to work with the next sheet.
6. Work quickly and gently, one sheet at a time.

What can be done to get a crisper phyllo?

Lightly smear the sheets between layers with honey, cover with a towel and roll flat.

What happens if the phyllo skin is rolled too tightly?

It will split apart when heated.

How can phyllo be kept from drying?

1. Cover with plastic and then place a damp towel over them.
2. Remove one sheet at a time and recover the skins immediately.

How can the fat content be reduced when sealing a phyllo roll?

Brush with egg white instead of melted butter. This will also result in a crisp texture.

Can olive oil be substituted for butter when stacking phyllo skins for baking?

Yes.

How should a stack of phyllo sheets be baked?

Place them on a lightly greased baking sheet, brush with melted butter and bake at 350 °F until golden brown.

How should phyllo triangles be baked?

1. Set the oven rack at the upper level.
2. Preheat the oven to 350 °F.
3. Lightly coat a baking sheet with nonstick spray or line the sheet with parchment paper.
4. May be baked up to 2 days in advance and then reheated at 350 °F for 10 to 12 minutes or until heated through.

Should phyllo be refrozen?

No, because refreezing dries the pieces, causing them to cling together.

Pies

What characteristics should pie pastry have?

Pie pastry, at its best, is light, flaky, tender and golden brown, with a fairly rough surface.

Will pie pastry keep?

The nature of pie crust is that it should be eaten within an hour or so after baking or the bottom crust can get soggy.

Must a pie have a top crust?

A pie may have a top crust, a lattice crust or be without a top.

Must the top crust, if used, be of sweetened dough?

No, either plain or sweetened will do.

In making pie crust, what can be used in place of shortening?

Finely ground pecans can be used for half of the shortening.

What are rules for handling the dough for pie crust?

1. Have all the ingredients cool.
2. Don't over-work the dough.
3. Refrigerate the dough before rolling.

How can you prevent a pie crust from getting soggy?

1. Sprinkle some graham cracker crumbs on top of the bottom crust.
2. Brush the inside of the crust with beaten egg white and let it dry.

How can pie dough be rolled round?

1. Pat the dough into a hamburger shaped patty.
2. Lightly pound it thin with a rolling pin.

How much fruit is required for a 9-inch double-crust pie?

About 6 cups or slightly more.

How should the fruit be chosen?

Choose firm, ripe fruit.

What should be done when berries are used for pies?

1. Spread them out and remove any leaf, stem or foreign material.
2. Discard those with any hint of mold.
3. Don't wash the berries until you're ready to use them; any amount of moisture will encourage the growth of mold.

Should fruit for pie filling be peeled?

It is a matter of choice and of the type of fruit. The skin of a peach can be easily removed with blanching. Plum skins can be left on but are better if finely diced. Because of tough skins, some plums should be peeled, especially if in larger pieces.

How do you get crusty pie dough?

1. Use fat (butter or lard) rather than vegetable oil.
2. Don't over-cut the fat into the flour. Stop as soon as the texture reaches the coarse, cornmeal stage.

Which is better, butter or lard?

Bakers disagree. A good compromise is a mixture of the two.

How can you get a browned crust?

Put in an initially hot oven then lower the oven to baking temperature.

What happens if pie pastry isn't refrigerated about forty minutes before baking?

It will shred and puff.

What is the advantage of butter for making a pie crust?

1. A lot of fat is necessary to have a good lift off (flakiness), up to 60% of the weight of the flour.
2. The fat that melts the slowest is most likely to create the biggest pockets. If the fat melts before the dough sets, the layers will collapse.
3. Butter melts fastest, then shortening, then lard.
4. Butter gives a beautiful flake and an incomparable flavor, but the crimped edge may lose definition and collapse more readily in the oven.

What does the flavor of the crust largely depend upon?

1. The flavor will largely depend on the type of fat used.
2. If lard has been used, the crust will taste slightly of that fat.
3. Butter or a combination of butter and lard may be used to give a different flavor.

What is the advantage of using lard instead of butter when making pie dough?

The crust will be flakier and have less saturated fat.

Is the taste of lard unpleasant in a crust?

Lard has a distinct, but not unpleasant taste.

Why is lard recommended?

Because it is best to work with, gives a tender crust and produces the lightest and flakiest texture.

How much lard should be used?

When using lard for butter or margarine, decrease the amount of lard by ¼ of the fat called for in the recipe.

How is the amount of lard measured?

You can measure the lard by the displacement method. For example, if ⅓ cup lard is called for, fill a measuring cup ⅓ full with water. Then keep adding lard until the water reaches the ⅔-cup level.

Why is vegetable shortening (such as Crisco) recommended?

1. Vegetable shortening has little flavor.
2. It is easy to work with.
3. It can be used in combination with butter.

What are important guidelines, regardless of which shortening is used?

1. It is important to keep the fat chilled before adding, and then to refrigerate the dough both before and after it has been rolled out.
2. Work quickly to assemble the pie and get it into the oven.

Why is the basic pie dough called the 3-2-1 dough?

Because it is composed of three parts flour, two parts fat, one part of water (by weight) and when properly made it should be flaky and crisp.

In making pie crust what is the end point for the dough?

It should resemble coarse meal with irregularly sized pieces of fat that are as small as a lentil and as large as a garden pea. The important thing is not to over-work the dough.

What are ways the juices inside the pie crust can be contained when using juicy fillings?

1. Add a teaspoon of tapioca to the filling before baking.
2. Before adding the fruit, brush the crust with egg white.
3. Sprinkle the bottom crust with corn flour or cracker crumbs.
4. Mix the filling with a few tablespoons of flour.

How can the crusts be sealed?

Leave an inch overhang of the top crust and then fold it underneath the bottom crust and press the two together.

How does the pie tin affect the bottom crust?

The shinier the pan, the longer the crust will take to brown, which is useful for a baked shell that gets baked again with its filling. Slow baking prevents over-browning.

How does this factor in a double crust pie?

This is especially good for a double crust pie where the liquids tend to leech out from the fruit and make the bottom crust soggy.

What criteria should be considered when choosing pie tins?

1. They should be sturdy.
2. They should have a rim wide enough to support a fluted edge.

What are the advantages of a glass pie pan?

Glass (pyrex) type pans give a beautiful color and allow the crust to brown rather quickly.

What is the advantage of an aluminum pie tin (not the disposable kind)?

It gives a crisp bottom crust.

What causes spots on the bottom of a pie to remain uncooked?

1. Inadequate blending of fat and flour.
2. Combination of warm and cold dough.
3. Insufficient mixing after the water is added so that the dough is unevenly moist.
4. Drops of water on the pie pan when the dough is put into the pan.
5. Uneven surface in the pie tin. This can result in either unbaked or over-baked spots.

What can be done to avoid spots on the crust?

1. Carefully and evenly roll the dough on a lightly floured surface.
2. Roll out from the center.
3. Roll it out a little wider than the pan.
4. Never stretch the dough.

What can be done with leftover scraps of dough?

1. Use them to make decorative pieces, moistening the bottoms before laying them on the top crust.
2. Use them to make cookies.

What are the advantages and disadvantages of nonstick pie plates?

Advantages: Don't stick, easy to clean.
Disadvantages: Can scratch easily when cutting the pie and when serving it.

What are two ways to ensure flakiness in the pie dough mixture?

1. Add a teaspoon of vinegar to the dough to prevent sogginess.
2. Spread a thin layer of butter on the pie plate before putting the crust on it.

What is needed after sugar or other sweetener has been added to the fruit filling?

Get the pie into the oven as quickly as possible. The longer the wait, the more the juice will run out of the fruit.

At what temperature should pie filling be before putting in the shell?

Cool.

Which is worse, more or less resting time before baking?

Less.

What does baking a pie crust "blind" mean?

Baking without any filling to avoid having a soggy crust when a moist filling, such as a custard, is to be added later.

Why prebake a pie crust?

It helps keep the crust crumbly.

How is it done?

1. Line a chilled pie shell with foil and fill with weights (metal pie weights, dried beans or uncooked rice).
2. Bake at 450 °F for 15–20 minutes on the lowest rack until set.
3. Then remove the foil or weights and bake another twelve minutes more until brown. (Some bakers omit this step and bake with the weights in until done.)

What happens if there are no weights used?

There will be a major shrinkage and sometimes distortion of shape.

What is the function of the weights?

To prevent puffiness.

How do you evaluate doneness and quality in baking pie dough?

1. Bake until it begins to take on a golden color.
2. The dough should appear dry.
3. If the dough was rolled out unevenly, the thicker portions may appear moist, indicating that the dough is not fully baked.

Why do you have to use a high-grade ice cream when topping a slice of hot pie?

A mediocre (cheap) ice cream will melt too quickly and waterlog the pie crust because it has so much air whipped into it.

What happens if patches are made over tears or holes in the crust?

When baked, there are apt to be holes that show where the dough has been pulled.

How can you guarantee a flaky, tender pie crust?

1. Chill the butter or shortening.
2. Add only enough water to form the dough.
3. Handle the dough gently to avoid over-activating the gluten.
4. Chill the dough before rolling.
5. Chill again to harden if the dough begins to soften.

What is an easy way to make a lattice top for a pie?

1. Line a baking sheet with wax paper.
2. Make the lattice on the paper but without trimming it to size.
3. Chill or freeze it.
4. Slide the lattice onto the pie.
5. Trim.

What adjustments should you make when using all-purpose or eating types of apples rather than cooking varieties?

1. Cut the pieces a little larger than usual to keep the fruit from disintegrating.
2. Add a little lemon juice to give balance.

How can the flavor of a fruit pie be enhanced?

1. Add a tablespoon or two of marmalade to the filling.
2. Substitute light brown sugar for granulated.
3. Add grated orange or lemon zest.

Why would a custard in a pie shrink away from the crust?

The pie was baked too long, or the temperature was too high.

How should unbaked pie crusts be handled for storage, and how long can they be kept?

1. Refrigerate at least 30 minutes, until firm.
2. Wrap in plastic.
3. Put into the freezer until quite firm. Then another crust can be put on top of it, thus conserving freezer space.
4. It can be kept frozen up to 3 months.

How should leftover fruit pies be handled?

1. Eat as soon as possible, ideally in the next day or two.
2. Warm before serving.

Pie Meringue

How can the highest meringue be achieved?

1. Add some baking powder to whites that are at room temperature before beating.
2. During beating add 2–3 tablespoons of granulated sugar for each egg used, beating continuously.
3. Add ¼ teaspoon white vinegar per three egg whites during beating.

How can weeping or cracking of meringue be prevented?

Leave the meringue in the oven until it cools.

What is Italian Meringue?

Boiling sugar syrup is whisked into stiffly beaten egg whites. The sugar cooks the whites, creating a topping of fluffy consistency. It can be flavored with vanilla, cinnamon, cocoa, orange liqueur, etc. It can be used as a frosting, a filling or baked as a meringue.

How can a meringue pie be transported?

Insert four toothpicks into the top of the pie and cover with wax paper.

Puff Paste (or Puff Pastry)

What is puff paste?

Puff paste is a crisp, light pastry consisting of many paper-thin layers of dough. These layers are prevented from sticking together by thin layers of fat (usually butter). When baking, the steam caught between the layers of dough evaporates and the fat is absorbed, leaving a high, crisp, flaky pastry.

What is the best flour for puff pastry?

Bread flour, although all-purpose can be used. Bread flour is made from hard wheat, which has a high gluten content that is necessary to achieve the thin layers that won't collapse when baking.

What is the best oven setting for baking puff paste?

While most recipes call for a very hot oven of 450 °F. or more, the safest is at 350 °F. Bake longer at lower temperature, so there is no danger of burned bottoms combined with raw insides.

What kind of butter should be used in making puff paste?

1. Use unsalted butter.
2. If the butter is stone cold when combined with the dough, it will break the dough within from the pressure of the rolling pin.
3. If the butter is very soft it will ooze out. It should be firm enough to be waxy yet approximately the same consistency as the dough.

What is the basic caution when making puff pastry?

Never make puff pastry in hot weather unless the kitchen is air conditioned.

QUICHE

Where did quiche originate?

It is generally credited to Alsace-Lorraine, where quiche Lorraine, made with bacon and cheese, originated.

Can a quiche be made without a crust?

Although a quiche is generally defined as an open-faced custard baked in a crust, quiches can be made without one. These are made usually with vegetables and cheese.

Should the shell for a quiche be prebaked?

Prebaked yes, chilled no. Warm is best.

What should be the texture of a quiche?

Smooth custard that is velvety on the tongue, rich but not too rich, fine taste, and a creamy-mouth feel.

What is a good baking temperature for a quiche?

The oven should be at 375 °F, although some start at 400 °F for 15 minutes and then reduce to 350 °F.

TARTS

What are the characteristics of a tart?

1. A tart is never covered with a top crust.
2. Tart pastry, even the bottom, is crisp but tender and flaky and stays so for days. It may outlast the edibility of its filling. Even after several days it will usually remain crisp and delicious.
3. The tops of tarts are colorful and bright with fruit glaze in contrast to the heaviness of most double-crusted pies.

Should a tart dough be chilled before baking?

1. Yes. Refrigerate for about an hour before rolling.
2. Freeze about twenty minutes after rolling, or refrigerate an hour or so before baking.

Will tart pastry keep frozen?

Unbaked tart pastry can be frozen for several months and will taste even better because of the extra chilling.

How must the crust be baked for a fruit tart?

1. It must be fully baked before the fruit is added.
2. Cover the crust with foil and add weights while baking to prevent shrinking or buckling.

How should tarts be placed in the oven for baking?

Oven position is critical. Always place them (especially when shell and filling are baked together) on the lowest rack, so the maximum heat will be directed at the bottom of the pastry.

PIZZA

In making pizza, why should cheese toppings (or other toppings that don't require much cooking, such as paper-thin prosciuto or blanched asparagus) not be added before putting into the oven?

If added when the crust is just lightly browned, it is impossible to tell if the other toppings are sufficiently cooked without over-browning and causing either leathery cheese or undercooked crust.

How can a crisp crust be obtained in a cheese pizza?

1. Put a thin layer of cheese on the crust first, then add the sauce, then any topping, then more cheese, if desired.
2. Use some cornmeal is making the dough, about ⅓ cup per cup of all-purpose flour.

What can be done to make certain that the bottom of the crust gets crisp?

Bake on a preheated baking stone.

Do sliced mushrooms have to be sauteed before putting onto a pizza?

No, they can be used raw, but are improved if first tossed with oil, lemon juice and salt and added before the cheese topping.

Are sweet pizzas made?

Yes, by using sliced fruits and topping with brown sugar, butter and spices such as cloves or cinnamon instead of the usual toppings.

PRETZELS

How are pretzels made commercially?

A stiff dough is sprayed with sodium hydroxide, which gelatinizes the surface starch. They are then baked slowly at a low temperature to dry them.

Are pretzels made at home different than commercially made?

Yes. A sourdough of only flour, yeast and salt is hand rolled and twisted, which results in uneven air bubbles. They are then boiled in a water and soda bath to help raise the gluten to the surface so as to heighten the deep color.

Are all pretzels salted?

No, some are made plain, and some are sprinkled with sesame seeds or other seasonings.

What are German pretzels?

German pretzels are dipped for ten seconds into boiling water containing a small amount of lye. They are then hand-salted or sprinkled with sesame seeds, baked and finally dried. As a result they will be very light in weight and very fragile but will last for weeks if sealed away from moist air.

Can pretzels be frozen?

Yes, in a plastic bag with the air squeezed out. They keep well but are best after thawing, when still a little chilled.

TORTILLAS

What is a tortilla?

A thin, round, flat unleavened Mexican bread that is made from wheat flour or cornmeal. (In Spain it refers to an omelet.)

How is it baked?

On a griddle.

What is the difference between wheat and corn tortillas?

Wheat tortillas are soft and pliable, while corn tortillas are stiffer and somewhat thinner. Corn tortillas also may be white, yellow or blue, depending on the variety of corn used, while wheat tortillas are typically white.

CHAPTER TWO

CHOCOLATE, COFFEE AND TEA

CHOCOLATE

What is the history of chocolate?

The cocoa tree originated in the river valleys of South America and was carried north into Mexico by the Mayans before AD 800. In Yucatan and Guatemala the *Cacahuaquchtl* (which means "the tree") grew and was the tree of the Mayan Gods. While chocolate is a word associated with sweetness, the name comes from the Aztec "*xocolatl*," which means "bitter water". Cocoa beans were used as currency, for instance, a rabbit was worth 10 beans; a turkey, 4; and a human slave, 100.

From Spain it spread throughout western Europe in the first half of the seventeenth century. During the first half of the 1600s, exorbitant taxes prevented ordinary mortals from enjoying chocolate. In 1690 it reached the Left Bank of Paris and one could drink it for eight sous (tea or coffee cost three). In 1770 the first chocolate manufacturing firm was established. In 1875 a Swiss, Daniel Peter, discovered milk chocolate. His company was later merged with three other brands to form the Nestlé Company in 1929.

Chocolate was not widely used in candy because the texture of the chocolate paste was crumbly, coarse and limited in its capacity to incorporate sugar until 1820. Conrad Van Houten in Amsterdam then developed a screw press that removed most of the cocoa butter from the bean, which made it smooth and easily dispersible. The first eating chocolate was introduced by the English firm of Fry & Sons in 1847.

Chocolate is now grown commercially in Hawaii on volcanic soil. This is the only place in the United States that can support it. This is the *Criolla* strain, a new variety with a low acid content.

How much cocoa does it take to make the 16 billion Oreo cookies consumed each year?

18 million pounds.

What are the nutritional values of chocolate?

1. It has no cholesterol except for the small amount in milk chocolate (from the added milk).
2. It has no appreciable amount of vitamins.
3. It has a small amount of minerals among which are magnesium, potassium, phosphates and iron.
4. Cocoa butter is high in saturated fat, but research has shown that it doesn't raise the low density lipoproteins (LDL, or bad cholesterol) like butterfat does, but fat is fat. There is a small amount possible from the added milk solids.
5. In 1.5 ounces of milk chocolate, there are approximately 200 milligrams of phenolics (the same amount in a glass of red wine). Phenolics prevent oxidation of LDL cholesterol into plaque that clogs the arteries.

What are the nutritional negatives of chocolate?

1. Cocoa butter is high in saturated fat, which does raise LDL levels.
2. It is high in fat, has plenty of sugar and little protein.
3. Its theobromine is a diuretic and may also cause an allergic response in some people.
4. Both caffeine and theobromine may produce heartburn, intestinal distress and allergic reactions in some people.
5. The headaches that some people have as a side effect comes from amines, another chemical in chocolate.

What is the relationship that chocolate has to acne in young people?

There is no proof that there is any relationship. Excess sugar is more of a suspect.

Does chocolate cause migraine headaches?

No, it only affects those with a chocolate sensitivity, and not all migraine sufferers have one.

What makes chocolate so highly craved?

1. Good taste.
2. Stimulants such as theobromine and some caffeine.
3. Its "texture." The cocoa butter gives it a smooth sensation of melting in the mouth.
4. Its attractive aroma.

What are the stimulants in chocolate?

1. A cup of chocolate milk or hot cocoa has only a few milligrams of caffeine, about as much as decaffeinated coffee or tea.

2. A chocolate bar or a piece of chocolate cake has less caffeine than a cup of coffee, but enough to give a buzz to someone who is sensitive.

3. The main stimulant is theobromine, caffeine's chemical cousin, but it is less of a stimulant than it is a powerful diuretic.

How does cocoa affect the heart?

It, like wine, contains flavonoids that protect against the oxidation of LDL cholesterol, which stimulates the production of plaque in the arteries.

What are the characteristics that should be looked for in judging chocolate as excellent?

1. It should look smooth, shiny and have a reasonable satiny gloss not an oily finish.

2. It should have a fragrant, chocolate, pleasing aroma that is deep and heavy.

3. It breaks with a clean "snap" to reveal a fine texture that doesn't crumble or produce splinters.

4. It will melt in the mouth quickly, evenly and smoothly.

5. The feeling on the tongue should be rich and moist with a slightly acidic flavor, but not leaving a film.

6. It will have a creamy texture.

7. Overall its flavor will be well balanced and complex.

8. The aftertaste should be long lasting and pleasurable.

What causes the surface of baking chocolate to turn partially gray?

Rub the gray surface with your finger. If that gives a dry feel, it is sugar bloom, which comes from moisture condensing on the surface when the air is cool and then evaporating when the temperature rises.

If it feels slightly oily, it is fat bloom, which comes from months of storage at higher temperatures, causing cocoa butter to melt.

How is cocoa processed?

1. The dried, fermented whole beans are roasted, and the shells are discarded.

2. The roasted nibs are then ground into chocolate liquor.

3. The chocolate liquor is refined and pressed, out of which comes cocoa butter and cocoa cake.

4. The cake is pulverized into sweet chocolate with the addition of chocolate liquor and sugar or with milk solids into milk chocolate.

5. After all the ingredients have been added, the chocolate is conched, which means that it is heated in tubs while huge rollers plow back and forth to smooth and refine it. In some European plants, this goes on for seventy-two hours to develop a special creaminess. This conched chocolate also has a more nut-like flavor.

6. Finally the chocolate is tempered. This means it is heated and cooled to develop a bright finish, durability and good melting quality. Chocolate that has not been tempered properly will melt into a sticky mess or tighten.

What are cocoa beans?

The pods from the tree contain twenty to fifty seeds (beans). The seeds are surrounded by a sweet-sour, whitish pulp. After picking they are left for four to six days to ferment and develop the cocoa aroma, then dried. They contain a great deal of fat, some starch and some protein.

What does roasting the beans accomplish?

Roasting the beans develops the flavor. Longer roasting periods create stronger flavor.

How are they roasted?

They are usually roasted at 435 °F for 7 to 8 minutes, but cooking chocolate is roasted longer and light colored chocolate is roasted at a lower temperature.

Does a product meet federal standards for chocolate if labeled chocolate-flavored?

Chocolate-flavored means that the product does not contain the minimum amount of cocoa fat required by federal definition, or that other ingredients do not meet the minimum requirements for labeling as chocolate.

What are the federal standards for labeling a product as chocolate?

Federal standards for labeling a product as chocolate say that the product must be made from finely ground cocoa nibs and must contain 50–58% cocoa fat. Emulsifying agents such as lecithin may be added, but they must be more than 0.5% by weight.

What is the difference between chocolate products made in Great Britain and those from Belgium?

In the British group the chocolate is made with some vegetable oil while the Belgian group uses only cocoa butter. Also the British group uses more milk (about 25% in their milk chocolate, while the Belgians use only about 14%).

What is Mexican chocolate?

It contains ground almonds and cinnamon. If a smooth product is desired it must be strained when liquified.

How is Mexican chocolate different otherwise?

It is higher in sugar than semisweet and has less binding capability in puddings and cakes.

Where does cocoa butter come from?

It is a naturally occurring fat that is pressed from refined chocolate liquor. The bean is more than half cocoa butter by weight. It is creamy and has a slight chocolate taste.

What is cocoa?

Chocolate with most (50–75%) of the cocoa butter removed, which results in an intensified chocolate flavor.

What are the types of cocoa?

It comes in two styles:

1. Non-alkalized, or natural, which is the traditional American type.
2. Alkalized, Dutch processed, or Dutched is the European standard, which is less bitter than natural with a diminished chocolate flavor.

What is the difference between alkalized and non-alkalized cocoa?

Non-alkalized: such as Hershey's, is simply chocolate liquor (nonalcoholic), with most of the cocoa butter (fat) removed by hydraulic pressure.

Alkalized: such as Van Houten, Droste and Barnsdorf, has a milder taste, reduced acidity and is somewhat redder in color than the non-alkalized.

How can cocoa be substituted for baking chocolate?

Use 3 level tablespoons of cocoa and 1 tablespoon of butter for each ounce of baking chocolate.

What is cocoa paste?

Beans are roasted to release and enhance the aroma, then they are shelled and crushed to extract the kernels. The kernels are ground to a bitter paste.

How is powdered chocolate made?

It's manufactured by grinding the residue of cocoa beans left after the paste has been pressed to extract some of the cocoa butter. Fat content of powder varies. The regulation is a minimum of 20%.

What is the difference between chocolate powder and cocoa powder?

Chocolate powder: A mixture of cocoa powder and sugar with at least 32% dry cocoa and 12% cocoa butter.

Cocoa powder: The powder left when most of the cocoa butter has been pressed out of the liquor.

What are chocolate bars made of?

A mixture of cocoa paste, cocoa butter and sugar with milk. Dried fruit, coffee liqueurs, nuts, etc. can also be added. Ingredients are ground (optional), strained and mixed while hot to give characteristic smooth and mellow consistency. May be molded or filled with other things such as fondant, caramel or praline in a proportion of at least 25% of its weight.

How does cooking chocolate differ from chocolate bars?

At least 30% of total is dry cocoa matter. It is the basic ingredient used by manufacturers for sweets or molded chocolate.

What is milk chocolate?

Almost 55% sugar, at least 25% dry cocoa matter (14% of dry matter is of lactic [milk] origin), and at least 25% fatty matter in all. Milk or milk solids replace some of the chocolate liqueur.

What is chocolate liquor, and how is it used?

A thick liquid of more than half cocoa butter and small particles of solid nibs suspended in oil. After the beans are roasted they are cracked, reducing them to small pieces, chaff is removed and the nibs milled or ground into chocolate liquor. The liquor is subjected to hydraulic pressure to remove part of the fat (or cocoa butter). Chocolate liquor is the base used for making various chocolate products. It contains what most people think of as chocolate flavor, but cocoa butter adds a great deal of flavor also.

Why must chocolate chips be made differently?

They must have more viscosity than regular chocolate, meaning that they are supposed to keep their shape when baked in cookies or cakes. They average 29% cocoa butter and 29% pure chocolate.

What must be watched for when melting chocolate chips?

Chips keep their shape when heated, so be careful to stir, for they will appeared not melted. Overcooking can result in scorching.

When chips or squares of chocolate are heated, will the melt indicate their doneness?

If they are heated to a runny melt they have been overcooked, because they keep their shape, especially when they were paper-wrapped.

What is meant by blooming?

When the surface of the chocolate gets pale gray blotches or streaks caused by excessive heat or humidity, which causes sugar or fat to rise to the surface.

Can bloomed chocolate still be used?

Yes.

What is the whitish haze that sometimes is found on chocolate?

Scuff marks from chips or pieces rubbing against each other. It is harmless.

What is compound chocolate?

A mixture of cocoa particles and oil (cottonseed, soy, etc.) but no cocoa butter.

What is meant by semisweet baking chocolate?

Unsweetened chocolate liquor blended with sugar and cocoa butter. Most manufacturers use a ratio of 35–38% pure chocolate to 28–32% cocoa butter.

What is the difference between bittersweet and semisweet chocolate?

Both are dark chocolates. The semisweet has sugar added, bittersweet (baking) chocolate has no sugar added.

Are various chocolates such as semisweet, milk, etc. the same for all brands?

No, they vary as to the amount of chocolate liquors, cocoa butter, sugar, milk solids and flavoring agents. If the recipe calls, for instance, for Hershey's and you use Nestlé's, the results might be quite different, not necessarily one being better than the other. Each company uses its own secret recipe.

What is the difference between sweet and semisweet?

Sweet must contain at least 15% chocolate liquor, while semisweet or bittersweet must have at least 35%. But one manufacturer's bittersweet may turn out to be sweeter than another's semisweet. Sweet chocolates vary greatly as to aroma, flavor, consistency and texture, and vary by both the quality and blend of the beans, the roast and the amount of cocoa butter added.

What is the percentage of chocolate necessary for a fine semisweet or bittersweet chocolate?

A minimum of 35% for USDA Standards, but the premium chocolates will contain over 60%.

What is the role of cocoa butter?

Cocoa butter adds smoothness and a velvety quality in the melting. Good chocolate contains a high percentage of cocoa butter. In lesser grades substitute fats and emulsifiers (mainly lecithin) have been added. The high cost of cocoa butter has led to the substitution of less expensive fats for the chocolate liquor but the result is a serious downgrading of quality.

What are the two types of cocoa powder?

Cocoa powder (cocoa after most of the cocoa butter is removed) is available sweetened or not. Most recipes do not specify and only call for cocoa powder.

How is premium chocolate defined?

By the percentage of chocolate (as opposed to sugar or other additives) it contains.

What is the problem with using Dutch-style alkalized cocoa?

Because cocoa is an acid product, it takes part in the leavening process by reacting with alkaline reagents such as baking soda, producing carbon dioxide gas. The alkalized type contains its own alkali and therefore it could cause an alkaline overload, which may result in a heavy texture. To create the correct pH (acid) balance, reduce the amount of baking soda and add some baking powder. There is no set formula. If baking powder is the only leavening agent, or if more baking powder than soda is called for, then use the alkalized type of cocoa.

What happens to melted coating chocolate if water is added?

A few drops of water or even steam from the double boiler will ruin the chocolate, meaning that often it cannot be repaired by reheating or reprocessing.

What are some guidelines for cooking with chocolate?

1. Chocolate should usually be melted before incorporating into a recipe. Chop chocolate into small pieces first.
2. Avoid water or steam.

3. Stir as it melts.

4. Do not melt over a direct heat because it is very easy to scorch and the flavor of burnt chocolate is impossible to disguise. It requires only 100 °F or so to melt (as you can learn by holding a piece in your hands).

5. An easy way to melt chocolate is to place a large skillet full of water on the stove, bring it to a simmer and remove to a burner that hasn't been heated. Place the chopped chocolate in a heavy bottomed saucepan, which is then placed above the hot water. At first, add no more than eight to ten ounces. If the recipe calls for more, then add the surplus (above the ten ounces) an ounce at a time into the *melted* chocolate and let this sit in the warm water bath for a few minutes until melted.

What is seizing?

When chocolate becomes a solid, dull, lumpy, solid mass.

What causes chocolate to seize?

Droplets of water or even steam coming into the chocolate will cause the chocolate to seize (stiffen) and become grainy and coarse.

What can be done if it seizes?

If this happens add a few drops of vegetable oil or clarified butter (both are fats with no moisture). This will help reverse the stiffness. If it doesn't, start over. During the melting, stir frequently to ensure even melting.

How can seizing be avoided?

1. Melt the chocolate with other ingredients in the recipe such as cream or butter. If it stiffens, add a few drops of clarified butter or vegetable oil.

2. Use the microwave at a medium setting, checking frequently, stirring occasionally.

3. When adding liquid to melted chocolate, add all at once rather than gradually.

What are some trouble areas when cooking with chocolate?

1. Never bring the chocolate to a boil by itself. It will lump up and then start to smoke as though it's ready to burn and develop a powdery sediment. When the chocolate so heated is allowed to cool, little white spots will appear on the surface.

2. When you try to add small amounts of liquid to various types of melted American chocolate instead of becoming a soft, smooth mass, the mixture tightens or develops sandy grains. This happens because of the large amounts of cocoa butter in domestic chocolate. One of the properties of this cocoa butter mix is that it will accept large amounts of liquid but not small ones. So add syrup or liquid all at once, not a little at a time.

What causes chocolate, when melted, to become tight and grainy?

1. Too high heat. Use a double boiler over barely simmering water.

2. Moisture in the melting pan. If liquid must be combined with the chocolate, make sure that there is at least one tablespoon of the liquid per ounce of chocolate.

How can chocolate be melted in a microwave?

1. Place chocolate in the microwave in a safe container.
2. Heat at medium level for 2–4 minutes, or until the chocolate turns shiny.
3. Remove and stir until completely melted.

How can a chocolate dip be prevented from melting when held before using?

Add a little fat to tempered chocolate using all-vegetable shortening to the warm melted chocolate.

How should liquid be added to melting chocolate?

Add it all at once, not a few drops at a time.

What is tempering?

The stabilization of chocolate by melting and cooling to increase glossiness of the surface and malleability.

What should you do when tempering chocolate?

1. Do the tempering in a room at about 68 to 70 °F.
2. Chop the chocolate into small pieces and put into a bowl.
3. Set the bowl over hot, not simmering, water, making sure that the bottom of the bowl doesn't touch the water. Make sure that no steam comes into the bowl.
4. Slowly heat to 120 °F so it will melt.
5. Then remove the bowl from its bath and dry the bottom.
6. Make sure that all the work surfaces and implements are dry, for moisture will cause the solids to separate from the fat and clump together.
7. Chocolate can be melted in a microwave at a medium setting, checking frequently and stirring occasionally.

How should cold chocolate desserts be served?

The flavor of chocolate will be more noticeable if you remove the dessert from the refrigerator for a brief time before serving.

How should chocolate be stored at home?

1. Store no longer than one year for dark chocolate, about six months for white or milk chocolate.
2. Keep wrapped lightly in a cool, dark, dry place (60–75 °F).
3. If the temperature exceeds 75 °F some of the cocoa butter may separate and rise to the surface, causing the development of a whitish cast known as bloom. It is still edible and there will be little change in flavor.

What is the best all-around chocolate to have on hand for cooking and baking?

Probably the best to have on hand for cooking or baking is one with good melting qualities and very little sugar, if any. This way you can adjust the sweetness to any particular taste simply by adding sugar. Also, a chocolate with no sugar added is apt to last longer (partly because you won't be tempted to nibble on it).

What is the quantitative relationship of cocoa to baking chocolate?

3 level teaspoons of cocoa + 2 tablespoons shortening = 1 ounce/square baking chocolate.

What needs to be added when chocolate is melted for an icing?

One teaspoon of butter.

What is the best chocolate for making slivers for topping a cake?

Sweet milk chocolate is best for this.

What is an easy way to make chocolate slivers to top a cake?

Use a potato peeler on a bar of chocolate. Dip the peeler in hot water to warm slightly and then run it along the smooth surface of a square of chocolate. If the curls chip or don't curl properly, dip the peeler in hot water again.

What can be done when fudge doesn't set up?

Try returning it to the pot, adding a teaspoon of water and cooking for a few more minutes.

How should milk chocolate be prepared for chopping in a food processor?

First, refrigerate the chocolate an hour or put it in the freezer compartment for fifteen minutes. Then use a pulse technique in the processor.

What is ganache?

Rich chocolate mixed with hot cream. As it melts, fine droplets of cocoa butter disperse into the cream, forming a shiny, silky smooth mixture.

What kind of chocolate should be used for making ganache?

Any bittersweet cooking chocolate, semisweet, milk or bar chocolate. But it should be good quality (a high cocoa butter content) so the chocolate flavor will come through.

What is a molé?

This delicious southern Mexican dish has unsweetened chocolate hidden in garlic, tomatoes, onions, chile powder and other spices and ingredients such as meat or poultry (such as turkey).

How can chocolate frosting that has dulled from drying be made shiny again?

Blow dry, using low heat and fan setting so that the frosting doesn't melt.

What is mocha?

A mixture of chocolate and coffee or coffee liqueur in varying proportions in sauces, cakes, drinks etc. It also refers to a Yemeni or Ethiopian bean that has a chocolate taste.

White Chocolate

What is white chocolate?

A mixture of cocoa butter, milk solids and sugar but no chocolate solids. It often has lecithin and vanilla added to it. Sometimes cocoa butter is replaced wholly or in part by vegetable fats to reduce cost, but that also means reduced quality.

What is the difference in flavor between white chocolate and milk or dark chocolate?

White: Rich, sweet, not very chocolatey.

Milk or dark: Bolder flavors.

What is the difference in the labeling of white chocolates from Europe and those from the United States?

Europe: Product can be labeled as white chocolate without the specified amount of cocoa butter.

United States: If the product does not have the required amount of cocoa butter, it cannot be labeled as chocolate. White chocolate is considered a confectionary coating.

Is there a strict formula for white chocolate?

No. It can vary in aroma, flavor, texture and consistency because of differences of sweetness, amount of cocoa butter, freshness, type of milk solids, the refining process, the length of conching and the quality of the flavoring used.

What is the new definition of white chocolate?

Effective as of 1988, there must be a minimum of 20% of cocoa butter.

What caution needs to be taken when melting white chocolate?

Excessive heat causes its milk proteins to clump and tighten, so keep the water in a double boiler below simmering, between 110 °F and 120 °F.

What is the melting point of white chocolate?

95 °F, below body temperature, which results in an even taste and smooth feel in the mouth.

What is critical about choosing white chocolate?

Avoid any brand that has substituted a vegetable fat for cocoa butter. Read the label.

What does it mean when white chocolate has "summer coating" or "compound coating" on the label?

A vegetable fat other than cocoa butter has been used, and therefore it won't taste much or anything like chocolate.

What does weather have to do with the use of white chocolate?

In humid weather, moisture is absorbed by milk proteins and results in a graininess when melted.

How should white chocolate be stored?

Never warmer than 65–70 °F, or the butter fats will turn rancid.

Can white be substituted for dark chocolate in a recipe?

No, because the white has no binding power.

COFFEE

Where does most of the world's coffee come from?

Brazil.

Where did coffee originate?

Tropical Africa and in Ethiopia, where the Arabs made the first use of it as a hot drink.

Is the drinking of coffee in America increasing?

No. Coffee consumption peaked in 1962, when it was thirty-one cups per person per day. In 1965 it had dropped to seventeen cups. There has been a resurgence in recent years, especially of the more expensive coffees, but the total is still less than it was in 1962.

What is the compound that gives the characteristic flavor of roasted coffee?

There is no single compound. There are more than seventy distinctive compounds involved.

What are the two main kinds of coffee beans?

Arabica: About three-quarters of production, the main one that comes to the United States. It is grown in high altitudes in tropical and subtropical areas that have plenty of rainfall.

Robusta: About one-quarter of production, a stronger flavored bean. It is grown at lower altitudes, also in tropical and subtropical areas. This varietal is easier to grow and is a heavier producer than the Arabica.

Which coffee has the highest caffeine level?

Robusta.

Does ground coffee easily absorb foreign odors and flavors?

Yes, such as from onions in the refrigerator.

What determines the quality of brewed coffee besides the quality of the beans?

1. Quantity, composition and temperature of the water.
2. The particle size (grind) of the ground bean.
3. The coffeemaker.
4. The extraction time.

Why is the use of Robusta increasing even if it is not the highest quality bean?

Because it is cheaper.

Does a stronger coffee require a darker roast?

No. Stronger coffee requires more coffee beans.

Does the name of the roast indicate the source of the bean?

No. For instance, Italian coffee can come from Brazil, and a Brazilian roast can come from Colombia.

What is the best way to store coffee beans?

In a tight container, preferably glass or glazed ceramic, to ban odors.

How long can coffee be kept?

If it is to be kept at room temperature, coffee can be stored for a week.
Coffee can also be kept in the refrigerator for a month, and even longer in the freezer.

What happens if you freeze coffee beans?

Freezing neutralizes the essential oils that reduce bitterness and improve richness. If you are going to keep ground coffee for more than a week, freezing is the lesser of the evils.

Should only distilled water be used to make coffee?

Tap water can have a disagreeable taste from metals and chemicals leached from the pipes and boiler. Heating tap water can make this bad taste even worse. If the tap water is drinkable, then distilled water is not necessary unless you have a finicky palate. Always start the process with cold water from the tap, as it will have less contamination.

How can cloudy coffee be cleared?

Reheat with an egg white added.

What is the best water for brewing coffee?

Cold, naturally soft water that is free of any water softener residue or odor such as chlorine.

What does adding milk to coffee do?

1. It masks or softens harshness.
2. It gives a creamier texture.
3. It varies with the roast. A lighter roast has a higher acid level and lighter body, and thus adding milk gives it a fullness comparable to darker roasts.

What is espresso?

Hot water is forced under high pressure in less than thirty seconds through finely ground and packed, very darkly (Italian) roasted beans to form a strong, thick, rich drink that is not acidic. It is served in a demitasse cup, which usually holds about an ounce of liquid.

Does espresso contain a higher level of caffeine?

Coffee prepared for making espresso has more caffeine than regular brews, but an espresso is served about one-quarter the size of a regular cup and therefore the total caffeine consumed is less. Also the brief steam-pressurized process for making espresso extracts less caffeine than does a percolator.

Which has more caffeine, instant or drip?

Drip coffee has twice as much caffeine as instant.

When a coffee bean is roasted what happens to its weight and volume?

1. It shrinks in weight about 15%.
2. It doubles in volume.

What does roasting do?

1. It develops oils, flavorings and aromatics.
2. Induces a chemical reaction that will lead to a loss of freshness when exposed to air.
3. Forms carbon dioxide gas, which protects against oxidation, but when the bean is ground, the carbon dioxide escapes and rancidity will slowly develop.

Does roasting change the caffeine content?

In a normal roast it doesn't change, but a darker roast slightly decreases the amount.

What are the caffeine amounts produced using various types of coffeemakers?

Per 8 oz. serving: Percolated 190–270 mg.
                    Drip   170–200 mg.
                    Instant   90–112 mg.

How much caffeine is in decaffeinated coffee?

From 3 to 7 mg.

What is the effect of coffee on the body other than the stimulation caused by the caffeine?

It tends to leach magnesium out of the body and minimize its absorption.

What are the main roasts?

The roasts are not clearly defined and vary considerably from one house to another.

American: The lightest, the least time in the roaster, but to a rich fullness.
Italian: Very dark, used for espresso.
French: Very dark with a heavy roasted flavor.

What is Chicory Coffee (also called Chicken Coffee)?

It is regular coffee with chicory in the blend, which adds bitterness. A favorite in the southern United States.

Which is more distinctive in flavor, light or dark roasted?

Lighter roasts are more delicate and individually distinctive.

What are the different grinds?

The terms vary from one store to the next, and some use numbers instead of names such as 1, 2, 2½, etc.

Fine: Used for drip, espresso.

Medium: Used for metal filters.

Coarse: Used for boiling types, percolators.

Extra fine: Used in vacuum types, for Turkish coffee.

Is there a limit of time between roasting and grinding?

Flavor decreases day by day. The warmer the storage temperature, the quicker the decrease in flavor from the roasting. In a tightly covered glass container the flavor will keep well for about three weeks.

Why should coffee not be ground in advance?

The grinding increases the surface area that is exposed to air and therefore the coffee oxidizes quicker. Also grinding releases some of the carbon dioxide gas that is part of the body and bouquet. Packing ground coffee in sealed cans slows coffee's deterioration until the can is opened. Refrigeration slows the oxidative process, freezing slows it even more.

How does the grind affect the flavor?

While different types of coffeemakers require different grinds, in general, the finer the grind, the fuller the flavor.

Is coffee ever ground powder-fine?

Yes, for Turkish and Greek Coffee.

What is Turkish coffee?

It is made by boiling together finely ground coffee, sugar and water to make a very strong brew.

What is cappuccino?

Espresso combined with steamed milk and topped with frothed milk.

What is instant coffee?

Brewed coffee from which the water has been evaporated out in either a vacuum or freezer-dryer to form crystals.

What can be substituted if a recipe calls for Postum?

Instant coffee.

Which is better, a single bean (type) coffee or a blend of several beans?

The blend is more complex and richer but hides the flavor of a specific bean. This is a matter of taste preference. Most prefer the mix.

Should white coffee filters be used?

No, as the dioxin used to bleach these filters may leave a harmful residue.

Why are freshly roasted coffee beans packed in non-airtight bags?

To allow the carbon monoxide formed during the roasting process to escape. If not, the coffee may have a poor taste.

What happens if coffee boils after brewing?

It becomes bitter and oily.

Why is a percolator not recommended as a coffeemaker?

Because it boils the coffee, which results in bitterness.

Should coffee be reheated?

Reheating is not recommended because coffee easily becomes bitter. If it must be reheated, don't let it come to a boil. Microwaving is a good way to reheat.

How long can brewed coffee be left on the warming plate of the coffeemaker?

It is best to pour brewed coffee into a preheated, insulated carafe because the flavors start to deteriorate within 10 to 15 minutes if left on the warmer.

Coffee will keep in a thermos almost an hour if the container has been preheated with hot water and drained.

What are the main factors in getting the best cup of coffee?

1. Choose a good grade of coffee.
2. Grind the beans to order and to the right grind for the coffeemaker.
3. Make sure the coffeemaker is scrupulously clean.
4. Use cold water that is free from minerals.
5. Don't let the coffee come to a boil.

Does coffee contain fat?

1. It is fat-free unless a small amount of oil is added when the coffee is flavored.
2. Flavored instant has about 2 grams of fat per cup of coffee.

Why is it essential that coffeemakers be scrupulously cleaned after each use?

Unless batches are made in succession, the residual oils will turn rancid and spoil the next batch.

How should a coffeepot be cleaned?

Scrub well with a mild detergent or baking soda solution and then rinse completely. However, some feel that soap should never be used as its residue remains and tarnishes the flavor.

How can iced coffee drinks be made without the melting ice cubes diluting the flavor?

Freeze strong coffee into cubes for chilling the drink.

TEA

What is the earliest evidence of tea being used as a beverage?

Used in prehistoric times, the first record dates from the first century in China.

What are the various kinds of tea?

There are about 3,000 variations of tea, depending upon where grown, the age of the leaf at which it is picked, the processing and whether it is fermented or not. All tea comes from the same plant species.

What is black tea?

The most popular are: Assam, Ceylon, Darjeeling, English Breakfast and Lapsang. The leaves undergo a nonalcoholic fermentation after being picked, in which the astringent elements are converted to more complex components and the leaves develop their reddish brown color and mellower flavor. It has the strongest flavor.

How does green tea differ?

The leaves are simply dried, not fermented. It has the most delicate flavor. It is the most popular in the Orient, particularly favored in China and Japan.

What is jasmine tea?

A scented green tea from China with jasmine petals added.

How is oolong unique?

It is a mix of black and green tea leaves from Japan or Formosa. The leaves are only partially fermented, which results in the development in some good-tasting oils while not changing naturally occuring oils. The result is a medium flavored tea.

What is the Earl Grey blend?

A blend of teas that is flavored with oil of bergamot (a bitter orange).

What is English Breakfast tea?

A loosely defined blend of Ceylon and Indian teas with a brisk flavor.

What does orange pekoe indicate?

That the leaves were picked from the top of the plant and are the smallest-sized leaves.

What is the difference between pekoe and orange pekoe?

The size and cut of the leaves used; pekoe are medium-sized, coarser leaves.

Is herbal tea a true tea?

Herbal teas are more properly called tisanes. They are not teas proper but are used as such. They are made from various herbs, flowers and spices and are caffeine-free.

Are herbal teas safe?

Most are safe, but a small percentage of people experience undesirable side effects from using them. For example, camomile tea has a laxative effect on some individuals. Some herbals have medicinal properties and so consumption should first be permitted by your doctor, particularly if there are medical problems and/or you are on medication. In any case, drink in moderation.

Where do the best teas come from?

Lapsang souchang from Taiwan; Assam and Darjeeling from Eastern India and Ceylon from Sri Lanka.

Which is the largest-selling tea in the United States?

Orange pekoe, a blend of different teas from Ceylon.

Is the quality of the water used for brewing tea important?

Very important. If the tap water is hard, then either filter it or purchase a bottled water.

What can happen if tea is brewed more than five minutes?

A bitterness will probably develop.

Should soap be used to clean teapots?

Yes, but only if the soap is carefully and thoroughly rinsed out.

How should bulk tea be stored?

In an airtight container that is not subject to heat, light or moisture.

How long will bulk teas keep?

Almost indefinitely.

Do commercial tea bags use a particular kind of tea?

Usually they contain a blend of teas.

Does the quality of tea depend on the size of the leaf?

The smaller the leaf, the younger it is and the finer the tea. Uniformity is as important as the size of the leaves.

What is a tea ball?

An infuser or strainer holding the leaves and through which the water is poured.

What are some considerations in using loose leaf tea versus tea bags?

1. Bags are easier to remove than loose leaves.
2. Some tea makers have strainers built into them.
3. A better choice of teas are available as loose leaves.

4. Often lesser teas are put into bags.

5. Loose leaves allow better water flow through tea.

How should tea be made?

1. Start with cold water and bring it to a boil (hot or reheated water contains less dissolved air, which can result in a flat taste).

2. Add the tea (loose leaves, tea bag or strainer).

3. Avoid long steeping, which may cause bitterness. About 5 minutes is ideal.

4. Don't stir the tea during the steeping process.

5. If a stronger tea is wanted, add more tea leaves.

What should the teapot be made of?

1. Use one made of glass, ceramics or porcelain.

2. Most nonporous ones work well.

3. Don't use metal as it can result in an undesirable reaction with the tea, which gives an off-taste.

What happens if the tea remains in the teapot too long?

It will stain the pot.

Why should tea for iced tea be made stronger?

To allow for the dilution that will result from melting ice cubes, double strength is often desirable (unless tea is cooled in the refrigerator and no ice is used).

What teas are best for iced tea?

Fermented black teas, such as Darjeeling, Earl Grey and English Breakfast.

What kind of iced cubes are best for iced tea?

Cubes made from tea.

How can cloudiness in iced tea be avoided?

1. Brew with cold water and refrigerate overnight.

2. If made with hot water, let the tea cool before refrigerating.

3. If made with boiling water and refrigerated while hot, it is apt to cloud. This can be cleared by adding a little boiling water.

Should Styrofoam cups be used to serve tea?

No!! The tea will react and affect the taste when served in Styrofoam. The reaction is accelerated if lemon juice is present.

CAFFEINE

What is the most commonly consumed drug in the world?

Caffeine. It is found in coffee, tea and cocoa and is added to soft drinks and other products.

What is caffeine?

A bitter alkaloid found in various plants and trees. It is used as a flavoring in soft drinks. It is not a normal part of plant metabolism, but rather is a defense the plant manufactures to inhibit insects or other predators from eating it.

What are the good effects of caffeine on the body?

1. It stimulates the cortex of the brain.
2. In small doses it improves attention, concentration, coordination.
3. It acts on the kidneys to increase water elimination.
4. It stimulates the action of the heart.
5. It causes blood vessels to widen everywhere, except in the brain where they are constricted.
6. It alters calcium ions so the contracting power of skeletal muscles are less susceptible to fatigue.
7. It can make for a better mood, i.e., cause a person to be more awake, eager for work and confident.
8. It fights drowsiness, so it probably can boost performance on monotonous tasks.

What are the bad effects of caffeine?

1. It can result in irregularities in the heartbeat.
2. It can cause overacute sensations.
3. It can result in hyperesthesia (oversensitivity of the skin or other sense organs).
4. There can be withdrawal symptoms if a heavy user (two or three cups of coffee a day, taking a caffeine-containing medication for more than a few days—more than 300 milligrams per day) discontinues use. Withdrawal symptoms usually start with headaches.
5. People with high blood pressure can have adverse reactions if caffeine is consumed before exercising, because it can excessively elevate blood pressure.
6. Too much consumption can cause restlessness, anxiety, irritability, sleeplessness, nervousness, diarrhea and increased heart rate. The amount needed to trigger these reactions varies greatly, depending upon individual sensitivity. Some can get these negative effects on a single cup. Even habitual users can have these reactions if they go above their usual amount.
7. It could affect zinc absorption, which could result in reduced sexual drive.
8. It could cause the skin to be dehydrated and thus promote premature aging.
9. Heavy caffeine use has been linked to infertility and miscarriages.
10. It reduces the body's ability to handle stress.

11. It has a negative effect on calcium metabolism.

12. There is currently debate over whether infants whose mothers consumed coffeine in pregnancy are at a higher risk for sudden infant death syndrome (SIDS).

Are there other sources of caffeine besides drinks?

Yes. Certain pain relievers, Excedrin for example, can easily supply as much caffeine in a day as five cups or more of coffee.

Which has more caffeine, tea or coffee?

Tea leaves are 2% caffeine by weight, coffee beans, about 1%. While tea has more caffeine, a pound of tea will make about 200 cups, while a pound of coffee will make only about 40 cups. Also a cup of coffee contains twice as much caffeine as a cup of tea because the caffeine is better extracted in coffee, thus there are 100 milligrams in a cup of coffee as opposed to 50 milligrams in tea.

How much caffeine is there in cola and cocoa?

A 12-ounce can of cola has about 35 milligrams, a cup of cocoa, about 15 milligrams.

Does the amount of caffeine in coffee and tea depend on the way it was brewed?

The amount can vary according to how coffee is brewed. Percolated coffee contains about 200 milligrams per cup, drip process about 108, instant around 100 and decaffeinated only 5. Black tea contains about 50 milligrams per cup, while its decaffeinated counterpart has around 10–12.

CHAPTERTHREE

DAIRY

BUTTER

What is the composition of butter?

There is no standard. It varies from batch to batch because of a cow's breed, feed, season, local legislation and dairy policy. Federal rules require at least 80 percent fat content.

What is the typical percentage breakdown of butter?

	UNSALTED/SWEET	SALTED
Fat:	81	81
Moisture:	18	16
Salt:	0	2
Other:	1	1

What other components are there?

Protein (casein), carbohydrate (lactose), minerals (other than salt).

What are the differences among butter grades?

AA: Made from fresh, sweet cream and has the best flavor, color, aroma and texture. Minimum 80% fat.

A: Excellent quality. Minimum 80% fat. Has lower flavor rating than AA.

B: May have a slightly acidic taste. Made from sour cream.

Is color a reliable indicator of quality of butter?

It is natural for color to vary from the palest yellow to deep yellow. Jersey and Guernsey cows yield the deepest yellow. The color is deepest in springtime and early summer when grass is rich in orange-yellow carotene, but because consistency sells, dairies use dyes such as carotene or annatto seed extract to get the same color all the time.

How are premium butters different from nonpremium butters?

They have a higher butterfat content, sometimes as high as 86%. They are made in small batches from the best quality cream. In some cases they are made from cream from cows not treated with hormones.

What is light butter?

This a relatively new product with a minimum of 52% fat and the balance replaced with whey, skim milk or other dairy ingredients. It is not to be used for cooking or baking.

What does the designation "sweet cream" on the label mean?

Only that the butter was made from sweet cream.

What is margarine?

A butter substitute made from hydrogenated vegetable oil or animal fat. It contains coloring, preservatives and food flavorings.

Is margarine more healthful than butter?

It was once thought so, but recent studies indicate that this is not valid. Margarine users, feeling safer, tend to use margarine more liberally, and thus ingest more fat.

Do blended butter spreads such as "I Can't Believe Its Not Butter" have less fat than butter?

It is a toss-up. Most combination spreads have little or no cholesterol, but their fat content is almost the same as butter and it is fat that plays a leading role in clogging arteries. Most blends also have trans fatty acids that are created when the vegetable oils are hydrogenated to make them solid, and it is these acids that contribute to heart disease.

Do white streaks in butter or margarine with or without multiple shades indicate quality?

Color is an indication of uniformity of a sample, not of its quality.

What is whipped butter?

Standard butter inflated with air by whipping for greater spreadability.

Why should butter be stored in a closed container?

To prevent the absorption of foreign flavors.

Can a heavy cream be whipped to butter in substitution of purchased butter for home baking?

Consistent results will be difficult because the amount of air and moisture will vary considerably.

Why is stick butter better for cooking than whipped?

1. If you use whipped butter, you must increase the amount by about one-third, because it contains 25 percent more air.
2. Almost all recipes are based on stick butter.

What can be done with the paper wrappers of stick butter?

They can be used to grease a pan and can be frozen until needed.

What are the advantages of tub butter?

1. It melts more quickly and is good for toppings, e.g., waffles.
2. It is easier to spread than stick butter.

What is the negative of tub butter?

It is more difficult to measure.

How much butter is required if the recipe calls for butter the size of a walnut?

The equivalent is 2 tablespoons, or 1 ounce.

Why can't butter be used for frying?

The milk solids settle to the bottom of the pan and will burn.

What can be done to prevent the burning?

Clarify the butter.

What is clarified (drawn) butter?

Clarified (drawn) butter is regular butter that has been treated by heating and the non-fat portion (water, salt, milk proteins) has been removed by decanting the clear yellow liquid (melted fat) into another container.

What are some uses of clarified butter?

It can be used for sautéing, tossing with steamed vegetables or for brushing on a piece of poached fish.

What are the advantages of clarified butter?

1. It is better than regular butter as a cooking medium.
2. It can be used to fry at a higher temperature (250–350 °F), for the absence of the milk proteins minimizes browning of the butter.
3. It can be stored longer because it loses its protein in the clarification process, protein is the first element to sour.

What are the disadvantages of clarified butter?

With both clarified butter and butter/oil mixtures you lose much of the butter flavor.

How do you clarify butter?

1. Cut butter in small chunks so it will melt at a lower temperature.
2. Melt slowly in a saucepan until the butterfat separating out is visible. Most of the solids will drop to the bottom, but a white foam layer will form on top.
3. Do not stir. Carefully remove the saucepan from the burner and spoon off the top foam.
4. Put in an ovenproof glass container in the oven at its lowest setting. Glass is better because it allows you to monitor the process. Do not stir!
5. Cool in the refrigerator for at least an hour. Do not disturb the bowl until the middle fat layer has solidified.
6. Lift out the solidified fat disk. Scrape off as much of foam and slimy bottom layer as possible without damaging the disk. Finish the cleaning step by quickly rinsing disk under cold, running tap water. Pat dry with a paper towel.

What is the yield in making clarified butter?

One pound butter yields about 1½ cups clarified.

What can you do if you must use it immediately?

After melting, scoop off the whey floating on top with a ladle and use the clear butter. Be careful not to take up the precipitated whey on the bottom.

How long can clarified butter be kept?

If kept covered in the refrigerator it can be stored for weeks, often longer.

How do you keep butter from scorching?

1. Use clarified butter.
2. Use half butter, half vegetable oil. The mixture has a higher smoke point than butter alone, less than oil alone.
3. Don't overheat, for that will change the character of the butter protein.

Why are some brands of butter sometimes watery?

Butter shouldn't vary much in water content, because by regulation it can have no more than 16% of its weight as water. Consistency varies according to the physical state of its fat.

What is summer fat?

Summer fat is usually softer than winter fat due to the change in the cows' feed, which affects the composition of their milk fat. The higher the percentage of free fat the more the butter will suffer from "oiling off," a premature separation of easily melted free fat from the crystals and globules. Besides being softer than the fat from winter, summer fat has more water in it.

Does this variation in moisture content make a difference?

This could have an effect in pastry and puff paste dough, which depend on the solid butter to keep the sheets of dough apart.

How long does butter keep?

It may be stored in its original carton or in a covered container in the *coldest* part of the refrigerator (not the door "butter keeper") for about a month or frozen in its original container for four months. Keep it in its original wrapper or wrap in foil or an airtight plastic bag for best results.

Why is salted butter a bane to cooks?

The salt content can vary from brand to brand, region to region. For example, one batch could be 1⅓% salt, while another could be 3%.

What is an easy way to measure stick butter?

Using the printed marking on the stick wrapper and making dents in the butter to indicate where to cut.

Can salted and unsalted butter be used interchangeably by varying the amount of salt added to the recipe?

1. It is difficult to calculate how much salt to take out of a recipe to compensate for the salt in the butter since almost all recipes are written based on unsalted butter.
2. Since salt acts as a preservative, unsalted butter is often fresher.
3. Salt is more of a flavoring agent than the preservative that it used to be.
4. On delicately flavored items such as a beurre blanc sauce, salted butter should not be used, but in strongly flavored items such as chocolate chip cookies it is acceptable.

What kind of butter should be used to make caramel?

Fresh, salted butter to create a balance of flavors.

What kind of butter should be used in making compound butters such as those containing red peppers, herbs or Roquefort cheese?

Use sweet (unsalted) butter of good quality.

How can herbed butter be made?

Melt the butter and then steep the herbs in it for a few minutes, depending on how strong a flavor is desired.

When heating butter in a microwave, why does it suddenly explode and make for a messy cleanup?

Butterfat, like all fats, is less dense than water. The watery portion of buttermilk collects at the bottom of the container as the lighter fat melts. The oven's energy is much more efficiently absorbed by the water. The small amount of water vaporizes, expands greatly in volume and suddenly propels the fat out of the container and onto the walls of the oven.

What is creaming and how is it done?

Creaming is beating butter (or a solid fat), usually at room temperature, with sugar until light and fluffy from the incorporated air.

Can creaming be done by machine?

This can be done by machine and will yield a fine-grained texture. The optimum temperature for the ingredients to be creamed is 70 °F.

What butter should be used for creaming?

Use unsalted butter.

How long before serving should flavored butter, such as with olives or walnuts, be made?

Make it the day before so that the flavors will meld.

BUTTERMILK

How much butter is there in buttermilk today?

None.

Why doesn't today's buttermilk taste like the old-fashioned kind?

Almost all buttermilk today comes from artificially soured skim milk, while the old-fashioned variety was made from whole milk and was the direct product of butter making. Traditionally whole milk is allowed to sour in order to make it easier for butter to coagulate. When sufficiently sour, the milk is churned to separate the butter from the nonfat components (which becomes the buttermilk). The few yellow specks of butter you see in buttermilk were too small to be removed.

In what other form is buttermilk found?

It is also available as a dried powder for baking.

What should be done to substitute buttermilk for regular milk in a baking recipe?

Add ½ teaspoon baking powder per cup of buttermilk.

What role does buttermilk play as a marinade for chicken?

It tenderizes the meat. Buttermilk also can help make a creamy sauce if more is added at the end of the cooking.

CHEESE

What is cheese?

A man-made food created by separating the milk solids (the curd) from the liquid portion (the whey) of milk, using enzymes and/or lactic acid bacteria.

Which is the world's largest cheese producer?

The United States.

How are cheeses classified?

Basically by moisture content. The moister and softer cheeses have more limited keeping quality.

What cheese has the largest percentage of saturated fat?

Cream cheese, with 90% of its calories from fat.

What is the volume relationship of milk to cheese?

It takes about 8 pounds of milk to make 1 pound of cheese, but it varies with type. One gallon of milk will yield 8 ounces of Camembert, while it takes 3 gallons to make 5 pounds of Brie.

How much grated cheese will a pound of cheese make?

From 4 to 4½ cups, depending on the coarseness of the grate.

How can a semisoft cheese, such as Monterey Jack, be grated?

Use a grater with large holes.

Why do the cheeses made from goat and sheep milk have a more pungent aroma?

The milk of these animals has a greater concentration of short-chain fatty acids than milk from cows, which creates a stronger smell.

Does this difference in aroma continue as the cheeses age?

The difference between cheese made from cow's milk and those made from goat or sheep milk will hardly be perceptible in aged cheeses.

Why does goat cheese go well with high acidity wines such as Sauvignon Blanc?

Because they are low in fat and high in acidity.

Are French cheeses sold in the United States different from those sold in France?

Yes. Most American cheeses are made from pasteurized milk. This also means that Brie coming here from France is made from pasteurized milk (but aged cheeses might not be). The taste of unpasteurized cheese is, in most instances, stronger and fuller.

When melted cheese is needed and a low-calorie content is desired, can low-calorie cheese be used?

Cheeses lower in calories contain less fat, so they don't melt very well.

Does the method of pasteurization make a difference in the quality of cheese?

There are two basic methods of pasteurization. The most common is to heat milk to 160 °F for about 15 seconds and then immediately cool. This results in a slight cooked

Dairy

flavor that can be perceived in unaged (fresh) cheese. The other method is to hold the milk at 144 °F for 30 minutes, which prevents a cooked flavor.

Why is coloring added to cheese?

To maintain a year-round consistent color. The natural color comes when the animals eat green plants and have greater vitamin D levels. Cheese made from milk gotten in winter when feeding is done inside would have diminished color.

When a cheese is listed as 50% butterfat does that mean that half the cheese is fat?

No. Most cheeses have 50% (to as much as 70%) water. It is only the solids which contain butterfat that count in this designation. Thus the 50% listed actually diminishes to about 25%.

Is the fat in cheese saturated or unsaturated?

Only about 60% is saturated.

Which cheeses are the highest in butterfat?

The semisoft and those labeled as double or triple cream.

What is the difference between ripened and unripened cheese?

Ripened: After a cheese is made it is given a protective covering or wrapping and stored at appropriate temperature and humidity to ripen to full flavor and texture.

Unripened: These are consumed soon after they are made, such as cottage cheese, and are not suitable for long storage.

What do the various ripening classifications indicate?

Soft unripened: High in moisture: cottage, cream, ricotta.

Firm unripened: Lower moisture: mozzarella.

Soft ripened: Slightly moist, mild to pungent, ripening occurs from outside to center: Camembert.

Semisoft ripened: Ripened throughout the cheese, mellow to strong flavor: Bel Paese, Muenster.

Firm ripened: Ripened throughout, mild to very sharp: Gouda, Cheddar.

Hard ripened: Ripened throughout, sharp flavor, low moisture: Parmesan.

Blue vein ripened: Semisoft, crumbly, slightly sharp to peppery: Roquefort.

Are smoked cheeses really smoked?

Not always. Sometimes liquid smoke or smoked salt is added instead.

What is processed cheese?

A cheese product (or a mixture of different cheeses) that has been pasteurized or cooked so that no further ripening occurs. It is made with stabilizers, coloring, gums or other chemicals. It is low in milk fat and high in moisture. Cheese mixtures plus the pasteurization destroy some part of its flavor.

Is pasteurized cheese ever flavored?

Yes, it is often mixed with pimientos, spices, vegetables or other foods.

How popular is processed cheese in the United States?

It represents more than half the cheese consumed in the United States.

What are government standards for processed cheese?

Only 57% of the final weight must be cheese.

What is fresh cheese?

Unripened cheese that has not been allowed to age and thus has a shorter shelf life than ripened cheese. Typically soft, it must be refrigerated. Flavors are close to fresh or whole milk.

What are some examples?

Cream cheese, mascarpone, fresh mozzarella, ricotta.

What is mascarpone?

An Italian cheese (though now also made in the U.S.) made from cream.

How is it used?

Like a cream cheese, in risotto or pasta sauces or with fruits and liqueurs in desserts.

What are the properties of soft cheese?

Made from cow's milk. Soft texture. Aged to some degree but not ripened, not made for aging. Fluffy, white rind, which becomes softer and creamier with age. Has a high moisture content.

What are examples?

Cottage, farmer's, pot, cream, Neufchâtel.

What is the difference between farmer's, pot and cottage cheese?

All three are made from pasteurized cow's milk, are low in fat and nutritious. Farmer's is cottage cheese from which most of the liquid has been pressed out. Sometimes the same cheese is called by any of the three names.

Farmer's: Grainy, firm enough to cut, curdless.

Cottage: Moist, milk, has curds.

Pot: Cottage cheese that has been drained of whey longer.

How is semisoft different from soft cheese?

Ripens from inside as well as on the surface. Little or no rind. Curing continues as long as temperature is favorable. High in moisture.

What are examples?

Brie, Camembert, Edam, Cheddar, Teleme, feta, Limburger.

What are blue vein cheeses?

These are cured with the aid of mold bacteria and specific mold culture that grows throughout the inside and produces familiar appearance and flavor.

What are examples of blue veined cheese?

Roquefort, bleu, Stilton, Gorgonzola.

What are firm cheeses?

Cheeses ripened utilizing a bacterial culture throughout the whole cheese. Slow cured with very low moisture and higher salt content.

What are the kinds of firm cheeses?

Brick, Cheddar, colby, Gouda, Gruyère, mozzarella, Muenster, Port-Salut, Havarti, provolone, Swiss, Emmenthaler.

What does the "weeping" of Emmenthaler indicate?

When the holes are moist and shiny from butterfat it signifies maturity.

How are very hard cheeses different from softer cheeses?

They are slow-cured with the aid of a bacterial culture with enzymes. Very low moisture content. Good for grating. Can be stored longer and can be frozen. Aged from several months to several years.

What are some of these cheeses?

Parmesan, Romano, Asiago, hard Monterey Jack, sapsago.

What are some good cheeses for melting in cooking?

Fontina, mozzarella, Romano, provolone, Parmesan, Gruyère.

How does Parmigiana Romano (Italian Parmesan) vary?

From the time of year the milk is taken.

Spring: Lowest butterfat, drier, complex flavor, softer, delicate.
Summer: Strongest, darkest color.
Fall: Highest butterfat, sweet, intense, dry, granular, full-bodied flavor.

What are the characteristics of fontina?

Semifirm, creamy, nutty flavor, melts easily and smoothly.

How you tell the age of fontina from the rind?

A light brown color says that it hasn't aged very long, while a darker brown comes with aging.

How can you tell age from the color of the cheese?

The color of the cheese does not indicate the length of the aging process. Yellowish color indicates that the cows were fed on fresh grass and that the cheese is rich in carotene from summer/autumn origin. It will have a higher caloric content and be richer in flavor.

What cheeses originated in the United States?

Monterey Jack (California) and brick and colby (Wisconsin).

Where are some of the American cheeses manufactured, and what are their distinctions?

Monterey Jack:	California (similar to American Mnenster)
Dry Monterey Jack:	California (similar to Parmesan)
Teleme:	California (unique tangy flavor)
Crowley:	Vermont (also known as Store Cheese, somewhat similar to Cheddar)
Colby:	Wisconsin
Maytag Blue:	Iowa (a creamy bleu)
Limburger:	Wisconsin (aromatic, pungent)
Brick:	Wisconsin (semisoft with tiny holes)

How should cheese be chosen at the market?

1. It should look clean and fresh.
2. The packaging should be intact, not stained or sticky.
3. Select a store with a good turnover.
4. Best bought when cut to order.

What is the best way to choose a cheese?

By taste.

Does real, authentic Parmigiano-Reggiano vary in quality, flavor, texture?

Made from winter milk:	Higher in butterfat, softer, best as a table cheese.
Made from summer milk:	Drier, better for grating.

How should Parmigiano be stored?

To avoid drying out and losing flavor, tightly wrap in plastic and after each use, use fresh plastic.

Should Parmigiano be stored in the coldest part of the refrigerator?

To the contrary, in the warmest part at approximately 40 °F.

What is the difference between an Italian and a domestic Parmesan?

Parmigiano-Reggiano is aged 2–4 years, while domestic is aged only slightly more than one year.

What are the characteristics of a good Parmesan?

No dry, white patches, a uniform, pale, creamy color. Crumbly, not rock hard. A mellow taste.

What is the best way to buy Parmesan?

Cut from the wheel, not precut, for when cut it dries and loses flavor. If immediately wrapped in plastic a good portion of its character will be saved.

Is it critical for quality to have freshly grated Parmigiano?

Yes, for dishes at room temperatures such as a salad. On hot dishes, such as pasta, the difference is hardly noticeable. This is especially true if the grated cheese has been frozen or refrigerated and kept in an airtight container.

Does Parmesan have to be grated "to order" or can it be pregrated?

Pregrated Parmesan will have a slight diminution of flavor.

Will grated Parmesan cheese deteriorate if stored in the refrigerator rather than grating to order.

No, unless kept for more than four weeks. There are disagreements about how long it will last. It will last a long time when frozen.

Can the quality of a cheese be determined by the regularity and smoothness of its rind?

No, for often the more uneven the rind the more attractive the cheese will be.

What is head cheese?

A sausage made from the head of a pig or calf.

What is ricotta cheese?

It is a cheese made from whey (watery liquid) after the cheese curds have been separated out. It is then reheated or cooked.

What can be substituted in a recipe for ricotta?

Cottage cheese blended smooth.

What is the difference between Italian and American ricotta?

Italian ricotta is made from the whey alone. American ricotta is made with at least some additional cow's milk and thus has a higher milk fat content.

What is ricotta salata?

Ricotta that is salted, pressed and drained of most of its moisture and then aged until it is hard. It develops a sharp flavor and a dry consistency. It has a very white color, no rind and is very good for grating or crumbling.

What is feta made from?

Originally of Greek origin, it was made from sheep or goat milk. It now comes from goat or cow's milk or a mixture of them. It has a strong, salty flavor.

What is the difference between a creamy and a crumbly feta cheese?

Feta is brine aged. The shorter time it stays in the brine the more crumbly it will be, while longer aging makes the cheese softer. Both are good quality.

What is baker's cheese?

A dry curd cheese something like cottage or ricotta. However, it is no longer on the market. Bakeries can get it by special order but only in a thousand-pound lot or larger which they use for making cheese cake.

What are the two types of Gorgonzola?

Dolce: Young, slightly sweet, soft, creamy, strong flavor, blue veined.

Piccante: Sharper, more pungent, warm-white color, soft, blue veined.

What is pecorino?

A general name for Italian cheese made from sheep's milk. It varies considerably in taste and sharpness from one region to another. A similar cheese with the same name is made in the United States.

What is the difference between Brie and Camembert?

They are difficult to distinguish in a blind tasting. They come from different areas of France and the names are also used for their counterparts made in the United States.

How is Cheddar cheese made?

When the curds are formed and then cut into small pieces they are scalded with the whey, then formed, cut into blocks and drained. This gives the cheese its texture. This slow process is called cheddaring which came from the English town of Cheddar.

What is the difference between orange and white Cheddar cheese?

The cheeses are the same. Annatto has been added to the orange version usually for aesthetic reasons only, for annatto is a natural product that is practically tasteless.

Should you buy a cheese with an ammonia scent?

No. Even though cheese stores sometimes claim that the ammonia scent of a surface-ripened cheese indicates the peak of perfection, the cheese is really over the hill because certain enzymes are attacking amino acids in the cheese and this spoils it. If it becomes ammoniated soon after purchase, unwrap, let it air and taste. The off-smell may dissipate.

How should a large piece of cheese that will be used for preparation of several meals be handled?

Cut off as much as you expect to use at one time and carefully wrap and refrigerate the remainder. Don't move it in and out of the refrigerator or let stand at room temperature any more than absolutely necessary.

When a cheese has been cut do you want to retain the moisture?

Yes, for the sake of texture. Keep it tightly wrapped (with fresh film), which also prevents the cheese from picking up odors from storage mates in the refrigerator.

Why can you store a hard cheese longer than a soft one?

Hard cheese has lower water content, and it is water that is conducive to the growth of spoilage-causing bacteria and mold. Cheddar is about 37% water, while cottage cheese is between 70 and 80% water.

What kind of cheeses have edible rinds?

Soft, ripened cheeses such as Brie or Camembert.

Which rinds are not edible?

Hard rinds (such as Parmesan or Stilton) or those that are wax coated.

Can Parmesan rinds be used?

Hard rinds such as those on Parmesan can be added to bean soup while cooking, which will give it special flavor, but they are to be discarded before serving.

How long can cheese be stored in the refrigerator?

Natural and pasteurized:	4–8 weeks.
Fresh:	Such as cottage, cream cheese: about two weeks since they have a high moisture content. Check the date on the container.
Hard, grated:	Romano, Parmesan, hard Monterey Jack: about 3–4 weeks or longer. They can be frozen much longer.
Hard, nongrated:	Several months, and it can be grated directly out of the freezer.

Can cheeses be frozen?

While not the ideal method of storage, most natural cheeses can be frozen without affecting the flavor, but it will result in texture changes, making it more crumbly. The best candidates are hard types such as Parmesan.

How should thawed cheeses be used?

Thawed cheese is best used in cooked dishes because of the change in texture, although the flavor and nutritional value essentially remain unchanged.

What is the best way to thaw cheese?

Thaw for use for about 24 hours in the refrigerator.

Is surface mold on the cheese dangerous?

No, just cut about a half inch off the surface from the affected side. Use the remainder within a week, because the mold spores are still there and will grow again.

Why does cheese sometimes refuse to melt in a sauce?

Probably because the cheese was heated to too high a temperature or for too long. This separates the protein from the fat and makes cheese tough, rubbery and stringy, especially if it is fresh cheese.

What if you just cook it longer?

Once the damage is done, further cooking only makes things worse.

How can you make sure that cheese will melt in a sauce?

1. Finely grate hard cheeses such as Parmesan.
2. Use a thick-bottomed pan or a double boiler, which will ensure even heating. Don't cook too long or at too high a temperature.
3. Add the cheese just before finishing cooking the sauce, continually stirring.

What causes cheese to curdle or string when cooked?

Overheating.

What should be done to prevent curdling?

1. Add the cheese grated.
2. Don't cook too hot.
3. Don't cook too long.
4. Incorporate a little starch (flour or cornstarch) into the cheese.
5. Add a little lemon juice or white wine to the cheese before mixing it into the sauce or dish to be baked.

What should be done when strands of cheese are wanted in the finished dish, such as a pizza?

Use a protein rich cheese such as mozzarella.

Why should cheese be carefully wrapped before refrigeration?

1. To keep the moisture in.
2. To keep cheese odors from getting out to other items in the refrigerator.
3. To keep other odors from permeating the cheese.

Where should cheese be refrigerated?

At the bottom of the refrigerator (vegetable tray).

How should cottage cheese be stored?

With the container upside down in the refrigerator.

What does aging do for cheese?

1. Gives time for the moisture in the cheese to evaporate and thus become firmer.

2. Intensifies flavors, thus aged Cheddar has a sharper taste than a milder, younger version.

3. Lengthens the time it can be kept.

What should be done before slicing or shredding a piece of cheese?

Chill the cheese well.

When should a cheese used as a topping be added?

In the last 5–10 minutes.

How should cheese be served?

Have it at room temperature; never serve it cold.

How can grilled cheese sandwiches be made for a group?

Butter two pieces of bread per sandwich, put the sliced cheese in between them and put them on a baking sheet, buttered sides out and bake at 350 °F, turning once.

What is Welsh rabbit (or Welsh rarebit)?

A British dish of melted Cheddar, beer or ale, seasoning and sometimes milk served over toast.

CREAM

What is cream?

Milk containing at least 18% butterfat.

Does heavy cream weigh more than light cream?

No. Fat has a lower specific density than water. Therefore, contrary to our palates, which are fooled by the viscosity, heavy cream is actually lighter in weight. Light cream is lighter then whole milk. Whole milk is lighter than skim milk.

What is clabber?

Soured, thickened, unpasteurized, unhomogenized milk that has become thickened and soured by the natural action of lactic acid bacteria.

What is clotted (Devonshire) cream?

This is made from fresh cream or milk that is heated (scalded) so that it is reduced in volume by 50 to 60% to intensify its sweetness and also its fat content. The heating makes the albumen coagulate. When it cools it clots.

What are the percentages of butterfat in various creams?

Half & half	10–12
Light (coffee)	18–30
Whipping	30–36

| Heavy | 36–40 |
| Clotted | 55–60 |

What is pastry cream (crème pâtissière)?

A thick custard of eggs, sugar, milk and thickener used to fill pastries.

What is the difference between crème brûlée and crème caramel?

| Brulée: | A rich custard with a crust of caramelized sugar. |
| Caramel: | Egg custard in caramel-lined molds, then cooked and unmolded. |

What is a flan?

Spanish for crème caramel.

What is crème fraîche?

A cultured cream of French origin that is slightly tart and has the consistency of sour cream. It is used in soups, sauces and desserts. It can be found in some delis. It has a slightly more rounded flavor than sour cream.

What can be done if the crème fraîche is too thin?

It will thicken as it chills.

How can crème fraîche be made?

1. Heat in a small saucepan 1 cup heavy (not ultrapasteurized) cream to 85 °F, transfer to a jar with a tight fitting cover.
2. Shake covered for a minute or so, and then let stand at room temperature for 8 hours or more until it thickens.
3. Another way is to add a small amount of buttermilk to heated heavy cream and then allow the mixture to ferment at room temperature until it thickens and is slightly sour.

How long can crème fraîche be stored?

It will keep in the refrigerator for 4–6 weeks.

What is ganache?

A heavy chocolate cream blended into a rich pastry or candy frosting.

Is it sensitive to heat?

It withstands heat well without curdling.

Why does homemade cream of tomato soup sometimes curdle?

Acid can curdle cream or milk. There will be more curdling as:

1. The ratio of acid to cream increases.
2. The heat of the mixture increases.
3. The salt content increases.

How can curdling be prevented?

1. Heat tomato and cream mixtures separately, then slowly add the tomato to the cream at the end of the cooking period.
2. Once mixed, do not heat very long and not above 180 °F.
3. Add the salt only just before serving.
4. Use the freshest cream possible because as cream ages it becomes more susceptible to curdling as its lactic acid content increases.

Why does cream sometimes curdle when poured into a cup of coffee?

1. Acid is the main troublemaker. Coffee may have too much acid, for the stronger the brew, the more acid the beverage contains.
2. Sometimes the cream is not fresh.

How can the fat content of sauces be reduced when cream is called for in the recipe?

1. Replace the cream with evaporated skim milk, which has more body and protein than regular skim milk.
2. Sauces can be thickened with cornstarch or arrowroot or flour dissolved in a little cold liquid.

How can creamy fillings be reduced in fat?

Replace the whipping cream with whipped, chilled, evaporated skim milk. This works best with strong flavors. Chill the beaters and the bowl. If flavors are more subtle, use an Italian meringue (a mixture of egg whites and cooked sugar).

Can soups be made less fatty?

Yes. Replace the light or heavy cream with low-fat milk thickened with cornstarch. A dollop of nonfat yogurt instead of sour cream can provide a good finish for the soup.

What happens when cream is being churned to butter?

The fat globules have their protective membrane ruptured and then the fat fuses into larger lumps that continue to grow larger, trapping along the way both moisture and intact fat globules.

When making crème caramel what should be done when making the caramel?

Make more than is needed so that it is easier to get enough for topping before it hardens.

Sour Cream

What is a good substitute for sour cream?

Low-fat cottage cheese pureed in a blender with a little fresh lemon juice.

What is the difference between buttermilk and sour cream?

Buttermilk: Originally, it was the liquid left over from churning milk into butter. Now it is pasteurized milk (nonfat or low-fat) that has been converted by adding bacteria to get an increase of texture and tanginess.

Sour cream: Is soured cream.

What is the difference between sour cream and creme fraîche?

Sour cream: Has 18–20% butterfat, is pasteurized and is made with bacterial starters.

Creme fraîche: Has 30–40% butterfat, is not pasteurized or made with starters.

Whipped Cream

What happens when cream is whipped?

Cream is whipped by incorporating air into the mixture in the form of tiny air bubbles. This emulsion is a delicate structure. What is sought is a procedure in which these tiny bubbles are supported most effectively.

How can you get the best whip from a cream?

1. Store the cream in the refrigerator for several hours before whipping.
2. Store the bowl and the beater for 30 minutes in the freezer, for if the bowl is at room temperature it can raise the cream's temperature 5 to 10 degrees.
3. If flavoring with sugar or vanilla, incorporate them just before the end of the whipping.

What happens if flavoring is added at the wrong time?

1. If added too early it hinders bubble development.
2. If added after whipping then you have to over-whip to get good dispersal of vanilla or sugar.

Why is light cream not good for whipping?

It soon loses its fluffiness because it can't hold the air bubbles.

What can be done if the cream is badly over-whipped?

Whip it some more and make butter. Then drain, mold and refrigerate.

What happens if the fat content is increased?

The higher the fat content of the cream, the better the whip.

How much butterfat is needed in order to whip?

A minimum of 30%.

What kind of sugar is best for whipped cream?

Powdered sugar because it helps form a stiffer foam.

What is the difference between heavy cream and whipping cream?

They are similar but heavy must have a minimum of 36% of fat, while whipping (may be labeled light whipping cream) must have 30 to 36% cream.

How do they vary in whipping?

Whipped, heavy cream is more stable and takes less time to whip.

What are the differences between pasteurized whipping cream and ultrapasteurized whipping cream?

1. Pasteurized is heated to 160 °F, while the ultra is raised to 280 °F.
2. The regular has better flavor and texture.
3. The ultra keeps longer.

How can cream be whipped without a whipper?

Put 1 cup of cream in a 2-cup plastic container. Cover and shake for 3–4 minutes until whipped.

Why should ultrapasteurized cream be avoided for whipping?

Because the high heat level of this pasteurization breaks down the fat molecules in the process and therefore the fluffiness and volume will not be achieved. It has poor whipping quality and is a less effective thickener.

Why is aerated (canned) cream a poor substitute?

1. It has a cooked flavor from pasteurization.
2. It has a different flavor from preservatives.
3. It is usually too foamy and unstable.

What will make cream whip faster?

Add 6–8 drops of lemon juice per pint of cream.

What happens when cream is over-whipped?

Butter forms.

Can cream be whipped a few hours before use?

Yes. Good quality whipped cream should last for about 24 hours in the refrigerator.

Can whipped cream be frozen?

Yes, if it is not to be reformed (for example, rosettes on waxed paper on a cookie sheet). Best if not frozen for more than 2–3 hours.

How should cream be whipped for storage?

1. Whip the cream until stiff peaks just form.
2. Turn into a cheesecloth-lined sieve.
3. Store in the refrigerator.
4. The liquid will drain, leaving the cream thick.
5. It does not have to be rewhipped.

What can be done if whipped cream is required and only thin cream is available?

Add 1 tablespoon unflavored gelatin dissolved in 1 tablespoon hot water. Then add this to 2 cups of low-fat cream. When whipped, this will keep 3–4 hours in the refrigerator.

How can calories be minimized in whipped cream?

Whip half the amount of cream called for in the recipe with an equal amount of stiffly beaten egg whites.

When should cream that is to be whipped be measured for a recipe?

Before it is whipped, for whipping increases the volume 2–3 times.

FROZEN DESSERTS

When did ice cream first appear on the scene?

There is no known specific date, but it is thought to have been during the sixteenth century in Italy. In England it was first called "cream ice." The first appearance in the United States was about 1700, and the first cone was produced in 1896.

What is ice cream?

A mixture of dairy ingredients, such as milk and nonfat milk, and ingredients for sweetening and flavoring. Functional ingredients, such as stabilizers and emulsifiers, are often included. It must contain a minimum of 10% milk fat before the addition of any bulky ingredients and must weigh a minimum of 4.5 pounds per gallon.

Are frozen custards or French ice cream different?

They must contain a minimum of 10% milk fat with at least 1.4% egg yolk solids. French vanilla is vanilla ice cream with egg fat in it.

What is gelato?

Italian ice cream. It has an intense flavor and is served in a semifrozen state. Contains sweeteners, milk, cream, egg yolks and flavoring.

How much fat is in a sherbet?

It has a milk fat content of between 1–2% and a slightly higher sweetener content than ice cream or ice milk. It must weigh a minimum of 6 pounds per gallon. Flavored with fruit or other ingredients, it is high in sugar but has very little fat.

What are water ices?

They are similar to sherbets but without any dairy ingredients.

What is frozen yogurt?

A mixture of dairy ingredients, such as milk and nonfat milk, which have been cultured, plus sweetening and flavoring ingredients.

What is the difference between a sherbet and a sorbet?

The names are often used interchangeably but a sherbet may have milk products, a sorbet cannot.

What is the difference between a sorbet and a granita?

The difference is mainly one of texture.

Granita: (*Grana* means grain): A fruit puree, made of simple syrup and perhaps a little lemon juice and a pinch of salt. This is frozen. It has less sugar, which means larger ice crystals.

Sorbet: Like a granita, plus beaten egg white and is usually finished in an ice cream machine, which gives it a silky, creamy texture.

Should a granita be made without ice crystals?

No, for the iciness prevents the granita from being cloyingly sweet.

What can be done if the granita becomes too hard-frozen?

Melt it until it can be broken into pieces, pulse in a processor so it is crushed and then refreeze.

What happens if too much sugar or alcohol is added to granita?

It won't freeze solid.

Why should granita be frozen in a freezer rather than in an ice cream machine?

Granita needs coarse textured crystals and a machine would eliminate them.

What is necessary to make a sorbet?

Pureed or juiced fruit and sugar syrup (sugar and water simmered together).

What can be done to enhance the flavor if fruit for a sorbet is not fully ripe?

Poach the fruit before pureeing.

Can frozen fruit be considered for making a sorbet?

Yes. It works very well, particularly if the fruit was flash-frozen.

How can an apple sorbet be made greener?

1. Use the juice of the apples extracted with the skin on.
2. Add a few leaves of green spinach.

Why is a little salt critical in making ice cream?

When making ice cream with egg yolks, salt gives a more silky finish.

What is critical for obtaining smoothness in making ice cream?

Make sure that the sugar is completely dissolved in the liquid ingredient.

Why is cream essential in making ice cream?

To get smoothness of texture, for it holds air that keeps ice crystals small.

What are ice creams of less than the minimum of 10% milk fat called?

Ice milk, but these are rarely seen on the market.

Why should only rock salt be used when making ice cream in a freezer?

The very coarse salt melts the ice more slowly, and therefore the ice cream freezes more evenly.

What are the differences between super-premium, premium, regular and economy ice creams?

There are no legal definitions, but generally the higher the quality, the higher the milk fat content, the heavier the weight, the better the flavor selection, the higher intensity and less overrun (percentage of aeration). This varies with the manufacturer.

What are the differences in the reduced fat ice creams?

Light:	50% less total fat than the average of the leading regional or national brands.
Reduced fat:	At least 25% less total fat than the average of leading products or of the company's own brand.
Low-fat:	A maximum of 3 grams of total fat per serving (½ cup).
Nonfat:	Contains less than 0.5 grams of total fat per serving.

Why is it important to control the amount of alcohol (liqueur or liquor) added to frozen desserts?

Alcohol is an antifreeze and will affect the texture and also lower the freezing temperature.

What is the butterfat content of commercial ice cream?

Vanilla ice cream must have no less than 10%, other flavors no less than 8% butterfat. Expensive ice creams may have as much as 30% or more.

Why does commercial ice cream have so much sugar?

1. The coldness of ice cream numbs the taste buds, diminishing their sensitivity. Therefore twice as much sugar is needed than if it were served at room temperature.
2. Sugar reduces the number and size of the ice crystals and lowers the freezing temperature. Thus it allows the beating of the mixture longer before it freezes,

decreases the possibility of ice crystals forming and thus allows more air to be incorporated into the ice cream.

Why do ice crystals form in ice cream that was smooth when purchased?

If ice cream travels too long from store to home freezer, makes too many trips in and out of home freezer or is kept too long in a typical home refrigerator freezer (which is not quite cold enough), then some of ice cream's water content, originally in the form of minute ice crystals, will separate from the fat and form larger ice crystals. Thus, a grainy texture.

How can ice cream in a partially empty container be kept?

Cover the remaining ice cream with plastic wrap pushed down onto its surface, and return to the freezer.

What causes a grainy or sandy texture in ice cream?

The grainy or sandy texture can come from too little water, while too much water results in iciness.

What are some of the additions to the milk in making ice cream commercially?

1. Dairy products: nonfat milk solids, skim milk.
2. Sweeteners: cane and beet sugar, corn sweeteners, honey.
3. Stabilizers: plant derivatives to prevent large ice crystals.
4. Emulsifiers: lecithin, mono- and diglycerides to provide uniform whipping qualities and a smoother texture.
5. Flavorings: vanilla, chocolate, etc.

Does higher butterfat content create creamier and smoother ice cream?

This is true up to about 20% butterfat, but over that level it can start becoming stiff and greasy.

Why is skim milk powder used in making good ice cream?

Together with the egg yolks, the milk protein helps to produce a smooth, rich, dense ice cream without adding fat. It also extends the longevity.

Should the ice cream mixture be cooked before freezing?

It should be cooked into a thick, smooth custard without lumps at a temperature of between 165 and 180 °F for 10 to 15 minutes and then quickly cooled to 65 °F. The cooled mixture should then be refrigerated overnight (or a minimum of 4 hours) before churning and freezing.

What is the purpose of heating and cooling?

The heating and cooling improves the texture and also protects against the danger of salmonella.

Why is ice cream made with egg yolks richer and creamier than that made without eggs?

1. Because the yolks are about 10% lecithin, which helps maintain the even dispersal of fat droplets throughout the mixture.
2. Eggs help keep ice crystals small, which helps trap air in the mixture.

Why do the yolks need to be beaten very well before being combined with other ingredients when making ice cream?

1. If the yolks are only lightly beaten the color of the finished ice cream will be too yellow.
2. Prolonged beating—two minutes with an electric mixture or four minutes with a wire whisk—ensures a lighter color, helps dissolve the sugar and, more importantly, evenly disperses the emulsifying agent in the yolk.

What is the percentage of air in ice creams?

It ranges from 10–20% in premium blends to as much as 50% in economy brands.

How can ice cream be prevented from leaking through a cone?

Put a piece of marshmallow in the bottom of the cone.

What precautionary measure needs be taken in making berry sherbets?

Strain the crushed berries, particularly raspberries and blackberries, to remove the seeds.

How can the crust be kept from becoming soggy when making an ice cream (or yogurt) pie?

Freeze the crust for a half hour, then spread the filling, then refrigerate for a half hour before serving.

How can you tell the overall quality of an ice cream?

1. Weigh equal sized samples of an expensive brand and the one you are questioning. The lighter weight will indicate the amount of overrun, or air beaten in.
2. Put a small sample in a bowl at room temperature. The quicker the melt, the less rich is the ice cream.
3. If stabilizers have been used, the melt time will not be appreciably different, but on the surface of the stabilized sample tiny air bubbles will appear, and also the poorer sample will have a chalky or gummy texture.

How should ice cream be selected at the store?

1. Make ice cream the last stop in the market.
2. In an open top freezer select a container from below the freeze line.
3. Avoid any package that is soft.

4. Put in a separate basket or on top of the other groceries.

5. Insulate the ice cream for the ride home with either a freezer bag or an additional brown paper bag.

What should be watched in storing ice cream at home?

1. Avoid repeated softening and refreezing.

2. Store in the main part of the freezer, not in the door, which is subject to greater fluctuation of temperature.

3. The best storage temperature range is −5–0 °F, at which it will hold its shape. The ideal serving range is 6–10 °F.

MILK

What is the difference between milk and cream?

The difference is the amount of fat.

Whole milk	3% milk fat or more.
Low-fat milk	1–2% fat.
Skim milk	less than 0.1% fat.
Heavy (or whipping) cream	35% fat or more, up to 40%.
Light cream	16–32% fat.
Half & Half	10–12% fat.

What are the new label regulations for milk?

Skim milk can be labeled "fat free" or "skim."

1% milk can be called "light" or "1% low-fat."

2% milk will be called "2% reduced fat."

What is the difference between milk fat and butterfat?

They are different names for the same product, namely the fat that comes in the milk from a cow, sheep or goat.

What is the meaning of the date stamp (also called pull date) on a milk carton?

It is set ten days from the point of pasteurization. It is safe for this period, although quality begins to decline in about a week after pasteurization.

How critical is the expiration date on milk?

Milk can retain its freshness, if under refrigeration, for up to a week past the date.

What is scalding milk?

Heating milk to just below the boiling point.

What is the best way to scald milk?

Heat the milk in a heavy saucepan until bubbles just form around the edge of the pan.

How should the pan in which milk has been scalded be cleaned?

To facilitate cleaning of the pan, rinse it in cold water before pouring in the cold milk.

Why scald milk before using it in a recipe?

1. To kill pathogens.
2. To destroy enzymes that would keep emulsifying agents from doing their job of thickening.
3. Scalding is useful to extract flavor from a vanilla bean or citrus peel.
4. Sugar dissolves rapidly and eggs disperse more evenly in hot milk, so scalding makes it easier to mix custard ingredients.
5. Because it instantly raises the temperature of the mix, scalded milk shortens baking time considerably.

Do all milks need be scalded?

Scalding is not needed for pasteurized milk even though some cookbooks don't specify this.

What causes milk to stick to the pan when heating it?

1. Heating at too high a temperature.
2. Heating too long.
3. Infrequent or incomplete stirring.
4. Thin-bottomed pan or one with hot spots.
5. The staler the milk, the more likely it is to stick.

What causes a film to form while heating milk?

The milk protein coagulates and yields lumpy texture and/or burnt taste.

How can the film be prevented?

A film can be prevented by stirring frequently, especially when the temperature is above 140 °F.

Why doesn't the cream of homogenized milk separate?

Dairies use high pressure equipment to force milk through fine openings that break up milk fat into tiny, well-dispersed globules than cannot recombine because of their minute size (1 micron or less = 1 millionth of a meter) and milk's casein (phosphoprotein) then acts as an emulsifying agent.

How is milk pasteurized?

Milk is heated: to 145 °F for 30 minutes, or
to 161 °F for 15 seconds, or
to 280 °F for 1 second.

When is the high temperature used?

The high temperature (280 °F) is used only for cream, which is usually kept longer than milk, as it is used more slowly.

Why homogenize milk?

1. It prevents cream separation so the cream won't float to the top.
2. The butterfat is evenly dispersed in the milk.
3. It makes the milk quite white.
4. It kills or inactivates pathogens.
5. It prolongs storage life because the population of bacteria (non-pathogens) is greatly reduced.

What are the negatives of homogenizing?

1. It changes the flavor slightly by evaporating away some volatile molecules and creating new ones.
2. The taste is blander.
3. It has an undesirable effect on the whipping potential.
4. Cheese-making is impaired.

Why do evaporated milks often have an unpleasant taste?

They are heated in the can, to 200 °F to sterilize. This process can give a cooked or burnt flavor.

What is condensed milk?

Whole milk from which half of the water has been evaporated and sugar (cane or corn) has been added. Then it is canned and often sterilized.

Does condensed milk have to be sterilized?

It does not have to be sterilized because of its high (more than 40%) sugar content, which serves as a preservative, and because the sugar concentration hinders bacterial growth.

How is evaporated milk different from condensed milk?

Evaporated milk is whole *un*sweetened milk from which about 60% of the water has been evaporated under vacuum at temperatures below boiling (to 200 °F). It is homogenized to evenly distribute the fat globules. Then it is sterilized in the can. A low-fat version has ½–2% butterfat. Because of the high heat it can have a cooked or burnt flavor.

Can evaporated milk be whipped?

Yes.

How can evaporated milk be whipped?

1. Place the can in the freezer until almost frozen.
2. The bowl and the beater should be in the refrigerator 30 minutes or more before use.
3. The whipping bowl should be placed in a larger bowl filled with ice that has a sprinkle of salt on top of it to keep it even colder.

What are the advantages of the two types of nonfat, dry milk?

Regular: Tastes better.

Instant: Mixes easier.

How should powdered, dry milk be stored?

Refrigerated.

What are the main constituents of nonfat dry milk?

About 35% of dried powder is protein (mainly casein).

About 50% of dried powder is carbohydrate (lactose, or milk sugar).

Why should nonfat dry milk be reconstituted the day before it is used?

Lactose does not dissolve quickly unlike cane sugar (sucrose). Instant dry powdered milk solves most of this problem.

Why are low-fat and skim milks reinforced with Vitamins A & D?

Because removing the fat has also removed the fat-soluble vitamins.

Why is a glass of warm milk before bedtime soothing?

It contains the amino acid tryptophan, which can reduce anxiety and stressful feelings, although it can cause insomnia if the drinker is lactose intolerant.

What is the advantage of the paper carton for milk versus glass or clear plastic?

1. Opaque paper blocks 98% of the harmful effects of light.
2. In plastic or glass just four hours of store light can destroy 44% of vitamin A in low-fat milk.

How can drips from pouring milk or cream from a pitcher be avoided?

1. Butter the underside of the pitcher's spout.
2. The drip is often due to an imperfect design of the pitcher. Try another.

How can sour milk be made quickly?

Add 1 tablespoon lemon juice or white vinegar to a cup of milk.

Which is the better milk for making the froth topping for a (coffee) latte?

Steaming alters the milk proteins in a different way than heating in a pot or in the microwave. Low-fat or skim milk makes a stiffer, more meringue-like froth than whole milk. Start with the milk cold.

YOGURT

What is yogurt? (also spelled yoghurt)

Curdled milk made with lactic ferments. Commercial yogurt is made from whole, low-fat and nonfat milk that is partially evaporated and then inoculated with a pure culture of Lactobacillus bulgaricus, a lactic acid fermenter. There are 200 million bacteria per cubic centimeter. Yogurt is mainly semisolid, but with heat or whipping it can be in a fluid state. It has renown as a cure for intestinal disorders, but this is not true for frozen yogurt or yogurt that has been heated above 127 °F.

What is the nutritional value of yogurt?

Yogurt is high in protein, calcium, phosphorous and riboflavin. Look for LAC on the label (live and active culture), which indicates a force for reducing cholesterol and possibly combatting the production of digestive cancers.

What are the fat content standards for the various low-fat yogurts?

Low-fat:	It must have no more than 3 grams of fat per serving.
Light fat:	Must have one-third less fat than the standard yogurt.
Reduced fat:	Must have 25% less fat than standard yogurt.
Nonfat:	Must have no more than 0.5 gram of fat.

What is the fat content of frozen yogurt?

It has less fat than ice cream but the range is 3–3.5 grams per serving (½ cup), while low-fat has 1.5–2.5 grams and nonfat has none. Caloric content ranges: 100–160 for regular, 70–100 for low-fat and around 70 for nonfat.

How should yogurt be used in cooking?

Heat it gently and keep it at less than 127 °F.

Can yogurt be substituted for sour cream in baking?

Yes.

Why do commercial fruit-flavored yogurts have so much sugar?

1. Sugar acts as a preservative and enhances the storage quality.
2. Panders to the public's sweet tooth.

When making yogurt why must gelatin be avoided?

Gelatin inhibits the whey from draining.

How is yogurt cheese made?

1. Put the yogurt into a filter and let it drain. The liquid (whey) drains out, leaving the thick and creamy milk solids and butterfat. Add salt (about 1 teaspoon/quart of yogurt) or to taste.
2. Controlling the draining time controls the density and spreadability of the cheese.
3. Use the freshest yogurt possible (check the expiration date).
4. Low-fat and nonfat yogurt make less rich cheeses. Nonfat cheese becomes crumbly and chewy when broiled.

How long can yogurt cheese be kept?

Use within a week, as it tends to become tart with age.

What are some uses of yogurt cheese?

1. It can be eaten plain.
2. It can be flavored with curry powder or fresh herbs (placed in the yogurt before draining).
3. It can be made into small balls and then rolled in chopped nuts or fresh herbs and served as canapés.
4. Marinated with olive oil and herbs, it can be added to a salad.
5. It can be piped onto vegetables for hors d'oeuvres.
6. Sliced on bread rounds and broiled, it can be used as croutons for soup.
7. Mixed with rice, it can be a stuffing for grape or cabbage leaves.
8. Mixed with cooked rice, it can be served as a starch.
9. Blended with pesto, it can be a sauce for pasta.
10. Mixed with honey, it can be used to make sandwich cookies.

Dairy

CHAPTER FOUR

EGGS

GENERAL

Which came first, the chicken or the egg?

Probably neither, they both evolved. But then there was this woman who said, "It must be the chicken because God would never lay an egg."

What is the surface area of the molecules of the phospholipids in an egg yolk?

One yolk contains two grams of phospholipids, which has a billion, billion molecules. The surface area of these molecules is 1,850 square yards or nearly one-third of a football field from just 1 tablespoon of yolk.

Are Americans eating more eggs now?

With eggs with less cholesterol available and publicity that shows that eggs are not harmful for persons without a cholesterol problem, the consumption is slowly rising after many years of decline.

What are the culinary functions of eggs?

1. Thickening, as in a custard.
2. Coloring, as in baked goods.
3. Adding moisture to baked goods.
4. Forming emulsions, as for mayonnaise.
5. Foaming, as for souffles.

6. Enriching and adding nutritive value to other foods.
7. Glazing, as an egg wash on baked goods.
8. Table service, as for breakfast cooking.
9. Bonding, as for meatloaf.
10. Clarifying, as for consomme.
11. Adhesive, as for breading.
12. Flavoring.

What is an egg wash?

Egg yolk mixed with a little water or milk to give color or shine to the surface of baked goods.

Can egg substitutes be used in all cases for eggs?

1. Can be used when the recipe doesn't call for the whites to be whipped separately.
2. Won't be quite as tender because the fat of real eggs acts as a tenderizer.

What is eggnog?

A flavored egg and milk drink.

NUTRITION AND HEALTH SAFETY

Are eggs safe to eat from a cholesterol/heart disease point of view?

According to current nutritional wisdom, the fear that the cholesterol that we eat goes straight into the bloodstream is unfounded. There is no direct connection. The body has a feedback system that adjusts internal cholesterol production, and it regulates the amount absorbed and recycled when dietary intake is high or low. How well this system works is largely determined by genetics. Eggs have less cholesterol that previously thought, revised from 250 milligrams/yolk to 200 milligrams/yolk. While they contain cholesterol, they also contain lecithin, which may provide enough good cholesterol (HDL) to counteract the bad (LDL).

A recent study of men eating 3, 7 and 14 eggs per week detected no significant change in the cholesterol level. Cholesterol problems seem to be a genetic predisposition. Probably two-thirds of the population can handle dietary cholesterol quite well. What is the most important is the fat content of your entire diet. The American Heart Association allows four whole eggs a week. One whole egg contains less saturated fat than a small roasted chicken with the skin.

What is the risk from eating uncooked eggs?

There is a small risk of getting salmonella infection. Reduce the risk by using only clean, un-cracked, fresh (less than a week old) eggs or by cooking them well.

Can the safety of an egg be evaluated by inspection?

Very often Grade A eggs, even when they are intact, can't be evaluated by visual inspection. This is true especially in eggs from the northeastern and central parts of the country. They can harbor a large number of salmonella bacteria from carelessly prepared chicken feed. Some infected hens are asymptomatic. These hens deposit the bacteria inside their eggs as they lay them. This is rare, but it happens. Cooking the yolk is the protection, but the whites should also be pasteurized or heated.

What should you do if you open an egg and there is a blood spot?

Spots don't affect quality, but if it bothers you, simply remove the spot with a cotton swab or the edge of a paper towel and proceed. Usually eggs with blood spots are detected during candling and removed from retail trade.

How can you be sure that the yolk or sauce made with yolks is salmonella-free?

By heating the yolks to 182 °F. A microwave works well for small amounts.

Why should uncooked batter with eggs never be tasted?

It may contain raw eggs with salmonella contamination.

Why should yolks not be passed back and forth from one half shell to another to separate them from the whites?

Because bacteria on an unwashed shell can be transferred in the process.

What is a safe way of separating uncooked eggs?

1. Once your hands are clean, crack the egg over a bowl that will hold the whites.
2. Have two bowls ready.
3. Use the thumb of one hand to pull the halves of the shell apart, being careful to keep the yolk fully contained in one of the halves.
4. Place the yolk in the other bowl.
5. When opening more than one egg, have a separate cup or bowl so that if one of the eggs is spoiled it won't contaminate all the rest that have been separated or opened.

When can the eggs be worked back and forth to extract all the white?

Working the yolk back and forth to extract all of the white should be done only if the egg shells have been cleaned.

Are double-yolk eggs better?

They are mainly curiosities, sometimes sell for more, but have no particular advantage or disadvantage.

Are fertilized eggs more nutritious than unfertilized ones?

No, just more expensive, and they don't keep as long.

Are brown eggs more nutritious and flavorful than white eggs?

No! Shell color is not an indicator of quality, just the reflection of the breed of the hen.

Should dirty egg shells be washed before storage?

No, because washing will remove the protective coating (most likely an oil spray) that has been put on after washing and sanitizing at the time of USDA grading. Without the coating they won't store as long. They can be washed immediately before using.

What can be done to loosen an egg stuck to the carton?

Pour a little cold water over the stuck egg and let it stand for a few minutes.

What do cracks in eggshells (before cooking) indicate?

They could indicate that either the egg has been contaminated or simply poorly handled.

Are the white strands that attach the yolk to the shell a problem?

They do not affect quality, but if the eggs are being used to make a smooth custard, then they might well be strained out because they can lump when cooked.

SELECTING

What should you look for when buying eggs?

1. Inspect for cracks, which could indicate bacterial contamination.
2. Shininess can indicate that they are not fresh.
3. Check the packaging date, if available.
4. Buy only eggs that are refrigerated.

What is the Julian system of dating that is used for eggs?

January 1 = 1; December 31 = 365. The package date on a carton stamped 59 would be February 28th, for there are 31 days in January plus 28 in February = 59.

If an egg carton is marked A or AA, does this mean that it has been officially graded?

Only if the USDA Grade Shield is printed on the carton.

What do the egg grades signify?

The amount the eggs spread when they are broken open.

How are eggs graded?

The grade is determined by candling, in which a light is held in back of the unbroken egg to illuminate the interior for visual inspection.

Why are eggs candled?

To see the size of the air space. The smaller the space, the better the egg. The older the egg, the bigger the space.

What are the different grades?

AA: Will have a small spread, be thick, a small amount of thin white, the white stands high, with a firm yolk.

A: Will have more spread covering a moderate area with a white that is a little less thick, yolk is round, stands high.

B: Will have a wide spread, a little thick white and probably an enlarged-looking yolk that is somewhat flattened.

C: Will have an even wider spread and a thin, somewhat watery white. Good for baking and general cooking with other ingredients.

Which are better, AA, A or B eggs?

1. AA cost more than A, which costs more than B.
2. The higher the grade, the plumper the yolk, and the thicker the white, which is desirable for frying or poaching, because the cooked eggs will be more compact and visually pleasing.
3. There is only a slight difference in flavor and practically none in nutritive value.

When is B grade the best?

For recipes calling for beating, such as in baked goods, B is the best buy but they are rarely available.

What should be the priority for egg quality?

Freshness.

Are eggs from free-range chickens better than those from birds raised in closed coops?

There is no discernible nutritional difference.

What does it mean if an egg in the shell floats when placed in a glass of water?

The egg is rotten, throw it into the garbage.

How can you tell how fresh an egg is?

Put it in several inches of water, if it lies on its side it's fresh; if it tilts it's about 3–4 days old, if it stands upright it's about 10 days old or more.

What is the importance of freshness?

A fresh egg has more flavor and nutritional value.

What are the advantages of freshness when cooking eggs?

A fresh egg:

1. has a thicker white and firmer yolk and thus is better for frying or poaching.
2. is better when a yolk is being used to thicken, leaven or emulsify.
3. is easier to separate because as the egg ages the membrane of the yolk weakens and tends to rupture more easily.

When is a week-old egg the best?

A week-old egg (if the shell is pierced with a pin) is preferable for hard-cooking (hard-boiled) because it will peel easier. In general, older eggs are better for hard-cooking.

How many eggs are needed to fill a cup?

	Large	Medium	Small
Whole Eggs:	5	6	7
Yolks:	12–14	14–16	15–19
Whites:	7–8	8–9	9–10

What is the ratio among different-sized eggs?

15 medium = 12 large = 9 jumbo

Which size egg should be selected?

Recipes, unless otherwise specified, are based on the use of large eggs. If not working with a strict recipe, purchase according to affordability.

How can you tell if an egg is large?

It should weigh 2 ounces in the shell.

STORAGE

What is the goal of egg storage?

To keep them as fresh as possible with the yolks centered.

How should eggs be stored?

1. Refrigerate as quickly as possible.
2. Store in a closed carton.

What is wrong with storing eggs in the refrigerator door (egg shelf)?

Repeated temperature fluctuations and the door slamming deteriorates the eggs.

How should eggs be placed in their carton or in an egg rack?

Store them large end up, pointed end down. This way they will stay fresh longer, for upright storage helps to retard spoilage, as it minimizes the distance between the yolk and the natural egg space. The gaseous space is potentially the more prolific environment for pathogenic bacteria.

How can you use yolks and whites?

Yolks: Sauces, custards, mayonnaise, enriched omelettes.
Whites: Meringues, soufflés, frostings, angel food cakes.

How can surplus yolks and whites be saved in the refrigerator?

1. Raw whites can be refrigerated for 4–5 days or frozen for several months.
2. Raw yolks, covered with water, can be refrigerated for a couple of days or can be frozen up to six months, but if frozen then add ⅛ teaspoon salt or ½ teaspoon sugar per 4 yolks before freezing to prevent gelatinization. The salted ones can be used in sauces, the sugared one in sweet dishes.

How can eggs be frozen?

1. They can be frozen (shelled) in plastic for future use. Be sure to label the number of eggs in the container.
2. Another way is to put each yolk or white into the individual compartments of an ice tray and then, when frozen, put them into plastic bags.

Can you freeze eggs in the shell?

No! Freezing usually expands the contents more than the capacity of the shell and it results in cracking.

What should be done before freezing the yolks?

Break the yolks.

What is a good use for frozen yolks?

Making mayonnaise.

Which keeps longer when frozen, the white or the yolk?

The yolks have a higher fat content, which gives them a shorter freezer life, while the whites seem to keep well for months.

Can cooked eggs or whites be frozen?

1. Yolks freeze ok.
2. Whites toughen and become watery.

COOKING

Why should eggs be cooked on gentle heat for a longer time?

1. Prevents yolks from becoming tough.
2. Prevents whites from becoming rubbery.
3. Allows even heat penetration.
4. Yolks will thicken well.

When should eggs be cooked on high heat?

High heat cooking is good for omelettes.

Can eggs be properly prepared in a microwave oven?

Yes, using very low power for unbeaten eggs. Use high power with beaten eggs.

When is the microwave not suitable?

For omelettes or soufflés. These need dry heat.

What are shirred eggs?

Eggs baked in individual ramekins, usually with a topping of butter. Can also be covered with milk or cream and baked until the whites are firm. Sometimes covered with bread crumbs. The yolks remain soft.

Why should you start cooking eggs at room temperature?

They will cook more evenly.

How can eggs with a cracked shell be boiled?

If the egg being boiled has a crack, remove from the boiling water, and pour salt on the crack generously, which will seal the crack and contain the white. Wrap in aluminum foil and twist the ends and continue boiling.

What is the best way to get egg residue off of plates?

Soak the dirty plates in warm (not hot or cold) water. The ideal temperature is just below 156 °F, as it is not so hot that the heat will set the yolk protein and bond it to the dish.

Hard-Cooked (Hard-Boiled)

Why is the term hard-cooked more appropriate than hard-boiled?

Eggs should not be hard-boiled but rather cooked with simmering water (always just below the boiling point) until the eggs are solid. Thus they should never be boiled. Hard-cooked, therefore, is a more accurate description and suggests proper cooking.

Should eggs be put into cold, lukewarm, simmering or rapidly boiling water?

Cold or lukewarm water, because otherwise the air space in the shell expands too fast and the egg may crack.

What is an alternate way of handling?

Remove the egg from the refrigerator and pierce the center of the larger end with a pin or other sharp point to keep the egg from cracking as it boils. Then put the holed egg into rapidly boiling water, lower the heat and simmer/cook for 12–15 minutes and then promptly submerge the egg(s) in cold water to stop the cooking process. Otherwise overcooking could produce a sulfurous odor and a greenish tinge in the yolk.

How are hard-cooked eggs best handled for removing the shell?

1. As the cooked egg white cools it begins to stick to the shell's innermost membrane, so peel soon after the cooking. If necessary, do it under running cold water to make the egg cool enough to handle.
2. Start peeling at the large end.

Why chill cooked eggs before slicing?

Whole, hard-cooked eggs will slice better and the yolks are less liable to crumble if refrigerated for at least 15 minutes after peeling.

What temperature should cooked eggs be at for easier separation of yolk and white?

Cool or cold.

When hard-cooking eggs, is it necessary to pierce the shell first?

Only if microwaved.

How can you avoid getting a green tinge to a hard-cooked yolk?

1. Don't overheat the egg, for that results in the formation of ferrous sulfate, which is green.
2. Use fresh eggs.
3. Don't cook more than fifteen minutes, stop further cooking with cold water.

How can yolks be kept centered when hard-cooking them?

Stir the water while the eggs are cooking.

How long should hard-cooked eggs be kept?

Three days should be the limit for health considerations, although they will taste good past that point.

How should deviled eggs be stored?

1. Place halves together with the filling in the middle.
2. Wrap tightly with aluminum foil and curl the edges of the foil or wrap with plastic.

What is the effect of adding salt to the water when hard-cooking an egg?

The salt makes it easier to peel when hard-cooked.

How can you get less wiggle on the platter when serving deviled eggs?

Cut a tiny bit off the bottom of the egg half so it will be more stable.

How can hard-cooked eggs (still in the shell) be marked to tell them from uncooked ones?

Put a little food coloring in the water when boiling the eggs, or put a drop of food color on each egg after they have been boiled.

What mechanical way can you use to tell if the egg has been cooked?

Spin it, if it rotates smoothly, it is hard-cooked. If it wobbles, the yolk is still liquid and it hasn't been cooked.

Soft-Cooked and Poached

What is the cooking time and process for soft-cooked eggs?

Cook only 5–7 minutes, starting them in cold or lukewarm water. Once cooked remove immediately and skip the cooling step.

Which are the best eggs for poaching?

Fresh Grade AA are the best candidates, since they have the largest proportion of thick white and will spread the least. As the eggs age the tendency of the whites to cling to the yolk relaxes and in poaching this detracts from the appearance.

What is the best way to poach eggs?

1. A couple of tablespoons of vinegar per quart of poaching water will help prevent the whites from spreading, and a little salt helps set the eggs and keeps them in shape. The acidic element holds the eggs together without flavoring them, toughens the albumin and helps keep it lily white.
2. Have the water close to but not boiling, as turbulent water will tease the thin albumen away.
3. Don't shell the eggs until just before they are cooked, because if they sit in open air they deteriorate quickly.
4. Carefully slide the raw egg from a bowl into a pan of simmering water where it slowly sets.
5. If only a few eggs are needed, use an egg poacher with its individual cups (if available) that have been lightly greased before adding the eggs.

What should the eggs look like when done?

The whites should be tender and glistening and jiggle just a little and the yolk, when cut, should run slightly.

What are Eggs Benedict?

A breakfast or brunch dish of two toasted English muffin halves on each of which is laid a piece of ham or Canadian bacon, covered by a poached egg and Hollandaise sauce.

Scrambled Eggs and Omelettes

What is the difference between scrambled eggs and an omelette?

1. Both are made by mixing yolks and white together. In the case of an omelette, they are mixed quite thoroughly.
2. Scrambled eggs are cooked slowly over low heat to avoid over-coagulation and stirred and scraped to break up the coagulating mass into large, soft lumps *and* to distribute the heat evenly. They should be removed from the stove top while slightly underdone since they retain heat and will continue to cook on their own for a bit.
3. Omelettes (ordinary or French) are cooked over high heat in a thin, intact sheet which is folded onto itself while its upper surface is still partly liquid.

How stiff should the whites be whipped to make a fluffy or souffléd omelette?

To a soft peak.

What is the difference if a small amount of milk or water is added to the mixture when making omelettes or scrambled eggs?

Milk products tend to harden the yolk. Water tends to slow down the coagulation but two or three teaspoons of either don't have a great negative effect. Cream will make it a little richer.

How should eggs be scrambled?

1. Heat the pan to melt the butter and then drop in the eggs and fork stir over low heat until done, or
2. Break into a bowl, beat briefly, mix in a teaspoon of water or milk and seasoning, scramble in the pan on low to moderate heat. Don't use high heat.
3. Remove from heat just before they are done as they will continue to cook.
4. Serve immediately, slightly underdone.

What can you do to make scrambled eggs light and fluffy?

Add a small amount of cream, milk or water when beating. The liquid steams upon cooking, creating tiny air pockets in the eggs. The result—the coagulating egg mixture lightens.

How can large, creamy curds be obtained?

Cook over low heat and occasionally pull the mixture from the edge of the pan towards the middle so that the uncooked portion runs to the edge of the pan.

What are the main cautions about beating and cooking eggs for scrambling?

1. They will have better texture if you don't over-beat them.
2. Cook slowly over low heat.
3. Remove from heat the moment they are done.

What is the best fat to use for an omelette?

Oil or butter will work. A combination of the two is even better. Try a teaspoon of heated oil and then a teaspoon of butter, or clarified butter, which has a higher smoke point.

When should the seasoning be added?

Just before cooking, for salting too early will tend to dry out the eggs.

How large should an omelette be?

Two to three eggs are the most manageable. For two people, make two omelettes.

What is the difference between the way French and American omelettes are folded?

The American way is once over, the French is a one-third fold, each side folded toward the middle.

What is the best way to mix eggs for an omelette?

1. Use fresh eggs at room temperature.
2. Use 2 or 3 eggs, no more. If more is needed then make another omelette.

3. Use a little liquid, either milk or water.

4. Use a fork to mix. Don't over-beat. A whisk doesn't help.

How should an omelette be cooked?

1. Stir lightly to shorten cooking time, shaking back and forth as you stir with a circular motion. Pull the eggs from the sides into the middle.

2. Spread the eggs evenly and let them stand cooking a few moments to set.

3. Add any filling.

4. Roll up with a fork, working gently.

5. Serve at once.

How can over-cooking a filled omelette be prevented?

1. Make sure all the ingredients of the filling are finely diced or grated.

2. If meat is used it should be sautéed before adding.

3. Cook over low heat but not too low, or it will toughen.

Can an omelette be cooked in advance?

Yes, if you want to serve it at room temperature cut up as an appetizer.

No, if it is to be served warm.

Can it be prepared in advance?

They can be prepared as much as two days in advance and baked later in a buttered glass or ceramic dish. This type frequently has a roux in it.

Should an omelette be browned?

This is a matter of choice.

When should the filling be added in an omelette?

1. When the curds begin to form, or

2. When the omelette is completed and on the serving plate, slit the top and add the filling.

What is the difference between an omelette and a frittata?

Omelette: A filling is spooned on top of partially set eggs, cooked a few seconds more, folded and then turned onto the plate and served warm. Can be made without a filling.

Frittata: The filling is prepared in the pan and the egg mixture is poured over it and then cooked until the eggs are set. It can be finished on the stove top or in the oven. Serve hot, warm or at room temperature.

How can good distribution of the filling be obtained in a frittata?

1. Fry the filling a little over halfway.

2. Add the egg mixture. Cook first at a low heat, then finish at a higher heat.

What kind of a pan is best for cooking a frittata?

A nonstick pan with a long, oven-safe handle and sloping sides.

How high should the heat be to cook a frittata?

Never more than medium; lower will give good results as well.

Fried

Why do some fried eggs have whites that are too rubbery?

Probably because they were cooked at too high a heat or cooked too long. Cook over as low a heat as possible.

How can you prevent spattering grease when frying eggs?

Drop a small amount of cornstarch or flour into the pan.

What is the best way to cook sunny-side up eggs with a firm yolk and perfectly cooked whites?

The coagulation temperature for the yolk is about 156 °F, for whites it is 149. So, the mixture doesn't work. If you want fried eggs with a firm yolk, then cook "over easy" or braise the eggs by covering the pan with a lid, and the trapped steam will hasten the cooking of the yolks.

What is the ideal temperature for frying eggs?

Ideal temperature for frying eggs is 244–280 °F, which can be approximated by heating the pan until the butter sizzles without browning.

What happens when frying eggs with too little heat?

The white will spread too thin before setting.

What results from too much heat?

The bottom will harden, while the rest remains liquid.

What will basting do?

Basting the egg with butter from the pan will even out the cooking of sunny-side up eggs. Another way to accomplish this is to put a lid on the pan for a moment or two at the end.

Which are the best eggs for frying?

Fresh ones.

Beaten Whites and Meringues

What difference does the type of bowl make when beating egg whites?

1. Copper is best, because its electrostatic force gives the biggest volume. This is not so important with electric beater. Nevertheless, the friction of the beater quickly warms the egg whites beyond optimum temperature and therefore the bubbles get bigger. Copper transfers the heat more quickly than other metals or glass. Copper

ions, which are released during beating, fortify the cream of tartar and give a desirable creamy color.

2. Stainless steel is next best.
3. Aluminum makes the whites turn gray.
4. Plastic is too porous and absorbs some of the liquid.
5. Porcelain and glass are too slick, so the mass that forms often won't hold on the side and may slip down.

When beating egg whites and whipped cream should they be cold or at room temperature?

1. It's better to have eggs at a cool room temperature, but this is not absolutely necessary. A cooler white is thicker, more viscous and thus traps the air more effectively even though it may take longer to attain optimum volume. The result is that, cool or cold, there is less likelihood of it being over-whipped.
2. Conversely, cream should be chilled.

What is the best way to beat egg whites?

1. The optimum flavor, aeration and structure comes from the freshness of the eggs.
2. It is best to crack open the eggs when they are cold because then the yolk is firmer and less likely to break.
3. Make sure the bowl is thoroughly clean and greaseless.
4. Use a copper or stainless steel bowl, not aluminum, plastic or glass.
5. Have the bowl at room temperature or slightly warm because if cold it will lengthen the time it will take for the whites to reach full volume.

Should the beating be at the fastest speed?

Start beating at a slow speed and then gradually increase it. This encourages the development of smaller bubbles, which are more stable than larger ones.

What will happen if the bowl is too small?

The foam will collapse if the bowl is so small that the foam tops touch the mixer, so use a big enough bowl. Otherwise the air gets beaten out of the whites instead of into them.

What is the volume equivalent of the beaten white of a large egg?

The beaten white from one large egg will fill about 1 cup.

What effect does fat or yolk have on the beaten whites?

A speck of egg yolk or fat will keep the beaten egg whites from reaching their full potential volume, because the fat emulsifies into the whites, weighing them down. If a speck of yolk falls into the bowl, remove it, for the fat lowers the surface tension and the bubbles can't form.

How can a yolk be removed?

If a speck falls into the bowl, remove it with a cotton swab or the corner of a piece of paper toweling.

How can you make sure that the bowl and beaters are grease-free?

Moisten a paper towel with vinegar or lemon juice and wipe them before using.

What are the stages that whites go through while being whipped?

Frothy: Start out at slow speed. Small bubbles appear in about 30–45 seconds. If sugar or cream of tartar are to be added, this is the point at which it should be done. Increase the beater speed to medium and add either one.

Soft peak: Soft, shiny peaks appear so that when the whisk is lifted, the peaks bend slightly.

Medium peak: Have a moist surface and form a rounded stable peak. Sugar and other flavorings can be added at this stage.

Stiff peak: If additional sugar is to be added, this is the time. A small amount of the foam rubbed between thumb and forefinger will feel smooth but *not* granular. Lifting the beater should leave stiff, shiny, smooth peaks with rounded tops.

How can you tell if the whites are over-beaten?

They will lose their glossy appearance and will not hold a defined peak.

What can be done to salvage over-beaten whites?

Stir in another egg white and beat some more.

Why do stable foams hold together?

Stable foams and egg whites have two things in common: the bubbles are very small, and the liquid that traps the gas is very strong. Albumin, the egg white protein, is thick and viscous, which gives it long life. In addition there are several types of protein in the whites. One acts as a "quick-setting cement," another, called ovalbumin, does its work later and helps to set the structure of the foam. These proteins have another physical property: they are curled up before beating and have one end that is attracted to liquid, the other repelled by it. This dual action helps create a lattice-work structure as the protein unfolds in different directions.

Why blend in a little beaten whites into the sauce before adding the rest?

To loosen the sauce so the whipped whites won't be crushed.

How should beaten whites be folded into a sauce?

1. First, blend a cup of the stiffly beaten whites into the heavier base.
2. Use a large rubber spatula or a flat whisk.

3. Use a gentle over and under motion to incorporated airy beaten whites or whipped cream into a stiffer mixture without deflating them.

4. Then put the rest of the beaten white mixture on top.

5. Cut straight down through the middle of the beaten mixture and bring up some of the heavier mixture from underneath. Repeat, rotating the bowl a quarter of a turn each time and repeating until the two mixtures are close to one.

What is the effect of sugar on beaten whites?

The sugar ties up the water that is part of the whites and thus slows its evaporation, and this retained moisture strengthens the bubbles.

When should sugar be added to egg whites?

Before beating, for the sugar helps to hold the white stiff. Adding later leads to over-beating and too dry a texture, but it is ok if the sugar is carefully folded in.

What happens if sugar or cream of tartar is added to egg whites to be beaten?

1. The net result is that it will take longer to whip but the foam will be softer and this will make the foam easier to fold into the sauce.

2. Make it easier for the whites to stretch and expand and at the same time retain their stability.

3. Firmer peaks will form with sugar.

What is the difference between confectionary sugar and granulated sugar when added to egg whites?

Confectionary (powdered) sugar has smaller granules that don't break the bubbles as much.

What is the effect of adding an acid component such as lemon juice, cream of tartar or vinegar to the whites to be beaten?

The acidity produces greater stability and smoothness.

When should other ingredients be added?

Near the middle of the whipping.

How can the highest meringue be achieved on a pie?

1. Have the whites at room temperature.

2. Before beating add some baking powder to the whites.

3. During the beating add 2–3 tablespoons powdered sugar for each egg used, beating continuously as it is added.

4. Add ¼ teaspoon of white vinegar per 3 whites during the beating.

What kind of sugar is best for a pie meringue?

Powdered instead of granulated.

How can weeping or cracking of a meringue be prevented?

1. Cook with a lower temperature for a longer time.
2. Leave the meringue in the oven until it cools.

What is a French meringue?

Raw whites are whipped until double in volume and they have shiny stiff peaks.

What is an Italian meringue?

Boiling sugar syrup is whisked into stiffly beaten egg whites. The syrup cooks the whites, creating a topping of fluffy consistency. It can be flavored with vanilla, cinnamon, cocoa, orange liqueur etc. and be used as a frosting or baked as a meringue.

Can egg substitutes be used successfully?

Yes, for cakes, cookies, muffins, quiches and omelettes, but not for meringues.

Are egg substitutes fat free?

Not necessarily, so check the label.

What needs to be done when using egg substitutes, since texture is dependent in part on fat?

To preserve the texture of some baked goods that are already low in fat, a teaspoon or so of oil might have to be added.

What can be done to reduce the yolks/fat besides using egg substitutes?

If a recipe calls for 3 whites, try 1 whole egg and 2 whites. If recipe doesn't depend on yolks use 3 whites only. This saves fat and money as egg substitutes cost up to six times more than eggs.

Which should be beaten first, if you need to beat both yolks and whites?

Whites first because they will stand up all right for several minutes, whereas yolks may not. This way you don't have to wash the beater in between.

What is the difference in whipping quality between fresh and older eggs?

The older eggs are easier to whip and rise to a greater volume but are not as stable as fresh whites.

How should a meringue be prepared?

1. Preheat the oven according to recipe.
2. Start with the whites at room temperature (warm).
3. Use an electric eggbeater to get the best volume.
4. Start slowly and then increase the speed gradually. Move the beaters around the edge of the bowl so all parts of the whites are beaten.
5. If it is a standing beater then bring the outer circle of eggs into the middle with a spatula.

6. Add the sugar in a slow stream without stopping the beating.
7. Fold the meringue very gently and under-mix rather than over-mix.
8. Put it into the oven immediately.

How can you tell if the mixing is correctly done?

If a little is rubbed between your thumb and finger it should feel smooth, not gritty.

How should meringues be baked?

Bake at a low oven temperature (225 °F) or at the most 250 °F for about an hour or so to let the exterior harden. This is what I recommend. Or put in a hot oven, turn off the heat immediately and let the meringue dry out in the cooling oven.

Can the rate of sugar to whites in a meringue vary?

Yes.

What is the usual relationship?

1. Basic: 2 parts sugar to 1 of whites (by weight).
2. For pie topping: 1 to 1.
3. For icing: 5–7 to 1.

Custard, Quiches and Crêpes

What is an egg custard?

A custard is a sweet, very moist, tender gel of egg protein. A basic custard contains an egg, 1 cup milk and 2 tablespoon sugar (more eggs or more egg yolks can be used for greater richness).

How should an egg custard be cooked?

1. Bake in a water bath in the oven at low heat until it sets, then remove from heat and bring down the temperature in a cold water bath (otherwise like scrambled eggs it will continue to cook with the retained heat).
2. A skewer is the traditional tester and, when inserted in the center, should emerge relatively dry.
3. The lower the heat, the greater the safety margin in preventing curdling. It is easy to overcook and make grainy curds. Don't raise the temperature.

What are the two types of custards?

Stirred: Such as crème anglais or zabaglione, stirred as it cooks.
Baked: Such as cheese cake or flan, not stirred during cooking.

How must a custard without any starch, such as cornstarch, be baked?

With a water bath.

How can weeping by a custard be prevented?

Don't bake at too high a temperature.

At what temperature should a custard be when making a top crust?

Very well-chilled to protect the center from overheating.

What happens if over-whipped?

If over-whipped, baking will result in a crusty, pockmarked surface.

Is scalding of milk necessary for a custard?

Not with pasteurized milk.

What happens if sugar is added all at once?

Lumpiness will result.

Can a custard be cooked in advance?

Cook just enough for one meal since refrigerator temperature will cause most custards to weep.

What can you do if a custard pudding develops a rubbery crust?

Scrape off the top layer and cover it with whipped cream.

What is crème caramel?

A custard baked with a caramel coat.

What can be used in place of caramelized sugar?

Maple syrup or dark brown sugar, although they will give different flavors.

What is a quiche?

An unsweetened custard that is baked in a crust.

What are the best known quiches?

Quiche Lorraine, which is made with bacon and cheese, and Quiche Florentine, made with spinach and seafood.

How do you make a quiche?

1. Blend the eggs with the milk or cream to make a smooth mixture.
2. Add the appropriate seasonings.
3. Pour the mixture into the prepared crust.
4. Bake in a moderate (350 °F) oven until set (a knife inserted in the middle should come out clean).

How should it be served?

1. Let the quiche set for a few moments before serving.
2. It can be served hot or prepared in advanced and then reheated in a conventional or microwave oven prior to serving.

What is the usual ratio of eggs to liquid?

Usual ratio is 6–8 eggs per quart of liquid.

What should you do with a quiche to prevent the crust from becoming soggy?

1. Reduce the liquid, or
2. Increase the yolks, or
3. Brush the unbaked quiche shell with beaten egg 10 minutes before pouring in the custard.

What is a flan?

A round pastry tart, with a custard or fruit filling.

How can the custard of a flan be made to achieve a smooth filling?

1. Blend the eggs until blended, not foamy, or there will be bubbles on the surface.
2. Remove from the hot water immediately upon finishing baking.

What is a crêpe?

A delicate, versatile, thin, smooth-textured pancake that doesn't break when folded or rolled.

How thick should the crêpe batter be?

Just a little thicker than a heavy cream.

Should crêpe batter be made in advance?

It is best if it rests refrigerated for an hour or more, especially if flavored with herbs.

Why should the batter be refrigerated this long?

To allow the flour to absorb the liquid and expand so that the batter will spread and make a smooth crepe.

Can the batter be prepared and then frozen?

Yes.

What can be done with leftover crêpes?

Keep refrigerated for several days or freeze.

How can crêpes be varied?

1. Use other finely ground grains, such as buckwheat or cornmeal.

Eggs

2. Bake, steam or grill them.

3. Change the form into different shapes such as triangles (after cooking) when filling and then cooking a little more.

What gives character to sesame crêpes?

A combination of sesame oil and sesame seeds.

What can be done with leftover crêpes (not filled)?

Stack them with a sheet of wax paper between each one and then carefully wrap the stack in foil or plastic. Refrigerate.

Are crêpes used for desserts?

Yes, filled with fruit or sweet sauces or ice cream.

What kind of a pan should be used for cooking crêpes?

A seven- or eight-inch, slope-sided skillet.

What can be done to expedite cooking if you are making a large number of crêpes?

Use two or three skillets over two or three burners.

What is a gateau de crêpes?

Also called a tower of crêpes. It is a layered dish, as many as twenty crêpes high, with a filling between each layer and covered with sauce. The fillings, which can be all the same or different, are bound with a sauce such as Mornay sauce, thickened tomato sauce, cheese sauce etc. Fillings can be mushrooms, shallots, lobster, crab, chopped poultry or meat. Before serving, the dish is baked about a half hour until lightly browned on top and bubbling hot. Served in wedges.

When the crêpes are to be served flambé, why must the crêpe and liqueur not be boiling hot?

If boiling, the alcohol will dissipate before burning, but the crêpes must be warm for the alcohol to burn and for good flavor.

Soufflés

What is a soufflé?

A soufflé is a sauce containing a flavoring or puree into which stiffly beaten egg whites are incorporated. It is then turned into a mold and baked in the oven until it puffs up and the top browns. The word "soufflé" comes from the past participle of the French words "to blow, to breathe, to whisper": meanings suggesting the fragility of soufflés. The basic soufflé is no more than a thickened, flavored sauce or puree of meat, seafood, vegetable, cheese or fruit that has been lightened with beaten egg whites and then baked.

Eggs

What are the three kinds of soufflés?

Regular: Beaten whites are folded into a thick yolk mixture and any cheese, meat, vegetable, chocolate etc. is added. Baked at 375 °F for 35–40 minutes, it will be fairly solid all through.

Dessert (or French dessert): The yolks are combined with sugar and flavoring (such as a liqueur), and the beaten whites are folded in. Baked at 500 °F for 12–15 minutes, it will be feather light with a moist/wet center.

Cold: This is really a mousse and is based on gelatin and stiffly beaten whites, which is then chilled or frozen. It is usually a dessert.

What is the soufflé sauce?

This is the base sauce into which the whipped eggs are folded.

How is soufflé sauce made?

Prepare a light roux by melting butter and then adding flour, stirring continually during the cooking, cooking for 2 or 3 minutes to cook the flour. Then add heated milk, a little at a time, whipping out any lumps. When smooth and thickened, about 15 minutes, remove this sauce (called a béchamel sauce) from the heat and let cool. To this base are added the flavorings such as nutmeg, cayenne, freshly ground black pepper, grated cheese (Emmenthaler, Gruyère, Parmesan, Jarlsberg or others).

Can it be made in advance?

The soufflé base can be prepared in advance and refrigerated or frozen.

What is the role of the egg whites?

The lightness of the soufflé is largely a matter of how much volume the whites have been beaten to and how lightly they have been folded into the body of the soufflé. It is the air in the form of tiny bubbles that expand as the soufflé cooks and pushes up into a puff.

How much do whites expand?

Correctly beaten, egg whites mount to seven or eight times their original volume.

What are the characteristics of whites besides good volume?

They should be perfectly smooth, free from granules and firm enough to stand in upright peaks but not over-beaten or dry.

How can you test for perfect stiffness?

Another test of perfect stiffness level is that the beaten whites will support the weight of a whole egg if one is placed on top of them. They will not if there is any particle of yolk or if the bowl they are beaten in or the beater is moist or slightly greasy.

How should the stiffly beaten whites be incorporated?

First, stir a big spoonful of whites into the soufflé mixture to lighten it. Then with a rubber scraper, scoop half the rest of the egg whites on top. Using the scraper, cut from the top of the mixture to the bottom of the pan and then to the left and out. You will be bringing up a bit of the soufflé mixture up over the whites. Continue the movement several times, rotating the pan until the whites are partially folded into the body of the mixture. Then add the rest of the whites and repeat the process. The whole process should not take more than a minute. Do not attempt to be too thorough. It is better to leave a few unblended patches than to deflate the whites. After you have smoothed the top or swirled it slightly, the top may be sprinkled with some reserved cheese (if a cheese soufflé).

When blending the beaten whites with the sauce, is over-blending or under-blending worse?

Over-blending, for the soufflé will suffer less from having some of the whites still visible than not having sufficient volume because of excessive folding.

Can the soufflé mixture be prepared ahead of time?

After the baking dish is filled and ready for the oven, you can set it aside in a warm place for no more than 30 minutes if it is free from drafts. Protect by covering with a big empty pot or soup bowl.

How high in the soufflé dish should the mixture be?

It should almost reach the rim of the dish.

What are necessary steps to get soufflés to great heights?

1. Start with the eggs at room temperature and whip the whites to their maximum volume. Beat the whites to get maximum air entrapment.
2. Don't over-mix when mixing the sauce and the whites together.

Are collars necessary in making a soufflé?

They are used to make a very high soufflé, that is, one that rises considerably above the level of the soufflé dish. They are necessary if the capacity of the baking dish is relatively small, otherwise they are not. An easy way of making a collar is to attach a double layer of aluminum foil around the lip of the dish and secure with a pin.

How can you get a crown or high hat for the souffle?

With a kitchen knife, cut a circle about 1½" deep about 1" from the edge just before putting it into the oven.

How should the soufflé dish be prepared?

1. Chill the soufflé dish or at least make sure it is not so warm that the butter greasing it melts prematurely and slides to the bottom.
2. Heavily grease the inside and bottom, including the side walls with butter or margarine. Without this lubricant (e.g., butter) the mixture will stick and not rise freely.

3. Coat the bottom *and* sides with flour, finely grated cheese, bread crumbs or sugar until all the surfaces are lightly but evenly coated.

4. Turn the mold upside down, knock on the table to dislodge any excess.

5. After filling the dish, run your thumb around the top of the inside of the dish, which will prevent the soufflé from sticking to the sides and helps it to rise taller and straighter.

How large should the soufflé dish be?

Either quart size or individual serving sizes.

How can a soufflé top be caramelized?

Sprinkle sugar over the top 5 minutes before finishing baking.

How should the soufflé be baked?

Put the soufflé in the middle level of a 400 °F preheated oven. This will produce a creamy center when the surface is done, while a 325 °F cooking temperature gives a more uniformly solid result. The cooking must be at temperatures high enough to set the proteins before the foam has reached its maximum expansion and begins to fall, but low enough to heat the interior without first burning the outside. My recommendation is 350 °F, which takes about 5 minutes longer but is safer.

Can the oven door be opened during baking?

No. Steady uninterrupted heat is necessary. If the oven door is opened as the air cells are expanding and the soufflé is rising, the air pressure and the temperature changes may be enough to collapse the whole structure. Plan on keeping the door shut 18–20 minutes before you open the oven door to check. It is best if you have glass door with interior light so that you can look in and see if the crust is browning well. If you can wait 25 minutes, that is even better. Don't leave the door open except momentarily. There is a saying that slamming the door shut will destruct the soufflé, but there is not great evidence for this argument. In any case, there is no reason the slam the door.

How long does it take for the soufflé to rise and brown on top?

About 25–30 minutes.

How can you tell when the soufflé is done?

If you like the center creamy, it can be served after 25–30 minutes, but it is fragile and will sink rapidly. In any case, don't overcook. The center should be softer than the out-side. Cook until a thin knife plunged into the center comes out clean.

What happens if the amount of yolks equals that of the whites?

The extra protein of the yolk causes the baking soufflé to set and brown prematurely.

What is the result of underbeating of the whites?

The volume, and therefore the tenderness, is reduced.

What is the result of overbeating?

The excess beating sabotages the delicacy of the texture and can also reduce volume.

When doubling a soufflé recipe, are all the elements doubled?

1. All are doubled except the whites, which need a boost. Example: if the recipes calls for 4 in the original go to 8 + 1 = 9 whites in the doubled.
2. Seasoning can never be unquestionably doubled and must be handled with care and tasting to get to the flavor desired.

How long should a baked soufflé rest before serving?

It can be served immediately, but in any case no longer than 5 minutes.

How should the soufflé be served?

A well-cooked soufflé will stay puffed for about five minutes in the turned-off but hot oven. The best way is to have the server standing by with the plates so that the dish may be taken immediately to the guests, or serve it at the table, but have your guests waiting for the soufflé, not the soufflé waiting on them.

Does the best soufflé have a moist or dry, firm center?

A moist center.

What are some variations on fillings or flavorings?

1. Different kinds of cheeses, such as Cheddar, Gruyère, Appenzeller, Parmesan, Asiago and Emmenthaler (Swiss), but avoid stringy kinds such as mozzarella.
2. Different meats, which should either be pureed or finely minced.
3. Different fish.
4. Different seafoods, particularly crabmeat.

How do you layer the mixture if adding meat or seafood?

If the chunks are slightly larger than a fine mince, turn half of the soufflé mixture into the dish, then layer the filling on top, making sure that the pieces do not touch the sides of the dish, then add the remaining half of soufflé mixture on top.

Should the added ingredients at least be partially cooked?

Yes, otherwise they will not be cooked enough when the soufflé comes out of the oven.

What are steps to making a perfect dessert soufflé?

1. Make the base and sauce in advance, but be sure the base comes to room temperature before assembling the soufflé.
2. Preheat the oven at least 15 minutes.
3. Position the rack in the lower third of the oven.

Eggs

4. Prepare a straight-sided mold by lightly brushing with vegetable oil or spraying with nonstick spray. Then sprinkle granulated sugar inside the mold, tilting to make an even distribution and tapping out any excess.

5. The soufflé is done when it puffs about an inch above the mold, the top is firm to the touch and the edges are slightly firmer and drier.

What does the sugarcoat give?

The sugarcoating will give a pleasantly crisp crust.

What extra steps are necessary to make a fat-free dessert soufflé?

1. Thicken the base with cornstarch.

2. Bake in a water bath to guarantee low heat and produce a slow, steady rise and a moist, creamy texture.

3. Use the proper cooking temperature.

    a. An instant thermometer is good and should read 160 °F 1″ from the rim and 140–150 in the center.

    b. If you don't have a thermometer, it should be puffed 1″ above the rim.

    c. The top is firm to the touch and the edges are slightly firmer and drier.

Why can't soufflés be cooked successfully in a microwave?

They need dry heat.

What is the best kind of cheese for a soufflé?

Any gratable cheese, such as a sharp Cheddar, Parmesan, dry Monterey Jack or any mixture of similar cheeses such as these.

What is a way of making a soufflé ahead of time?

1. Bake the soufflé, remove from the oven into individual baking dishes.

2. Refrigerate for several hours.

3. Coat each with a light, white sauce and then sprinkle with grated cheese.

4. Rebake.

What is a soufflé omelette?

An omelette in which the yolks and whites are separated and the stiffly beaten whites are then folded in. It is cooked in a pan until puffed and browned on the bottom and then finished in a 375 °F oven until the surface is dry to the touch. It is also called a puffy or fluffy omelette.

What is Salzburger nockerl?

A light Austrian desert soufflé made by baking a stiffly beaten egg white mixture in a shallow layer of flavored milk.

CHAPTER FIVE

FRUITS AND NUTS

FRUITS

Which are the most popular fruits?

Apples, oranges and bananas.

What is most important in selecting fruit in the market?

Use your nose more than your fingers or eyes.

Why are canned juices usually enriched?

Because the heat of processing destroys most of the naturally occurring vitamins.

What are mandarins?

Mandarin is the general name for many varieties of small citrus fruits, including tangerines, clementines and satsuma.

What are the kinds of citrus fruits?

Citron:	Looks like a lumpy, furrowed lemon. The pulp is sour, but the peel can be candied. From the Mediterranean area.
Clementine:	A variety of mandarin, good for sorbets.
Grapefruit:	Improved variety of pamplemousse. Both juice and segments are good.
Kumquat	Like a one-inch, pale orange with orange flesh. You can eat the thin skin, too.
Lemon:	Bright yellow acidic citrus fruit. There are nine major varieties.

Meyer lemon:	A lemon-orange cross.
Lime:	Most acidic of all citric fruits, very fragrant.
Mandarin:	Small, sweet orange fruits. Satsuma and King are best-known varieties in the United States.
Orange:	Navel is the best eating; Valencia, the best juicer; Temple, a new Florida entry, is good for eating. Blood orange is mainly from Arizona and California; its dark-red flesh is slightly bitter.
Satsuma:	A mandarin orange, easy to peel.
Tangelo:	A cross between a tangerine and a pomelo. A common variety in the United States is the Minneola.
Tangerine:	Mandarins' other name. Robinson, sunburst, dancy, honey are some of the varieties.
Ugli:	A variety of tangelo from Jamaica, a cross between a grapefruit and a tangerine.

What is the zest of lemons and oranges?

The yellow/orange outer covering (not the bitter white pith). It's full of fragrant oils and has a rich flavor; it also contains natural pectin, which helps thickening.

What is pith?

The white material under the zest, most often bitter.

How should citrus fruit be prepared for zesting?

Wash with warm water, scrubbing with a brush to make sure any wax is eliminated.

How should zest be removed?

1. Use a small-hole grater.
2. Use a five-prong zester.

How can discoloration of fruit such as apples be minimized or avoided?

After slicing or cutting with a stainless steel knife, sprinkle with lemon or lime juice and refrigerate.

What is a compote?

A mixture of fruits cooked slowly with a sweetener, such as sugar syrup, served chilled.

What is a cobbler?

A baked, deep-dish fruit dessert similar to a pie with a bottom crust and topped with a biscuit-type cover and sprinkled with sugar.

What is a fool?

The English name for a mashed or pureed fruit. It may be mixed with sugar. Most often served cold.

What is most critical in making a fool?

Using the ripest, best-tasting fruit.

Should fruits for making a fool be pre-cooked?

This is optional, some, such as a mango, are lessened in flavor by cooking.

What is the difference between a "betty," a "buckle," a "crisp," a "crumble," a "grunt" and a "slump"?

All are cooked fruit desserts.

Betty:	Fruit baked with a topping of buttered bread crumbs.
Buckle:	A cake containing fruit, with a sweet, crumbly topping.
Crisp:	Fruit baked with a sweet, crumbly topping.
Crumble:	Same as a crisp.
Grunt:	Biscuit dough is dropped onto boiling fruit and steamed.
Slump:	Same as a grunt.

What are some additional flavorings that can be used with fruit?

Fruit-based liqueurs, such as Triple Sec, citrus zest, mint, salt.

How should acidic fruits such as berries be pureed?

Press through a nylon sieve, since some metals will discolor the puree.

What are muskmelons?

The name for the melons that include cantaloupe, casaba, honeydew. The other class of melons are the watermelons.

Storage

How long will dried fruit keep?

In an airtight container, six months in a cool, dry place and up to a year in the refrigerator.

How can dry, hardened fruit be plumped?

In water, fruit juice, wine or liqueurs.

What fruits should not be stored in contact (in the same container) with other fruits or vegetables?

Those that emit ethylene gas, such as melons, apples, bananas, avocados. They will promote spoilage. The exception to this rule is when they are being used as a ripening agent for other fruit.

What happens when tropical fruits (mangos, pineapples, papaya, kiwis) are refrigerated too long?

They lose their sweetness.

What foods are susceptible to the odors given off by other fruits and vegetables?

Dairy products, apples and cherries absorb odors.

Which emit odors?

Those that emit odors include onions, garlic, lemons and melons.

Ripeness

How can you tell if a melon (other than watermelon) is properly ripe?

1. Sniff the blossom end. If the fruit is ready to eat, you should be able to smell its good fragrance.
2. A melon is overripe if it feels soft when squeezed between the palms of your hands.

Which melon is an exception?

One exception is the casaba, which remains odorless. All others should have an inviting fragrance.

What fruits are regularly picked for commercial distribution before they are ripe?

Apples, pears and bananas, among others.

What can you do with melons that are picked before they are ripe?

They won't ripen unless they are only slightly under-ripe. These can be stored at room temperature in a pricked paper bag with an apple in the bag.

What are some fruits that don't ripen after being picked?

Berries, cherries, grapes, citrus fruits, pineapples and watermelons.

Which are the fruits that improve in color, juiciness and texture without sweetening after picking?

Apricots, blueberries, other melons and nectarines.

What is more important in selecting fruit, size or weight?

Weight, for the heavier for its size, the better.

Which are the sweeter fruits?

Apples, kiwi, mangoes and papayas.

Using

What percentage of nutritional content is in the skin of fruits and vegetables?

At least 10–12%.

What is a good way to peel a thick-skinned fruit?

Cut a small amount of peel from the top and bottom then on a cutting board cut off the peel in strips from top to bottom.

What can be done to peel thin-skinned fruit more easily?

1. Place the fruit in a bowl with boiling water, let stand for 1 minute, drain and cool in ice water. Or, spear with a fork and hold over a gas flame until the skin cracks.
2. Quarter and peel with a sharp paring knife or use a potato peeler.

What can be done to prevent iced fruit juice, lemonade, punch etc. from becoming watery?

1. Use ice cubes made from the drinks instead of from water.
2. Put ice in a tightly sealed plastic bag and put in container. Add the juice to the container.

What can be done if refrigerated citrus fruit has shriveled?

Soak in hot water for 20–30 minutes.

What happens when sugar is added to cut berries?

It softens them, so don't add sugar until just before serving.

What can be done with overripe fruit?

1. Puree it (peel first if necessary) and use as a topping for waffles, pancakes, ice cream or blend with yogurt.
2. Add liquid to the puree (juice, cream, yogurt, wine, liqueur) for making a sauce or drink.

How can wax be removed from the surface of fruits or vegetables?

Washing with a mild dishwashing soap and then thoroughly rinsing will remove most of it.

What are sure ways of removing surface contaminants?

If the fruit has been treated with pesticides, only peeling will remove both the wax and the pesticide. This means that the zest of citrus fruit may contain some pesticide.

What function does poaching achieve for fruit?

1. Softens fruit cellulose or fiber.
2. Concentrates natural sugars.
3. Allows the fruit to retain its shape and most of its texture.

How should fruit be poached?

For firm or under-ripe fruit, bring the combined fruit and syrup to a simmer and then allow it to cool in the syrup, thus permitting the fruit fiber to soften and absorb the maximum flavor from the syrup.

Why should fruit be poached in syrup and not in plain water?

Osmotic pressure (the process of the cell walls of the fruit seeking to equalize the concentration of molecules on both sides of the cell wall) will expel the fruit's sugar, making it less sweet when water alone is used. Therefore, use syrup, which instead allows the fruit to absorb some of the sugar and thus keep its structure.

What about soft, delicate fruit?

Make the syrup first and pour it over the peeled fruit. The water trapped on the cell walls cools slowly enough to cook the fruit.

How does sugar syrup affect flavor?

If not excessively sweet, the syrup will intensify the existing flavors of many fruits.

APPLES

How many varieties of apples are there?

The ancient Romans knew of 37, but now there are more than 7,000 in the United States alone, of which about 150 are commercially grown. However, local markets usually stock only a dozen at most.

What should be looked for when buying apples?

1. The best buys are usually the medium-sized ones.
2. The best flavor is often indicated by markings on the skin such as spots, streaks, different colors.
3. Shiny appearance usually means the apple has been waxed.
4. Slightly greasy surface means the apple is old.
5. Select firm, well-colored fruit.
6. Avoid over-ripeness.
7. Apples that are soft may have been frozen.
8. Avoid bruised or slightly shriveled apples.

Is the smell important?

1. A fermented odor means the apple is too old.
2. No aroma suggests that the fruit is not mature.

What are some varieties that are best for various functions?

Pies:	Granny Smith, Rhode Island Green, Newton Pippin, Gala.
Baking:	Rome Beauty.
Eating:	Jonathan, Granny Smith, Delicious, Newton Pippin.
Applesauce and applebutter:	McIntosh, Jonathan, Winesap, plus pie apples.
All-purpose:	Baldwin, McIntosh, Newton Pippin, Winesap, Granny Smith.

How does an under-ripeness affect the apple's digestibility when eaten raw?

If the apple is eaten raw and hasn't reached its flavor peak, it contains indigestible starch.

Why choose a slightly under-ripe apple for cooking?

Cooking needs extra tartness and firmness and the cooking will make the starch palatable.

What is the best way for storing apples?

1. Wipe dry and pack in dry sand or sawdust.
2. Don't let the apples touch each other.
3. They lose their flavor ten times faster at room temperature, so refrigerate and they will keep for weeks, even months.

What kind of knife should be used to cut an apple?

Stainless steel or ceramic, because carbon steel can cause the apple to brown.

How can cut apples be kept from turning brown?

1. Sprinkle the cutting board with a little lemon juice.
2. Store the cut pieces partially submerged in a little orange or pineapple juice.
3. Completely submerge the pieces in a double strength acidulated water (1 tablespoon lemon juice or ½ cup vinegar) per cup of water.
4. Soak the apples in a solution of ¼ teaspoon salt per cup of water.
5. If making a salad containing oranges, simply toss the apple with the orange, which is acidic.

How can wrinkling of the skin be minimized when baking apples?

By cutting a few slits in the skin to allow for expansion from the heat.

When should you add sugar when cooking apples?

Sugar helps to maintain the shape of the pieces as they cook, so incorporate the sugar at the beginning unless making applesauce or puree.

Can more than one variety of apple be mixed when making applesauce?

Yes, and the results can be a more interesting flavor.

What is apple wine?

Fermented apple juice with sugar added to produce an alcohol content of 10% or slightly higher. It is often clarified.

What is the difference between apple juice and apple cider?

Although the terms are frequently used interchangeably, if the juice has not been filtered, pasteurized or otherwise treated, it is cider. The clear product is juice.

What is the difference between sweet cider and hard cider?

Sweet: Nonfermented juice, usually not pasteurized or filtered.
Hard: Fermented juice with about 6% alcohol content, and it may be clarified.

Crab Apples (Cox's Orange Pippin)

What are they?

A tart apple variety with a crisp texture that comes in various colors and sizes.

How are they used?

Too sour to be eaten raw, they are good for jellies and preserves and go well with pork.

APRICOTS

What is the origin of apricots?

They are originally from China and were brought to California by Spanish explorers for the first production in 1792. Now more than 400 California growers with 21,000 acres produce about 95% of the country's stock.

How should apricots be selected?

1. Look for plump, well-formed fruit.
2. They should be slightly yielding when pressed, but not soft.
3. They should have a fragrant bouquet.

What varieties should be chosen?

Select the variety best for each use, such as Royal and Blenheim for eating or cooking, Tilton for canning or Patterson for drying.

How should dried apricots be stored?

Refrigerate or, if for not too long, in a closed, plastic bag at room temperature.

BANANAS

What are the main kinds of bananas on the market?

Yellow:	Large, vary from green to deep yellow, from semiripe to very ripe.
Green:	Use for cooking; semiripe: pale yellow, semisweet, use for cooking and eating; very ripe: brown spotted, soft, fragrant, use for cooking.
Red:	Plump, dull skin with black spots, very sweet, slightly dry. For cooking and eating.
Lady Fingers:	Short, stubby, sweet, slightly dry, for cooking and eating.

Why are bananas harvested under-ripe?

They ripen less well if left on the tree, and also they ship better green. When harvested green they contain about 1% sugar and 20% starch, but when they are fully ripened the starch is converted to sugar and only about 1% starch is left.

What is a "banana hand," and how many fingers does it have?

A bunch cut from the stock is a "hand," and it is composed of a variable number of fingers or individual bananas.

How should bananas be chosen?

1. Choose firm, plump ones (for they are better than skinny ones) that are uniformly yellow without brown spots.
2. Select according to planned usage: green tipped for cooking; all yellow, for cooking or eating; flecked with brown spots, to eat now or use for blending into baking goods.
3. Those with a dull gray skin won't ripen properly.

How should they be ripened?

1. Put green ones in a perforated paper bag at room temperature.
2. Those in a hand (bunch) will ripen slower or a little slower than those that are separated.

Are banana leaves of any culinary value?

They can be used to wrap foods for cooking and give a delicate flavor and maintain moisture.

What volume will sliced bananas yield?

One medium sliced will yield about ½ cup.

What will happen if a banana ripening at room temperature is refrigerated for 1–2 days?

The ripening process will stop even though the peel will darken.

How ripe should the bananas be for baking and sautéing?

Slightly soft for the most intense flavor. A full ripe banana has 15–20% sugar, unripe ones only about 2%. Brown patches on the skin are not negative indicators. The fruit must be firm for sautéing.

How can over-ripe bananas be used?

Peel, puree, stir in a teaspoon of lemon juice per banana and freeze. Use in bread, puddings, cake etc.

BLACKBERRIES (BUBBLE BERRIES)

What should be looked for in blackberries?

1. Choose fresh, ripe, glossy, completely black berries.
2. The first berries of the season that come on the market are often very tart and sour.
3. Watch out for mold.
4. If possible, choose those without stems.

Are the seeds edible?

The seeds are apt to be tough, and if the berries are cooked it is usually desirable to strain them out.

BLUEBERRIES

How should blueberries be selected?

1. Choose ones that are plump, uniformly blue with a silver haze and are practically free of leaves, stems and mold.
2. The containers they are in should not be juice stained.

What should be done when taken home?

1. Sort and discard any squashed or moldy ones.
2. Keep them dry until you use them, then wash and dry.

How should they be frozen?

Put a single layer on a cookie sheet in the freezer. When frozen, put in a plastic bag or container.

How long will they keep refrigerated?

About a week or so.

Why do fresh blueberries in muffin tins turn greenish brown?

The baking soda in the recipe causes an alkaline balance in the batter that creates the discoloration.

How can this discoloration be avoided?

Use 1 teaspoon of baking powder for every 1¼ teaspoon of baking soda in the recipe.

How can the bleeding of blueberry juice be prevented or at least minimized?

1. If frozen, add to batter in their frozen state.
2. If canned, drain very well and dry on paper toweling before adding to batter.

CANTALOUPES

What criteria should be used in selecting cantaloupes?

1. They should be round and smooth.
2. They should have a depressed, smooth scar at the stem end. If the scar appears round or the stem is still attached, the melon hasn't ripened well and it won't improve much with standing.
3. It is best if the netting is an even yellow color with little or no green.

4. The melon is immature if the natural netting doesn't stand out in relief from the underlying skin.
5. The aroma is a good indicator of ripeness and sweetness.

Will the melon ripen at room temperature?

It will; but they should be refrigerated as soon as they ripen.

How can you tell if they are ripe?

You should be able to hear the seeds rattle inside when shaken.

CASABA MELONS

Can you tell ripeness by smelling the melon?

The casabas are different from most melons in that they remain odorless even when ready to eat.

CHERIMOYA

What is a cherimoya?

1. A heart-shaped fruit that is green when ripe.
2. It has a rough skin with indentations.
3. Its texture is that of a sherbet.
4. The taste is of strawberries, bananas and pineapple all at once.

How should it be enjoyed?

When fully ripe, like a peach, cut in half, remove the seeds and eat raw by the spoonful. Another way is to skin, cut in pieces or puree it and mix in a drink or with ice cream.

CHERRIES

What are the two main types of cherries?

Sweet: Bing, Lambert, Royal Ann.
Sour: Montmorency, Morello, Early Richmond.

What are choke cherries?

A wild, sour, astringent cherry mostly used for preserves.

What is the maraschino cherry?

A pitted cherry dyed red or green, marinated in Maraschino liqueur and used in cocktails or baked desserts.

What are criteria for buying cherries?

1. They should be firm, good-sized, blemish-free and plump with a glossy appearance and good color for the variety.
2. The stems should be fresh looking.
3. They should have a well-developed flavor.

When are they at their best?

They are at their best in late spring or early summer, but this varies greatly from one growing area to another and by variety.

Will they ripen further?

Buy them ripe because they won't ripen at home.

How should they be stored?

Put them unwashed in a shallow, paper-lined bowl in one layer with a plastic cover or in a plastic bag and then refrigerate.

CRANBERRIES

What should you look for when selecting cranberries?

1. A good, ripe berry will bounce when dropped on a hard surface.
2. They should be hard, bright and light to dark red.

What should be looked for if they are packed in a plastic bag?

They will keep well, sealed in plastic bags for a month if refrigerated and up to a year if frozen.

Since the fresh are on the market for such a short time, how can you have cranberries at other times of year?

When you see these American natives, buy them, refrigerate or freeze them in the bags they come in, and they'll keep for 4–6 months.

How should they be defrosted?

They don't have to be defrosted to use, just wash and pick over.

How should they be cooked?

1. Add 1 teaspoon of butter per pound of cranberries to eliminate overboiling and excess foam.
2. Cook only until they "pop," for longer than that will make them bitter.

How can cranberry dishes be made sweeter without adding calories?

Adding ½ teaspoon of baking soda when they are cooking will mean less sweetener will be required.

CURRANTS

What are currants?

A small berry, mainly from the gooseberry family, that comes in white, black and red.

How are they used?

1. The black are used mainly for preserves, syrups and liqueurs.
2. The red are made into jelly, which can be served with lamb or croissants.
3. Other uses are for puddings or as a base for Cumberland Sauce (used on venison and ducks and with various baked goods).

DATES

Where do they come from?

From the Near East and from California, which, together, produce some 46 million pounds a year, 99% of the world's production.

How should they be chosen?

They should be plump, soft, no off-odors, without sugar crystals or mold on the surface.

What are the main varieties available on the market?

Deglet noor: The most common in California.

Medjool: Large, soft, fruity, more expensive.

What can be done if they harden?

They can become hard with storage. Soak in a little hot water for about 5 minutes, drain and pat dry.

What happens when they are finely minced?

They will form a sticky paste.

How can they be stored?

Nonrefrigerated. Best in a plastic bag where they will stay soft.

How can dates be cut when they are so sticky?

Oil the knife blade or shears and cut or snip into pieces. Don't finely mince them or they will form a paste.

FIGS

How should they be chosen?

1. The softer, the riper and the sweeter.

2. If slightly wrinkled, the sugars in the fruit have concentrated.

3. They should smell sweet, not sour.

How can they be served fresh?

1. Eaten as is, including the skin and seeds.

2. Served with cream.

3. Wrapped in prosciutto.

What is the main season for figs?

There are two seasons, the first in June and the second from mid-August to September.

Is there a difference in the fruit between seasons?

The later-season fruits are usually riper and sweeter.

GRAPEFRUIT

What are the four variations of grapefruit?

Seedless or seeded, white or pink.

What variety is the best eating, white or pink?

White has a stronger flavor, but the pink is sweeter.

What are the heavy skinned ones best for?

Candied peel or grating.

Will grapefruits improve in taste if you hold them longer?

They do not ripen further after harvesting.

How should they be selected?

1. The heavier, the juicier.

2. Choose those that are symmetrical in form.

3. They should be firm.

4. They should not be discolored.

How can you make grapefruit taste better?

Some people think adding a little salt will make them taste better.

GRAPES AND RAISINS

What are the best-selling grapes in the United States?

Thompson Seedless.

How should grapes be stored?

1. Don't wash them until you are ready to eat them, because the surface moisture accelerates bacterial growth.
2. Store them in a plastic bag in the vegetable crisper or bowl along with a dry sheet of paper towel to absorb any moisture.

What does it indicate if when a bunch is shaken and a few grapes drop off?

The bunch is not fresh.

How are they best served?

While cold grapes are refreshing, to enjoy the full flavor serve at approximately 60 °F, just below room temperature.

How should grapes be frozen?

1. Rinse, stem and dry.
2. Freeze on a cookie sheet or in plastic bags.

How long will the frozen keep?

Several months.

How should frozen grapes be defrosted?

They can be eaten frozen, or they will defrost at room temperature quickly.

Which have a better flavor balance in baking and cooking, raisins or currants?

Commercially sold raisins tend to be too sweet, currants have a better flavor balance.

How should currants and raisins be stored?

Keep them plump and moist by transferring them to a tightly sealed jar and then refrigerate.

How can they be plumped?

Marinate them overnight in dry sherry or Madeira wine.

Do raisins have more iron than grapes?

One grape = one raisin, and therefore they have the same iron content. However, one cup of raisins equals ten cups of small grapes.

How are golden raisins produced?

They are treated with artificial heat and sulfur dioxide, which yields plumper, moister raisins.

Which grapes are dried for raisins?

Thompson Seedless, Muscats and Black Corinth.

HONEYDEW MELONS

How should they be selected?

1. Best when creamy white or pale yellow with a silky finish.
2. A faint sweet smell indicates ripeness.
3. The bigger, the better.
4. It is mature if the skin shows a little texture.
5. The blossom end (end opposite from the stem) should be slightly soft.

How should they be stored at home?

1. If whole, they will taste better if left unrefrigerated for a few days.
2. Store cut sections in the refrigerator with the exposed area (including the seeds still in the cavity) covered with plastic wrap, which should be pressed onto all the exposed surfaces.

KIWIS (CHINESE GOOSEBERRY)

What is the kiwi?

A member of the cucumber family that is a native of New Zealand but now grown in the United States. Has fuzzy, greenish-brown skin, edible seeds and a sweet-tart flavor.

What should be looked for in kiwis?

Choose ripe fruit that yields to gentle pressure, or let them ripen at room temperature in a perforated paper bag.

How should they be stored?

When ripe, store in the refrigerator up to about three weeks.

How should they be prepared for eating?

Peel before eating by slicing off the ends, then separate the skin from the fruit with a spoon and push the flesh out from the skin. Or, simply scoop the flesh with a spoon.

KUMQUATS

What are kumquats?

Small, plum-sized citrus fruits with the rind often sweeter than the flesh, which is tart.

How are they prepared?

Usually whole, cooked in a sugar syrup or eaten raw.

How are they served?

Both the peel and flesh are served in salads, or they can be candied.

LEMONS

Are lemons or limes more acidic?

Lemons are more acidic, while limes are sweeter.

Do lemons vary with the season?

Those from spring and summer are usually sweeter.

Is the acid of lemon juice stable when squeezed from the fruit?

No. It will break down if the juice is stored (when it is to be used in a filling) for more than one day.

What kind of lemon should you select?

1. Spongy, thick-skinned lemons offer less juice than firm-skinned ones, and thick-skinned ones are the best for candying or zesting.
2. Buy those that are full-shaped and heavy for their size.
3. The smaller the bulb or protuberance on the end, the less mature and therefore less full-flavored it is likely to be.
4. Smell the lemon and choose ones with its characteristic, fresh scent. Avoid those with a fermented smell or with no smell at all.
5. Avoid those that are green or partially green.

How should they be stored?

In the refrigerator in a plastic bag, or in an open bowl. They will last for several weeks if the surface is kept dry.

What is the nutritional value of a lemon?

It is mainly a source of vitamin C, which will be lost within a few hours when squeezed out as juice.

What are the best ways to juice lemons?

Rolling the lemon on the counter with the palm of your hand to create gentle pressure increases the amount of juice available.

What temperature should the lemons be before juicing?

Bring them to room temperature before squeezing to increase the volume of juice extracted.

How can this be done more rapidly?

1. Submerge them in hot water for 10–15 minutes.
2. Warm for 10–30 seconds in the microwave.
3. Put in a warm oven for a few minutes.

What can be done if only a few drops of juice are needed?

Make a deep X-shaped cut into the fruit with a paring knife, then squeeze out the juice needed and store the cut lemon in plastic wrap in the refrigerator.

How much juice can be squeezed out of a lemon?

This varies with the size of the lemon, the texture of its skin, and its temperature; but a medium lemon should give from 2–3 tablespoons.

How many lemons are needed for a cup of juice?

About 5 medium-sized ones, which will run about 4–5 per pound.

How can lemon juice be used in a recipe in place of vinegar?

Double the quantity of juice, so if the recipe calls for 1 teaspoon of vinegar, use 2 teaspoons of lemon juice.

What should be done if using the skin as a garnish or flavoring?

Scrub the skin well, as it is liable to have been coated with insecticides.

What are Meyer lemons?

A variety of lemon thought to be a cross between a lemon and an orange with a very complex, fruity aroma. Its zest is more delicate and sweeter than that of the regular lemon. Both zest and skin are often edible, so it can be eaten like an unpeeled apple, but this varies considerably.

What is the season for Meyer lemons?

From December to February.

What are nine things you can do with lemons besides making lemonade?

1. Make gremolata, which is a mixture of grated lemon zest, chopped garlic and chopped parsley that is used over osso buco and in soups and stews.
2. A lemon will remove the stain from your hands after pitting cherries or slicing beets.
3. Lemon juice, a little grated zest and a pinch of sugar will make a dressing for fruit salad.
4. Hot lemon juice and honey will soothe a sore throat.
5. Rubbing the cut side of apples or artichokes with a slice of lemon will prevent browning.
6. Lemon juice, olive oil and fresh herbs make an easy marinade.
7. Grind used lemon rinds in the garbage disposal to get rid of odors.
8. Rub a lemon half and coarse salt over copper to clear stains.
9. Add lemon juice to powdered sugar in icing for a light, white color.

What can be done to provide a citrus flavor without too much acidity?

Bake lemons wrapped in foil at 350 °F for 1–2 hours.

How can lemon zest be grated without losing much of it in the holes of the grater?

1. Lay a piece of parchment paper over the grater and this will act as a barrier.
2. Use a zester if a fine grate is not necessary.

What is lemonade?

Sweetened, watered lemon juice.

LIMES

How should limes be chosen?

1. They should be bright in color.
2. They should feel heavy.
3. Avoid dry-skinned ones or those that are soft and moldy.

What are the best-known uses for limes?

Key lime pies and tequila-based drinks.

Should limes be bright green?

They are fully ripe when yellow, but tradition in this country is to use them green when they have plenty of acidity.

How should they be stored?

They keep their vitamins and aroma if stored in a sealed plastic bag in the vegetable crisper of the refrigerator.

How should they be prepared?

Scrub them well, since they frequently have insecticide residue on their skins.

Are lime and lemon juices interchangeable?

They can be substituted in most recipes, although they have different tastes. Try them in guacamole.

MANGOES

How should mangoes be selected?

1. Choose firm, unblemished ones that yield to gentle pressure.
2. Reject any that are almost entirely green-skinned and hard. They will rot before ripening, even though they will soften.
3. Those that are very soft are past their prime.

How can you tell if a mango is ripe?

If the skin is mostly red or orange and yields slightly to pressure then it can be ripened at home if not already completely ripe.

How should it be stored?

They ripen at room temperature. Store in a pierced paper bag for one to several days. When ripened, refrigerate.

What size is the best value?

The most economical are the larger ones, because the flesh/pit ratio is better, that is, more to use for the money.

What can be done with raw mangoes?

1. If green, let stand to soften.
2. They are good with ice cream to make a sundae.
3. They are good in salads, such as with fennel or endive.

MARION BERRIES

What are marion berries?

A cross between a blackberry and an olallieberry. It is named from the county of origin in Oregon.

What are they used for?

They are excellent for jams, syrups and fudge sauces.

NECTARINES

What are nectarines?

Fruits that are members of the peach family, smooth skinned and taste something like a cross between a peach and a plum.

How should they be selected?

1. Choose full-colored, plump ones with a fragrant aroma.
2. Avoid those that are hard and green or those that have blemishes.
3. They can be somewhat green, for they will mature at room temperature.

How can they be peeled?

Peeling is easy if dipped briefly in hot water, but they need not be peeled to be enjoyed.

ORANGES

What are the best oranges to use?

The thin-skinned Florida (Valencia) are best for juice, while the thicker-skinned California (Valencia) are best for eating out of hand. Both, however, are grown in both states and are good for eating and juicing.

How should you select oranges?

1. Choose those that are heavy for their size.
2. A green tinge on a Valencia does not necessarily indicate lack of ripeness.

3. They should be firm, not soft or spongy, with no evidence of mold, cuts or blemishes.

4. There should not be the slightest hint of fermentation.

5. Avoid those with a very rough peel.

Is the size of the orange critical?

Yes, for the larger ones can be dry and without flavor.

What does the color indicate?

Color is not an indicator of quality, because they are often dyed to improve appearance, and also the color varies with the variety.

Does the deeper color indicate better quality?

When they look green they have undergone a natural process called regreening, especially with thin-skinned Valencias. In this stage, orange pulls chlorophyll pigment from the leaves. These are usually very sweet and good tasting.

What is the nutritional value of oranges?

They contain vitamin C (a 6-ounce glass of juice provides 100% of the recommended daily allowance of carotene, folic acid and potassium).

Is freshly squeezed juice more nutritious than store-bought?

1. The vitamin and mineral content of fresh juice, juice sold in a container and that reconstituted from frozen concentrate is virtually the same. The vitamin C content may diminish slightly when it sits, but only slightly.

2. The flavor of fresh-squeezed is the best.

What is the shelf life of the juices on the market?

Freshly squeezed:	About two weeks, but the flavor begins to lessen almost immediately.
Frozen (not from concentrate):	About six months.
Juice from concentrate:	Pasteurized, about two months in the market.
Frozen concentrate:	About one year at 6 °F.

What is the nutritional difference in canned or frozen fruit juice of U.S. Grade A (Fancy), Grade B (Standard) and Grade C (Commercial) oranges?

None. The lower grade fruit juice comes from fruit that has more blemishes.

Which of the market juices taste best?

That from frozen concentrate.

How can oranges be made easier to peel?

Soak in boiling water for 5–6 minutes, which also shrinks the white pulp.

What does the liqueur Campari add to fresh juice?

It produces a slightly bitter taste and an alcoholic kick.

What are blood oranges?

Medium-sized oranges with reddish flesh or red streaks. They are sweet and less tart than other oranges, but slightly bitter.

What gives color to blood oranges?

It comes from anthocyanin which is the same pigment in red grapes.

How are blood oranges used?

To color cocktails, mixed with other fruit juices, in salads, made into sorbets, eaten as a fruit or drunk as a juice.

PAPAYAS

How should they be chosen?

1. Choose ones that are mostly yellow, that yield to gentle pressure and have a pleasant perfume.
2. They should not be too soft or mushy.
3. Avoid fruit with rotten spots.

Can they ripen at room temperature?

Yes, if a little unripe but well-colored, but not if they are completely green or hard.

How should they be stored?

1. Once ripe, in the refrigerator.
2. If only a portion is used, cover the balance with plastic wrap, leaving the seeds in and pressing the plastic wrap down into contact with the exposed flesh and seeds.

Can they be cooked?

Yes, while they are still green (immature).

What is a good use for papaya puree?

Meat tenderizer. Spread the puree over meat, refrigerate for about 3 hours, then scrape off and dry the meat.

PEACHES

What are the two main types of peaches?

Cling: Their flesh clings to the pit. They come on the market the earliest in the season and are mainly used for canning, although they are enjoyable fresh.

Freestone: As the name indicates, they separate from the pit easily and are better tasting fresh.

Should peaches be peeled before pureeing?

Yes, if the skin is thick, but not necessarily if it is thin. However, a thin skin left on will result in some color flecks in the puree.

What are some ways to peel peaches?

1. You can use a vegetable peeler or paring knife, but a lot of fruit is lost this way.
2. Cut an X in the bottom of the fruit, then blanch quickly, usually for less than a minute.
3. Put in a pot of boiling water (with ¼ cup baking soda per quart of water) and simmer two or three peaches at a time until the skin begins to shrink. Quickly chill in cold water, then slip off the skin.

What does overcooking do to peach skin?

It will toughen the skin.

Should peaches be peeled before cooking?

Yes, unless you will be poaching them.

PEARS

How should pears be selected for purchase?

They should be fragrant, free of blemishes and firm but not hard. It is unfortunate that at most stores they will be on the hard side.

Will pears ripen at home?

Yes, slowly, if wrapped in a brown paper bag.

How should they be ripened?

1. Place in a perforated brown paper bag, if possible with a ripe apple.
2. Place the bag in a cool, shady place.
3. Handle carefully as they bruise easily.
4. When fully ripened, refrigerate (without the apple).
5. They will usually ripen, but much more slowly, on a plate at room temperature.

What are the main kinds of pears on the market?

Bartlett:	The first pears on the market, usually can be had until the middle of December. They are bell-shaped and their skin is green with an occasional red blush. As they ripen they turn golden yellow, juicy and sweet. Good eating raw or baked or poached.
Bosc:	Peaks from October through February. Has a long, tapered neck. Good for baking or poaching, because they don't become mushy in the process. Also good for eating.

Anjou:	The late ripener known as the winter pear. Oval shaped and shorter than the Bartlett but not as flavorful. Smooth texture. Good for baking.
Comice:	Generally available from October through December. Squat shaped. Loaded with flavor and almost chewy in texture. Bakes well and good for pies.
Winter Nels:	Available from October through April. Coarse to medium texture as they ripen. Use fresh, cooked or baked.
Asian (also Chinese):	Sweet, firm, crunchy, granular texture, varying in size and color.
Seckel:	Small, russet color, sweet, spicy, crisp.

Which are best for poaching and baking?

Bosc, Anjou, Comice, Seckel, Bartlett.

How should a pear be tested for baking?

Press the stem end, and if there is a slight give, it is ripe enough. Don't use fully ripened pears or they will mush.

Can pears be poached in advance?

Yes, and save the poaching fluid for its intensified flavor.

Does yellow skin indicate ripeness in pears?

Not all ripe pears are yellow. Bartletts and Comice are most often yellow when ripe, but Anjou, Bosc and Seckel are not.

Should pears be canned whole or cut?

For best results, cut in half (lengthwise), for the core is then visible and less of the pear will be lost when it is removed.

Should a pear be peeled before eating?

It is not necessary, but be sure to wash it if you don't peel it.

PERSIMMONS

What are the types of persimmons?

There are two basic types, astringent and nonastringent. The small astringent is found in the United States in the Midwest. It is a small fruit that was used for medicinal purposes. Both types have limited acidity.

What is the Hachiya variety?

Japanese in origin, shaped like an acorn and about the size of an apple. Considered an astringent type until fully ripe.

How can persimmons be judged ready to eat?

They should be completely softened before they can be eaten.

How should they be used?

Either baked (they are good for puddings) or raw.

How should they be enjoyed?

Chill and cut out the top and spoon the translucent flesh into a bowl. They are sweet and delicious as is, or they can be served with cream, ice cream or plain yogurt.

What is the Fuyu variety?

Persimmons that are shaped like a flattened, lobed tomato. They need to be completely softened before they can be eaten.

Should the Fuyu be peeled?

The skin is edible but tough. They taste better when peeled. Peeled wedges are excellent when tossed with lettuce, toasted pecans and halved ripe figs with a balsamic vinaigrette.

What is the chocolate variety of persimmons?

Those having dark orange skin and brownish-orange flesh. They must be quite ripe to be enjoyed.

How about the Goshu variety?

These persimmons are shaped like a plump Fuyu, and they can be eaten either firm or soft.

What is the nutritional contribution of persimmons?

Vitamin A and some C.

PINEAPPLE

How should pineapples be selected?

1. Sniff. Unless there is a sweet smell it won't taste sweet.
2. Press gently with the palm of your hand. It should feel firm yet springy.
3. Choose ones that are large for their variety, as they will have the most edible fruit.
4. Pineapples should be heavy for their size, indicating juiciness.
5. Most varieties are ripe when the skin is a lively golden orange or yellow, but the color may vary from green to gold.
6. If there is mold or decay at the base, odds are that the interior has started to deteriorate.
7. The crown leaves should be small for the variety and bright green without signs of browning.

Must they be ripe when taken from the field?

Yes, for the fruit does not ripen once it is picked, although it will soften.

If the fruit is not quite ripe, can it be salvaged?

If it is just short of being ripe you can increase the sweetness while decreasing the tartness by storing it in a pierced storage bag at room temperature for a couple of days. Those that show no signs of ripeness can't be rescued.

Is the traditional test for ripeness (being able to easily pull out a leaf) valid?

Ability to pull out the leaves is not an indicator of ripeness.

How should ripe pineapples be stored?

Refrigerated, but they are best used within a week.

How should pineapples be prepared?

If you want rings or cubes but have trouble with skinning the fruit, cut it into the desired shape first, such as slices, then removed the skin.

Do pineapple and gelatin mix well?

Don't add pineapple to gelatin, because the enzymes of the fruit will hinder the gelling, unless the pineapple has been parboiled.

Can you mix pineapples with cream?

A mixture of the two will cause the cream to curdle.

What is another use for pineapples besides eating?

Use the juice as a tenderizer, they are especially good with pork.

PLANTAINS

What are plantains?

Members of the banana family, but they are never used without cooking, because their texture and flavor are not palatable when raw. Cooked, their starchy flavor tastes like a cross between a potato and a squash. The riper they are, the sweeter they are, but they are never as sweet as regular bananas.

What are their nutrient value?

They are high in potassium and vitamins A and C.

What does the color indicate as to ripeness and use?

Green:	Unripe, very starchy. Should be peeled, sliced and added to soups or fried.
Flecked yellow:	Semiripe, after sautéing or boiling, can be served as a vegetable.
Very black:	Very ripe, sweet, often baked with skin intact, served as a dessert.

How should a plantain be peeled?

The tough, stringy, lengthwise fibers make it difficult to peel. Cut the ends, then cut it lengthwise through the skin along the inside curve and, beginning in the center, pry the skin away.

How are they handled in cooking?

Much like a potato. They may be fried, mashed, pureed for soup or baked in breads.

PLUMS

How should they be selected?

Buy only firm to slightly soft fruit.

Will they ripen at room temperature?

1. Let them stand at room temperature in a perforated bag until fairly soft.
2. Very hard plums won't ripen well.
3. Under-ripe ones don't improve much but will soften and lose some of their tartness.

How should they be stored?

Refrigerated.

What is the season for this fruit?

1. In California, where most are grown, it begins in August and goes until early January, peaking in October and November.
2. The season is a long one with different varieties following each other and overlapping. With fruit coming from various growing regions there is practically no time when they are not available.

What variety of plums are best for plum pudding?

No plums are used for it is made from dried currants, suet, almonds, raisins and other ingredients.

POMEGRANATES (CHINESE APPLE)

How should they be selected?

1. Blemish free.
2. Heavy for their size.
3. Brightly colored or pinkish yellow.
4. Firm to touch.

What is the season?

September through January.

How can they be used?

1. Eat as a fruit, spitting out the seeds.
2. Made into an excellent marinade for meat, poultry or seafood.
3. The juice makes an excellent colored and distinctive flavored sorbet.

How can the seeds be removed?

1. Cut the crown end off without piercing the seeds, lightly score the skin in quarters from stem to crown, then firmly break the sections apart. Then hold the fruit under water break the sections apart, separating the seed cluster from the membrane, then drain and dry on paper toweling.
2. Bend back the skin and gently scoop out the seeds, removing any pith.
3. Gently, but firmly, roll the pomegranate with the palm of your hand on a flat surface.

How can the seeds be used?

1. As a garnish for a pudding.
2. Eating uncooked.
3. A source of juice.

How can they be juiced?

1. Place the seeds in a blender or food processor, blend until liquified, then strain through cheesecloth.
2. On a hard surface roll and press with your hand until the seeds are broken (when done the crackling sound will stop). Then pierce the rind and squeeze out the juice or poke a straw into the hole. Rolling the fruit inside a plastic bag will contain any leaks.

PRUNES

What are prunes?

Dried red or purple plums, usually those with the most sweetness and flavor.

How are they enjoyed?

1. By themselves as a snack.
2. Pitted and stuffed after being blanched in boiling water.
3. As a garnish for pork or duck.

4. Chopped and added to baked goods or applesauce.

5. Pureed into prune butter.

What happens if overcooked?

They become mushy and not very appealing.

Can prune butter be used in baking?

If pureed into prune butter they can substitute for butter in baking, measure for measure, up to about 75%. If a greater amount is used the texture will tend to be rubbery.

How should a package of prunes be handled?

Once a package is opened, store in plastic or a covered container in the refrigerator. Before that they can be kept at cool room temperature.

QUINCE

How should they be selected?

1. Choose large, smooth, yellow ones, sometimes with a green tinge.

2. They will be hard even when ripe, but they bruise easily.

What is quince season?

Fall.

How should they be prepared?

1. Wipe off any fuzz on the surface or scrub under running water with a brush.

2. They need to be pitted, cored and peeled before cooking.

3. They have an astringent, tart taste that requires sweetening.

What are good uses for quince?

1. They make good jams and jellies because of their high pectin content.

2. They are an excellent complement to meat.

3. They give a subtle taste improvement to condiments.

4. They amplify the flavor of apples when baked together.

How should they be stored?

They will keep several weeks refrigerated.

How should they be cooked?

1. Baked or poached like apples.

2. Stewed or braised.

3. Cut up, as in pies or tarts.

4. Grated into baked goods such as breads or cookies.

5. Made into preserves or jellies.

6. Made into ice cream.

7. Sliced used to stuff a chicken.

What does heat do to quince?

The acidic flavor becomes sweeter, the flesh more tender and the color turns from yellow to pink.

RASPBERRIES

How should they be selected?

1. Choose brightly colored black, red (most common) or dark purple.

2. They should be plump, not shriveled.

3. If the stems or hulls are still attached, the berries were picked prematurely.

4. Never buy a box that has even the slightest speck of mold because the fungus spreads quickly.

5. Sniff the fruit. It should have a fresh, fruity aroma rather than moldy or fermented one.

6. Dull-skinned ones indicate over-ripeness.

7. Examine the container bottom, if it is stained red, some hidden berries probably have been crushed and may be decaying.

Should they be washed?

1. Don't wash them until time for using because surface moisture shortens their life.

2. There will be less crushing or bruising if the berries are washed cold rather than at room temperature.

3. After washing, refrigerate, preferably in a single layer.

STRAWBERRIES

How should they be selected?

1. Choose brightly colored ones that are red from top to bottom.

2. They should be firm and have the hull (leaves) attached. Hulls should be fresh, green and not shriveled.

3. Avoid any sign of mold.

4. They do not ripen after being picked. White portions will stay hard and flavorless.

5. Store in a colander or plastic basket to allow for best air circulation.

When should they be hulled?

Just before using and after washing or they will absorb too much water and become mushy.

What should be done if they are to be used for pies?

Drain well and let dry for a half hour after washing.

Will they be good if they are frozen and then defrosted?

They will have lost their texture but can still be excellent in flavor.

What can be done if they become soft?

Puree them and then cook briefly in a simple sugar syrup for use as a topping on biscuits, cakes or ice cream.

What happens when they are sweetened with sugar?

They will be softened, so add it as late as possible.

How can the flavor of fresh strawberries be enhanced when they are not quite ripe?

1. Clean them with a damp paper towel.
2. Halve or slice them.
3. Put in a shallow pan with a sprinkle of sugar.
4. Cover tightly and let stand several hours.
5. Sprinkle with a little balsamic vinegar about a half hour before serving.

TANGELOS

What are tangelos?

A cross between a tangerine and a pomelo that is a sweet, juicy citrus fruit that ranges in size from that of a small orange to a small grapefruit.

What is their main season?

November through March.

Which is the main variety found in the United States?

Minneola, which is distinguished by a nipple-shaped stem.

TANGERINE (MANDARIN ORANGES)

What are tangerines?

Loose skinned, orange-like with fruit segments that are easily divided. Most are a shade of orange color.

What are the main varieties?

Honey:	Aromatic, rich-flavored, sweet, juicy, January–April.
Satsuma:	Mild, juicy, seedless, sweet, October–December.
Clementines:	Rich-flavored, very juicy, seedless, November–April.
Dancy:	Sweet, mellow, similar to clementines, December–January.

What is the difference between a mandarin orange and a tangerine?

The tangerine is a variety of mandarin orange.

WATERMELON

What is the song of a ripe melon?

Snap against the melon with the thumb and third finger.

1. If the melon says "PINK" in a shrill high voice, the melon isn't ripe.
2. If the melon says "PUNK" in a deep tone, the melon is ready to eat.
3. If the sound is HOLLOW it may be too ripe.

Is a watermelon a fruit or a vegetable?

Some botanists classify it as a vegetable but it is considered to be a fruit by most. The watermelon is a member of the cucumber family.

How do you select a good watermelon?

1. They don't mature once they are picked, so choose carefully.
2. If the melon is mature and ripe, it should have a creamy, white underbelly.
3. It should be heavy for its size.
4. Press the two ends of the whole melon, they should yield slightly.
5. The surface of the rind should be dull, not glossy, and your fingernail should leave visible traces when you lightly scrape the rind.
6. Avoid those with a flat side.

When buying a cut, seedless melon what should you look for?

Seedless varieties, which cost more because they are more expensive to grow, have a better edible yield and often have small edible seeds that are often white but sometimes black.

NUTS

What kind of nuts can be used in baking?

Almost all with the exception of cashews and peanuts.

How can nuts be roasted for use in a recipe?

Spread on a baking sheet in a single layer and roast until lightly brown (10–15 minutes at 350 °F.) While hot, stir in butter and salt. For 1 cup of nuts use ¾ tablespoon butter and ⅛ teaspoon salt.

What can be done if nuts have been soaked in hot water to remove skins and have become soggy?

Toast them at 350 °F for about 10 minutes.

What are the nuts with the highest fat content?

Pecans, with more than 70% fat.

What is the protein content of nuts?

Ounce for ounce, peanuts and almonds have almost as much protein as red meat but without cholesterol.

How can nuts be finely ground (into a flour) without having it clump together?

1. In a food processor, using the pulse key only a few seconds at a time.
2. If the nuts are toasted, make sure they are completely cool before grinding.
3. If the recipe calls for sugar, then use a little oil on the sugar before combining with the nuts.

How are nuts best chopped?

When warm, so microwave or oven warm them for a few minutes before chopping.

How should nuts be toasted?

1. In an ungreased skillet over medium heat until golden brown.
2. In a medium oven for about 15 minutes, stirring constantly.
3. Microwave for 3–4 minutes.

What are edible seeds?

Sunflower, pumpkin, sesame, squash. They are available with or without seeds, salted or not, whole or ground, as a paste or a flour.

What is a special use for sesame seeds?

As a base for halvah candy.

Is the ratio of weight to volume the same for all nuts?

One pound of unshelled, whole nuts will yield 4 cups of walnuts or pecans, but only 3–3½ cups of almonds.

How should nuts be stored?

Preferably in the shell, in a tightly covered container and in the refrigerator or freezer. Shelling should be done only as needed to prevent rancidity.

What should be looked for when buying nuts?

1. Buy them in a store with a good turnover so they won't be stale.
2. If you find many particles or much dust in the packaged nuts, they are probably not fresh.
3. Individual nuts (with the exception of peanuts) should rattle when shaken.
4. The shells should be solid and free from cracks or holes.
5. They should be heavy for their size and uniform in color.

Which packaging for shelled nuts is the better quality buy?

Those that are vacuum packed in glass, hard plastic or cans, as they are more likely to be of better quality.

How much should you buy?

Don't buy much more than what you will use in a month or so.

How can shell bits be removed?

Put nuts in a bowl of cool water, and the shell fragments will float to the surface where they can be skimmed off.

ALMONDS

What are the two types of almonds?

Sweet: Delicate, these are the most available in the marketplace.

Bitter: Illegal in the United States because they contain a trace of poisonous prussic acid, even though practically all of the acid is destroyed by the roasting heat.

Why can't almond paste be made in a home kitchen?

True almond paste contains oil of bitter almonds. Both bitter almonds and apricot pits contain a toxic chemical that must be neutralized by commercial processing. The FDA prohibits the importation or sale of bitter almonds to consumers.

Should almonds be blanched and skinned before roasting?

If it isn't too bitter, leave the skin on, as it adds to the flavor.

How can almonds be skinned?

1. Put them in a bowl, cover with boiling water and let stand for two minutes, then drain and dry.
2. Press the nuts between the thumb and forefinger to pop the meat from the skin.
3. Spread them on a baking sheet and dry for a few minutes in a 325 °F oven.

What are some of the ways that almonds can be used?

1. Plain, blanched or roasted.

2. Whole, sliced or chopped.

3. Ground to a paste.

How should the nuts be prepared when making almond ice cream?

Flavor the ice cream base with almond extract (or vanilla) and freeze until just firm, then stir in toasted nuts and complete the freezing.

What is the difference between almond paste and marzipan?

Marzipan is almond paste with added sugar and is often made with added egg whites.

Can they be used interchangeably?

No.

CASHEWS

Why are cashews sold shelled and toasted?

1. They are encased in a double shell that is separated by a toxic oil (prussic acid) that must be burned off.

2. Toasting make them more digestible.

How are cashews best used in cooking?

They are best in quick cooking such as stir-fry, because prolonged heating or baking will over-soften them.

Why is refrigeration so necessary for an open package of cashews?

Because they contain almost 50% fat, they can easily become rancid.

CHESTNUTS

Why do chestnuts turn rancid in a short time?

1. They have a high moisture content.

2. They are susceptible to mold and bacteria and therefore perishable.

How should they be stored?

Refrigerate if bought in advance. Freeze for best results.

How are chestnuts used?

1. Roasted whole as a treat.

2. Cut up as part of poultry stuffing.

3. As flour for cakes and sauces.

How should they be prepared?

Before roasting cut an X in the skin on the round side without cutting the meat of the nut in order to allow the steam to escape.

How should they be roasted?

Cut side up at 425 °F for about 1 hour with a sprinkle of water every 15 minutes.

When should they be peeled?

Peel them while still warm, for as they cool, the brown skin sticks to the meat.

How do chestnuts taste best?

They are best eaten cooked (roasted, boiled or pureed).

What is the season of availability?

Their peak is from October to February, but in one form or another they are available year-round.

When shelled what is their yield?

One pound in the shell yields about two cups shelled.

COCONUTS

How do you select a coconut?

1. Lift it. It should be heavy for its size.
2. Shake next to your ear. If it is fresh, you should hear the milk inside sloshing.
3. Examine the three eyes, which should be dry and without any trace of mold.
4. Reject any with cracks, since bacteria can enter through them and spoil the flesh.

How should it be prepared?

1. To open, first pierce the eyes and drain the liquid.
2. Crack open the shell with a hammer and pry the meat from the shell.
3. Peel off the dark skin.

How should prepackaged coconut meat be selected?

If you buy pregrated, choose the product that is packed in a tin can, which will protect it from oxidation. Plastic bags are not as effective.

Does coconut meat keep well?

No. It becomes rancid quickly when exposed to air, since it is high in oil content.

How can you revive dried coconut meat?

Soak it in milk for a half hour.

What is the water that comes out of the pierced eyes of the coconut?

A sweet liquid that is good for drinking but only infrequently used for cooking.

Is coconut cream a part of the water?

No, the cream is made from the white meat of the coconut, which is grated and moistened with water.

How is coconut cream made?

The liquid from the coconut is drained off from the grated white meat which is then left to stand until the cream rises to the surface and can be scooped off. This is put into cheesecloth and wrung out. This thick, rich cream can be used for sweet dishes or as a thickener for sauces.

What is coconut milk?

After the cream has been extracted, water is added and a second pressing yields a thick milk, which is parallel in consistency to half and half. A repeat of the process yields a medium milk parallel in consistency to whole cow milk. A third pressing will give something like a low-fat milk or a no-fat milk.

How can coconut milk be made?

Combine the water, peeled meat milk and a cup of boiling water. Then puree in the blender and squeeze the pulp dry.

How long will coconut milk keep?

About two weeks refrigerated, frozen almost indefinitely.

What is canned coconut cream?

This is pasteurized coconut milk with sugar or other ingredients added. If poured into a tall glass container and left to settle, the top can be skimmed off as a cream. The remaining liquid is comparable to a thin coconut milk.

What is coconut meat used for commercially?

It is pressed for its oil, which is used for making margarine, soaps, candies etc.

HAZELNUTS, FILBERTS

What is the difference between hazelnuts and filberts?

Hazelnuts grow wild, filberts are cultivated. Hazelnuts are the smaller of the two. Sometimes the names are used interchangeably.

What does roasting accomplish?

It intensifies the flavor.

How can you get rid of the bitter brown skin?

Put nuts in a 350 °F oven for 10–15 minutes or until the brown skin is dark in color. Then rub the nuts in a towel or between your hands to get rid of the flaky skin.

MACADAMIA

What are macadamia nuts?

Of Australian origin, now mainly cultivated in Hawaii. They are buttery, rich, high in fat and have a hint of sweetness. They are usually sold shelled and roasted.

PEANUTS

What are peanuts?

While commonly considered a nut, they are really a legume (such as beans, peas). They originated in South America (probably Brazil but possibly Peru), and were brought to Europe by the Spanish Conquistadores and to the United States by slave ships. There are two main types currently on the market: Virginian the most common, is oval; the Spanish is small and round. There are many subvarietals.

What should be looked for in selecting peanuts?

1. Choose shelled if in vacuum sealed containers. They are usually roasted and very often salted.
2. Choose unshelled, which have unbroken shells and are without blemishes.

What is the yield?

One and a half pounds unshelled will yield about 3½–4 cups shelled.

How should they be stored?

Well wrapped, in the refrigerator.

How should they be roasted?

Roast raw nuts at 350 °F for about a half hour. Spread out in a single layer on a pan and stir occasionally.

What is peanut butter?

A ground blend of peanuts, vegetable oil, salt and perhaps other additives to enhance the creaminess and to prevent separation of the oil.

What is natural peanut butter?

Consists only of peanuts, oil (usually peanut oil) and may have added salt.

What should be expected in peanut butter?

It cannot contain artificial flavor, coloring or added vitamins but it can have 10% added salt, honey, corn syrup, hydrogenated oil or preservatives.

What oil is added?

Soybean and cottonseed oil are among those used to keep the peanut oil from separating and floating to the top.

How should peanut butter be stored?

1. It should be refrigerated to prevent fats from becoming rancid once opened.
2. Put the container upside down so that it will remain fresh longer.

What percentage of its calories come from fat?

About 75%.

Can peanut butter be made from red-skinned Spanish peanuts?

Yes, even with the skins.

How is peanut oil used?

For making margarine, soaps, candies etc., and for frying because it has a high smoke point.

PECANS

Should pecans be purchased shelled?

Buy with or without shells.

What is their nutritive value?

Although they have a fat content of more than 70%, almost 90% of the fats are heart-healthy. Pecans also contain protein, vitamins A, B and E, folic acid and a number of minerals.

How can pecans be sugared?

1. Adjust the oven rack to the middle position and preheat to 325 °F.
2. Toss the pecan halves in egg white until completely covered.
3. Stir in the sugar (1 cup of sugar to 1 egg white).
4. Bake on a baking sheet, single layer.
5. Stir every 5 minutes until nutty brown, about 25 minutes.
6. Immediately transfer to a clean pan and cool in a single layer.
7. Store covered at room temperature.

How can pecans be cracked?

Cover with water, bring to a boil, cover the pot and let cool. Dry and crack.

PINE NUTS

What are pine nuts?

The oval, small, sweet nut from pine trees.

What are the two main pine nuts on the market?

European (Pignole):   Long, narrow, delicate, expensive.
Chinese (Pine Kernels):   Shorter, darker, stronger flavored.

How should they be stored?

Because they have a high oil content they turn rancid early, so keep them refrigerated. Will last for about 3 months or frozen for 9 or 10 months.

PISTACHIO NUTS

What color are pistachios?

The natural color is light brown, but they are often dyed red in the Middle East to cover blemishes.

What is their nutritive value?

Pistachios are rich in calcium, thiamin, phosphorous and vitamin A.

What does it signify if the shell is not cracked open?

That the nut is immature.

WALNUTS

How should walnuts be prepared for use in baking or cooking?

Lightly toast them in a skillet at medium heat for 4–5 minutes until the nuts begin to sizzle, or toast in a baking pan in a medium oven until they begin to darken and feel crisp.

Must walnuts be bought shelled?

Buy with or without shells. They will keep very well, frozen either way.

How should walnuts be used in pilaf or other rice dishes such as with shrimp or feta cheese?

Coarsely chopped and lightly sautéd.

How should walnuts be prepared for salads?

Roasted on a baking sheet at 350 °F until lightly browned, takes about 10–15 minutes.

Fruits and Nuts

What is the white walnut?

Better known as the butternut, it is a native American nut mainly used in baking.

WATER CHESTNUTS

What are water chestnuts?

A tuber from a water plant with white flesh and a dark skin.

How are water chestnuts used?

1. Eaten raw or cooked.
2. The fresh (as opposed to canned) are very sweet and rich in flavor.
3. They are excellent chopped in stir-fry.

Fruits and Nuts

CHAPTER SIX

GRAINS, BEANS AND PASTA

GENERAL

What is a simple test for the nutritive quality of a batch of grains?

Pour a quantity into a pot of water. If the majority of the grains sinks to the bottom, they still contain most of their nutrients.

What are legumes?

Seeds grown in a pod, such as beans. They can serve as a food both in and out of the pod.

What are pulses?

Edible seeds from leguminous plants that make pods, such as beans, garbanzos, peas and lentils.

What are some of the grains that benefit from presoaking?

Scotch barley, buckwheat, bulgar, wheat, hominy.

What are wheat berries?

Whole, unprocessed kernels that can be cooked as cereal, used in breads etc.

How should these berries be prepared?

Soak in water for a half hour, drain, combine with fresh water, bring to a boil and simmer until just tender.

What are enriched grains?

Processed grains or cereal products to which vitamins and iron have been added to replace that lost during processing or to add to a normally low level.

What is filé?

Also known as gumbo filé it is a fine, starchy powder made from sassafras leaves, which acts as a thickener for dishes such as filé gumbo and, importantly, gives its own flavor.

What is a pilaf (pilau)?

A dish made from rice, bulghur, barley, quinoa or other grains that have been lightly browned in butter or oil and then cooked in added stock. It can also have chopped vegetables, particularly onions or cooked meat and seasonings.

What is a tortilla?

Spain: A thin omelet or thin oven cake. The full name is tortilla de huevos (omelet of eggs).

Mexico: A thin, unleavened, flat pancake made from corn or wheat flour.

What are grits?

Crushed grain cooked like rice. May be from barley, corn, oats or rice. Most often the term refers to hominy, which is from corn.

How can grits be cooked smoothly?

Add the grits slowly, a little at a time, to the cooking liquid.

When a mixture of different grains are to be added to a salad, what precaution should be taken in preparing them?

Each type must be cooked separately (can be in advance), and then they can be mixed together.

What is tapioca?

A starch extracted from the cassava root.

What are the kinds of tapioca?

Pearl: Used in puddings, needs to be presoaked to soften.

Flour: It is cooked enough when the solution is clear.

Starch: Good thickener for soup, glaze.

Quick-cooking: Granular, mainly used as a thickener.

What precaution should be taken when using tapioca in cooking?

It is heat-sensitive and should not be boiled.

What is farina?

A bland, fine flour from cereal grain that is used as a hot cereal and in puddings for thickening.

What are its nutritive values?

Easily digestible and high in protein.

How can cooked legumes (soybeans, lentils etc.) be handled for storage?

Cook, cool, refrigerate in their cooking liquid and then reheat later in the liquid or sauté in butter or oil.

What is amaranth?

Once thought to be a weed, its leaves can be used in cooking or in salads, and its seeds can be ground into flour. Used as a cereal with an almost peppery flavor.

What are its nutritive values?

A high source of protein.

BARLEY

What are the types of barley?

Hulled (whole grain):	Only the husk has been removed, a nutty taste, similar to rice in use.
Scotch:	Coarsely ground, harshest.
Grits:	Hulled and cracked, medium coarse.
Pearl:	Bran removed, steamed and polished; most common on market.

What is pearl barley?

The grain is covered with two inedible outer husks, a thin layer called the aleurone, and the outer layer, a starchy endosperm. When the barley is processed, these are removed and the result is called "17 pearled."

Does pearl barley have any nutritive value?

The pearl has been stripped of much of its nutritional value. The barley still retains an enzyme that controls and reduces cholesterol in the human body.

What other form is it sold as?

It is also milled into barley flour.

How should barley be cooked?

Add 1 cup of barley to 3 cups of boiling liquid (broth or water). Lower the heat to simmering and cook about 40 minutes, covered. Check after a half hour to see if more liquid is needed.

Can barley be added to soups directly without presoaking?

It may be added to soups directly and simmered in the soup until done.

Can barley be used as a substitute for rice?

It can be made into a pilaf or a risotto in place of rice, but the cooking time and liquid requirements will differ.

DRIED BEANS

How do beans rank in the human diet?

Beans are used second only to grains in the human diet and have been cultivated for about 9,000 years.

How should dried beans be stored?

In an airtight container in a cool, dry place or frozen in a plastic bag.

What happens to the cooking requirement when they get old?

When they are old they tend to cook unevenly and require long presoaking of 4–7 hours.

What are the main dried beans?

Black, navy, lima, pink (kidney) beans and garbanzos (also called chickpeas or ceci beans).

What are Boston baked beans?

Navy beans cooked with molasses and salt pork or bacon.

What should be looked for in selecting dried beans?

1. The loss of characteristic color or faded beans indicate improper or prolonged storage.
2. If you see pinholes in a bean, it has been attacked by bugs.

What is the yield of dried beans when cooked?

1 cup dried equals 5 or 6 cups cooked.

How do beans compare in protein content with beef?

Beans have 22% protein, while beef has 18%.

Why do beans cause gas?

Beans contain carbohydrates (oligosaccharides) that humans cannot fully digest. When bacteria in the intestine start to ferment the undigested substance, gas (flatus) results.

What foods besides beans cause flatus?

Broccoli, Brussels sprouts, cabbage and spinach also create gas, as do fibrous foods such as cereal bran.

Is food always to blame for gas?

No. Swallowing air by gulping water, wolfing food down the gullet or chewing gum are major sources of gas for many people.

What can be done to minimize or eliminate gas production?

Since about 80% of the flatulent-causing chemicals are water soluble, soak the beans overnight, discard the soaking water and rinse before cooking.

What is the first step in preparation for cooking beans?

Examine for possible pebbles or other foreign matter before soaking and/or cooking. If foreign matter is not removed, the diner could break a tooth.

When should tomato be added when cooking beans with tomato sauce?

The beans should be fully cooked before tomato or other acidic elements are added, for they will prevent the beans from softening.

Can different batches of beans be cooked together?

Don't mix two batches of beans, even if they are of the same variety. If one batch has been stored longer than the other, it may be considerably more dehydrated and, therefore, require longer cooking time.

How should dried beans be seasoned?

1. Add herbs or aromatic vegetables when the beans come to a simmer.
2. Adjust the seasoning when the beans are fully cooked.

Can different varieties of beans be prepared together?

If different varieties are used, cook them separately, because they will have different cooking requirements.

Do all dried beans require presoaking?

Most dried beans need presoaking in water.

What is the best way to soak them?

Soaking the beans overnight in cold water is best.

Which are the hardest of beans?

Relatively hard beans are the soybeans, navy beans, black beans and pinto beans. These require overnight soaking (a minimum of 3 hours or more) and up to 3 hours cooking time.

What can be done if overnight soaking is not possible?

Cover with cold water, bring to a boil and simmer for 5 minutes, then turn off the heat. Let the beans soak for 2 hours before starting to cook. Remove any "floaters." Always discard the soaking water.

Does the age of the beans make a difference in cooking?

The older, the harder the bean and the longer it has to be soaked and cooked.

How should beans be soaked?

1. The evening before cooking, put the beans into a sieve.
2. Pick over to remove broken, discolored beans or little stones.
3. Toss under cold water to wash off dirt and dust.

4. Select a large bowl for soaking as the beans will usually more than double in size.
5. Turn into the bowl, cover with water and let stand, covered lightly, at room temperature until morning.

Which beans do not require presoaking?

Red and green lentils and split peas which are relatively soft require no soaking or, at most, minimum soaking and ½–¾ hours cooking time.

What is the effect of cooking beans that are not presoaked?

1. Cooking times lengthened about a quarter hour.
2. They will need more water.

What is the difference when cooking beans between using a covered pot and using an uncovered pot?

Covered: Yields a more creamy texture.
Uncovered: Beans stay separate, don't break.

How can you tell when beans have been soaked enough?

Bite one. It should have a crisp raw texture but no hard core.

How should beans be cooked?

1. Put the saucepan to moderately low heat or the casserole into a 225 °F oven.
2. If during cooking the liquid sinks below the surface of the beans, add driblets of boiling water so that the beans are just submerged at all times.
3. After an hour, stir in salt, bay leaves, oil, garlic etc.
4. Start tasting after about 2½ hours.
5. Total time: about 3–4 hours, depending upon the freshness of the beans.

At what heat should beans be cooked?

Simmer (don't boil) beans for the sake of tenderness and texture. The violent movement in rapidly boiling water causes the beans to fall apart.

How much water should be used for cooking dried beans?

The beans should always be covered with water during the entire cooking period, so use plenty of water in a pot large enough to handle their almost doubling in size.

When should beans be salted, and why?

Salt toughens the beans chemically as they cook. Therefore, salt only during the final half hour of cooking time at the very earliest. This is also true for acid additives such as tomatoes or lemon juice.

Is the rule about adding salt an absolute?

The proper time for the addition of salt is a source of disagreement. Some say that unless it is added at the beginning, correct seasoning is impossible. The toughening is due to the presence of calcium, but modern manufacturing practice doesn't add (or leave in) much calcium in salt. In any case for beans that will be pureed, don't salt until the water comes to a boil, the point at which the beans begin to soften.

How do acidic additives affect cooking time?

Tomatoes, wine, vinegar or other acidic elements will slow down the cooking, so allow enough time or add the acid elements when the beans are almost done. It is all right to add garlic or onions at the beginning as they won't interfere with the softening.

Can tap water be used for cooking beans?

Avoid hard water as a cooking medium because it lengthens the cooking process. To soften hard water add ⅛ teaspoon baking powder per cup of dried beans, but this is advisable only with extremely hard water.

How can you tell when beans are cooked?

To tell if the beans are adequately cooked cut one in half and examine the center for a chalky interior. Beans are ready to eat when the chalky interior disappears. Another test is to blow on several samples in a spoon. If their skins split, the beans are ready. Best of all, taste a bean to see if they are done.

What will cause cooking time to vary?

Cooking time will vary with the age of the beans and the size of the pot.

How long should dried beans be simmered?

There can be no set time since some batches are older, drier and harder than others. Test by tasting. They should be firm but not mushy and without a hard core.

Why do dried beans sometimes not soften?

1. If cooked with acids such as tomatoes or vinegar.
2. If cooked in hard water (excess of minerals).
3. If none of the above, the beans are probably too old.

When should seasonings be added?

Towards the end of the cooking process add the dried seasonings such as herbs, bacon etc. Add fresh parsley, basil, dill etc. at the last moment to preserve their flavors.

What happens when beans are cooked in advance?

Cooking a day in advance will improve flavor and texture. Be sure to cool and refrigerate them when storing, for otherwise they may ferment.

Are canned beans reduced in nutritive value compared with dried, uncooked beans?

No. Nutritive profiles are similar. Both are fine sources of protein, vitamin B and iron. Both have one gram of fat per cup, and both have more fiber than other foods except cereal bran. Canned beans are higher in sodium. Rinsing them will reduce the salt content somewhat. The taste difference is slight.

What is a caseload?

A rich, baked casserole of white beans cooked with a variety of vegetables and seasonings and then layered with sausage, roasted pork, pork rind, pressed duck or duck confit or a selection of meats.

What can be made with leftover beans?

They can be used as the base for soups, added to salads or recooked in a stir-fry.

BRAN

What is bran?

The ground outer layer of either wheat or oats. Mixed with wheat flour, it adds flavor and fiber.

What is bran used for?

Baked goods and breakfast cereal.

What are its nutrient components?

Fiber and vitamin B_1.

BUCKWHEAT (LE BLE NOIR, SARACEN CORN, KASHA)

What is buckwheat?

Actually it is not a true grain but a fruit of a plant that is a distant cousin of rhubarb. When dried and split it has a kernel or groat, which is usually roasted.

What are the types?

It is ground into two types, a dark and a light. The dark has more seed hulls. Both are low in gluten.

Is its use the same in different cuisines?

In the United States it is mainly used for bread and pancakes, in Denmark to make a liqueur, in Germany as an ingredient for soups, puddings etc. and it is also is brewed into beer and distilled into a spirit. Its most extensive use is in Russia. Also used for making pilaf for stuffing for poultry or fish. In Japan it is used to make noodles. When coated it is used in a Jewish dish with noodles known as *kasha varnishkes*.

What is kasha?

In the United States it refers to roasted, whole, buckwheat groats. In Russia it refers to various grains.

Does buckwheat have much flavor?

1. Roasted buckwheat groats have a toasted, nutty flavor.
2. If coated, it has little flavor of its own and is used as a stuffing.

What herbs and spices work well with buckwheat groats?

Use pungent ones such as ginger, sage or rosemary.

What are its nutritional components?

High in vitamin B, protein, fiber and complex carbohydrates. Low in gluten, more fat than wheat or rye.

BULGHUR (BULGUR)

What is bulghur?

Originated in the Middle East, it is a wheat that is parboiled or steamed until it increases in size by three times, dried on a screen, then dehulled by sifting. Finally it is ground into extra fine, fine, medium or coarse granules.

What is the difference between bulghur and cracked wheat?

Bulghur:	Whole wheat berries parboiled or steamed, then dried and crushed and some of the bran is removed. Cooks in a short time. Good in salads and pilaf.
Cracked wheat:	Whole wheat berries cracked between roller. Good for porridge.

Is there a single grind for bulghur and cracked wheat?

Both are available in coarse, medium and fine grinds.

How does whole grain bulghur differ?

Whole grain bulghur, with the bran layer intact, is darker in color and has a nuttier, chewier texture. It has little fat.

How should bulghur be prepared?

Pour boiling, salted water (or stock) in a ratio of 2 cups liquid to 1 cup of wheat over the bulghur and let stand 30–45 minutes or until almost all of the water is absorbed and the grains are puffed. Then drain very well in a fine mesh sieve or colander.

What are the four cuts of bulgur used for?

Extra coarse (also half-cut):	Steamed dishes.
Coarse:	Pilaf.
Medium:	Stuffing, with vegetables such as cabbage.
Fine:	Salads.

Are there other ways of cooking bulgur?

It can also be cooked by adding it to boiling liquid and simmering for 20–30 minutes, then let stand for 10–15 minutes before serving. Some prepare it by adding cold water, heating and skimming off any film that forms.

Can raw bulghur be added to a dish?

It can be added uncooked to meatloaf and meatballs.

How should it be stored?

Store in the refrigerator or a cool room.

CORNMEAL

What is the history of corn?

The first corn had no husk. About 2,000 years ago a husk-type developed, which improved the quality and quantity of kernels, and as a result the standard of living of the population improved. Civilizations in the Old World fed by wheat grew slowly, while the fertility and rapid mutation of maize (corn) allowed the American Indian civilizations to develop relatively faster. To the American Indians maize was both the source of life and the reason for living, for maize was the staple food of ordinary American Indian as a thin porridge sweetened with honey, spiced with peppers, supplemented with any available vegetable, meat or fish. Very rich Aztecs would flavor it with cacao. The Quichna Indians of Peru drank phenomenal amounts of *chicha*, a fermented beer made from germinated maize.

In Africa, where it was introduced by the Portuguese, it grew well and one woman, unaided, could produce enough food to ensure that her family did not go hungry. In Central and South America it was eaten with tomatoes, peppers and fish, which are rich in the elements corn lacks (particularly nicotinic acid). Venetians introduced corn to the Near East, the Spanish to the Mediterranean.

What are the uses of corn?

1. Cornmeal.
2. Cornflakes.
3. Corn syrup.
4. Bourbon.
5. Wine.
6. Corn sugar, cornstarch or corn oil.
7. Cornbread.
8. Popcorn.
9. Hominy, grits.
10. Stalks and leaves can be made into paper or be used as cattle feed.
11. Tortillas.
12. Best of all is to eat it as a vegetable.

Which has a larger amount of oil or fat—corn or wheat?

Corn has almost twice as much oil as wheat.

What is the nutritive value of corn?

Starch, of course, but some protein, vitamins A, B and C, potassium and dietary fibers. It is low in the amino acid lysine. It is also low in sodium.

What are the two types of cornmeal?

Stone and de-germinated. Stone (or water) ground is more nutritious and tastes better than steel roller ground, because it still contains the germ (embryo) and is softer in texture, richer in flavor. It has a shorter shelf life and needs to be refrigerated to prevent rancidity.

De-germinated (steel roller ground) can be stored in airtight containers in a cool, dark place.

What are ways that cornmeal can be toasted to give a better flavor?

1. Saute it in a little oil until golden brown.
2. Dry roast in the oven at 300 °F for about 10 minutes.
3. Cook it in a dry sauté pan, tossing/stirring frequently until golden brown.

Should salt be added before the cornmeal is added or after it is cooked?

Add it before cooking, because the salt not only adds flavor but slows the swelling of the starch and therefore the meal won't overcook before the interior of the granules are done.

Should corn tortillas be frozen?

No, because freezing dries them out. Flour tortillas will hold well, however, in the freezer.

How should tortillas be warmed?

1. Microwave, unwrapped 15–20 seconds.
2. Wrap in a damp cloth and heat in 200 °F oven.

How can tortillas be used in salads?

Lightly brush with olive oil, cut into narrow strips 1–2″ long and toast in the oven or in a heavy skillet.

What are some other uses for corn tortillas besides making tacos?

1. Cut into pieces, bake or fry, and use in salads or as toppings for soup.
2. Use to make a pizza—best when stale or more dried out.

What is polenta?

Polenta is a mush made from cornmeal. It is a staple in Italy.

What is instant polenta?

Instant polenta is commercially produced cornmeal that has been partially cooked and dried.

What grind of cornmeal is best for polenta?

Either coarse or medium grind. Fine is too smooth. Medium is most popular.

What is hominy?

Dried kernels of white or yellow corn with the hull and germ removed.

What are hominy grits or grits?

Hulled kernel coarsely ground or crushed and boiled in milk, water or stock.

What can be done to lower salt consumption and still enjoy popcorn?

Use herbs, such as garlic powder, chili powder, basil or oregano, to replace the salt.

What is the nutritional difference between regular popcorn and gourmet popcorn?

The gourmet type makes the largest blossoms but usually they are slightly tougher and less crisp. It is just the size of the popped kernel. So the answer is very little or none.

What is the advantage of air-popped popcorn?

It makes larger blossoms but usually it is tougher and less crisp. It has minimal fat, and none need be added, although most often it is.

How can kernels that don't pop well be treated?

Freeze the kernels.

How much will a cup of popcorn kernels expand to?

About twenty cups of popped corn.

COUSCOUS

What is couscous?

A finely cracked semolina wheat or millet that has been processed by steaming and drying. Native to Asia and Africa where it is widely used as a staple.

Is it uniform in size?

It ranges in size from the tiny Moroccan to the larger Lebanese, the size of small peas.

What is Israeli couscous (also called pear couscous)?

A large form, more rounded in shape. It is most often made into a risotto-style dish with vegetables, meats or seafood. The grains are rolled, dampened, rolled in flour then moistened, lightly oiled and dried.

Is it used for desserts?

It makes a good dessert sweetened and seasoned with cinnamon, nutmeg etc.

How is couscous prepared?

1. Wash 1¼ cups in cold water, drain, rake grains with fingers and let rest 10 minutes, giving time to swell.
2. Steam, uncovered for 20 minutes but only the steam, not the water, should touch the grains.

3. Remove from steamer, put in pan, sprinkle with ½ cup salted water, lift with a wooden spoon, separate grains and break up any lumps and let rest 10 minutes.

4. Simmer slowly until fluffy, about 15–25 minutes. This step is often repeated several times.

Is there an instant variety of couscous?

An instant variety on the market is precooked and requires only a short soak in a hot liquid before serving.

What is the yield of 1 pound dried couscous?

Steamed: 10–12 cups.

Quick cooked (instant):   5–6 cups.

May couscous be prepared in advanced?

Yes.

Can couscous be served cold?

Yes, particularly in combination with vegetables and spices such as cumin.

FARINA

What is farina?

Polished, medium ground wheat berries used for breakfast cereal and baked goods. It will soak up any syrup that is poured over a cake.

What are its nutritional values?

It is rich in protein and easily digestible.

GARBANZOS (CHICKPEAS, CECI BEANS)

How are garbanzos used?

Soups, pastas, salads, as a starch with grilled sausage or vegetables and with roasted eggplant to make hummus.

How should they be cooked for making hummus?

Longer than for other uses, so that they will puree better.

Are garbanzos good nutritionally?

They are among the fattest of the beans. A cup contains a little over 4 grams of fat and 270 calories. They are high in fiber and folic acid, fair in protein and iron.

What is the key to cooking garbanzos well?

Maintaining a constant temperature in the cooking liquid.

How much longer cooking time do garbanzos require when they have been frozen?

Freezing actually shortens cooking time.

LENTILS

What is the earliest written mention of lentils?

In the book of Genesis, Esau sold his birthright in exchange for a dish of lentils.

What are the kinds of lentils?

Because they are easily grown and inexpensive, they became known as "the poor man's meat." There are more than fifty varieties known, but most in the United States are the brown ones known as U.S. Regular. Others range in color from black to orange and are found in speciality stores.

What are the tastes of the different lentils?

Yellow or brown:	Intense flavor.
Peeled red:	Slightly sweeter.
French le puy:	Robust flavor.
Whole red (brownish seed coat left on):	Best flavor.
Green (French):	Delicate.

How can lentils be used?

They are good as a warm dish or in soups (whole or pureed), cold with a vinaigrette as a salad, sweet as a preserve or in cookies.

What is the nutritional value of lentils?

High fiber, vegetable proteins, complex carbohydrates and fairly good in iron and protein, low in sodium and fat-free.

How long should lentils be soaked before cooking?

They don't have to be soaked for tenderness, but presoaking helps to keep them whole.

What should be done before cooking?

They should be rinsed and picked over for small rocks or pieces of hull.

How should lentils be prepared?

1. Cover with cold water and salt and slowly cook for 30–40 minutes, checking periodically to make sure that they are just covered with water.
2. When soft, drain well and rinse.

How will acidic items such as tomato or wine affect the cooking time?

If tomato or wine is being used, add it at the end of the cooking cycle or increase the cooking time.

How should they be cooked?

In salted water.

Can cooked lentils be kept?

After cooking they will keep well in the refrigerator in a sealed container for several days.

MILLET

What is millet?

A seed from a hardy grass, a cousin of wheat but with a smaller seed.

What is its main use in the United States?

Fed to small birds as birdseed.

How is it used nutritionally?

When hulled it is a good source of protein, B vitamins, phosphorous, iron, manganese and copper. It is useful for those who are unable to digest wheat.

How is millet used?

1. Cracked, it is one source of couscous (in North Africa).
2. Ground into flour, it can be made into porridge by cooking with milk or water.
3. Good in stews, soups, salads (with vegetables), meatloaves, timbales, polenta-like dishes and can be combined with rice or quinoa.
4. Works as a stiffener of puddings.

How is millet cooked?

1. Simmer in broth or water with a little added butter or margarine for about half an hour.
2. Its flavor will improve with a light toasting in the oven before simmering.

What will sautéing the millet before simmering it accomplish?

It will yield a nuttier flavor, the light oil coating will keep the grain distinct and prevent mushiness.

Does millet need seasoning?

Yes. It has a bland flavor without seasoning.

What is millet meal?

Ground millet. It has a crumbly richness but is bland tasting.

How should millet be stored?

Freeze it.

OATS

Where do oats come from?

They are mainly grown in the Midwest United States.

What is the main use of oats?

Cattle feed.

Which is the grain with the highest fat content?

Oats. It contains 2–5 times the amount of wheat.

How can it be used in bread-making?

It has no gluten-producing enzymes and therefore no light breads can be made from oats alone.

What is the use of oats if the bran is removed?

It is used for making oatmeal or heavy cakes.

What is the effect of adding rolled oats when making bread?

Gives a sweet, chewy moistness.

How can oat flour be made?

In a blender, work rolled oats to a fine meal consistency.

QUINOA

What is quinoa?

(Pronounced keen-wa). Not a grain, although it acts like one. Instead it is the dried fruit of the herb family *Chenopodiaceae*. It is from the Andes of South America but now is grown in the Rocky Mountains of the United States.

How is it used?

Quinoa can be used in place of rice or couscous. It contains healthful unsaturated fats and is low in cholesterol. It has a light, nutty flavor and a slightly chewy texture.

How should quinoa be handled?

1. Rinse under running water to remove any residue of its outer coating.
2. Remove any black grains, as they will not become tender.
3. It will have a richer flavor if toasted to a light golden.

How should it be cooked?

Cook like rice with 2 cups of liquid to 1 cup of quinoa.

How should it be stored?

Store in cool, dark place or refrigerate. Because it is high in fat, it can become rancid.

What is the yield when cooked?

One cup uncooked will yield four cups of cooked.

What is the nutritional value of quinoa?

1. Twice as much proteins as rice or barley.
2. High in B vitamins.
3. One cup has as much calcium as one quart of milk.
4. The calories are about the same as in rice.
5. It has all eight essential amino acids.

RICE

Did rice originate in China?

The cereals initially grown in China were millet and wheat. Rice was introduced in the Yangtze delta from India, carried overland by birds or wind or by sea on flotsam. Archeology shows that rice reached Shanghai nearly 3,000 years ago. In Japan it was introduced somewhere between 300 BC and AD 300. Around the tenth century, Arab and Indian traders brought rice to Madagascar. In Africa, rice is important only in Senegal, Gambia and the Ivory Coast. Much of the rice eaten in Africa is imported. Persians and Mesopotamians first encountered rice around the fifth century BC as result of trading with Chinese and Indians. Rice reached Egypt and Syria during the next two centuries. Rice water as a treatment for digestive disorders was written about in the first century AD by the Greek doctor Pedanius. Southern Spain owed its first rice fields to the Moors in Andalucia. At end of the thirteenth century rice was brought to the Po River delta of Italy. Portugal was not introduced to rice until the fifteenth century.

How did rice get to the United States?

The Portuguese and the Spanish in South America introduced rice from the beginning of the sixteenth century, especially south of Brazil, lower Peru and Suriname. Carolina rice dates from seventeenth century when a ship was wrecked on a beach in South Carolina, then a British colony. Rice is now grown in Arkansas, California, Louisiana, Texas, Florida and Mississippi. The United States has been the sixth-largest rice producer for the last thirty years.

How many varieties of rice are there?

The 8,000 different varieties of rice worldwide can be classified by the length of the grain into three main kinds, plus sticky rice.

What is short-grain rice?

Almost as wide as long, it contains lots of starch and tends to stick together after cooking. Decreasing use in European countries, used mainly in soups and puddings. Grown in Camargue (France), Italy and Spain.

How does the medium grain differ?

The grains are slightly longer, contain quite a bit of starch and stick together after cooking. It is used in same way as short-grain. Cheapest of the varieties.

What is sticky rice?

Very popular in Asian nations and used to make noodles and cakes. Main basis for making saki. Rich in nitrogen. Also known as glutinous or sweet rice (but isn't sweeter than any other). It is clingy, moist and sticky when cooked. It comes short, medium and long grained and in brown, white or black. The Thai type is long grained and has more aroma, the Chinese type is short grained.

Is the stickiness of a rice related to the shape of the kernel?

The stickiness is related to the length, i.e., the shorter the kernel the stickier it will be.

What are the characteristics of the long-grain varieties?

Six mm or more in length, very slender and contain a different kind of starch. Grains remain separate when properly cooked. More expensive.

Why is the Arborio variety so highly regarded?

Arborio, which is grown in northern Italy, is used for making risotto because it can absorb a lot of stock while remaining al dente. It is also used in Valencia for making paella, for it has a soft, creamy texture.

What are the best-known varieties?

Carolina:	Most widely grown in the United States.
Basmati:	An expensive, aromatic rice from India and Pakistan.
Jasmine:	From Thailand, emits a wonderful scent when cooked.

What are the problems with cooking the different types of rice?

Short:	It becomes mushy if cooked too long.
Medium:	Can clump during cooking.
Long:	It hardens as it cools and thus needs to be served warm.

What is pecan rice? (also wild pecan rice)

It comes from southern Louisiana and has an intensely nutty flavor and aroma.

What are uses for rice besides cooking for the table?

Rice is used to make dietary flours, starches and thickening; either short-grain or broken kernels are used. Rice flour does not rise and so will not make good bread on its own.

Why is short-grain rice more sticky than long-grain rice?

The starch amylase produces a less sticky rice, and it is dominant in the long-grained varieties, while amylopectin, which increases water absorption by the starch, is more dominant in the short-grained type. This stickiness makes short grain the selection for dishes to be eaten with chopsticks, for risotto, puddings and sushi.

What is the advantage of enriched rice?

A few of the vitamins that are lost in the milling process are added back in the enrichment process, but much of them are lost again when the rice is washed and cooked.

Is rice perishable?

Yes. It should be stored in airtight containers. It will last for several months in a cool, dark place without deterioration. Brown rice should be refrigerated, since it contains the nutritious germs, which become rancid easily at room temperature.

What must be done with rice that has been stored for a long time?

Allow extra cooking time if rice has been stored for a long time, because it will have lost its moisture.

Why should white rice not be rinsed before cooking?

It will wash away the nutrients that have been added to it during processing.

What is dirty rice?

Rice cooked with ground poultry liver, gizzards, onion, garlic etc.

What are some precautions to take when cooking rice?

1. Don't wash before cooking.
2. Add salt at the beginning of cooking.
3. Don't stir while cooking, or the outside covering of the rice will break, causing the starch to leave the exposed kernel and be dissolved in the cooking water.
4. Don't remove the lid prematurely, even to sneak a quick peek, because that lets the steam escape, which, in turn, lowers the quality of the finished rice and increases cooking time.

What happens when rice is cooked with added butter?

It yields a softer, more flavorful, move moist rice, using about 1 teaspoon butter per cup of uncooked rice.

How can rice be tested for doneness?

1. Cut or bite a kernel in half. If the core is still hard, it needs additional cooking time. If the kernel is soft throughout, it has cooked too long.
2. If the kernel has only a slight resistance, it is time to turn off the heat. Lightly fluff the rice with a fork, being careful not to crush the grains.

When the rice is done, should it be served immediately?

Let the rice stand 5 minutes before serving.

Why is rice so nutritious?

1. It is rich in complex carbohydrates.
2. While limited in protein content, it contains more than most other grains.
3. It has all eight essential amino acids—the protein building blocks—and in proper balance.

How do instant and minute rices compare?

Both minute and instant rices are the lowest in nutritional content of any rices.

What is basmati rice?

Known as the queen of fragrances! Basmati is a long-grain rice grown at the base of the Himalayas in India and is valued for its nutty, earthy scent. It is aged to enhance its rich aroma and nutty flavor. Unique in that when cooked it will double its length, which is much more than it widens when cooked.

How should basmati rice be prepared for cooking?

1. Check for stones, bugs, or unhulled grains by spreading on a plate or cookie sheet.
2. Wash two or three times with cold water in a large bowl, pouring off the water each time. This will remove excess starch or particles and thus when cooked it will be light and fluffy.
3. Soak ½–1 hour so the rice will absorb the most moisture when cooked and also minimize the breaking of the kernels.
4. Use the soaking water for cooking to save nutrients.

How long can basmati rice prepared in an electric cooker be kept?

Only an hour, or the kernels will dry out.

How much salt should be added when cooking in an electric cooker?

Do not add any salt.

What is pilaf?

A dish made with rice (or bulghur or barley) that has been sautéd before the cooking liquid is added and then cooked with stock or other liquid until the liquid is absorbed or evaporated. Other foods are often added, especially onions.

How should basmati rice, pilaf style, be made?

1. Heat a little oil (canola or vegetable).
2. Add thinly sliced onions, stirring until they are translucent.
3. Stir in the rice, mixing well, so that each grain is coated with oil, and cook, stirring, for 1–2 minutes.

4. Then add water (1½ cups per cup of rice) and 1 teaspoon of salt per cup and bring to a boil.
5. Reduce the heat, cover well and cook until all the water is absorbed—about 15–20 minutes.
6. Let stand ten minutes off the heat, then fluff with a fork and serve.
7. It can be seasoned by adding spices such as cloves and cinnamon at the beginning.
8. True basmati kernels (from India) will double their length.

What can be substituted for basmati in pilaf?

Other rices, barley, millet or wild rice can also be used, but the cooking time will vary.

Which is better for pilaf, brown or white rice?

Chefs disagree. Although white is traditional, from a nutrition point of view, brown or wild rice is better.

What procedures will enhance barley or millet in making pilaf?

Dry toasting first will prevent mushiness and bring out their nutty flavors.

What can be done with leftover pilaf?

1. Make a salad with a vinaigrette.
2. Use for Chinese fried rice.
3. Add cooked meat or shrimp and reheat into a main dish.

What is Valencia rice?

A variety that comes from the Spanish area of that name. A medium grain, it is used in paella and can be substituted for Arborio or vice versa.

What is black rice?

A long-grained rice that is similar in appearance to wild rice but is sticky when cooked. From Indonesia and Philippines.

What is "converted" rice?

This is a trademark name for parboiled long-grain white rice that has been processed so that it doesn't stick together when cooked.

How is it made?

A treatment with steam pressure ensures that the grains cook up fluffy and separate. Soaking, steaming and drying gelatinizes the starch in the center of the grain and removes some of the starch from the exterior, making it less likely to be starchy or sticky when cooked.

What are its cooking differences?

"Converting" toughens the kernel and therefore adds at least five minutes to the cooking time, compared to regular long-grain rice. It also requires 2½ cups water per cup, compared to 2 cups with regular.

What is instant rice?

White rice that is cooked, dehydrated and scratched slightly to decrease the cooking time to about 5 minutes. It also comes as instant brown.

What is brown rice?

Rice, when harvested, has an inedible straw colored hull to protect it. When these hulls are removed by mechanically passing them through a sheller, if the outer bran layers are left intact, the grain is called brown rice. It comes in short, medium or long grain. It has a warm color, a nutty flavor and chewy texture.

How do its cooking requirements differ from those of white rice?

Brown rice requires more water for cooking than white and 2–3 times more cooking time.

Will the microwave cook brown rice well?

It saves a little time, but the rice tends to be sticky.

What is the nutritional difference between regular and instant or precooked brown rice?

It is much the same. The instant costs 3–4 times as much.

How brown is brown rice?

Once cooked it is only a light brown in color.

What are the types of brown rice?

Long grain:	Gives fluffy and separate kernels.
Medium and short grain:	Tends to dry or become starchy because of the ratio of the two main starches (amylase and amylopectin). Amylase content in long grain is 23–26%; medium 18–26%; short 15–20%.

What are the differences among brown rice, white rice and converted rice?

Brown:	Has only the husk removed. A half cup cooked has 1.6 grams dietary fiber.
White:	Has the nutritious bran coating removed by milling. A half cup cooked has 0.3 grams fiber.
Converted:	Has been parboiled to remove the surface starch. A half cup cooked has 0.2 grams dietary fiber.

What are the advantages in nutritive value of brown over white rice?

1. Has twice the fiber of white but still only about ½ gram per cup of cooked rice.
2. Has slightly more protein.
3. Has 2–3 times more vitamin E, magnesium, potassium and phosphorous.
4. Has volatile bran oils, which have been linked to cholesterol reduction in humans.

What are the disadvantages of brown rice?

1. Since it has volatile bran oils that can oxidize, it should be purchased in limited quantities, no more than you can use in a couple of months. It should be stored in the refrigerator.

2. It may also contain numerous green or broken kernels, which will cook differently, giving an uneven texture. These variants are nutritionally sound. Modern top processors limit immature or broken kernels to less than 4%.

Why does brown rice take approximately three times longer to cook than white rice?

The bran covering of brown rice hinders the absorption of water by the starchy interior. It also requires 1½ times more water to steam it, partly because of the longer cooking period.

How does long grain differ nutritionally from most standard rice?

Long grain contains more protein but fewer minerals.

What does the addition of butter or oil do to the cooking of rice?

Produces a less dry, softer and a bit more flavorful product.

How much butter or oil should be used?

Use about 1–2 teaspoons per cup of raw rice.

What does the addition of salt do to the cooking of rice?

Without salt the rice tends to be softer, almost mushy, because the salt slows down the absorption of water, as water, is attracted to the salt and resists penetrating the rice. Slowing water absorption increases cooking time.

How much salt should be used?

Use about ½ teaspoon per cup of raw rice.

How can rice be cooked so that it is more fluffy and dry?

A few minutes before the rice is done place a double layer of paper toweling just under the lid and finish cooking.

How can rice be tenderized?

Soak for an hour or two before cooking. This is *rarely* needed.

How can rice be prevented from becoming mushy in a soup or stew?

1. Add the rice only long enough to cook.
2. Cook the rice separately and add just long enough to heat.

What is steamed rice?

Steamed rice refers to rice that has been cooked over low heat and allowed to steam dry with the lid on.

How can leftover cooked rice be kept?

1. Put it in a sealed container.
2. It will be all right for 3–5 days in the refrigerator. It can be stored in the freezer for up to a month.

How can leftover rice be reheated?

1. To reheat, add a few tablespoons of water in a sauce pan and heat over low heat for 3–5 minutes, stirring occasionally. Add more water as needed or sprinkle with water and cover.
2. Microwave on high power for 1–2 minutes.

Why is sticky rice not suitable for quick cooking?

It needs to be soaked for 3–8 hours before cooking.

What happens when long-grain, sticky rice is cooked by boiling in water?

It disintegrates to mush.

How should long-grain rice be cooked?

It should be steamed. Spread the grain evenly over a towel in a steamer and cook over simmering water until soft.

What are the goals in making risotto?

1. The cooked kernels must be separate, that is, not mushy or stuck together and are bound together not by the starch of the rice but only by the sauce.
2. The kernels should be al dente when cooked. This is most important.
3. Leave the risotto just a little soupy since the rice will continue to absorb liquid along with any additional butter.

Is a creamy risotto high in fat and calories?

The creaminess comes from the starch in the rice, so the calorie and fat content is low, unless butter or cream is added.

What kind of rice should be used for risotto?

Use first quality short-grain rice. Arborio from Italy is by far the first choice, Japanese short grain or California medium grain can be used with somewhat lesser results.

How should risotto be made?

1. Cook finely minced onions (or shallots, or leeks) in butter to obtain a sweet, rich flavor.
2. The quality of broth used is critical. It should be high in flavor and not too salty.

3. If wine is used, add at the end of cooking so the rice kernels will not over-soften.

4. It may be served with additional butter.

5. Don't cover the cooking risotto, for this will steam the kernels.

Why shouldn't stock be used as a cooking liquid?

Stocks are usually too strong in flavor so that they will dominate the taste.

Why add the rice to the butter/onion mixture before adding the stock or other liquid?

In order to keep the kernels separate and allow the heat to gelatinize the starchy rice coating.

Why stir constantly?

Frequent, almost constant, uninterrupted stirring is required to prevent the rice from burning and to liberate the amylopectin (rice starch) of the rice that then will swell and help make the sauce. Gradual release of this starch gives the dish the desired creamy texture.

What happens if the rice starts to brown?

The kernels will harden and not emit the starch that gives the risotto its creamy quality.

How should broth be added?

Add broth a little at a time but only when the previous pour has been absorbed.

What are rules for adding cheese?

Use good quality cheese (Parmigiano-Regiano, Asiago, fontina) that is freshly grated and add at the last moment.

How can leftover risotto be used?

1. To thicken soups.

2. To make fried rice cakes or rice balls.

What is the cooked yield of one cup of long-grain white rice?

About three cups.

Should rice be rinsed before cooking?

No: 1. Almost all white rice grown in the United States has been enriched by coating the surface of the kernels, and this layer would wash off in the water.

2. Most white rice milled abroad has not been enriched unless it is sold in California, New York or several other states.

3. Brown rice has not been enriched, but some soluble nutrients will be lost with long-term soaking.

Should cooked rice be tossed before serving?

Tossing with a fork will let any steam escape, which makes for separate kernels. Don't toss while cooking (after the initial quick stir). This rule does not apply when making risotto.

What kind of rice is best for salads?

Long grain that is cooked to be fluffy and firm.

How should rice salad be seasoned?

Season while still warm, just after draining.

What is rice paper?

Rice paper (Bahn trang in Vietnamese) is made from sheets of cooked rice pounded into dough and then formed into paper-thin sheets.

How are the rice papers used?

They are used to make fried spring rolls or to wrap grilled meat or vegetable fillings.

How should they be kept?

Keep unused papers in their original bag or in a self-sealing plastic bag with the air squeezed out.

How are rice papers prepared for use?

1. Dip the papers into lukewarm water (not cold or hot water), do not soak. Then put them on a damp towel and let sit for 1–2 minutes until pliable.
2. Remove from the towel one at a time, put in the filling and roll. Then serve as-is or fry or steam as the recipe indicates.
3. Keep covered with a damp towel while using.

Can they be made in advance?

Rolls can be made ahead, but don't refrigerate them, as this will toughen the skin.

RYE

What is rye?

A grain that originated in Central Asia and has been indigenous to northern Europe. It has a low gluten content and is usually mixed with wheat flour.

What is rye used for?

Used for breads such a pumpernickel. It has a high water-retaining capacity, which results in heavy, moist breads.

What is pumpernickel?

Bread based on rye flour. Often the rye is mixed with other wheat flours.

How can rye be used?

Whole berries or flakes:	Cooked in a liquid to make a hot cereal.
Cracked berries:	To make grits.
Flour:	To make bread such as pumpernickel.

What are the nutrients in rye?

Calcium, phosphorous, riboflavin, iron, thiamine, potassium and niacin are present, but their quantities are greatly diminished if the flour is made from rye that has had the bran removed.

SESAME (BENNE SEEDS)

What is sesame?

The seeds from a plant that originated in India or Africa and was brought to this country by slaves.

What are its forms that are used for cooking?

Seeds:	Tiny flat seeds that make a good coating for breads, rolls, fish. Toasting brings out full flavor but pretoasting is not needed for foods that will be cooked in the oven.
Oil:	From crushed seeds, is light brown with a rich, nutty flavor. Used in cooking and dressings.
Oriental sesame oil:	Pressed from roasted seeds, is darker and stronger in flavor and is used by itself or with regular sesame as a flavor enhancer.

SOY BEANS

How are whole soy beans used?

Soaked and roasted for snacks or baked beans.

How does natto differ from whole soy beans?

Natto is made by fermenting and mashing cooked, whole soy beans and is used as a rice topping, in miso soups or with vegetables.

What is miso?

Soy beans fermented under pressure and mixed with rice, salt and a mold culture to make a rich, salty condiment as a smooth paste.

What determines the color of miso?

If miso is light or white it has been aged 2–6 months and is sweeter and milder. If the color is dark or red, it has been aged 6 months to 3 years and is stronger and saltier.

How is miso used?

For soups, sauces, pâtés. A substitute for salt or soy sauce. It is thick, spreadable and salty.

What are the kinds of soy sauce?

Soy: Made from fermented beans.

Tamari: A by-product from making miso, a naturally brewed, sugar-free soy that may be wheat-free.

Shoyu: A blend of soy and wheat.

How is tamari used?

As a condiment.

What are the characteristics of soy oil?

Light in flavor with a high smoking point, it is used in making vegetable oil. It is cholesterol-free and low in saturated fat.

What is soy milk?

A creamy milk made from the liquid strained from whole beans made by pureeing soybeans with water. It is sometimes sweetened with a nutty flavor. Served hot or cold, with flavorings or with vegetables to make a soup.

What is tofu?

It is a custard made from soybean curd with a bland flavor. Tofu was invented somewhere in China about a thousand years ago. It is now an integral part of the Japanese and Chinese cuisine and is used in other parts of Asia as well. Called the "Cow of China," it is a creamy, cheese-like product made from cooked, strained and jellied soy beans (soy milk). Similar to cheese, it ranges from soft to quite firm and is available in a low-fat form.

What are tofu's nutritional values?

High in calcium and magnesium and low in fat.

How is tofu used?

As a meatloaf, in soups, sauces, cream pies. It is served hot or cold, plain or marinated, grilled, fried, scrambled as a substitute for eggs, in salads and other dishes as a substitute for chicken. It is easily digestible.

What are the styles of tofu?

It is offered in various styles, such as extra firm, firm or hard and soft. It is also sold flavored.

What are the forms of tofu?

Fresh: Either soft or firm (sometimes in-between), packed in a tub with water. Will keep 4–5 days if refrigerated. Best if the water is changed daily.

Fried: Puffy, honeycombed. If store-bought it is often too greasy.

Marinated: Use sliced or diced in a stir-fry or shredded in a spring roll.

Smoked: Similar to a smoked mozzarella. Good in salads and with pastas.

What is tempeh (also tempe)?

It is chunky cakes of pressed, fermented soy cake and sometimes grains. Absorbs flavor when cooked. Marinated or grilled and added to soups, pasta, casseroles. It is also used as a meat substitute. It looks and feels like cheese. Tempeh comes from Indonesia.

How should it be stored?

It must be refrigerated and used within a week of purchase, or frozen.

SPLIT PEAS (FIELD PEAS)

What are they grown for?

Specifically for splitting and drying. Field peas have high levels of amino acids lysine and tryptophan and contain 21–25% protein. They are an excellent source of vegetable protein.

How long should split peas be soaked?

They don't need presoaking.

TRITICALE

What is triticale?

It is a hybrid of wheat and rye that is hardier than either of the two.

What is its nutritional value?

It is nutritionally more valuable than wheat and, in fact, is one of the highest nutritional flours and is high in protein.

How is triticale used?

1. If the berries are crushed they can give crunchiness to bread.
2. As a flour it works well with breads, muffins or pasta but the gluten is very delicate and is easily broken up if over handled.

WHEAT BERRIES

What are wheat berries?

Hulled, whole berries of wheat.

What are their nutritive value?

Wheat berries are almost fat-free and have a high protein level with hard wheat and a low protein level with soft wheat.

How are wheat berries used?

In place of pasta or rice.

When should wheat berries be salted?

After cooking, because the salt prevents them from absorbing liquid.

WILD RICE

What is wild rice?

Rice that comes from a grass-like plant that is grown wild in shallow water and is now cultivated. The kernels are long grained, longer than regular rice and more slender. It has more flavor and texture than regular rice.

How is wild rice sold?

As a whole grain. It is never refined. During preparation it is fermented to develop its nutty flavor. It has more protein than does white rice.

How should "select" or short-grain wild rice be best used?

In soups or baked goods, for the grains are often broken.

How is wild rice cooked?

It can be baked or simmered in liquid with the pot covered.

Does wild rice combine well with other grains?

Yes, with rice or bulghur.

What needs to be done before cooking?

Soak in a bowl or pot with ample cold water. Let it stand 5–10 minutes, scoop out any floating debris, drain and cook. Without soaking, the cooking time is much longer.

What happens if wild rice is overcooked?

It becomes mushy, loses color and the flavor diminishes.

PASTA

Did the Chinese invent pasta?

There is evidence that the Chinese made some form of pasta in about 5000 BC. Marco Polo brought some back to Italy from this China trip, but pasta was made on the Italian peninsula some 1,700 years earlier. It was probably invented in several places independently.

Why is pasta a healthy part of the diet?

It is made without fat or cholesterol, and it does not cause blood sugar to rise, stimulating the release of insulin, which causes the body to store more fat. The fattening effects come only from adding cheese, cream and other fats and proteins.

What is the nutritional value of pasta?

Two ounces of dry pasta has no cholesterol or sodium, 210 calories, less than 1 gram of fat and is high in complex carbohydrates.

Why are most pastas good for those on a low sodium diet?

They are made with very little or no salt.

Why is semolina the best flour for making pasta or noodles?

1. It is made from the durum wheat berry, so it has lots of protein and cellulose and is high in gluten.
2. Pasta made from it keeps firm and doesn't get so mushy, for it absorbs less water.
3. It isn't necessary to wash the pasta before cooking.

Are products made from semolina worth their higher price?

The semolina products usually are more expensive, but they are worth it because they taste better and hold their shape better.

Should semolina be mixed with other flours?

A mixture of 2 parts all-purpose, nonbleached flour to 1 part semolina works well for making pasta.

Why is unbleached flour better for making pasta?

The bleaching process reduces the gluten content of flour.

Should semolina flour be used in making egg pasta?

No, because the flour is too hard.

What are other materials used to make pasta/noodles?

Buckwheat, corn, mung beans, yams, rice flour, seaweed, shrimp paste.

What is the negative of pasta made from corn?

It tends to be gummy.

What should you look for in buying packaged pasta?

1. Choose one that is made from semolina flour.
2. Make sure the box or package is tightly sealed, for otherwise it might have suffered from oxidation or pest damage.
3. Check that the pieces aren't broken or crumbly.

4. If there is more than a smidgeon of dust inside avoid the package because it signals that it has been improperly stored or stored too long.

5. Look for an amber, sunny color.

6. It should be slightly textured and speckled.

Are the more expensive brands worth the extra price?

1. Quality brands are preferable to less expensive ones because of taste and texture.

2. Higher quality pasta also has a less starchy exterior. This is desirable because excess starch can cause pieces of the pasta to stick together after cooking.

Which is better to buy, fresh or dry packaged pasta?

1. Fresh is more expensive.

2. Fresh cooks faster.

3. The difference in quality varies with the manufacturer. I like both styles but think the fresh is often better. Still many dried are excellent, especially the wider, larger forms.

When is the dried form preferred?

1. If serving a dish at room temperature (rather than heated) use dried pasta because it will retain its texture better when it cools.

2. If serving with a thick sauce the dried pasta is probably better that fresh because the firmer the pasta, the more likely the sauce will cling to it.

What is the volume relationship of fresh and dried pasta?

One pound dried = 1½ pound fresh.

What is the difference between dried pasta made by the larger commercial producers (here and in Italy) and those made by the small Italian manufacturers?

The small producers extrude the dough through bronze discs rather than through teflon discs and get a rougher texture on the surface of the pasta, which results in better adhesion of the sauce.

What can be done to avoid excess liquid when using vegetables with a pasta?

1. Caramelize the vegetables, such as onions.

2. Chop, blanch and saute higher moisture vegetables such as mushrooms.

How can oven-ready, no-boil pasta be used?

1. Use more sauce than with regular pasta.

2. Have the sauce fairly thin.

3. Cover lasagne with foil when baking and then remove it for the last 15 minutes.

4. Precook the vegetables.

5. The best type of sauce for this is made from tomatoes.

Should the pasta be thick or thin?

Either can be good depending on the nature of the sauce. There is no hard and fast rule. For a dish such as lasagne it can be either, although a thin sauce is most often preferred. Creamy sauces go best with wide pastas.

What does al dente mean?

In Italian, it translates "to the tooth," which means that when you bite the pasta there is texture and some resistance.

What are signs of quality when cooking pasta?

1. During cooking it should retain its color and emit a nutty aroma.
2. It should not cause the cooking water to cloud, which would indicate that a lot of starch is being given off.
3. When al dente, drained and tossed with sauce, it should remain firm and have a discernible wheat flavor.

How can you go about finding a quality pasta?

The only way is to try several brands, and when you find a brand that works for you, stay with it.

What should be ready before adding pasta to water?

1. The colander should be in place for draining.
2. The sauce should be ready to serve.
3. A warm bowl or plate should be at hand for serving.

Why is such a large amount of water recommended?

1. So the strands will be separate.
2. To keep the pasta from being starchy.
3. So the cooking water will return to boiling quickly after adding the pasta.

How long should pasta drain?

Not until absolutely dry. The warmth will continue the cooking.

Should cooked pasta drained in a colander be shaken until dry?

Shake only a couple of times, not to make it bone dry, for the small amount of water remaining will help spread the sauce.

How can pasta be reheated if held too long after draining?

Keep the cooking water for reheating.

What happens when pasta is overcooked?

It doesn't taste as good. Can become gummy, doesn't have the desired chewy texture and loses some of its nutritional quality.

What are the main problems in making a pasta dish?

1. Overcooking.
2. Oversaucing.

What are the governing factors in choosing a sauce for pasta?

1. Essentially, the more delicate the pasta, such as angel hair, the lighter the sauce should be.
2. Creamy sauces do well on broader forms.

Should there be more or less sauce with pasta?

It depends on where the emphasis is. When the sauce is to be spooned over the top of the pasta, use less.

How much sauce is needed?

Don't over-sauce, just enough to coast each strand.

What is the difference between noodles and pasta?

Noodles are a flat style of pasta that must, by law, be made with eggs. Those labeled egg noodles must have no less than 5.3% eggs.

What does "lite" on the label of pasta products mean?

These pastas are lower in calories due to their ability to absorb more water.

How can pasta dough be stored?

Be sure it stays moist by wrapping it very tightly in plastic.

What kind of sauce should be used if pasta is to be served at room temperature?

One made with oil and vinegar, not one with cream or melted cheese.

How can a tight seal be achieved in making stuffed pasta, such as ravioli?

1. Make a dough-to-dough seal.
2. If the pasta must be moistened, do not paint the surface with water with your finger or a brush but moisten it with egg white or very lightly spritz with water from a spray bottle.
3. Never use whole eggs or yolks as a sealant, because their fat will prevent a proper seal.
4. After stuffing and sealing, let the pasta dry from 20–30 minutes to form a leathery skin. This will prevent it from sticking in storage or when cooking.

How should pasta be cooked?

1. Have lots of water, 4–6 quarts per pound of pasta, so adding the pasta will not cool the water too much.

2. Have the water boiling vigorously before adding the pasta.

3. Add a little salt after the water is at the boil and before adding the pasta.

4. You can stir the pasta a couple of times after adding but when the water is boiling vigorously the water currents will do the job of separating the pieces.

5. Cover the pot after adding the pasta to hasten the reheating of the water back to rapid boiling. Watch out for foaming or boiling over.

What will adding oil to the cooking water achieve?

A tablespoon of vegetable oil can be added to keep the pasta from sticking together but mainly to keep the water from frothing. However, if the pasta is served with a thin sauce, the oil will prevent the sauce from adhering, and therefore adding oil is not recommended.

Besides adding oil to the cooking water, what can be done to keep pasta from sticking together?

To prevent sticking, make sure there is enough water and stir the pasta after adding to the boiling water. For lasagne noodles, cook only a few at a time and remove them with tongs when done.

Is it necessary to break pasta to fit the pot?

No. As you add the pasta it will quickly soften and fit. But you may find it easier to serve or eat if the strands aren't so long. The longer the strands of the pasta, the more difficult it is for the diner to lift it off the plate. Breaking pasta is contrary to Italian practice.

How should partially thawed pasta be handled?

A large fork used to loosen the block in the water will work well.

How should pasta be tested for doneness?

1. Fresh pasta (i.e., not dried) needs only a minute or two of boiling to be ready. With dried pasta, start testing at eight or nine minutes and repeat every minute or so to see if it is tender. When almost al dente, there will be some chewiness, but the pasta will not be hard or gummy.

2. Don't overcook, and remember that pasta will continue to cook off the heat and after it is drained but still hot.

3. Cook until soft but still firm. When you bite into a piece it should be tender but with no starchiness even in the thickest part.

How should pasta be drained?

1. Immediately drain in a colander or sieve, reserving some of the cooking liquid.

2. If the cooked pasta has stuck together after draining, mix in a little of the hot cooking water.

3. Quickly place on a warm, thick platter or in a warm bowl and serve.

How should the drained pasta be rinsed?

Don't rinse, except when making pasta for a salad, because it will lessen the quality and cool the pasta. Then rinse only briefly in cold running water. If you have used enough water it should not be gummy.

If sun-dried tomatoes are not available for calzone or other pasta sauce, what can be substituted?

A roasted red pepper, cut into strips.

How should pasta be sauced?

1. Have the sauce hot before cooking the pasta.
2. Toss the sauce and pasta together immediately.
3. Or, do it at the table, letting each diner add as much sauce as desired, as they do with the grated cheese.

What should be done if the sauce is too thick?

Add a couple of tablespoons of cooking water to thin it.

Which pasta is best for lasagne?

Fresh, paper-thin, handmade pasta.

What are oven-ready (no-boil) lasagne noodles?

Thin, rippled noodles that have been precooked and dried at the factory. They need no parboiling if enough sauce is used when assembling the lasagne.

How should pasta be cooked that will then be baked with a sauce?

Under-cook it so that it just softens but is quite flexible.

How should stuffed pasta be cooked?

1. Use a lot of water, a minimum of 7 quarts per pound of pasta, because they exude excess starch as they cook and will leave a gummy coating if there isn't enough water.
2. Foam on the surface of the cooking water indicates insufficient water.
3. When the water comes to a rolling boil add plenty of salt, about ¼ cup per 7 quarts. This will season the water, not the pasta.
4. After the water returns to boiling, stir the pot gently to prevent the pasta from settling to the bottom.

What is the end point for cooking pasta that will be stuffed?

Cook until the edges of the pasta are tender, about 4 minutes.

Can buttermilk be used instead of heavy cream for a pasta sauce?

No, because buttermilk is not heat stable, and the sauce may separate or curdle.

What are gnocchi?

Italian dumplings usually made from potatoes and formed into small balls.

What are the kinds of gnocchi?

From pureed potato dough:	With flour and eggs, may have cheese or other ingredients.
From ricotta cheese:	Bound with flour and eggs.
From semolina:	Made with hard flour with milk and Parmesan cheese, it is cut into crescents and baked with sauce or butter.

What are the best potatoes for gnocchi?

Russet, Yukon Gold or sweet potatoes. The moister the potato, the more flour is needed and the less delicate they become.

What are guides when making gnocchi?

1. Bake (rather than boil) potatoes to have the least amount of moisture possible.
2. Have the potatoes warm.
3. If sweet potatoes are used, the dough will require more flour.

What happens if too much flour is used?

The gnocchi will become tough and chewy.

When should sauce be added to pasta salads?

At the last minute, as the pasta absorbs it.

How should pasta be used in salads?

1. Don't used large, hollow forms such as macaroni.
2. Make sure the pasta is not gummy.
3. Toss with dressing while still warm.

What is the yield relationship of uncooked to cooked pasta?

1 cup uncooked = 2 cups cooked.

What precaution should be taken if zucchini and pasta are to be served mixed together?

Make the sauce thicker than usual, for the zucchini will release moisture which will thin the sauce.

Noodles

What are rice noodles (Stick Noodles, Sha He Noodles or Somen Rice Sticks)?

Made from rice flour, most are thin and off-white. Mainly seen in Southeast Asian dishes.

How are rice noodles prepared?

Soften by soaking in hot water before cooking, then drain and rinse to get rid of excess starch. Cook quickly.

How are bean noodles (also bean thread noodles) different?

They are made from Mung bean starch, not rice flour.

How are bean noodles used?

Soften a few minutes in warm water and drain. They don't need rinsing. Simmer about 10 minutes. They have little flavor but take the flavor of the sauce.

What are the main Japanese noodles?

Soba:	Round, almost as thick as spaghetti, made from buckwheat, light brown in color, usually square with a dense structure, a nutty flavor and have a high protein content.
Mugwort soba:	Green, iron-rich from the mugwort plant.
Jinenjo soba:	Contains dried Japanese wild mountain yams.
Udon:	Made from hard wheat or sometimes from corn flour. Thick, white, round or square, used interchangeably with soba. Used in soups.

What is the difference between rice noodles and bean threads?

Rice:	Bland, plain, absorb flavors well. Vary in thickness. Drained after cooking to get rid of excess starch. Good for cold salsa, stir-fry dishes, soups.
Bean:	Made from mung bean starch, vary in thickness. Good for soups, stir-fry, slow-cooked, braised dishes.
Somen:	Delicate from wheat flour and oil. Served cold with a dipping sauce or in hot soups.

What are the best known Chinese noodles?

Chinese egg noodles:	Available dried or fresh, of varying thickness, made with or without eggs, often colored with food color.
Chinese wheat flour noodles:	Mainly available dried, vary in thickness, round or flat. Used in soups and casseroles.

How can bean threads, or cellophane noodles, transparent noodles, shining noodles, stick noodles or mung bean sticks be used?

1. Blanch about 30 seconds and drain.
2. Deep fry and use in salads.

They are translucent with little taste, have a good texture, and flavor comes from the cooking sauce.

How can a clear noodle soup be prepared?

Cook the noodles separately and drain before adding to the soup.

What are egg roll wrappers (also called egg roll skins)?

Thin pastry sheets used for encasing savory fillings. Sold refrigerated in the produce section. Can be steamed or deep fried to make egg rolls.

Grains, Beans and Pasta

CHAPTER SEVEN

MEAT

How is meat inspection by the government indicated?

Meat inspectors stamp meat with a round purple mark U.S.INSP'D & P'S'D. Meat packaged in an inspection facility will have a stamp that identifies the plant. Grading is done only if the packer requests it.

Is a USDA inspection stamp for meat wholesomeness mandatory?

Yes, unless there is a state stamp. However, when meat is cut for retail display and sale the stamp won't be visible of most cuts.

Should you cut off the meat, fat or skin where the purple stamp of the inspection has been placed?

No, it is a harmless purple vegetable dye.

What is "the net"?

A netting of twine or elastic used to contain a rolled piece of meat.

Does red meat always have more fat than chicken?

Modern slimmed-down cows and pigs have cuts that are lower in fat than the dark meat of chicken. Roasted, served without skin, the dark meat of chicken is 10.9% fat for a thigh and 8.4% for a leg. Even a low-fat chicken breast at 3.6% fat has competition from the broiled top round which has only 3.7%.

How much fat is allowed in Extra Lean meats by the USDA Standard?

Less than 5 grams of fat per 100 grams of meat, 2 grams saturated fat, or less and 95 milligrams of cholesterol.

What happens when meat is frozen?

The freezing and subsequent thawing cause the meat to lose some of the internal juices that contribute to flavor, texture and nutrition and help keep the meat moist and tender as it cooks. Don't keep frozen steaks too long, less than a month at most, if you want them at their best. However, they will be edible, even good tasting, for many months if well wrapped.

What is marbling?

Streaks or flecks of fat throughout the meat. This does not refer to the fat around the outside of the cut or wide fat bands in a steak.

Why is marbling important?

Because flavor is generated as the meat cooks and the fat melts. Marbling occurs as the animal ages, and thus there is very little marbling in veal.

What are the basic cooking methods with moist heat?

Boiling, braising, microwaving, poaching, pressure cooking, simmering, steaming and stewing.

What are the main methods with dry heat?

Baking, broiling, deep-frying, microwaving, pan frying, roasting, stir-frying and toasting.

What is poaching?

Simmering in a small amount of fluid (stock or water).

What are the temperature differences for poaching, simmering and boiling?

Poaching: 160–180 °F.
Simmering: 185–205 °F.
Boiling: 212 °F.

Will alcohol lower the boiling temperature of water?

Alcohol will lower the boiling temperature, for it has a boiling point of 175 °F. So if you substitute a fair amount of wine for the water, extend the cooking time by 5–10% to compensate for the lower temperature.

Is there a difference in temperature between lightly and vigorously boiling water?

No, for at the boiling point the temperature remains constant within one degree. However, with vigorous boiling more heat is transferred, which shortens the cooking time. The negative is that there will be a loss of fuel, nutrients and flavor because boiling water violently knocks the food pieces against each other, but this is not negative for some foods such as pasta.

What does poaching of meat accomplish?

1. Helps hold shape.
2. Makes it easier to remove tough membranes.
3. Prepares meat for final cooking.
5. Removes slight odors, such as in kidneys.

What is barbecuing?

Low, dry heat coming from below the food for inexpensive meats that need long, low heat to tenderize by breaking down the tough connective tissue.

What is the difference between barbecuing and grilling?

Often the words are used interchangeably and usually refer to meat done on a grill. Barbecuing is most often done outdoors. The term "broiling" is also used for grilling, even though broiling refers to a heat source above the food.

What are the forms of grilling?

Broiling, barbecuing, pan broiling.

What is pan broiling?

On top of the stove in a heavy, cast iron pan over high heat. Juices or fat are released, which, if not removed, changes the cooking process into what is known as sautéing.

What is the difference between a pâté and a terrine?

Both are usually made from meat or fish that is minced or chopped and spiced. The terms are used interchangeably, although technically the pâté has a pastry crust, while the terrine is cooked in a baking dish without a crust.

What is a terrine?

Forcemeat baked in a mold in a hot water bath.

What is forcemeat?

A combination of lean meat and fat put through a sieve or ground together.

Must the texture of forcemeat be fine?

It can be either fine or coarse, but the mixture must be an emulsion.

Should the meats and fats be forced through with a tamper so it will go through the grater easier and quicker?

No, it should not be mashed, so the resulting meat can be cut into strips or diced.

What kind of meat should be used for making mincemeat?

It used to be usually beef, but now meat is not used, only chopped fruits, nuts, spices, liquor or liqueur, suet.

What is jerky?

A cured and dried meat (also salmon), often smoked.

What do the terms "variety meats" or "by-products" on the label of a hot dog mean?

That almost any part of the animal may have been used in making the hot dog (stomach, tongue, fat, tripe, etc.).

What do the terms "added water" and "natural juices" mean on a label?

The weight has been increased by the addition of the liquid up to 10%.

What are the criteria for grading meat?

Age, texture, appearance and marbling.

What does naturally raised meat mean?

According to the USDA, all meat, regardless of how the animal was raised, can be labeled natural if after slaughter no artificial ingredients or antibiotics were added and the meat has been minimally processed.

How can you get meat that is natural?

Look for written claims such as "raised without hormones or antibiotics" or "no antibiotics."

What is the chine bone?

The backbone of an animal.

What is marrow (or bone marrow or marrow bone)?

The soft substance found in the center of bones, mainly from legs, that is very fatty and has an excellent taste.

What is a paillard?

A thin piece of meat pounded for quick grilling.

What is tripe?

The first and second stomachs of cattle, pigs or sheep.

What is fell?

The connective tissue covering the animal carcass, just under the hide.

What is a cubed steak?

A steak, often from the chuck, pounded to tenderize it and then scored on the surface before cooking.

What is confit?

Meat cooked in its own fat and stored in a pot with a fat covering.

What is brining of meat (also seafood and poultry)?

Immersion of meat in a saline solution (together with herbs and spices) causes the muscle fibers to absorb salt, which denatures the meat protein. In essence it is seasoning inside the meat rather than only on the surface.

How much salt should be added when cooking brined meat?

It should not be salted because it will have salt throughout.

How long should pork or chicken be brined?

Pork chops:	1 day.
Whole chicken:	8–12 hours.
Shrimp:	½ hour.

Can stew and casserole recipes be halved?

Yes, but when halving, reduce the amount of liquid by ⅓ instead of ½.

Can they be doubled?

Yes, but when doubling multiply the liquid by 1½, not twice, to avoid a soupy dish.

What is deglazing?

Dissolving food particles in a frying or roasting pan with a liquid, such as stock or wine, for use in making a sauce or gravy.

What is the difference between mincing meat and mincing vegetables?

Vegetables:	Finely chopped.
Meat:	Cut into strips no more than ⅛″ thick, ½″ wide and 1–2″ long.

SANITATION

Since hot dogs are processed foods, are they safe to eat without cooking?

No! The Food & Drug Administration has recently announced that a large percentage of them have pathogenic bacteria in them, and they should be cooked first.

Need smoked meats be refrigerated?

Yes.

What is dangerous about allowing properly cooked meat and poultry to cool to room temperature?

While the bacteria will have been killed by the cooking, if the cooked meat contains spores of the bacteria that survive and multiply, they create a toxin that causes food poisoning. So when the product has cooled down and is not served immediately, refrigerate it, then reheat to 165 °F for serving.

If there is a power failure and frozen meat thaws, is it safe to refreeze it?

Yes, even for fully cooked meats, but only as long as the temperature remained below 40 °F. If it goes above that temperature for more than two hours there is danger. Further, even if the bacteria don't grow to a dangerous level, the fats in the meat may become rancid. If you have any questions about the quality or safety of a meat, the best thing is to throw it away.

What happens to the flavor with refreezing and thawing?

Both the texture and flavor will diminish.

How can you keep the foil on meat that is to be frozen from sticking to the meat and/or tearing?

Coat the foil with a cooking spray before wrapping for freezing.

How should meat be thawed?

1. Thaw in the refrigerator, not at room temperature.
2. When thawing a steak, defrost in the refrigerator until the surface has partially thawed and the steak can be bent. Then cook. This will be a good procedure for rare and medium-rare. For medium and well-done, defrost until completely thawed.
3. If in a hurry, put the meat in a plastic bag, seal and then immerse the bag in warm water.

How should you refrigerate meat that was prewrapped at the market?

After 2–3 days at most take off the wrapping and rewrap.

When should you begin marinating frozen meat?

Marinate it while it thaws by placing both the meat and the marinade in a sealed plastic bag, turning the bag occasionally.

Why bring meat out of the refrigerator an hour or so before cooking to allow it to come to room temperature?

Otherwise the surface of the meat will be too cold, and it will therefore dry out before the cold interior will cook.

Is prior warming necessary for stew or braising?

No.

Is leaving the meat out for warming safe?

The USDA says that less than 2 hours is safe. If in a marinade, the acidity of the vinegar or yogurt will inhibit, although not absolutely prevent, bacterial growth.

What makes a meat kosher?

It is from healthy animals with split hooves that chew the cud (cattle, sheep, goats, deer), killed so as to not cause pain or suffering and inspected by trained personnel for adhesions, cuts or bruises.

What part of the animals can be used?

Only the forequarter.

How is the meat koshered?

It is soaked for a half an hour, salted, drained and washed.

TOUGHNESS

How does an animal's activity affect the meat's toughness?

The more the animal exercises, the greater the connective tissue development, and therefore the tougher the meat. Thus, if the animal roams free instead of being confined, the meat will have more connective tissue and be tougher.

What does the age of the animal have to do with the tenderness of the meat?

The older the animal, the less tender the meat will be.

How do ranchers minimize the toughness of their animals?

1. They keep them cooped up, e.g., calves for veal.
2. They castrate them, since a steer (desexed male) is less active physically.
3. The Japanese (famous for their Kobe beef) regularly massage the animal along its back to keep the animal relaxed, because tension flexes the muscles and toughens them.

What will make one cut of meat naturally tougher than another?

Connective tissue is the key. The more or the firmer the connective tissue in the raw meat, the tougher the flesh is likely to be. The quantity of connective tissue is dependent upon the location of the cut, the animal's activity and the animal's age.

What is the goal in handling tough meat?

The goal is to tenderize without drying so that the meat will not be stringy or fibrous. This depends on the meat's temperature, which should not be cooked above 160 °F internal temperature, and is achieved over very low heat over a relatively brief time.

What does this slow cooking achieve?

It helps the collagen to shrink, and maintaining this low temperature promotes the conversion of collagen to gelatin.

What is the goal?

To cook the meat so that the juice does not run out and the fat does not melt and run out.

Why are older animals more desirable for braising or stewing?

Slow, moist heat will tenderize even a somewhat tough meat by breaking down its connective tissue. The benefit is that the meat of the older animal has more flavor.

AGING/TENDERIZING

What is the purpose of aging meat?

To tenderize it and improve flavor.

What is dry aging?

This type of aging means that the meat (top quality beef or lamb) has been in constant, dry refrigeration (hanging without covering) at 34–38 °F for 2–3 weeks for beef and 1 week for lamb.

What happens when meat is dry aged?

If the meat is stored for up to several weeks in an ideal aging environment (between 34–38 °F plus ultraviolet light to minimize mold), there is a natural enzymatic change that softens some of the connective tissue. 10–20% shrinkage occurs, which also intensifies the flavor.

How does it enhance flavor?

1. The meat proteins break down into amino acids, which have a stronger flavor.
2. The meat loses 1% of its water content (by weight) per day, therefore the flavor is more intense.

Should all meats be dry aged?

Only top quality, whole pieces that are well covered with fat may be aged because the surface must be discarded after the aging and it would be too wasteful to use small cuts such as individual chops or steaks for this process.

What is the difference in appearance between aged and unaged meat?

Fresh, i.e., unaged meat is a bright cherry-red with the fat a creamy white. When aged the color darkens and the surface dries.

Should hanging meat in a refrigerated room be wrapped?

No, but food should not be stored under it because of the fluids that drip down.

What is wet aging?

This refers to meat that is wrapped and sealed in Cryovac (or equivalent polyethylene bags). Many butchers claim that this is not real aging and that little tenderizing or improvement results.

What good does it do?

It accomplishes some aging with less shrinkage, and the meat ages while it is being shipped. It is less expensive but less effective than dry aging.

What method do most butchers use?

Few, especially retailers, have the facilities for dry aging.

What is instant aging?

Aging done by applying two minutes of electrical shocks to a hanging carcass. It has limited effectiveness.

Do cut steaks in the butcher's meat case that have darkened represent an aging process?

No! There is nothing wrong with darkened fresh meat, but unless they have been improperly aged, the darkened steaks are no better or worse than the bright red ones.

How can the consumer avoid the natural toughness of connective tissue?

1. Buy young meat.
2. Buy U.S. Prime, if possible.
3. Buy aged meat.

What are ways of tendering meat at home?

1. Use papaya juice or puree.
2. Pound the meat.
3. Add strong black tea to a stew.
4. Cook longer (with moist heat).
5. Cook in a pressure cooker.

What preparatory steps can be taken to overcome toughness?

1. Trim out the connective tissue, if feasible.
2. Gently pound the meat with a mallet or the flat of a large knife blade.
3. Make gashes in the meat.
4. Marinate the meat.
5. Use commercial meat tenderizers. (I do not advise this since most tenderizers extract some of the natural juice. Avoid those with MSG or salt in them. Add salt after the meat is almost done or fully cooked.)
6. Use papaya juice or puree (but remove the puree before cooking). This is especially good for steaks.
7. Presoak and simmer the meat in strong tea.
8. Grind the meat.

How should the cooking be done?

Cook slowly with moist heat such as braising or stewing. However, heat and prolonged cooking both soften connective tissue and harden muscle fibers. The first action more than compensates for the hardening.

What is a serving procedure that will make for tenderer meat?

Cut the meat against the grain since this shortens any connective tissue, therefore the meat will be more tender.

Why must tough meat be cooked longer and to a higher internal temperature?

To melt some of the tough connective tissue.

Which is the more effective, the commercial tenderizer or a marinade?

The commercial tenderizers do not tenderize uniformly, and when the meat is cooked the surface tends to be mushy. Marinades have only limited tenderizing ability. They are good for flavoring, but if overdone they too also cause mushiness in the meat.

How does marinating tenderize meat?

The marinade's acidity (lemon juice, wine, etc.) chemically softens the connective tissue. It also reduces the time required for heat to convert collagen to gelatin.

Why is meat pounded before cooking?

1. To increase the surface for searing.
2. To improve caramelization of the surface.
3. To tenderize.

How does slow, moist heat soften connective tissue?

The main connective tissue is the protein collagen. In a hot moist environment (boiling water, for instance), the collagen is partially transformed into gelatin and the tissue softens and dissolves, making the meat more tender.

Why does a piece of meat toughen as it cools on the plate?

As the meat cools, the gelatin (from the collagen) cools and thickens, therefore, the meat loses some of its tenderness.

How can re-toughening be minimized?

By using heated dinner plates.

COOKING MEATS

What are the two basic methods of cooking meats?

Dry heat: For meats that naturally contain moisture such as fat or liquid. This includes broiling, baking, sautéing and some microwaving.

Wet heat: For meat that requires the addition of moisture. This includes pressure cooking, stewing, braising, poaching, boiling and some microwaving.

Does the dry heat method tenderize meat?

No, so the meat must be naturally tender.

What are the most effective ways to flavor meats for smoking?

Use dry rubs, pastes or marinades.

How can smokiness be induced from the wood?

Soak the wood for a half hour or more so that the wood will smoke rather than burn.

What kind of wood should be used in smoking meats?

Hard woods such as oak, cherry or hickory.

What woods should be avoided?

Soft woods such as cedar or pine.

Is a surface seal formed on the food in moist heat cooking?

No, and as a result some of the juices/flavors of the meat go out into the pan liquid.

Does searing meat seal in the juice?

No, the juice still comes out.

What effect do tomatoes have in the cooking process when combined with meat?

Their acid tenderizes, and they give flavor.

What is the similarity between barding and larding?

Both are ways of adding fat to meat to help it keep moist in dry cooking.

What is barding?

Covering the meat with a piece of fat, e.g., covering a meatloaf with strips of bacon.

What fat can be used for barding?

1. Fat trimmed off the meat to be cooked.
2. Pork fat.

What is done with the fat?

When roasting barded meat, remove the fat 15–20 minutes before the finish so that the surface will brown.

What is larding?

Larding is inserting fat into the body of the meat with special needles. This is particularly useful with lean cuts such as the round.

How can juices be retained in meat (and fish or chicken) when cooking?

1. Use tongs or a spatula instead of a fork to turn the meat, so that the juices won't ooze out of the fork holes.
2. Quickly brown over high heat, then finish cooking at moderate heat.
3. Turn only once.
4. Don't overcook.

What are two methods of flavoring meat before cooking?

Marinade: A liquid of herbs, spices, vinegar, lemon juice that both seasons and tenderizes a little.

Dry rub: A mixture of herbs and spices such as salt, pepper, cayenne and thyme. It has no tenderizing action.

What controls the effectiveness of a marinade?

Time, temperature, thickness and type of meat and the quantity and strength of the acid component.

What are the advantages of dry rub versus wet marinade?

The dry rub will flavor the meat as do marinades but because they don't drain off, all the flavor stays with the meat and the rub will cook into a crisp crust.

What types of meat are best for dry rub?

Cuts that are fat enough to hold their moisture when cooked a long time.

When should a dry rub be applied?

It can be added long before grilling or just before.

What is the goal of sautéing?

Food is sautéd to make it crisp and golden on the outside and moist inside.

How should sautéing be done properly?

1. First dry the meat (or poultry) throughly.
2. Coat the meat with flour.
3. Make sure the fat is very hot, but not smoking, before adding the food.
4. Do not allow the pieces of meat in the pan to touch each other.

When cooking en papillote, what special step can be taken with thick meat pieces?

Sear the meat in advance so that it will be fully cooked when served.

Why does the color of cooked beef indicate its doneness?

The myoglobin (red) pigment undergoes chemical changes as the temperature rises. At rare (approximately 135 °F) it retains most of its redness. At (145 °F) medium-rare it is pink, and at (160 °F) well it has turned a drab brown.

What are some hints for barbecuing meat?

1. If the meat is low in fat keep the lid on to retain moisture.
2. Use a nonstick spray on the grill and then preheat for about 5 minutes or brush the meat with a light coating of vegetable oil.

What is a way of easily reheating slices of cooked meat?

Place the pieces of meat in a casserole with a lettuce leaf in between slices. Then heat in the oven or microwave. This will retain tenderness and moistness of the meat.

Grilling

What is grilling?

Cooking with the heat source below the food, usually outdoors.

What is skillet grilling?

Use a skillet (cast iron) with bottom ridges so that it will leave grill marks. Get it very hot, brush with oil and don't overcrowd.

Why should the grill be very hot when cooking fish fillets?

It keeps the fish from sticking to the grill by melting any fat or heating the oil to form a coating and thus keeps the fish from falling apart.

Deep Frying

What happens if the oil is at the wrong temperature?

Too hot: Oil will smoke, food will burn.

Too low: Food will be greasy, it will take too long to cook.

Why should only limited amounts of food be added at a time in deep frying?

To prevent lowering of the oil temperature.

Why are some vegetables greasy when deep fried?

1.   Usually it is because the oil was not hot enough (375 °F or more).
2.   The temperature was not maintained.
3.   The food was not added gradually enough, so the temperature decreased.

What happens if the oil is old and deteriorated?

1.   The food will be greasy.
2.   The color of the food will be dark.
3.   A rancid taste will develop.
4.   A toxicity may develop.

What conditions cause the fat/oil to deteriorate?

1.   Heat.
2.   Sunlight.
3.   Iron and copper pans.
4.   Exposure to air (oxygen).

How should food be prepared for deep frying?

1.   The pieces to be fried should be uniform in size.
2.   The foods should be almost dry.
3.   If coated with batter, any excess should be removed.

Can items to be deep fried be prepared in advance?

Yes, but it is best if they are refrigerated until cooking time.

Why should an item to be breaded first be coated with flour?

To seal the surface so that the batter will adhere better and not fall off as easily when fried.

How can you tell if the cooking temperature is correct?

The best way is with a thermometer with the bulb completely immersed but without touching the sides or bottom of the pan.

What happens if re-used oil is not strained before using it again?

The debris from previous cooking will scorch and give a bad flavor.

How can you tell if reused oil should be discarded?

When it begins to smoke at 360 °F or lower.

What kind of crumb breading should be used in deep frying meat?

Coarse crumbs: Crisper.

Fine crumbs: Absorb less fat.

Sautéing/Pan Frying

What is the difference between pan frying and sautéing?

There is no difference. "Sauté" is the French word for pan frying; it comes from the verb "to jump."

Should the pieces be shaken or moved when browning meat or vegetables?

Don't keep moving them, or they won't brown.

When should spices be added during a sauté?

It is not wise to add chile powder, black pepper or like seasonings at the beginning as they may either become bitter or lose their bite. Add towards the end.

What does the higher heat accomplish?

The higher heat seals in the juices more effectively so that fewer of the internal juices of the meats and vegetables are lost. This means a crisper texture. It also means that the cooking time is shorter and there is, therefore, less color fading.

How can burned particles be avoided when sautéing?

1. Shake the food to be sautéd before cooking to rid it of excess flour.
2. Sauté in oil, oil and butter or in clarified butter.
3. Add food in batches.

4. Keep adjusting the heat as needed so the food doesn't scorch.

5. If there are any burned bits, quickly remove them from the pan with a moistened paper towel.

Why should food to be fried be dried before cooking?

To avoid spattering the fat and to avoid steaming the food.

Stir-Frying

What should the preparation for stir-frying include?

1. Assemble all the ingredients, including the seasonings before starting.

2. Remove all bones, skin, excess fat.

How should vegetables be prepared for stir-frying?

After cutting them to small size, blanch them in boiling water for a minute or two, then drain, plunge into iced water to stop further cooking and drain again.

Is this preparation used for meat?

This process is sometimes used for meat that has gristle or fat.

What are good procedures for stir-frying?

1. Be sure that the pan is hot before adding the oil.

2. Don't overcrowd the pan.

3. Cook in sections, that is, first meat, then carrots and onions and at the end bean sprouts and/or jicama, removing each unit from the pan at it is cooked and returning it for the final seasoning.

4. Add the sauce last, but very tender items such as bean sprouts, which are good raw, can be the last item into the pan, even after the sauce has been added and the pan is removed from heat. Then let rest covered for a few minutes.

What is a wok?

A round-bottomed utensil that is also good for deep frying and steaming, made from rolled steel, stainless steel, etc.

Does a kitchen need to be equipped with both a small and large wok?

It is easy to cook a small amount of food in a large wok, so only a large one is required.

What should be looked for when choosing a wok?

1. Deep sides and rounded bottom.

2. Large: 12–14".

3. Heavy carbon steel that will take high heat and not scorch food.

4. Thin steel that will heat quickly.

What kind of stirring tool is best for a wok?

A long-handled spatula shaped like a small shovel, but any kind of long-handled spoon will work.

Can you stir-fry in a skillet?

Not well.

1. If you must use a skillet, then use an old-fashioned cast iron skillet.
2. Be sure to do your cooking in small batches with each batch immediately removed, not piled up on the sides.

How should meat be cut?

Either sliced thin or cut into small cubes.

Why should meats be marinated first?

To protect them from overcooking.

Why can't you replicate exactly the wok dishes of Chinese restaurants at home?

The difference is the heat used to prepare the dishes. Restaurant stoves have more than twice the heat production as do home ones, both by the amount of gas to the burner and the design of the burner itself. The restaurant burners are often concave, so the bottom of the wok is down closer to the flame. Home gas stoves range from 7,000 to 10,000 BTUs (British Thermal Units) while a Chinese restaurant stove will go as high as 40,000 BTUs.

Will a wok work well in an electric stove?

Stir-frying in a wok on an electric stove is practically impossible, because only a limited amount of heat is produced and it hits only the very bottom of the wok. An electric wok works better but only to a limited degree.

What are good oils for stir-frying?

Those with a high smoke point: peanut, canola, safflower.

Why not use olive oil?

It can produce too strong a flavor and smokes at a low temperature.

What is important in the preparation of the meat and vegetables for stir-frying?

1. The pieces should be taken up with chopsticks, so each should be small enough to be eaten in one bite.
2. They should be sized evenly, thin and small, so they will cook quickly and evenly.

Is there an order to adding the vegetables?

Yes, add the carrots and cabbage (or any that require longer cooking) first.

How can the sauce be thickened?

Use a little cornstarch, stirred into cold water and added at the end, but be careful not to overdo it.

Should noodles or rice be used in a stir-fry?

Either: Chinese egg noodles or short-grained rice.

Braising

What is braising?

Braising consists of browning food in hot fat and then simmering it in scant liquid in a tightly covered pan so that the steam is not lost and thus is pressured into the meat. Braising in the oven is usually preferable.

What kinds of meats are best for braising?

It is mainly used for lean, sinewy cuts, such as brisket, chuck of shoulder roasts.

What was the origin of braising?

The method originated in France as a way of cooking on an open hearth with a tightly sealed pan called a *braisere,* which was set into hot embers and topped with more hot coals on the special lid. In old French recipes the meat was larded with fat bacon before braising and bacon rind was added to enrich the sauce.

What is the best use of braising?

Mainly for red meats (especially good with lean cuts such as briskets), but it can also be used for vegetables.

What is the contribution of braising?

This method's best contribution is the quality of the sauce it produces. It also tenderizes.

What can be done to get good browning in braising?

1. Start with dry meat (blot with paper toweling).
2. Make sure the cooking fat in the pot is hot.
3. Dust the meat with flour before starting.

What is a daube?

French braising of beef and vegetables in which the meat is browned and then simmered in red wine.

When should meat to be braised be browned?

Before any liquid is added and before steaming.

What are some rules and tips for braising?

1. Wait until the dish is nearly cooked before adding the salt.
2. Make sure the spices are fresh and the aromatics (celery, onions, carrots) are crisp.
3. Cubed meat, stew and poultry require less time and liquid than larger pieces.

What sized pan should be used?

Use a pan that is only slightly larger than the food being braised, for this minimizes the air space and therefore reduces the amount of steam. If there is too much steam the food will have the taste and texture of steamed food.

What happens if braising is done on the stove top?

1. The liquid in the pot will boil, and as a result the texture and flavor will suffer.
2. If the liquid is kept below the boiling point the part resting in the liquid will cook significantly faster than the part above.
3. It is difficult to control temperature this way.

Why is braising best done in the oven?

1. Oven heat more uniformly engulfs the pot, resulting in more even cooking.
2. Because the need to generate steam is not so critical, the food can be cooked at a slower pace and therefore at a lower temperature.
3. The texture and the flavor will be the best.
4. It will require less pot watching than on the stove top.

Can marinated meat be browned?

If you wish to brown meat that has been marinated, first drain it well, then pat dry with paper toweling.

What cuts are not recommended for braised dishes?

1. A roast with lots of fat.
2. Poultry with the skin on.

What cuts of meat are best for braised dishes?

The tougher meats (less tender), such as those cut from the leg, shoulder, rump or neck, which are suited for long, slow cooking. In this slow process, those muscles release natural gelatin, which both tenderizes the meat and enriches the stock. Make sure the meat can be cut into regular, larger pieces (don't use scraps).

What are some guidelines for braising and stewing low-fat cuts of meat?

1. Increase the flavoring power of oil-based marinades by first sautéing the onions and spices in oil.
2. Avoid temperatures that will bring the liquid to a boil, as this will toughen the meat. The oven is best for achieving and maintaining low temperature.
3. Don't salt the meat until the end of cooking.
4. Don't marinate too long in an acidic marinade, or the meat will become chewy.

Stewing

What is the difference between braising and stewing?

They are similar procedures, but braising is done with a large piece of meat, such as a roast, while stewing is the same process with small pieces.

What are the best cuts for stews?

Most stew meat comes from the forequarters or chuck (shoulder, ribs) or the upper hind leg or round. The round is best for tenderness and flavor.

What are these cuts in different meats?

Beef: Short ribs, large end of brisket, top round, chuck.

Veal: Shoulder.

Lamb: Shank or shoulder.

Pork: Butt, hock.

What does flouring the meat before starting to cook a stew accomplish?

The cooking liquid thickens, so when the meat is done the sauce is ready.

Which is better for breading, eggs or milk?

Eggs have more sticking power.

How can the fat content be minimized in a stew?

Cook very gently at a bare simmer so that the fat will melt off the meat and flow into the liquid. Then chill and skim off the hardened fat.

What can be done to enrich the flavor of a stew?

The secret of a rich-tasting stew is to be sure that the meat, vegetables and flour are browned before the addition of any liquid.

How can the sauce of a stew be thickened?

1. Concentrate (reduce) the volume of the sauce.
2. Flour the meat before browning, but this is less desirable because the meat will not brown as well.
3. Use cornstarch or arrowroot as thickeners.
4. Puree some of the potatoes of the stew with a little of the sauce. The more potatoes pureed, the thicker it will be.
5. Add a small amount of instant potatoes or rolled oats.

How can you speed the cooking of a stew?

Cut the meat into smaller pieces.

Why should stews be thickened at the end of cooking?

Because thickened mixtures easily stick and burn.

What happens if a stew is over-cooked?

The protein will toughen along with the meat.

What wines can be used for making a beef stew?

Use a young, fruity, full-bodied, inexpensive red of decent quality, such as a California Cabernet Sauvignon, a red Zinfandel, a Chianti, a red from southern France or a Shiraz from Australia.

Should wine labeled cooking wine be used?

I do not use any labeled cooking wine, for they are usually not very good.

What is the best way to proceed if you have not browned the stew meat?

Bring the liquid to a simmer before adding the meat, which will help seal the meat juices and flavor at least to some degree.

How can the cooking time of a stew be reduced?

1. Add a half cup of strong tea.
2. Cut the meat into smaller pieces.

What should a stew be served with?

Serve with a starch with which you can enjoy the sauce, such as dumplings, rice, potatoes, noodles or pasta.

Roasting and Broiling

What is the difference between oven roasting and baking?

No difference in method, just in terminology. Baking is usually used for breads, pies, cakes etc., roasting for meats.

Should a roast be boned before cooking?

A boned roast will be easier to carve, but will be less flavorful, since the bone adds flavor.

How close to the burner flame or electric coil should the meat (or fish) be?

3–5".

Why should a roast not be too small?

Cooking in dry heat, if small, it will lose its moisture and will be less tender.

What are the best cuts for roasting?

The tender parts of the animal. The neck, shoulder and hips are tougher because they are the most active. The loin or tenderloin are the best. Young animals, such as lambs or calves (veal), are good for roasting. The closer the cuts to the head, horn or tail, the less tender.

How many servings can you get from a rib roast?

About two generous servings per rib.

What are the advantages and disadvantages of slow roasting?

Advantages:
1. There will be less shrinkage.
2. A uniform doneness can be achieved.
3. There will be better flavors.

Disadvantages:
1. The exterior will not be as well browned.
2. It will take longer.

What happens if the meat to be roasted is cold or semi-frozen when put into the oven?

1. If it is a larger piece, the outside (surface) will be done before the center is warm.
2. If it is a small piece, the exterior browning can result in a rare to medium-rare center.

How long should the roast sit before serving?

Don't let the roast sit indefinitely, 20–30 minutes at most. If you must wait longer, then remove the roast from the pan and wrap it tightly in foil and put it in a warm spot. It will stay warm a couple of hours. If you must keep it longer, then reheat it in a barely warm gravy.

What is the effect of adding tomatoes to a roast?

Its acidity will help to tenderize the roast.

What can be used for deglazing the pan besides stock?

Try wine or cream.

What is the advantage of a high-temperature oven for roasting?

1. Shorter time required.
2. Creates a good crust.
3. Better, juicier flavor.

What is critical when roasting meat?

That there be air space around the roast, therefore, best done on a rack and not covered.

What are the disadvantages of roasting at a high temperature?

1. More shrinkage.
2. Greater chance to over-roast.

How should a roast be served?

1. Let it rest before serving. This can be done while making gravy out of the pan drippings (after degreasing).
2. Carve as thinly as possible against the grain. If not feasible, then cut on a bias.

How can a fatty roast be made to look better?

1. Refrigerate until the fat solidifies, then cut off the fat.
2. Baste and cook until hot.

Why tie a roast?

1. To ensure even cooking.
2. So it retains its shape.

What happens to a roast after it is removed from the oven?

The internal temperature will increase by about five degrees, therefore, remove it just under the desired internal temperature (as measured by a thermometer).

Should meat be roasted in the same pan with vegetables, such as potatoes or corn?

No! The vegetables will yield moisture that will partially steam the meat, which should be cooking in dry heat.

Why should a roast be at or near room temperature before cooking?

1. Mainly as a precautionary measure so that the roast's outside doesn't overcook and dry out before the inside is warmed and cooked.
2. Since a room temperature roast cooks more quickly than a colder one, energy and time is saved.

How should a roast be prepared for roasting?

If there is no fat layer, cover the roast with bacon or a slab of fatback.

Why is an oven rack important?

If the roast is elevated on a rack in a roasting pan, hot air gets to all surfaces. Without it the bottom will be sautéd instead of roasted. Without air circulation all around the roast, steam can accumulate, forming a liquid pool, which will prevent browning.

What are some of the tricks in roasting meats?

1. Have the oven preheated and the roast at room temperature.
2. Cook the roast fat-side-up, so that the melting fat will baste the meat.
3. Turning the roast once or twice will help brown it evenly.
4. Baste frequently.
5. Don't use a covered pan. Uncovered means dry heat. When the meat is covered the steam is trapped, and this results in a mushy rather than a crisp surface and a pale brown color rather than deep brown.
6. Let the roast stand 10–15 minutes before carving.

Why should a roast be allowed to rest prior to carving?

When first removed from the oven the surface of the roast has less juice than the meat at the core. If you carve immediately the edges of the slices will be unnecessarily dry and the meat's juices will seep out because the saturated muscle tissue in the interior cannot absorb and hold the excess liquid. The resting period gives the liquid a chance to redistribute and settle throughout. The meat becomes firmer, making it easier to cut thin slices.

Does cooking the roast in a convection oven change the requirement for standing?

Standing is less necessary or even unnecessary if a convection oven is used.

What does slow roasting accomplish?

Slow roasting (a lower temperature for a longer time) will result in less shrinkage, but high temperature for a relatively short time will give a browned crust and a rare to medium-rare center. A compromise is to start at 450 °F for about 20 minutes and then turn the heat down to finish cooking.

Why is the surface of a roast cooler than the oven temperature, which makes measuring the surface temperature an inaccurate way to determine degree of doneness?

1. The air molecules are hotter than those of the roast because they come in direct contact with the heat source and the very hot oven walls.
2. The meat's cooler interior absorbs heat and thus relatively cools the surface.
3. As the meat cooks, some of the internal juice flows to the surface, and its evaporation occurs, which has a cooling action.

How should a roast be browned?

Sear all the surfaces brown over high heat in a skillet with a little bit of hot oil in order to develop a rich color and a surface crust that will intensify flavor. Turn as necessary. Or, brown at high temperature in the oven and then reduce the heat to finish roasting. If the heat is not reduced, the interior won't be cooked by the time the exterior has to be removed from the oven.

What is the best way to sear a roast?

Chefs disagree. Either start with a hot oven and then reduce it to roasting temperature after it browns or sear it in the roasting pan (if sturdy enough) or in a frying pan on top of the stove.

Will the browning be as effective if done at the end of the roasting?

No.

What adjustment should be made when time is not available to bring a roast to room temperature before cooking?

Set the oven temperature slightly lower and roast slightly longer.

When cooking meat with dry heat, should it be salted, before or after roasting?

Before. Unless salted before starting, the salt will not have a chance to infuse the meat and trigger chemical flavor-enhancing reactions. Otherwise the meat will be unevenly salted.

Pot Roasting

What is the best meat for pot roasting?

Well-exercised muscles that contain a good deal of connective tissue. Even though these muscles contain considerable collagen (connective tissue protein), which is a major factor in toughness, it can be pot roasted to change the collagen to gelatin.

What are the best beef cuts for pot roasting?

Chuck, boneless shoulder, eye of the round, rump. Chuck is the most tender and flavorful.

How else is chuck labeled in the retail markets?

Beef chuck, mock tender roast, top chuck roast, chuck shoulder, beef chuck, boneless roast.

How good is the round for pot roasting?

The bottom round is next best to the chuck.

If you buy only a portion of the round, which part should be selected?

The pointy end, which contains some muscle.

How should a pot roast be cooked to achieve the most tenderness, juiciness and flavor?

1. Tie the roast to make it compact and as evenly shaped as possible.
2. Dry the tied roast thoroughly with paper toweling and then season.
3. Use a heavy pot with a tight lid to retain moisture and distribute the heat evenly.
4. Brown the roast to a deep mahogany color.
5. Brown the vegetables.
6. Keep the heat moderately high for browning and keep an eye on the roast. Don't blacken the pot or the roast will have a bitter flavor and the surface may be leathery.
7. Add just enough liquid to film the bottom of the pot, about 2–5 tablespoons. Don't submerge the meat.
8. The liquid used should match the meat, such as a rich red wine for beef, a white wine for chicken.
9. Use a very low heat for the duration of the cooking.
10. Turn the roast every 20–30 minutes.

What will happen if the roast is not browned well?

The gravy will be pale and lacking in flavor.

Which fat should be used for browning?

Beef or pork fat is better than oil.

How can very low heat be attained on the stove top?

1. Turn the flame way down (some newer stoves have a low-heat setting).
2. Use a way to block the heat such as a flame turner, stacking two burners.
3. Use one or two beat-up pizza pans or cookie sheets over the burner.

How should the temperature be set if pot roasting in the oven?

No higher than 175 °F.

How can you tell if the heat is too high?

Bubbling of the liquid is a certain sign the temperature is too high, as is a steaming pot.

How long should a pot roast be cooked?

Flat chuck should take 2 hours, plus or minus a half hour, rump 2½–3 hours.

How can doneness be tested?

1. Poke with a fork in several places. If the meat yields to moderate pressure and the juice bubbles out clear or just faintly pink it is done, or nearly so.
2. At one end make two very thin slices. Taste the second. It should be a little chewy, faintly rosy, compact, nicely juicy but not dry, stringy or falling apart.

BEEF

What are the grades of beef?

Prime: The best in tenderness, juiciness and flavor with moderate marbling or better. Limited availability to retail markets, mainly sold to upgrade restaurants. Only about 2% of the production is Prime. The best for dry heat cooking.

Choice: The best available to most consumers and less expensive than Prime. The cuts are tender, juicy and flavorful. Less marbling than Prime but still high in quality. Many less tender cuts, such as those from the round, rump or blade can also be cooked with dry heat.

Select: (Formerly called Good, which is still used by some markets.) Less expensive than Choice and not quite as good. Less marbling. May lack some of the juices and flavor of Choice. Only the most tender cuts should be cooked with dry heat.

Utility, cutter and canner: Rarely if ever sold at retail, they are used for making ground beef.

What internal temperature will give a rare beef?

130 °F.

What is corned beef?

Beef brisket cured in brine or by salting.

Where did the term "corned beef" come from?

In England, originally, where the meat was covered with whole grains of salt, which were known as corns, hence the name.

How is corned beef used?

It is eaten hot cooked with vegetables, such as cabbage, or cold, as in sandwiches.

What is pastrami?

Beef prepared by curing in brine and preservatives or coated with salt and seasonings for several weeks, more often cured, then smoked for several hours, then cooked.

What cuts are used?

Usually brisket or round.

What is brisket of beef?

The first part of a cow's breast. The thickest part is the most tender.

Why are kosher loins and legs of beef not found in the market?

To be kosher all veins and arteries must be removed, and to do this would disfigure these parts of meat too badly.

What is osso buco?

Veal shanks braised with stock, wine, tomatoes, and carrots and garnished with gremolata.

What are the best cuts for osso buco?

The larger, meatier shanks (shoulder), which are often cheaper than the hind legs, which are smaller and tenderer. Since the dish is wet-cooked for a long period of time, the relative lack of tenderness can be overcome.

How do beef cuts compare as to calories and fat for a 3-ounce portion?

	Calories	Fat
Top round	153	4 grams
Top sirloin	165	6 grams
Top loin	176	8 grams

What are guidelines for choosing and cooking oxtails?

1. They have a vivid red hue and a clean scent when freshly butchered.
2. They need slow, moist cooking such as braising or simmering.
3. The older the animal, the longer the cooking time required.

4. Once cooked, remove meat from bone, shred it and add back to the soup.

5. Use it to make hash.

What should be done first to cut a piece of meat for a paillard?

Make sure it is well chilled.

How can a cutlet or a paillard be pounded?

1. Cover it with wax paper.

2. Lightly pound it with a pan bottom, the flat of a cleaver or a meat mallet until evenly smooth.

How can a paillard or cutlet be flavored?

1. Marination.

2. Cover with some mustard before pounding.

3. Salt and pepper the meat before cooking.

4. Bread the meat.

Steak

Where does the name "steak" come from?

When the Saxons conquered Great Britain, they came as skilled cattlemen who liked to cook beef on a stick over a campfire. The Saxon word "steik" means "meat on a stick."

How can you determine whether a steak or chop is rare, medium or well done without cutting into it?

Touch it. Rare: Soft with very little resistance.

Medium: Slight resistance that springs back into place.

Well: Firm to touch.

What are thermometer readings for the various degrees of doneness of a steak?

120 °F   Very rare.

130 °F   Rare.

140 °F   Medium-rare.

160 °F   Well done.

Why is a fresh cut of meat red on its surface and brown inside?

When myoglobin is denied oxygen it first turns purple, then to a brown tinge. When the butcher makes a retail cut then wraps it in plastic, the newly exposed surface has had access to oxygen and turned red. If you cut open a piece of meat it, too, will turn red. But with further aging it starts to brown again.

What is the reason for always browning the exterior surface of a steak?

For flavor, because the light heat results in a reaction similar to caramelization of sugar.

Why is a "bloody red steak" not really bloody?

Most of the blood is bled out in the slaughterhouse or butcher shop. Myoglobin, the principal pigment in raw meat, gives it color and is found in the muscles, while hemoglobin, the red pigment in blood, is found in the arteries.

What kind of a pan should be used for searing a steak?

A heavy, unlined pan.

Why should the pan be very hot when pan searing a steak?

To prevent it from sticking.

What does sprinkling the pan with salt before adding the steak accomplish?

Helps to prevent sticking and also favorably affects the flavor.

How should steak be seasoned with salt?

There are conflicting views as to when to add salt, before or after cooking has begun, and how much to use. Compromise: cook the steak on one side, turn it over and salt one side. Finish cooking and salt the other side.

How can a steak be grilled rare and still get the center warm?

1. Start with the grill clean and very hot, the meat at room temperature and sparingly coated with oil.
2. Cook the meat over the center of the fire until it shows just a little resistance when poked with your finger. Then slide the steak over to the edge of the grill for a few minutes over the warm heat to finish cooking.

Why should a well-marbled but tough steak, such as skirt steak, be cooked no more than rare or medium rare?

To limit shrinkage of the muscle and the loss of juiciness, both of which would increase toughness.

What is a skirt steak?

A thin cut from the belly of the steer. Also called beef plate skirt steak.

How should flank or skirt steak be handled to make a tender dish?

Cook very briefly; never overcook it.

How should it be served?

1. Cut the meat in thin slices across the grain.
2. Angle the blade of the knife at a 45-degree angle to the cutting board to create wider slices.
3. Let the meat rest a few minutes before serving but keep it warm.

What are optional steps for cooking skirt steaks?

1. Marinate the meat for a few hours.
2. Pound the meat lightly to break fibers, but avoid pounding too much or the meat will tend to break apart, develop holes and lose its juice during cooking.

Will searing a steak reduce the juice loss during cooking?

Not appreciably.

What is the purpose of searing meat?

The meat will taste better. The same is true for poultry, fish and even vegetables. Browning adds new and exciting flavors.

What preparatory steps should be taken before searing?

Have the meat at room temperature with both the broiler and the broiler pan preheated and the meat should be patted dry.

How far from the broiler's heat source should food be placed?

1. Most foods between 3–6″ (flame or electric coil).
2. Generally, the thicker the food, the closer to the heat.
3. If too close for its thickness it will be dry and overcooked on the outside before the inside is properly cooked.
4. If too far below, the exterior will not develop the deep color and somewhat crusty texture.

How can you tell when a steak should be turned over on the grill?

When the upper surface begins to be very moist.

What is the best way to pan broil?

Rather than pouring oil onto the pan, coat the meat with oil. The browning will be even and the other side will brown almost as well. The pan must be very hot to start.

What is a hanger steak?

This is a piece that hangs down as an extension of the tenderloin. There is one per animal. It is about an inch thick, about 12″ long, 5″ wide, is boneless, diagonally grained, well marbled and very flavorful.

What is the difference between New York and strip steaks?

The name only. In the Midwest and West it is called a New York steak, but in New York it is called a strip steak. Both are porterhouse without the fillet. Other names include Delmonico, Kansas City, shell, boneless club and sirloin strip.

What are the difference in fat standard for ground beef and steak?

Steak: Lean: no more than 10% fat.

            Extra Lean: no more than 5% fat.

Ground: Lean or Extra Lean: as much as 18% fat.

Are standard and commercial grades of beef safe?

Both are just as safe as the more expensive Prime and Choice cuts.

What is a London broil?

A steak that is broiled with a crisp crust.

How should it be served?

Cut against the grain, sliced very thinly.

How can you give it a crust yet keep it rare or medium-rare?

Start it in a very hot skillet and cook it in a very hot oven, turning once, and then finish it in a 120 °F oven (using an instant-read thermometer).

What is the best cut for a London broil?

Shoulder round, second choice top round.

Ground Beef

What are the fat contents allowed from the different labels on ground meat?

Ground or standard:	Can contain up to 30% fat.
Lean ground	Up to 18% fat.
Hamburger	Up to 14% fat.

What do labels mean as to the source of beef?

Ground beef:	Must contain only beef, but may be from any part of the cow.
Hamburger:	May be from any animal.

How can you get leaner meat?

1. Buy pieces of meat and trim them carefully.
2. Have the butcher grind it for you, instead of choosing prepackaged.
3. Grind a lean cut at home.

Why is ground meat more perishable than a steak?

1. Ground is subjected to bacterial growth that may be on the butcher's hands or grinder.
2. Grinding enlarges the surface area many times, thus making the meat more accessible to bacterial growth.

Beef hamburger can be sold as "100% pure beef" but can contain offal. What does that include?

Lung, heart, lips, bone, ears, esophagus. In other words, edible offal.

What are the rules for selecting ground beef?

1. In all cases choose beef that is bright, rosy red for it gradually browns as it sits.
2. Buy it only for consumption within a short time.
3. It will be juicier and more tender if you chop the meat in a food processor rather than having it preground because the store ground tends to be pasty as it has been pressed through small hole of the grinder. If done at home, don't over-chop.

What meat should be chosen for hamburger?

Choose chuck instead of round or sirloin. The burgers will be more tasty because the meat is more flavorful to begin with. It will also be juicier because of the extra fat even though most of the fat will drain out by the time the burgers are finished cooking.

What are safety factors in handling hamburgers?

1. Store the fresh ground meat in the coldest part of the refrigerator.
2. Patties prepared ahead, wrapped well and stored in the refrigerator should be used within 8 hours or, if frozen, within 2 months.
3. Defrost in the refrigerator, not at room temperature.
4. Do not refreeze defrosted, uncooked ground meat.
5. Cook as soon as possible after thawing.

What can be added to regain moisture in low-fat hamburgers?

Grated onion, cottage cheese, stiffly beaten egg white.

At what temperature should they be cooked?

Cook to medium (160–165 °F). The center will be a light grey and the juice will run clear.

Is steak tartare a potential source of bacteria and therefore potentially dangerous?

Yes, because of both the raw meat and the raw egg. But in a good restaurant where the meat is chopped fresh, and hamburger is ground ahead of time in a properly cleaned grinder, then danger diminishes. Raw eggs, however, have a danger ratio in the neighborhood of 1 in 10,000. If proper sanitation precautions in home cooking are followed the possibilities can be diminished to improbably.

What are the results of using ground meat that is high in fat?

1. Flavor is better.
2. More fat will drain off when cooked so the fat content will decrease.
3. Greater shrinkage.

What will result from a low fat content of the meat?

1. The beef will be dried out.
2. The fat content in the finished meat will be lower than for regular beef.

How can meatballs be prevented from falling apart when cooking?

1. Refrigerate them 20 minutes before cooking.
2. Handle carefully when forming so you don't over-compact them.
3. Add a little flour to the meat before shaping into patties.

How should hamburger meat be ground or chopped?

1. Remove as much fat as possible before grinding.
2. Double grind to break up fat into smaller globules, thus allowing more fat to be lost in the cooking.

What else should be done when grinding meat at home?

1. Make sure the grinder is very clean.
2. Trim out all gristle and fat.
3. Chill the meat to minimize the loss of juice.

How can meat be handled so that the grinder won't clog?

Cut the meat into small pieces and freeze it slightly so the chopper won't clog and the loss of meat will be minimal.

What happens if a hole is poked in the center of a hamburger when shaping it?

The center cooks first but the hole will be gone by the time the meat is done.

How can hamburgers be cooked faster?

Make a few punctures in the patty before cooking.

How can burgers be made that are low in fat but taste good?

1. Buy lean meat that is labeled "90% lean" or, better yet, "fat-free."
2. Combine the meat with grain or beans.
3. Mix in the seasoning before cooking.
4. When shaping the patties handle as little as possible, for a loosely packed burger is juicier.
5. Don't press the burger down when cooking.

What can be done to make a reduced-fat burger less dry?

1. Add one stiffly beaten egg white per pound of meat.
2. Add one large, grated onion per half pound of meat.
3. Form the patties with one tablespoon of cottage cheese in the center.
4. Use potato flakes in the mixture.

Meat

What meat should be chosen for meat loaf?

Choose ground round, because it has less fat, and the fat in meat loaf does not drain out as well as it does with burgers, being absorbed by breadcrumbs and other ingredients. Ground round also has more flavor than ground sirloin.

What other meats make a flavorful meat loaf?

Use a mixture of meats, such as beef with pork or veal, or beef with ground turkey or ground chicken.

How can cracking be avoided in a meat loaf?

Don't over-mix. Form the loaf with your hands, gently, so the result will not be dense and heavy.

How can cooking time of a meat loaf be shortened?

Make individual portions and bake them in a muffin tins. They will be ready in 15–30 minutes at 375 °F.

How should meat be ground for meat loaf?

Use coarsely ground rather than finely ground meat.

How should meat loaf be prepared for roasting?

1. Add a little moisture, such as wine, broth or tomato juice, to the mix to make the loaf juicier.
2. Add flavoring elements, such as grated cheese, soft breadcrumbs, grated carrots, onion, potato, mashed potatoes or drippings.
3. To ensure a moist loaf, take about ¼ of the meat together with the seasoning and hard-cooked eggs and chop finely, then blend with the rest of the meat.
4. Level the surface of the loaf in the baking pan with the back of a spoon.

What is the difference between a meat loaf baked in a loaf pan and one baked free form?

The one baked free form will have a more glazed crust.

How should the loaf be baked?

1. To make it juicy and tender, slow bake (lower temperature) and baste it with its drippings.
2. Check the internal temperature, baking until it reaches 170 °F.

Can the loaf be cooked in the microwave oven?

Yes.

What can be substituted for breadcrumbs as filler?

Rolled oats or cornflake crumbs.

Should a meat loaf have a center filling?

This is optional. A filling will give it an added dimension.

What are some such fillings?

Hard-cooked eggs, pickles, cheese, chopped vegetables.

What are some glazes for meat loaf?

Cranberries, ginger, chutney, maple syrup with allspice and/or ground cloves.

How can meatballs of equal size be achieved?

1. Form the meat into a sheet that is thick enough to allow you to cut it into squares of the size desired. Cut into squares of uniform size. Roll the squares lightly with moist hands.
2. Use an ice cream scoop.

What kind of breadcrumbs should be used?

Soft crumbs instead of hard.

How should cheese be added?

1. Mix grated cheese into the meat.
2. Put a piece of cheese inside the middle.
3. Sprinkle grated cheese over the exterior just before finishing cooking.

What is a ragu (ragout)?

Traditionally an Italian meat sauce, mainly used for pasta. Usually made from ground beef, wine, celery and seasoning. Nowadays the term is used for stews made with many different ingredients.

What is the secret in getting a crust in hash?

The crust is formed on the bottom of the pan. After 10–15 minutes stir the bottom so the crust comes up into the meat. Then cook 10–15 minutes more and repeat. The crust will end up throughout the hash. Some chefs believe that there should only be a crust on the bottom so they don't stir.

Variety Meats/Organs/Entrails

What are variety meats?

Brains, feet, kidneys, livers, sweetbreads, tongues, tripe, esophagus, spleen.

How are variety meats used?

Liver:	Pâté, sausage, sautéd.
Heart:	Braised or stewed.
Brain:	Poached, fried, baked, broiled.
Kidney:	Broiled, braised, stewed.
Sweetbread:	Braised, sautéd, poached, in soufflés.

How long does it take to cook tripe?

Low simmering, some 5–12 hours, depending on the age of the animal it came from.

How should a pickled tongue be handled?

Soak overnight to get rid of excess saltiness.

How should tongue be selected?

1. For more tenderness, select a relatively small tongue (veal or lamb).
2. The tongue should feel soft to the touch.

How should it be cooked?

Cook it with slow, moist heat by braising or simmering.

How should a cooked tongue be sliced to serve?

Slice it thinly across the grain starting at the tip end.

What are traditional ways of serving tongue?

1. Serve it hot with a mustard sauce.
2. Serve it cold, in smaller pieces, in a salad with a vinaigrette.

What are sweetbreads?

The thymus glands of beef, pork or lamb, usually taken from young animals.

What are the best sweetbreads?

Those from milk-fed animals, especially from lamb.

How should they be selected?

Choose those white in color, plump and firm.

How are sweetbreads prepared for cooking?

1. Soaked in several changes of acidulated water (lemon juice or vinegar added).
2. Remove the outer membrane.
3. Wrap in cheesecloth, roll up and tie with a string.
4. Place in a rectangular container and top with a board with a weight on top of the board.
5. Refrigerate.
6. Any excess moisture will be forced out and the sweetbread formed, compacted, shape and ready for cooking.

How can they be made firmer?

Some chefs blanch them to make them firmer.

What is the difference in kidney from an older versus younger animal?

The older the animal, the stronger the odor, the less delicate its flavor and texture.

How should kidneys be selected?

Avoid those with blotches and dry skins. Choose those with an even, rich color.

How should kidneys be prepared?

1. Skin and remove fat.
2. To reduce the strong flavor blanch them or soak in cold water.

What is the difference in livers between younger and older beef?

1. The color goes from pale pink-brown in calves to a full reddish brown in older cows.
2. The texture is tougher with age.
3. The flavor and odor intensify with age.

What happens if liver is overcooked?

It becomes tough.

How can a liver be tenderized?

1. Soak in milk for several hours in the refrigerator.
2. Use tomato juice, refrigerate for 3 to 4 hours.

What is the best way of preparing pork liver?

In a pâté.

How should it be chosen?

It should be plump and red without a grey hue.

Since the heart is a tough muscle, how should it be treated?

Slice it then braise. Those from young animals can be roasted after blanching.

What are rules for choosing brains?

1. They are best when from very young animals.
2. They are very perishable, so buy only if pinkish-white, free from off-odors and plump.

How should they be cooked?

1. They are quite delicate, therefore, handle with care.
2. Soak in acidulated water in the refrigerator for an hour, which will make their membranes easier to remove. This also draws out any blood, which would turn brown when cooked and spoil the appearance.

What should be done if they are to be sautéed?

Blanch them first in acidulated water, which will also firm them and whiten the flesh.

VEAL

What are the differences among veal, baby beef and beef?

Veal: Traditionally from a calf under three months, but now up to twenty-six weeks.

Baby beef: From three to twelve months of age.

Beef: One year or older.

What are clues as to the age of beef?

Much of the baby beef is sold as veal. You can tell the difference by appearance. If it is creamy pink, it is veal, if creamy red, it is baby beef. The deepening of color comes from the calf's increased consumption of iron in its diet. Another indicator is the color of the surrounding fat. The whiter and less yellow, the younger the animal.

Will veal keep as well as beef?

Veal is more perishable, so buy only for immediate use.

What is the difference between very young veal (less than four months, called milk-fed) and the veal available in most markets?

The flesh of the very young is very white and without much flavor. While very tender it needs seasoning to be attractive. The older calves are weaned and on a normal diet. Their meat is darker with much more flavor and while tender it is not as tender as milk-fed.

What is the relationship of fat in lean veal to that in lean beef?

Lean veal can have as little as one-tenth the fat of lean beef but its cholesterol content may be the same.

How should veal be pounded?

Use a steady, moderate stroke, starting at the center and moving outward.

What are cooking hints for veal?

1. Even tender cutlets benefit from pounding before cooking.
2. Veal needs ample but gentle cooking to develop its delicate flavor.
3. Overcooking can toughen it.
4. A roast is best at an internal temperature of 160 °F, when the juice begins to run clear.
5. Cutlets are best if breaded or floured, which enhances the flavor and helps to seal in the juices.
6. Breading adds texture.

What must be done to get good adhesion of the breading?

Air-dry the cutlet fifteen minutes or so before cooking.

Why is the leg the most desirable cut?

It has solid, lean, firm-textured meat.

What is the saddle?

The complete unseparated loin from both sides of the animal.

LAMB

What are the USDA grades of lamb?

Prime: High in tenderness, juiciness and flavor, with moderate marbling. Chops and roasts in this grade do well with dry heat cooking. Almost all goes to restaurants.

Choice: A little less marbling than Prime but still high in quality. What is found in most markets. Has less fat than Prime.

Good: One of the market grades, leaner than Prime.

Utility: Useable, but inferior grade. If sold at retail, the grade is seldom stated.

Cull: Applies only to mutton, and mutton does not qualify for Prime and is mainly used to make processed meats.

What is yearling lamb?

From 12–20 months old. Too young to be called mutton, too old to be called lamb. Usually used ground for sausages or the like.

What should be looked for in buying lamb?

1. The younger the animal, the more tender the flesh. The quality varies with age. Choose the smallest, for it will be the youngest.
2. The loin chops are more tender than shoulder chops.
3. If the meat has been frozen, it will be less tender.
4. As the lamb ages, the flesh loses its paleness, and the white fat picks up a yellow tint and a dry, crumbly texture.
5. Look for finely grained flesh that still has a fresh glow.
6. When buying a half a lamb leg, the sirloin is more tender but yields less meat per pound of weight and is more difficult to carve than the shank half. The shank is best.
7. The whole leg of lamb should be plump, for scrawny legs have a lower meat to fat and bone ratio.

How thick should lamb chops be?

Chops should be 1⅓–1½" thick, so they don't curl or dry out.

Why is roasting such a good cooking method for lamb?

Because of the meat's high fat content.

What is the calorie/fat content for a loin lamb chop (trimmed of fat)?

178 calories and 9 grams of fat.

Should the lamb shoulder be boned before or after roasting?

Best if the blade bone is loosened from the flesh before so that when roasting is done the bone can be easily removed.

How are Australian and New Zealand lamb different from that produced in the United States?

1. It is against the law there to use hormones or tenderizers.
2. Most domestic (U.S.) animals are at least partially grain fed, which produces a milder flavor, while the imported lamb graze only on grass.
3. The imported are usually aged longer.
4. U.S. lambs are larger and meatier animals and tend to be fatter.

What is spring lamb?

Spring lamb used to be those animals born from March through October, but new breeding technology has made the term useless. It has no legal meaning since lamb is on the market now all year round.

When does lamb become mutton?

According to the USDA, lamb is from an animal under twelve months old. Also called yearling or winter lamb. More than a year old it is mutton. Usually what the butcher sells is from an animal 5–6 months old.

What is milk-fed or hot house lamb?

Meat from an animal that has no grain or grass food and is milk-fed only. Also it is under three months of age.

What is a crown roast?

A dish made from two or more racks of lamb. The back bones are removed without separating the chops. With the meat turned inward they are tied together and stood bottom side down to make a circle. The trimmed ribs on top are wrapped with ham or covered with foil or a small potato while roasting to protect against charring, and the coverings are then often discarded before serving.

What other meat can be used for a crown roast?

Pork ribs.

With a rack of lamb, how much is left after trimming out the backbone and fat?

A 3½-pound rack will yield about 2 pounds. Trimmed, it will serve four people.

What is the tenderest cut of lamb?

Double loin (saddle).

What is the fell of lamb?

The outer membrane that keeps the lamb together when stuffed.

What are the best cooking methods for getting good flavor from lamb?

1. Trim off excess fat before broiling, sautéing or roasting to lessen the smell and "lamby" taste.
2. Avoid overcooking, because that causes the meat to toughen and lose its subtle flavor. The interior meat should have a pink color.

Should lamb be cooked in a slow or fast (higher) temperature roasting?

Fast, for with a slow roast the meat can become mushy.

What are the temperature guidelines for cooking a lamb roast?

Remove the meat from the oven when the internal temperature registers:

120 degrees for very rare.

125 degrees for rare.

135 degrees for medium-rare (pink).

140–145 degrees for medium.

How does butterflying change the cooking time?

Cuts the time by almost two-thirds.

Should a butterflied leg also be cut across the grain?

It is almost impossible since the grain goes different ways.

What is the effect of butterflying a leg?

While a butterflied or boned leg is easy to serve, it loses some of its flavor by having the bone out. This can be partially remedied by marinating the meat.

What can be done with the bones after butterflying a leg?

They will make good soup when cooked with carrots, onions and celery and seasoned with salt, pepper, garlic and rosemary. After the soup is made, strain, degrease and add the vegetables back plus barley, rice or other grains.

What should be known about stuffing a lamb roast with garlic cloves?

Don't insert a lot of garlic cloves into a roast, as they will have a toughening effect by blocking channels for internal juices to escape.

What is an arm chop?

The shoulder or round chop.

How should a roast be sliced?

Across the grain, because when cut with the grain the meat is tougher and chewier.

What is the best meat for shish kebab?

Leg or sirloin steaks.

What can be substituted when wooden skewers are not available when making kebabs?

Try branches of rosemary, from which half of the leaves have been removed. This will add a special flavor.

How can lamb sausage be made without casing?

1. Knead the ground meat with its flavoring mixture.
2. Refrigerate thirty minutes to firm it.
3. Mold the mixture around oiled skewers.
4. With a brush or oiled hands coat the outside of the meat.
5. Broil.

PORK

What are the grades of pork?

There are only two USDA levels of quality: Acceptable and Unacceptable.

What should you look for when buying pork?

1. The younger the animal, the more delectable and tender.
2. Unless very young, the flesh should show evidence of marbling. These minute pockets of fat embedded in the lean meat help keep the meat juicy and tender when cooked.
3. The skin of a young animal will be thin and light hued.
4. The fat layers next to the lean meat of young pigs are bright white without yellow pigmentation.
5. Since pork is usually produced from young animals, it is much less variable in tenderness than beef.

Why is freezing more damaging to pork than to other meats?

Because the flesh is so lean it will become unnecessarily dry when cooked.

What is the leanest cut of pork?

The tenderloin, with only 4 grams of fat in a 3-ounce serving of roasted meat.

What is a safe temperature for cooking pork?

The trichinosis organism dies at 137 °F, but the pork tastes better at 160–165 °F. All traces of pink do NOT have to disappear. The meat is safe when the color of the interior changes from a rose pink to a blush of pink. Further cooking toughens the pork. Cook to 145 °F and let the roast stand 20 minutes before slicing and the temperature will rise to 160 °F and therefore be safe.

How does pork marketed today compare to that of a decade or more ago?

Modern pork is higher in protein and has 32.5% less fat and 14% fewer calories.

How should modern pork be cooked?

Slowly, because it is quite lean.

What does this lean pork need to be succulent?

Fat to replace the 4–5″ of fat that used to be on the pig. Now it needs some added fat or some substitute to avoid producing a dry roast.

What is the advantage of precooking the vegetables used in stuffing a roast of pork?

The meat can be roasted without worry whether or not the stuffing has been cooked enough, and thus overcooking can be avoided.

What is the advantage of butterflying a loin of pork?

It will cut cooking time almost in half. Roast for about half the cooking time at 375 °F and then finish under the broiler for about twenty minutes.

What flavors a roast faster than a marinade, if you're in a hurry?

Tie rosemary sprigs around the roast.

What is the difference between leaf lard and regular lard?

The leaf lard is the fat around the kidneys, while regular lard is fat from any part of the pig and has a much stronger flavor.

Pork Chops

What should be avoided when selecting pork chops?

Look for meat that is solidly pink without white streaks. The white is not fat but connective tissue (elastin), which doesn't break down when cooking.

What are the best cuts for pork chops?

The center cuts are the best (center ribs or center loin do best). Avoid cuts from the ends of the loin even though they are often cheaper. Those from the rib are more tender.

Why should the chops be about 1″ thick?

Otherwise they too often dry out when cooked.

What is the best way to cook pork chops?

1. Tenderize with a few mallet strokes.
2. Sautéing is best to avoid dryness and toughness. Brown them gently about 1 minute on each side and then cover and slowly cook about 10 minutes. Turning once. Be careful as to temperature for they will toughen if the temperature is too low or too high.

What methods of cooking chops are not recommended?

Baking, broiling or braising are usually not satisfactory. Boiling draws out the juice and toughens them.

Why should a pork chop have the bone left in when broiling or sautéing?

There will be less shrinkage.

How can you tell when pork chops are done, since use of meat thermometers is not practical?

Press the chop. If it is firm but not hard it will be medium rare. This will be about 137 °F, which will kill any trichinosis parasites. Above 165 °F the meat will be harsh and dry. While modern techniques of raising and butchering have practically eliminated the trichinae, they are still in existence so be careful.

Which marinades are good for pork?

Acid marinades (such as white wine or lemon juice based) will flavor the meat but won't affect the texture. A dry, salt-based marinade will give good flavor.

Why is the Boston butt such a good selection for barbeque?

Because it has enough fat to keep the meat moist and juicy during the long cooking.

How can modern-day pork chops that are quite lean be prepared?

1. Choose chops that are about 1″ thick, even though they take a little longer to cook.
2. Leave the bone in and also the thin layer of fat around the edges, which is easy for the diner to trim off at the table.
3. Season before cooking (although this can be done afterwards).

How can they be cooked so that they don't become tough and dry?

1. Sear the meat in a heavy (cast iron is best) skillet on the stove top. First get the skillet very hot, then add a tablespoon of oil. Add the chops and after 1–2 minutes use a spatula (not a fork) and turn them over and sear the other side.
2. Finish cooking in a 400 °F oven, which will take about 8–10 minutes for a 1″ chop.

Sausage

How fatty are pork breakfast sausages?

They can be up to 50% fat.

How can shrinkage and/or splitting of sausages be minimized?

1. Make a few skin punctures before cooking.
2. Boil 3–5 minutes before frying.
3. For link sausages, precook (simmer) until the juices run clear. This will also prevent shrinkage.
4. Roll in flour.

How can you judge the seasoning level when making sausages, since you shouldn't taste the raw meat?

After the meat and seasoning have been combined make a small patty, fry and taste it, then adjust the seasoning as necessary.

Should link sausages have their casings removed?

As a general rule, yes.

Bacon

Should you buy the leanest bacon?

That could be counterproductive, as the fat gives the bacon most of its desirable flavor and crispness. Most of the extra fat melts off during cooking.

What is Canadian bacon (back bacon)?

Lightly smoked, boneless, cut from the loin that has been cured. Best known as an ingredient in Eggs Benedict.

How should Canadian bacon be cooked?

While it can be eaten raw, much like ham, it is best prepared fried or baked when thickly sliced.

What is pancetta?

Italian bacon made from the pig underbelly and is unsmoked. Salted and cured in slab form for 2–3 weeks, it is then seasoned, rolled and placed in a casing to be cured for several months. It has a high fat content and is rarely eaten raw.

How does pancetta differ from American bacon?

1. Both come from the belly of the pig.
2. Pancetta is cured with salt and spice (usually cloves and peppercorns) and then rolled into a log shape.
3. Bacon is smoked, pancetta is not.

How is pancetta used?

1. Mainly as a flavoring agent, not as a meat component.
2. Chopped pancetta is used in Tuscany for enriching pot roast (as a stuffing into crevices of the roast).
3. Wrapped around a pork tenderloin and then grilled.

How long will bacon keep in the refrigerator?

Once the vacuum pack is opened, it will usually keep only about a week, although sometimes for a couple of weeks.

What can be done with leftover, cooked bacon?

1. It can be recrisped in a skillet, a microwave or an oven.
2. It can be used crumbled in salads, pasta or on baked potatoes.

Can you save bacon by freezing it?

It does not freeze well, since its high salt content will prevent satisfactory long-term freezing. In addition the freezing causes ice crystals, causing the bacon to splatter when fried.

How can splattering be minimized when cooking bacon?

1. Pour off the fat as it is rendered. This will also produce crisper meat.
2. Start the frying in a cold pan and cook over moderate heat. If it starts to smoke, lower the heat.

Why use paper towels over and under the meat when cooking bacon in the microwave?

Over: To prevent splattering.

Under: To reduce the nitrosamine level, which is considered to be a carcinogen in animals but does not seem to be an important problem for humans.

Why is burned bacon dangerous?

The burning will produce carcinogens.

How can bacon be prevented from curling?

1. Soak the raw slices in cold water for two minutes but dry them well with toweling before cooking.
2. Sprinkle with flour.
3. Polk a few holes in the slices.

How can you reduce the salt level when using bacon or salt pork in cooking?

Blanch it by covering with cold water, then bring to a boil, simmer 5 minutes, drain, rinse in cold water and towel dry. This will remove both saltiness and smokiness.

Can crisp bacon be achieved in a microwave?

Yes if cooked on a bacon plate, i.e., one with ridges so that the melting fat drips off.

Ham

What can be labeled as ham?

The smoked or cured leg of a hog, mainly the hind leg. No water has been added and 20.5% is protein, or more after the fat has been removed.

What is picnic (or California) ham?

The meat from the front leg. It is tougher than regular ham.

Meat

What is country ham?

Ham cured with a dry crust made from salt, sugar, black pepper and other spices, much like Italian prosciutto.

How can country hams be handled so that they aren't too salty?

1. Soak them about 12 hours, changing water twice to reduce saltiness and soften the meat.
2. Partially bake them, then drain off all the juices, then pour a small bottle of ginger ale over and finish baking.

Why should country ham be thinly sliced to serve?

They are usually salted and this will reduce the level of saltiness in a mouthful.

What is city ham?

Cured in a liquid (salt and sugar) brine. This is the most common ham on the market.

When must the phrase "water added" be stated on the label?

When the water content (total weight) is more than 8%. Up to that point it can be labeled as ham with natural juices

What does the label "cook before eating" mean?

Heat to 160 °F internal temperature.

What is a ham hock?

The part of the pig's back leg between the foot and the ham.

How should cured ham be handled?

Soak in milk for several hours before broiling or sautéing to improve tenderness and flavor.

How should ham slices be cooked?

Slowly, so that they will remain tender and juicy.

What should be done to be able to slice a ham thinly?

Chill the ham before slicing.

What is prosciutto (Parma ham)?

This is a salted and cured ham made from the hindquarters of a young pig.

How does it differ from American ham?

It is not smoked and is pressed to form a dense, firm texture.

How is it used?

It can be enjoyed raw, with a piece of melon, or cooked for flavoring or stuffing or for larding meat.

Meat

How does Italian prosciutto differ from that made here?

Most on the market is domestic and is less expensive than the imported, which is slightly salty and sweet.

What are the types of prosciutto?

P. Cotto: Cooked type.
P. Crudo: Raw but ready to eat.

How long should prosciutto be cooked?

Normally it shouldn't be, but if put in a cooked dish then add it at the very end of cooking.

Are large cans or smaller cans the best buy when buying canned ham?

The best ham is put into large cans. The smaller ones are usually bits and pieces or small chunks of meat that have been pressed together.

Is a canned ham that requires refrigeration better than one that doesn't?

Generally, yes. In order to sterilize the ham in the can so that it doesn't require refrigeration it will be heated to a very high temperature, which negatively alters the flavor, aroma, texture and nutritive value.

What are some guidelines for cooking ham?

1. If you stud the ham with cloves, insert them near the end of the cooking, otherwise the clove flavor can be overwhelming.
2. Don't forget to remove the cloves before slicing, as biting into one can break a tooth.
3. Glaze the ham, fat-side-up, because the luster of the caramelized coating appears more striking on fat than on flesh. Brush with a glaze, repeating 2–3 times, enhancing appearance.

What are some serving guidelines?

1. Remove the skin of the ham soon after it is cooked, because the longer you wait the more difficult it becomes.
2. Allow the roast to rest about half an hour. It can be served warm or at room temperature.
3. Slice across the grain.

How can ham rinds be removed easily?

Slit the rind before placing the ham in the oven. As it bakes, the rind will pull away and then can easily be removed.

Why doesn't ham become gray brown when cooked?

A cured ham contains nitrite salt, which reacts with the myoglobin to create nitrousmyoglobin, which stays rosy red even when exposed to high temperatures.

Meat

Spareribs

What are the cuts of pork ribs?

Spareribs: From the lower rib cage next to the bacon. Good amount of meat, considerable fat, best for barbeque. The long ribs have less meat and are less tender. Cut in slabs of thirteen ribs, varying in size. The younger the animal, the more tender the ribs.

Baby back ribs: Low ribs, smaller, meatier than spareribs. Work well grilled. Good tasting, tender.

Country style ribs: From the upper side of the rib cage. More like chops. Highest in fat, not suitable for long cooking.

What measure of spareribs are needed per serving?

From the brisket: 1 pound will give 1 serving. From the baby loin (also called back ribs or baby back ribs), which is meatier, 1 pound will give 1½–2 servings.

How should spareribs be cooked?

This varies with regional cuisines, but generally slow cooking, just long enough to take on flavor but not so long that the sweetish sauce (barbeque) develops a burned flavor. Some cooks like to parboil the ribs, but if they are boiled it is usually necessary to cut the ribs in half to fit in the pot.

How can you tell when the ribs are done?

1. If meat tears when you pull it in opposite directions.
2. If you pinch the meat, it should feel soft and pliable.
3. A probe or skewer should go in easily.
4. Hold the piece in the middle with a pincer and if both ends droop, it is done.

DEER

What is venison?

Technically the meat from large game animals, although in modern practice it refers only to the meat from a deer.

What is a fallow deer?

A farm-raised deer.

What are some different ways to prepare venison?

As a rack, roasting (leg or shoulder), in sausage.

What are the best cuts?

1. Loin and ribs are quite tender and suitable for roasting, grilling, sautéing.
2. Haunch, legs are more exercised and need moist heat, or a combination of moist and dry.

What is roasting time for venison?

About 15–20 minutes per pound for a 6-pound roast, which should bring it to an interior temperature of about 175 °F.

How can gaminess of venison be eliminated?

Soak in a cola beverage overnight.

How does venison compare to beef in fat content?

The venison meat has less fat and less cholesterol than beef.

Meat

CHAPTER EIGHT

POULTRY

What is the origin of poultry as part of the diet?

The chicken reached the Western world about the fifth century BC, in Greece. It was a descendent of a russet-color bird of Malaysia and was first domesticated in the valley of the Indus and then went to Persia. With the exception of the turkey, which came from America, all domestic fowl we eat today were found on Roman tables. The duck was domesticated by the Chinese 4,000 years ago, the chicken, about 2000 BC in India.

What is the main source of contamination for poultry?

Most chickens and turkeys are processed and defeathered in 125–132 °F water, which is where bacterial growth is at its highest level, for the warm water opens the pores and thus allows undesirable matter floating in the hot bloody water of the commercial tank to be absorbed into the skin.

How can you make sure that a bird is safe?

1. Store at below 40 °F.
2. Thaw in a microwave oven or in the refrigerator, never at room temperature.
3. Make sure it is well cooked.
4. Cook a whole bird to 170–180 °F.
5. Refrigerate or freeze any leftovers within 2 hours.

What is the difference in the way kosher birds are processed?

Kosher birds are submerged for thirty minutes in very cold water, then hand-salted inside and out and allowed to soak for the removal of any remaining blood, then washed three separate times to remove the salt. They sometimes taste salty and have a somewhat different taste.

How long can fresh, packaged poultry be kept?

Use within two days, or freeze immediately after purchase.

What is a squab?

A domesticated pigeon before it has started flying, it weighs less than a pound.

Should poultry be roasted in a covered pan?

No, for that will result in a steamed bird, not a roasted one.

How can you test to see if the bird is young?

1. The younger the bird, the easier its bones will snap and the less jagged the edges will be.
2. Examine a cross section of a bone. The pinker the tone, the younger the creature. The bones are more porous in the young and become denser with age.
3. The skin of a young bird is smoother and finely grained.
4. The feet of young birds should be slender, shiny and covered with thin scales and have supple nails that do not look badly worn.
5. Relative size is the easiest known gauge, for the larger the animal, the older it is likely to be.

How can you tell a bird's age when poultry is prepackaged so that its condition is obscured?

1. The heavier the package, the older the bird.
2. The smoother the skin, if visible, the younger the bird.

Does the flavor diminish when a chicken ages?

To the contrary, it heightens, even though most meat toughens with age.

What determines the method of cooking poultry?

This is generally a matter of preference, but the younger the bird, the more tender and more suitable for dry heat, such as roasting. The older bird is less tender but more flavored and usually does best with moist heat such as braising.

What is velveting?

A two-step process to add a protective coating to chicken or fish in order to hold in the juices. The food is blanched in barely simmering water for 10–30 seconds and then dipped in a mixture of cornstarch, egg white, salt and sometimes wine. It is particularly used in stir-frying.

What should be done once coated?

Let it rest in the refrigerator for at least an hour or longer. Longer refrigeration yields better results.

When should the velveted food be added in stir-frying?

Toward the end of frying.

What is a caution when preparing wild birds such as a duck?

Over-marinating will mask the flavor of the bird.

How can you test the bird for doneness?

1. Prick the thickest part of one thigh with a fork, the juices should run clear.
2. A meat thermometer, without touching a bone, should read 170 °F. Boneless birds should register 160 °F on the thermometer.

What is the "done" indicator if the bird is stuffed?

The center of the stuffing should register 165 °F.

Should you serve a roasted bird immediately after taking it out of the oven?

Chefs disagree, but it need not stand very long.

What is the comparative calorie content of duck, chicken and turkey breast (skinless)?

Calories:	Turkey	135
	Duckling	132
	Chicken	165

What precaution must be taken when making a chicken or turkey salad?

Wait until the meat is fully cooled before adding any type of salad dressing or mayonnaise.

How should poultry be barbecued?

Leave the skin on during cooking and then remove it, or skin the bird and marinate it well.

What will happen if you reduce the amount of oil in the marinade?

A half to three-quarter reduction won't reduce the flavor, just the calories.

Why choose a meaty, full-breasted bird?

To obtain best value for your money.

How should leftover cooked poultry be handled?

Deboning it will help it hold its flavor longer.

What is a confit?

Meat that is salted, slowly cooked in its own fat, then pressed and immersed and covered with some fat. Made most often from goose or duck.

Poultry

What is foie gras?

It is the fatted goose liver traditionally from Alsace or Perigord in France. Foie gras produced in the United States is mainly made from ducks. The birds are force-fed to increase the size and fat content of the liver.

STUFFING/DRESSING

What is the difference between stuffing and dressing?

They are the same thing, except that the stuffing is cooked inside the bird while the dressing is baked in a separate cooking pan.

What are some of the carbohydrates that can be used as a basis for stuffing?

1. Barley.
2. Bread, or mixtures of breads.
3. Chestnuts.
4. Pasta.
5. Rice or wild rice.
6. Quinoa.

How can you safely stuff a bird?

Since the stuffing expands as it cooks, don't overfill the bird—about 80% of the capacity of the cavity is the maximum, or it will begin to ooze out.

What must be done before refrigerating or freezing a stuffed bird?

If you refrigerate or freeze a cooked bird, remove the stuffing and freeze it separately. Otherwise the stuffing cools down last and bacteria may have time to develop. Remove the stuffing as soon as possible after the meal.

Are commercial breadcrumbs suitable for making stuffing?

Most are too fine. What is needed is bread cut in cubes and dried in a low-temperature oven (200 °F). It can then be cut smaller in a food processor if desired.

Can breadcrumbs be dried at room temperature?

Yes, but of course it takes much longer.

Do stuffed birds require longer roasting, and if so, how much more?

Yes. About 15–20 minutes longer than unstuffed of the same weight.

What is the precaution to take when cooking stuffed breasts?

Make sure the breasts are in a single layer, using two baking dishes, if necessary.

Is 140 °F a safe temperature for cooking foods such as poultry stuffing containing meats?

No! For poultry or poultry stuffing containing meats it is important for the temperature to register at least 165 °F with no interruption in the cooking process.

How can you be sure that all the stuffing of a bird comes out?

1. Line the cavity with a piece of cheesecloth before stuffing, then pull the cloth out after cooking.
2. Scrape it out very methodically.
3. Bake the stuffing separately.

What happens to stuffing baked outside of the bird?

It will be good but will lack some of the flavoring from the juices of the bird.

How can the cavity be used for flavoring when roasting a turkey or chicken without stuffing?

Fill it with a lemon, whole onion or a bunch of herbs. After roasting, discard flavoring items.

CHICKEN

Why is there light and dark meat in chickens but all dark meat in ducks and geese?

The coloration comes from oxygen-storing myoglobin. The muscles that require a lot of oxygen have more myoglobin to retain the oxygen brought by the blood until needed by the muscle cells. Since chickens do a lot of standing and walking and practically no flying, the breast muscles aren't exercised, don't need much oxygen and thus have little myoglobin. The legs do more exercise. This distinction is also true for turkeys. Ducks and geese fly, using their breast muscles, therefore the breast meat is dark.

Is it necessary to skin the chicken before cooking to reduce fat?

Most of the fat does come from the skin or under the skin, but the fat does not transfer to the meat as it cooks. Cook it with the skin on to retain moisture. It will baste the meat as it cooks. Then remove and discard the skin if you wish.

Why is the flesh and leg bone of a fully cooked chicken sometimes bloody?

Chicken bones contain hemoglobin, the red pigment of blood. Sometimes this protein leaches out after the bone is cooked. This is especially likely to happen either if the chicken is quite young or has been frozen. Don't put the bird back in the oven for the meat will then dry out. The hemoglobin is not blood, just an element of blood, and is neither dangerous nor bad tasting.

How should a bird that is cut into pieces be cooked?

Partially cook the dark meat first, then add the white because it cooks faster.

What is a fricassee?

A term mainly used for braised chicken.

Choosing the Bird

Why do chickens in a foreign country taste different than those from the United States?

Many foreign countries don't allow fowl to be raised as they are in this country. In the United States great coops hold ten thousand or more birds housed in a box with food and light available day and night so that they can eat at any hour.

What are poussins?

Small baby chickens about 4 weeks old that weigh about 1 pound. Great for grilling and roasting.

What is a paillard?

A boneless breast of chicken that has been pounded thin. The term is also used for veal or pork.

What are Cornish hens (also called White Rock, Cornish, Cornish game hens and Rock Cornish game hens)?

They are a hybrid of Cornish and White Rock chickens and are usually on the market as babies about 5–6 weeks old and weigh no more than 2 pounds. Best for roasting and grilling.

How can you plan how many Cornish hens to prepare?

Usually figure one bird per serving, because they run considerably less than 2 pounds.

How are they best cooked?

1. Tie their legs.
2. Space them so they are not touching.
3. Place breast down.
4. Roast or grill them.

How can they be made even better?

Marinate for 2 hours prior to roasting.

What sort of glaze helps their appearance and flavor?

A soy or a soy and jelly mix.

If stuffing them, what should be done?

Warm the stuffing before using.

What are broiler-fryers?

These are the most popular and plentiful birds found in markets and weigh between 2½ and 4½ pounds. They are generally 6 to 8 weeks old, although many are slaughtered when 9 to 12 weeks old. Great for broiling, grilling, frying, roasting, poaching, braising and stir-frying.

What is the difference between a broiler and a fryer?

None except for the name. However, many stores separate chickens as broilers (2–2½ pounds), fryers (2½–4 pounds) and roasters (more than 4 pounds). These are not exact or legal measurements.

What are roasters?

Plump hens of 5–7 pounds. Good for stuffing and roasting. Meaty and tender and have enough fat to brown beautifully during roasting. Can also be poached or braised. Slaughtered when 10 to 20 weeks old.

What are capons?

Surgically castrated roosters that grow plump and tender. Slaughtered when about 10 weeks old and weigh 8–10 pounds. More white than dark meat and are good stuffed and roasted. To save grain the Lex Faunia (law) of 162 BC forbade Romans to eat fattened hens. Breeders got around this by castrating cockerels, which, as a result, grew to twice their normal size and put on a lot of weight.

What are stewers?

Mature hens usually over 1 year old and weighing 4–8 pounds. Require long simmering but have plenty of flavor and are good for stocks, soups, fricassees and stews. Slaughtered when more than 10 months old.

What can be substituted if a stewing hen is not available?

A heavy roaster over 5 pounds.

What are free-range chickens?

Chickens allowed more living space and that have access to outdoors, i.e., the door to the coop must be open so they can roam and forage on their own. Generally speaking they taste better, have better development and a more pronounced flavor than those raised in pens, but often, when free to leave the coop they are fed the same as those that are caged.

How is the commercial handling of the free-range chickens different?

Usually sold whole and are only occasionally available as parts. More expensive than those mass-produced. Usually not frozen and wrapped for the market before shipping, and therefore they will weep blood and fluid and end with better flavor.

What does the term "organic" signify?

Not tightly defined, but fed only pesticide-free and chemical-free grains and raised on land that has not been treated with pesticides, herbicides or chemical fertilizers for at least 3 years. Organic chickens are almost always free-range and of high quality.

Poultry

How must chickens be handled to be labeled kosher?

Kosher: slaughtered under rabbinical supervision according to Jewish law. Usually free-range and very high quality. They are slaughtered, rinsed and sold fresh or frozen.

What kind of fowl are usually on the market?

Mass produced, commercially raised on a large scale at lowest prices. In general they are meaty, well proportioned and of good quality. Sold whole or cut up.

What is the advantage of buying chicken whole, not as cut up parts?

1. Intact birds are usually cheaper than when buying parts.
2. Many organic and/or free-range birds are sold only whole.
3. The backbone, wing tips and giblets can be frozen for later use in making stock or used right away to serve or to enrich the sauce making, and many people enjoy giblets.

What about a chicken suggests the most suitable cooking methods?

The age and the size.

How do you choose the right chicken?

1. For roasting, braising or stewing, choose a mature chicken, because it has more meat per pound.
2. For broiling or frying, select a young bird, one that is relatively young for the variety because it is tender enough so that it will cook quickly in high heat.

How should the chicken be selected?

1. Sniff! If not enclosed in plastic, don't buy it if it has even the slightest off odor.
2. The skin should be moist, smooth and free of abrasions and discoloration.
3. Look for symmetrical structure and firm, plump flesh.
4. The legs should be squat for its size.
5. The more flexible the breastbone, the younger the fowl.
6. If the head is still attached, the comb should be a bright, vivid red.

Why are fresh birds better buys than frozen?

Choose fresh birds because the frozen ones lose a fair portion of their internal juices during thawing. The catch is that federal regulations say the bird is *not* frozen until it reaches 0 °F. Sometimes the price of the frozen will be low enough to compensate for the juice loss on a strictly cost basis.

What should be looked for when buying parts?

The color of the exposed flesh should have a fresh blush and not be dull or grayish.

Is the expression "stew an old chicken, fry a young one" justified?

Yes. A mature chicken, especially an old one, has considerable connective tissue that is best tenderized with slow, moist cooking, while a lengthy cooking process on a young bird can coagulate and toughen the muscle fibers.

How does a free-range chicken compare in fat content with a regular commercial bird?

Free range has 11–24% fat compared to standard supermarket birds with 15–18%.

How much fat does chicken skin contribute to a portion of cooked chicken?

Baked with skin equals about 20% fat, skinned about 5%.

What is the difference in quality between a chicken with a yellow skin and one with a white skin?

The only difference is that of appearance. It used to be true that the yellower was better, but in the last decade or so the mass-marketing chicken farms are feeding marigold petals, corn and other sources of gold, yellow and orange pigments, which make both the skin and egg yolks a more vivid yellow or orange.

What is the yield of finished chicken from the raw bird?

A 3-pound chicken yields about 2½–3 cups of cut up meat, which is about 1 pound 5 ounces edible meat.

What are giblets?

The internal organs of chickens or other birds, including gizzard, heart, liver and neck.

Which has a higher fat content in the fast food outlets, the coated fried chicken or most hamburgers?

The chicken. A Burger King cheeseburger has 42% of its calories from fat, while the Kentucky Fried Chicken breast has 57%.

Are contaminated chickens really much of a danger?

Studies show that 48% of food poisonings are caused by contaminated chickens. This affects approximately one in fifty persons in the United States. Americans consume more than 6 billion chickens a year, of which, perhaps, 2 billion are contaminated.

Why must you be careful in the handling of chicken?

They can carry pathogenic bacteria like salmonella. Work on the chickens in a confined area that is easy to clean, or spread a plastic or paper bag on the work surface and use poultry shears to cut the chicken. Then discard the bag. When through, wash your hands and all surfaces that the raw chicken has touched with hot soapy water. Store in the coldest part of the refrigerator.

Is a plastic cutting board safe?

Yes, if it is cleaned afterwards with a bleach solution or put through the dishwasher drying cycle.

How should birds be refrigerated?

Store in the coldest part of the refrigerator, usually the meat tray, for no longer than 2 days. If longer, then freeze-wrap, squeezing out any air, seal tightly and freeze. Birds will keep 4–6 months at 0 °F.

How should frozen chickens be thawed?

Thaw in its wrapping in the refrigerator. Whole, frozen chickens that weigh 4 pounds or less will take 12–16 hours, parts take only 4–9 hours.

How can thawing be accelerated?

Put in a watertight bag and submerge in cold water for a quicker thaw.

Can thawed birds be refrozen safely?

Once thawed do not re-freeze! The texture will suffer.

What are other safety precautions in preparing a chicken?

1. Wash the bird in hot water, inside and out, then dry.
2. Don't touch any other food until you have washed your hands.
3. When finished, wash everything connected with the preparation: utensils, cutting board, toweling, hands.
4. Cook to at least 165 °F throughout.

Preparation

What is another quick way to thaw a frozen chicken?

Place in a pan of cold water with at least ¼ cup of salt added.

What is the best way to refrigerate a chicken?

Wrap in waxed paper instead of plastic wrap.

Why truss a chicken?

1. So that it will have a smooth, compact shape.
2. Trussing retains moisture.
3. Trussing retains the stuffing, if filled.

How can a bird be trussed?

There are many ways. Perhaps the easiest is to place the chicken (stuffed or not) breast-side-up in front of you. Press the wing tips down and bend them backwards, forcing them under the bird. Then pull the drumsticks together, cross slightly and tie them together with string or unflavored dental floss.

What is the difference between cooking a chicken with the bone and without the bone?

With the bone in, the meat will be juicier and tastier. This is also true for beef, lamb or fish.

What should be done if cooking is delayed?

If tightly wrapped in plastic and cooking is deferred more than a few hours, remove the plastic so air can circulate and dry the skin. Otherwise bacteria are more apt to grow. Before refrigerating, rewrap loosely in butcher or wax paper.

How should a refrigerated bird be prepared for roasting?

Bring it to near room temperature before starting to cook.

Why does salting the exterior of a bird inhibit the skin from crisping?

If you want a crisp skin, do not salt the exterior until near completion of the cooking, since the salt draws out the juices, keeping the skin moist, which hinders browning and crisping.

How can lemon juice/flavoring be added to a chicken without the juice spilling out?

1. Cut a lemon in half and rub the bird all over.
2. Use the lemon halves as stuffing.

What is the advantage of butterflying a chicken?

It results in a more even thickness, which means it will cook faster and have all parts done at the same time, whether roasted, sautéd or grilled.

How does the size and age of the bird affect the cooking?

The older and larger the bird, the lower the temperature and the longer the roasting period should be.

When should the bird be peppered when sautéing or broiling?

Don't add pepper until near the end, as the pepper can scorch, making it bitter.

How can boning of a chicken be made easier?

By partially freezing the bird first.

Should a chicken be cut up first to skin it?

It is easier to skin before cutting up the bird. The skin can be pulled off in one piece, with the exception of the wings, which are very difficult to skin before they are cooked.

How can chicken be tenderized?

Baste with white wine as it cooks. This also gives a unique flavor.

How can chicken breasts be pounded to an even thickness?

Remove the breast tender, place between two sheets of waxed paper and pound.

Roasting

How do you prepare a bird for roasting?

1. Remove giblets, neck and any large, visible pieces of fat from inside the whole chicken.
2. Rinse the bird inside and out with cool water and pat dry (optional).
3. If unstuffed, season the cavity with herbs and lemon juice.

How should a bird be stuffed?

Loosely fill the main cavity, then truss. A 4½-pound bird requires about 2–2½ cups of stuffing. Increase the stuffing by ½ cup per pound for larger birds. In any case, stuff only about three-quarters full to allow for expansion, as the stuffing absorbs the bird's juices.

Why not skin the bird to reduce fat?

Don't skin the bird before roasting even if you plan to serve it skinned, so that the juices will stay in the meat and the chicken will taste better.

What is the best way to roast a chicken?

There is considerable difference of opinion among chefs on this subject.

1. On a horizontal rack, initially sear in a hot (400 °F) oven and then finish at 325 °F. This will quickly cook the skin and outermost flesh, which holds the juices in. Salt and pepper when the roasting is almost done in order to get a better browning and crisping of the skin. Many cooks do not use an initial 400 °F, searing and instead cook at 325 °F a bit longer.

2. My preference is the vertical roaster, which is easy and quick to use, although it will not result in a really crisp skin. I use one that is cone shaped, narrow on top and broad on the bottom. After cleaning out the inside cavity, rinse and then dry and season the bird, including the cavity. Place the coned bird on a pie tin with a half inch or so of water (to make cleaning afterwards easier) and put into a pre-heated 375 °F oven. Check after about thirty minutes, for a 3-pound chicken is usually done in 45 minutes. The skin should be fairly well browned, and both the white and dark meat juicy and tender. The bird can also be placed upside down, i.e., with the neck down on the cone. This can give an even roast.

What can be done to improve the roasting process?

1. Oil the rack.
2. Turn the bird once, finishing with the breast up.

What besides temperature reading tells if the bird has been cooked enough?

The juice will run clear.

What is an easy way to give rich seasoning to a chicken for roasting?

1. After removing the giblets and neck trim off the excess fat.
2. Starting at the neck, loosen the skin from the breast and legs with your fingers.
3. Slip under the skin seasonings such as sliced garlic, rosemary, marjoram leaves etc.
4. Put into a hot oven (400 °F or more) for twenty minutes and then reduce to 350 °F to finish.
5. Salt and pepper the outside of the bird towards the end of the roast.

When roasting a stuffed bird how can the stuffing be protected from burning?

During the last part of the roast cover the cavity with a small piece of foil.

What happens if a chicken is cooked with a low to moderate temperature?

The chicken will be juicier since more fat and moisture is retained, but the skin will be less crisp.

Is basting desirable?

While it prolongs cooking time, it increases the attractiveness of the skin.

What can be used for basting?

Melted butter, pan juices, milk, fruit juices.

How should a roasting chicken be turned?

With a large kitchen fork in the main cavity so that no holes are made in the meat, which would cause loss of juice.

Breasts/Cutlets

What color should be looked for when buying chicken breasts?

The color itself is not critical, rather look for consistency of color.

Why are boneless cutlets pounded before sautéing or grilling?

So they will cook faster and more evenly. Pound about 5–6 minutes. If uniformly pounded, no one part will be over- or undercooked.

How should cutlets be prepared?

1. Moisten the pounded cutlet with buttermilk or water.
2. Coat with fine cornmeal flour, regular flour or a mixture of the two and desired seasonings.
3. Sauté in a mixture of butter and oil, starting at a high temperature.
4. Lower the heat as they cook.
5. Cover the sauté pan for the last half of the cooking.

What are the main considerations when cooking chicken breasts?

1. Season the breast with salt and pepper, a marinade, a rub or a coating.
2. Don't overcook. Take off the heat when they are firm to the touch and the juice runs clear, not pink when a fork pierces the meat.

What should be looked for when buying chicken breasts?

1. Check for liquid in the package, which is a sign that the breasts have been frozen.
2. Choose symmetrical breasts for even cooking.

What preparation can be done to get tender, moist chicken breasts?

1. Add a few slices of lemon when stewing.
2. Submerge the breasts in buttermilk 3–4 hours under refrigeration before cooking.

What ingredients are good for coating chicken breasts before roasting?

1. Grated cheese (such as Parmesan) and breadcrumbs.
2. Crushed crackers and finely chopped nuts.
3. Grated cheese and corn flake crumbs.
4. Crushed potato chips and herbs.

Sautéing

How can a chicken be sautéd so it will brown properly and be crisp and golden on the outside?

1. Thoroughly dry the pieces.
2. Make sure that the fat in the skillet is very hot but not smoky before the meat is added.
3. Don't let the pieces touch each other in the skillet.

Can chicken be sautéd ahead of time?

Yes, if you expect to serve it at room temperature.

Can you reheat sautéd chicken?

Yes, but it will not taste as good reheated.

When should pepper be added when sautéing or broiling a chicken?

Near the end of the cooking so that high heat won't scorch the pepper.

What is the best way to get coating to stick to the chicken?

Chilling the coated parts for thirty minutes to an hour before cooking.

Barbecuing

What causes so many home-barbecued chickens to be black-crusted and bitter?

This comes mainly from the sauce. High heat readily burns the sugar, a major sauce ingredient. The sauce may also have lots of spices that become bitter when scorched.

How should BBQ sauce be added?

1. Brush on the sauce only 15 minutes before finishing cooking.
2. Use more cooking time and less heat, at least 4–6″ above the briquettes.
3. The thicker the food, the greater the distance it should be from the coals, and therefore the longer the cooking time.

Chicken Stock

What is chicken stock?

Made from chicken meat, it is clear and generally served as a soup. If it is made with a combination of bones and meat, it has a milder flavor and is more full-bodied than the stock made from just meat because of the effect of gelatin from the bones.

How is stock used?

It serves as a base for sauces or soups.

What are steps in making chicken stock?

1. Rinse the bones, blanching them if frozen.
2. Combine the bones with cold water.
3. Bring them slowly to a boil.
4. Add a mirepoix (a mixture) of vegetables, spices and salt.
5. Simmer for about 5 hours.
6. Skim the surface as necessary.
7. Strain, cool, de-fat and store.

What does blanching a chicken do when making chicken stock?

The blanching will keep the chicken from releasing foam into the stock.

What is a good way to save leftover chicken stock?

Freeze in ice cube trays, then put the cubes in a plastic bag. When a recipe calls for bouillon cubes thaw as many as desired in the microwave.

DUCK

What are the two main varieties of duck found on the market?

Muscovy: Very popular, lean, limited availability, most often available as packaged breasts. A South American variety that weighs more than the pekin, about 4 pounds. Its meat is gamier and fatter.

White pekin: Also called Long Island, low fat with lean meat, mild flavored with a generous breast size. It is most readily available.

How do wild and domesticated ducks differ?

Wild birds are often gamey in flavor and very low in fat.

Why is trussing not necessary for ducks?

Because they have very short legs.

What are some sauces that go with duck?

Olive, orange, red currant (bigarade), plum, tomato, herb, wine. These sauces should be full-flavored.

Can a duck be microwaved?

Do about ¾ of the cooking in the microwave and then finish in a very hot oven.

How should wild ducks be handled prior to use?

Wild ducks are best hung refrigerated several days before using, even as much as a week.

How should wild ducks be prepared?

1. They often require basting to overcome the gaminess and the use of a rich sauce, such as a fruit sauce or one that is rich with herbs and spices, to handle the low fat level.
2. Rub with lemon juice.
3. Fill the cavity with onions, celery or citrus fruits.

What is the average weight of a farm-raised duck?

About 3–6 pounds.

How many servings should a 3-pound duck give?

Five to six or more.

How should you shop for a duck?

1. Look for one that is small for the variety.
2. Select a fleshy, broad-breasted, fairly plump bird.
3. The skin should be elastic, not soggy.
4. If frozen, make sure the package is complete, not broken, and that there are no signs of thawing.

How should domestic birds be prepared for cooking?

1. They are fatter than wild ducks, so remove as much fat as possible.
2. Rinse the bird and then dry with paper towels.
3. Puncture the skin all over without cutting into the flesh so fat can escape.
4. Refrigerate overnight, uncovered, to dry.

How should duck be stored?

Refrigerated: Loosely covered, with the giblets removed, for 2–3 days.
Frozen: Thaw in the refrigerator.

What is the purpose of stuffing a duck?

To reduce the fat in the meat and mainly to flavor the bird, not to create an edible stuffing since the stuffing will absorb too much fat from the bird.

How should a duck be prepared for roasting?

1. If frozen, thaw in the refrigerator for 1–2 days.
2. Remove the giblets and the neck fat.
3. Rinse the bird and dry.
4. Gently scratch the skin lengthwise with a sharp knife to aid in the basting process.
5. Prick the skin all over at one inch intervals.
6. Stuff only a short time before roasting.

Why should the skin be pricked before roasting?

The juices and fats can escape to the surface where they will caramelize in the heat and coat the skin with flavor and crispness.

How should the duck be roasted?

1. Roast in a 350° oven for 30–40 minutes per pound.
2. Basting is unnecessary for farm-raised fowl, because they are so fatty.

What precaution should be taken when cooking wild duck?

Don't overcook. Like all game birds, they can easily become dried out if overcooked.

Will basting be enough to ensure moistness in a wild duck during roasting?

No. The birds are often so lean that they need to be barded with a layer of fat.

What is barding?

Covering the breast with salt pork or bacon.

When is the roasting complete?

The breast should register 165 °F for medium and 180 °F for well-done. Before carving, let it rest on a warm platter, covered loosely with foil for about 15–20 minutes.

Are duckling breasts high in calories?

A hundred grams of skinless meat will have 140 calories, with 2.5 grams of fat. In comparison, a comparable serving of chicken breast will have 165 and 4, a trimmed beef sirloin 209 and 9.

How can the duck breasts be prepared for cooking?

Deeply score the skin in a diamond pattern.

What should be the color of a duckling breast when properly prepared?

Just pink.

What is the cooking time for sautéing a 4–6-ounce skinless, duckling breast?

From 4–6 minutes per side over medium heat, a little longer for well-done.

How long should a breast be left before slicing?

About 3–4 minutes to allow the meat to equalize in temperature and minimize the loss of moisture.

How can the duck be deboned after roasting and resting?

1. With the bird breast down, insert the tip of a sharp knife into the neck cavity and cut through the wishbone.
2. Then turn the bird over so the breast is up.
3. Cut along the breastbone, following the contour of the rib cage.
4. Where the wing comes out of the socket, cut through and continue cutting along the bird towards the thigh joint.
5. Gently pull the thigh bone out of its socket.

Poultry

6. Continue cutting until one-half of the duckling has been removed from the carcass.

7. Remove the wing portions.

8. Repeat the procedure on the other side.

GOOSE

What should you look for in selecting a goose?

1. The breast should be plump, meaty and symmetrical.

2. The younger the goose, the more tender the meat, so choose one that is small for its variety.

How big a bird is needed?

Since geese have a lot of fat, figure at least one dressed pound is needed per diner. For a holiday occasion, figure 1–2 pounds per person.

How long will it take to defrost a frozen goose?

Up to four days in the refrigerator.

What are preparation rules to follow before cooking a goose?

1. Have the bird at room temperature.

2. Slip your finger underneath the skin between the fat and the meat (not next to the skin for it might tear) and press gently on the fat. This is called ballooning when done by pumping in air. This will separate the fat from the skin so it will be released more easily.

3. Cut away with scissors or pull out the fat pockets in the body cavity and discard.

4. There is more than enough fat to make a bread stuffing too heavy. Stuffing with lemon wedges, prunes, apples, parsley and the like will heighten the flavor but absorb so much fat that it is best discarded.

5. Don't stuff the neck cavity. That will allow the fat to drain better.

6. Season with salt and pepper.

7. Punch the skin all over with a sharp fork to allow the fat to escape.

How should the goose be roasted unstuffed?

1. Start at a low temperature and finish on high.

2. There is no need to baste since there is plenty of fat.

3. Roast in a preheated 375 °F oven for 20 minutes, plus 20 minutes per pound. Thus a 6-pound bird would need 6 × 20 minutes plus 20 minutes more = 140 minutes, or 2⅓ hours.

What is another approach?

1. Put in a preheated 475 °F oven on a rack, unstuffed.

2. After a half hour, spoon the melted fat out of the pan.

Poultry

3. Repeat the de-fatting after another 40 minutes.
4. Turn the oven off but keep the oven door closed.
5. Let the goose continue to cook in the retained heat for 1 hour. Pour off the remaining fat. The goose will be done.

How does stuffing affect the cooking time?

Add four minutes per pound if stuffed.

What can be done to get a crisp skin?

Raise the oven temperature to 400 °F a half hour before finishing the roast.

TURKEY

How much does a 12-pound turkey actually weigh?

After removing the packaging, giblets, tail piece and allowing the bird to drain, there could be a variation from the sticker weight as much as 1½ pounds. If you calculate timing for a 12-pound bird that is actually closer to 10 pounds, then, allowing 20–25 minutes per pound, the bird could be done 40–50 minutes earlier.

How big a turkey should you buy?

Figure about 1½–2 pounds of whole turkey per person. Thus, for ten people a bird of 15–20 pounds is adequate, larger if the focus is having leftovers. It also depends on how many side dishes will accompany it. The larger the turkey, the lower percentage of the weight is bone, so the more there is for eating.

What is the advantage of serving two smaller birds?

1. Two small ones will give more wings, thighs, drumsticks, giblets and will require a shorter cooking time.
2. The younger the bird, the more tender it is and the more elegant the flavor.

What are the drawbacks of smaller birds?

1. Smaller birds have a higher bone to meat ratio than large birds, therefore, using two small birds will cost more per usable pound than using one large bird.
2. Two younger birds are apt to cost more.
3. Two birds are sometimes difficult to handle in a small oven.

How should a frozen bird be stored?

1. Don't remove the wrapper.
2. Keep in the freezer until 2–3 days before using.
3. Thaw in the refrigerator.

How should a nonfrozen turkey be handled?

1. Remove the giblets and neck (usually stored wrapped together in the body cavity).
2. Rinse and pat dry with paper towels.
3. Refrigerate at or below 40 °F. Don't keep longer than three days, less is preferable.

What should be done to prepare the bird for roasting?

1. Have the turkey at room temperature.
2. Don't stuff the bird until just before roasting, as late as possible.
3. Season before stuffing.

Should the turkey breast be covered with foil while roasting?

It is not recommended, as this will trap the steam and prevent the skin from crisping, but if foil is used, crinkle it so that it is not laying flat on the skin.

What is an alternative to foil covering?

A better alternative to foil would be a double layer of cheesecloth that has been soaked in melted butter, which would eliminate the need for frequent basting.

How long should stuffing be baked if baked separately?

1. Cook in a casserole until a metal skewer inserted into the center of the stuffing is hot to touch.
2. An instant-read thermometer in the center should read 165 °F.

How should leftover stuffing be handled?

Scoop leftover stuffing out of turkey and refrigerate separately.

What are the advantages and disadvantages of cooking the stuffing separately?

Baking separately will reduce the cooking time and make it easier to handle, but dressing cooked inside the bird will have a special flavor that is much desired.

How much stuffing is necessary?

10-pound bird	8 cups
15-pound bird	12 cups
20-pound bird	16 cups

How should leftovers be refrigerated?

Double wrap them, to prevent drying out.

Should leftover turkey be boned before refrigeration?

No. Keeping the bones in will keep the flesh moister.

What is the advantage of a disposable roasting pan?

It doesn't have to be washed, just thrown away.

What are the disadvantages of the disposable?

1. They are often not sturdy enough, so that they bend easily. This can be overcome by using two of them, one inside the other.
2. Most of these pans can't be put on the stove burner for gravy preparation.

Are pop-up timers a good deal for turkeys?

1. They are often broken when the bird is handled.
2. The leg timers are calibrated to pop up at 178 °F, which will result in the legs being well-done and the breast meat overcooked.
3. Breast timers that are sold separately are calibrated for 163 °F, which will give better results.

What indicator is best?

Rely on an instant-read thermometer. The stuffing should read 165 °F.

Are ground turkey products low in fat content?

Read the label! Some brands have almost as much fat as equivalent lean beef.

What are pen-raised wild turkeys?

They are genetically wild but are raised in barns on generic feed and so taste more like domesticated birds.

Poultry

CHAPTER NINE

SEAFOOD

Which seafoods do Americans like least?

Squid, shark and snails.

What is Bombay duck?

This is not a duck but comes from the Bumalo, a smelt-sized lizard fish off the coast of India. It is served dried with curries.

What is Asian fish sauce?

It is made from fermented fish from southern Asia, especially Thailand and Vietnam. Look for anchovies on the label, for that is a sign of better quality.

Are all shellfish cholesterol builders and therefore bad for the heart?

No! Some shellfish, such as squid and shrimp, are high in cholesterol, but those that primarily feed on microscopic plant life, for example, the bivalves (mussels, scallops, clams, oysters), are not. More importantly, all shellfish are very low in both total fat and saturated fat.

What is imitation shellfish?

It is a look-alike made from mild, flavored fish, which has been processed to remove color and flavor and then recolored and flavored. Usually has a high sodium content. Most are not very tasty.

How much whole fish should be bought per person to be served?

About 1–1½ pounds per person. About 45% of a whole fish will be edible. Thus a 2-pound fish will yield slightly less than 1 pound, which is equal to two servings.

What should you look for when selecting a fish market?

1. The market should have a brisk business and thus have a fast turnover.
2. It should be spotlessly clean and well maintained.
3. It should be free from fishy odors.
4. The fish is separated from seafood in the refrigerated counters to reduce the chance of bacterial cross contamination.
5. Whole fish should be well iced with ice that is clean and white, which will indicate that the ice is changed regularly. The fish should be practically buried in the ice.
6. The market cuts its own fish, and the fish servers are knowledgeable about their product.

What is the effect of air on frozen seafood?

1. It will dehydrate it by drawing out moisture, thus diminishing flavor.
2. Causes freezer burn.
3. The oxygen of the air reacts with the oil of the fish or seafood, especially oily fish such as tuna and salmon, which then causes a rancid, unpleasant, sour flavor.

What should be looked for when buying frozen seafood?

1. Avoid any with white or yellow spots, which indicate freezer burn.
2. Make sure that the packaging completely encloses the product and that there are no holes or abrasions or signs of rough handling.
3. If the food has been vacuum packed there will be a clear view for inspection.
4. Check to see how it has been handled. Frost on the package is a good indication that there has been at least partial thawing during storage or handling.

How should IQF packages be chosen?

IQF (instant quick frozen) fish should not clump together if properly stored, with the exception of very small shrimp, which may clump even if properly handled.

Where does most viral and bacterial disease from shellfish originate?

In sewage-polluted waters on the East Coast. Shellfish harvested from such waters are often contaminated.

What should be the preparation for pan steaming?

1. Select fish that aren't too thick (½″ or less for fillets, and if thicker, sauté before steaming).
2. Before starting to cook, chop or slice all the vegetables to a size that will cook quickly.
3. Have everything in place, including seasoning.
4. Shell seafood and debone all fish before starting.

How should pan steaming be done?

1. Use a heavy pan or skillet, since there needs to be heat retention at the end to continue the cooking off the heat source. If using an electric stove (with coil heater) the pan should be moved away from the heat.

2. Set the pan over high heat.

3. Add a couple of tablespoons of oil.

4. Wait 2 minutes, or until a drop of water bounces around when it hits the oil. Make oil even hotter for scallops, since they should be browned.

5. Briefly sauté the fish or seafood together with the ingredients that need more cooking time, such as onions.

6. Ingredients that don't need much cooking time, such as red onions or citrus slices, should be added just before covering the pan.

7. Cover the pan with a tightly fitting lid and steam until done.

What happens to shellfish when they are overcooked?

The flesh will toughen.

What can be done when sautéing shellfish and too much liquid is released into the pan?

Remove the seafood temporarily with a slotted spoon, cook the liquid until it reduces to the desired consistency, then return the seafood and finish cooking.

UNIVALVES (GASTROPODS)

What are univalves?

Creatures with a single shell and single muscle.

What are the main univalves?

Abalone and sea urchins.

What are the colors of abalone?

Black, pink, red or green.

Where are abalone found?

Mainly in the Pacific area with limited availability.

How should fresh abalone be chosen?

It should not have a fishy aroma, and the relatively smaller ones should be chosen.

How is it prepared?

It should be pounded to tenderize and then briefly sautéd (30 seconds at most) per side. The extra large ones should be flattened.

SQUID AND OCTOPUS (CEPHALOPODS)

What are cephalopods?

Creatures with the tentacles or arms attached directly to the head.

What do you look for in squid?

Get fresh ones, not frozen, that are semifirm, slime-free and with the purple dappled outer membrane reasonably intact.

How are squid prepared for cooking?

Remove the quill by pulling it out.

Do squid need to be cooked?

Young squid are tender enough to be eaten raw, but most of us prefer them cooked or at least marinated.

How do you cook young squid and still keep it tender?

Cook a young one very quickly at high heat (sautéd or fried) only to augment the flavor. Sauté or fry for no more than a minute or two, for longer than that toughens the meat.

What can you do if you over-cook squid?

If over-cooked, cook an additional twenty minutes or more to regain tenderness, for there is a rubber-like phase that occurs between instant and long cooking.

Is it necessary to remove the ink sac?

No, that is optional. The ink can give a briny taste. Most cooks do remove it, however, and if they use the ink, they incorporate it into a sauce.

How should mature squid be cooked?

1. Mature squid should not be sautéd or fried but rather gently simmered for 20 minutes to 2 hours, depending on the thickness of the pieces.
2. They can also be deep fried or stuffed and braised.

How should squid be handled in the microwave?

They shouldn't be microwaved, because they will get tough.

How are octopus usually sold?

Cleaned of ink and beak.

How should octopus be cooked?

1. It needs long cooking (boiling or steaming) to become tender.
2. Wine or vegetables in the fluid are good additions.

How should octopus be served?

Cut into bite-size pieces and serve warm with a sauce or cold in a salad.

BIVALVES

Why are oysters, clams, mussels and scallops known as bivalves?

Because they have two shells that are hinged together with a small, strong adductor muscle for opening and closing the shells.

Why are bivalves known as filter feeders?

They ingest about 100 gallons of water a day in order to filter out the one-celled organisms that are their food. This is why they must come from certified waters. Anyone selling live bivalves in the shell must have a certificate to that effect.

Why should you buy a few more bivalves than the recipe calls for?

Because a few might have to be discarded. Use firmly closed shells, or, if open, they should close tightly when squeezed or rapped on the counter. Discard those that remain open or have cracked or broken shells.

When should mussels, clams and oysters be purchased?

They should be bought the day they are to be used and should be the last purchase of the day.

How should mussels and oysters be stored?

1. Refrigerate immediately on arriving home.
2. Store the mussels and oysters in a colander nested in a bowl that is covered with a damp cloth.

How is the storage of clams different from that of mussels and oysters?

Store the clams without the damp cloth.

What happens if you store them in fresh water?

Never put them in fresh water, as that will kill them.

How long will they keep?

They will keep for 5–7 days at the proper temperature, 34–40 °F, but are best cooked and eaten within a day or so.

Clams

How should clams be selected?

1. Make sure hard-shelled clams are tightly closed.
2. If they aren't, then snap the shell with your finger and, if still alive, it will close.
3. If they float, discard them.
4. Select those that are small for their variety to get the most tender and delicately flavored ones.
5. Once opened, the liquid inside should be clear, not cloudy.

How should they be cooked?

1. Cook at low heat to prevent toughening.
2. Add to chowder or stews at the end of the cooking to preserve the texture.

Which should be used for making chowder?

In making clam soup use fresh or frozen, not canned clams. Add minced clams only at the last minutes of cooking. Simmer, don't boil the soup, or clams will toughen.

Do clams need to be purged of sand and grit?

1. Yes, if you harvest them yourself.
2. No, if commercially sold, for then they are usually purged before reaching the market.

How can clams be purged?

Soak in a generous amount of lightly salted water with a couple of tablespoons of flour or cornmeal stirred in. After a few hours the clams will have purged themselves of sand.

What does it mean if the shells don't open while cooking?

It indicates that the clams were not alive in the first place.

Is wine a good addition to a clam sauce?

It works well with the juice but does add flavor to cooked clams, so use in moderation and use wines without intense flavors.

What are geoducks?

Large Pacific Coast soft-shell clams with a rich flavor.

Mussels

How do you select them?

1. Choose the smallest of the variety and even sized for even cooking.
2. Avoid very heavy ones, because they may be full of sand.
3. Avoid very light ones for their size, because they may be dead or dying. Also avoid ones with broken shells.
4. If an open shell doesn't close when lightly tapped, don't buy it.
5. Rope-cultured mussels are grit-free but they are often more expensive.

When is the best time for mussels?

Mussels are the meatiest before they spawn, so the best time is October to May.

Seafood

How many mussels should be bought?

About 12–15 medium sized mussels per person for a main course, with a few extra so that any dead ones can be thrown out. Mussels are heavy, so count, don't depend on weight.

How can you tell the sex of a mussel?

Female mussels have orange colored flesh, males, white.

Are mussels poisonous?

No. They can absorb toxins from contaminated water or when the level of plankton in the water is high. Watch for Public Health warning signs (mainly May through October). Those offered on the commercial market will be safe. Most do come from mussel farms and are not harmful.

What is the beard of a mussel?

The beard is a small bundle of dark fibers the mussel uses to attach itself to its home base as it grows. They are not harmful but not tasty either.

What should be done with the beard?

Remove it just before cooking with the aid of a small knife or a scissors. If there is no beard then it was probably removed by the processor in a way that didn't negatively affect the tissue.

How should they be stored?

1. For as short a time as possible.
2. Refrigerated.
3. Put in a strainer or perforated bowl, which is set on a bed of ice.
4. Store mussels in a single layer for best results.

How should mussels be prepared for cooking?

1. Soak in cold water (⅓ cup salt per gallon of water) for an hour or two so that they will extrude their internal sand. Wild ones (as opposed to rope-cultured) sometimes need several soakings to clean them.
2. Scrub well under running water.
3. Discard the beard.

How should they be cooked?

1. Steam gently in broth (or wine) until the shells pop open and the meat inside is plumped. If overcooked they will be tough.
2. They make wonderful soups.
3. Broil with garlic butter.
4. Don't over-cook.

Oysters

What are the main varieties of oysters?

Atlantic: From all along the Eastern seaboard, difficult to open, mild, fresh briny flavor.

European: Better known as belons, a slightly metallic (coppery) flavor.

Olympia: From the Pacific Northwest, very small, soft texture.

Pacific: From the West Coast, mainly toward the north, easy to open, strong somewhat fruity flavor.

What is the nutritive value of oysters?

They contain vitamins, phosphorus salts, chalk, iron, copper and manganese that are easily assimilated by the human body.

Is it ok to buy/eat oysters in warm weather?

When the water in which the oysters are growing warms they tend to be soft and bland in taste rather than firm and bright tasting. While not at their best for eating raw, the softer ones are excellent cooked or barbequed. Often the oysters offered in stores in summer come from the far north where the seawater has not warmed.

What amount of oysters should be bought per person?

About ½ to ⅔ pound per person.

How should oysters be bought and handled?

1. Live oysters should be as fresh as possible.
2. Choose ones with intact, not broken, shells.
3. Avoid those whose shells are not closed, unless they close when tapped with a fingernail.
4. Choose the smaller oyster of the species.

What should be looked for if the oysters are shucked (out of shell)?

1. They should be uniform in size once shucked, smell fresh, be plump.
2. The liquid from them should not be cloudy but rather clear or slightly opalescent.

What happens if you soak oysters in club soda for about 5 minutes?

The oyster will usually be more easily removed from the shell.

What should be done to oysters before opening?

Thoroughly scrub them under running water with a brush to remove all sand and dirt.

What happens if they are overcooked?

They toughen.

Scallops

What are the kinds of scallops?

1. Sea: The meat is about 1½" in diameter. The most common type.
2. Bay: Small, about ½" in diameter. The tenderest and best tasting but most expensive.
3. Calico: Small. Often sold as bay scallops, but they are not as sweet or as flavorful as bays.
4. Diver: Scallops harvested by hand, not dredged, coming mostly from the Maine coast. Of excellent quality. Not soaked in phosphate solution for marketing.

Why are bay scallops the most expensive?

They are the most tender and delicious, about ½" in diameter, more succulent, sweeter and less chewy, and they are not as abundant.

How do some merchants cheat customers with regard to selling scallops?

1. They soak their sea scallops so that they will weigh more.
2. They cut sea scallops to the size of bay scallops so they can charge more.

How should you choose scallops?

They should smell ocean fresh and be plump and resilient when pressed.

What are processed scallops?

Scallops that have been treated with a phosphate/citric acid mixture to inhibit discoloration and extend shelf life. They will be exceptionally white and sitting in a pool of their secreted water. Dry or fresh scallops will be beige or ivory. They sometimes are sitting in their juices.

Should scallops be frozen?

They freeze well and are good eating when thawed.

Why are calico scallops so white when offered for sale in the market?

Because they are steamed to open them.

Should you buy scallops in the shell or shucked?

Unlike clams, oysters or mussels that can remain live and healthy out of the water, scallops die quickly when harvested, so they are usually sold out of the shell.

How should they be prepared?

To prepare, peel off and discard any white membrane, if any, that originally held the flesh to the shell.

How do you keep scallops from getting tough when you cook them?

1. First, dry them with paper toweling, then quickly sear them in butter or oil to seal in the internal juices.

2. Don't over-cook. Once seared, reduce the heat to moderate. Bay scallops need to cook only two to three minutes, depending on their thickness. Use minimal shortening.

3. Try to get uniformly sized scallops so they will cook evenly or cut them vertically to make them equal in size.

CRUSTACEANS

Crabs

What are the types of crabs?

There are 4,000 species of crab, of which 4 are generally seen in our markets.

Which are the main ones are found in the United States?

Dungeness: Hard-shelled, found on the West Coast from Washington down through mid-California.

King: Hard-shelled, found off the coast of Alaska, large with a spread of two feet or so. Most often the claws are the only part sold.

Soft-shell: Found on the East Coast and Gulf from New Jersey (blue crab) south and on the Gulf Coast to Texas.

Stone: From Florida, with very hard shells that must be hammered to crack. Their pink and white claws tipped with black are the only part eaten.

What should be the characteristics of cooked crabs?

The cooked shells should be a bright red color, not orange, and the crab should have little or no odor.

What should be done if the gills are spongy?

Discard them, they are diseased.

How should cooked crabs be displayed in the market?

They should be displayed on a bed of ice.

How should live crabs be stored?

Keep in the refrigerator up to 24 hours, but not in water or on ice or in an airtight container. Temperature of 40 °F is excellent for hard-shelled crabs, 50–55 °F for soft-shelled.

What are soft-shell crabs?

They are blue crabs (*Callinectas sapidus*), which shed their hard outer shell eighteen times during their 3-year life span, as they mature and outgrow each shell.

When are they available?

They are available fresh from May through September and all year when frozen. They will keep frozen about a year. Best if bought alive with soft, moist shells.

How long will fresh ones keep?

If fresh they should be used within a couple of days at most.

How should frozen ones be thawed?

If frozen, they thaw quickly in the refrigerator. Don't thaw them under cold running water as they easily break apart. Remove spongy gills where shell comes to a point.

How should they be cooked?

1. Sauté, deep fry, grill or broil but don't cook in the microwave.
2. They do well when basted or coated with a batter or dusted with flour.

Are crabs better when boiled or steamed?

They can be done either way, but steaming results in a better, less watery taste.

What are the grades of crabmeat?

Lump: Large chunks, good for salads.
Backfin: Smaller chunks.
Flake: Smaller pieces still, good for soufflés, least expensive.

What should be done before serving crabmeat?

Pick over carefully for small pieces of shell.

Should crab be served hot or cold?

Either way: warm with melted butter or at room temperature, with mayonnaise or lemon or just plain.

What is the yield of edible meat from a Dungeness crab?

About 20%.

What is the Dungeness crab season?

Since only the males are kept, the season is over when the males have been cleared from the spawning grounds. This means a short season for locals (San Francisco) but it is extended as the fisherman move north. Its starts in early fall and goes into spring.

What are crab cakes?

Crabmeat, freshly chopped, mixed with salt, pepper and beaten eggs, which is shaped into small patties and fried in butter. There are, however, numerous variations in ingredients (for example, onions and green peppers).

What are some other ways crab can be prepared?

1. Stir-fried with black bean sauce.
2. In crêpes.

3. In soup.

4. With pasta.

What is the advantage of the male crab?

It is best for the white meat of the claw.

What about the female?

For the pink coral (roe, or eggs).

What can be done if canned crabmeat has a metallic taste?

Soak for a few minutes in iced water, then drain and pat dry.

Lobsters

How can you identify a true lobster?

Only a true lobster has two hard-shell, forward claws.

Are lobsters left-handed, right-handed or ambidexterous?

They can be either left- or right-handed. The larger claw has coarse teeth for heavy-duty crushing jobs. The smaller claw is for lighter ripping or tearing tasks. A lobster is left-handed or right-handed, depending on which side has the larger claw.

Is this an important factor in selecting for purchase?

No.

Which claw tastes better?

1. The smaller is sweeter and more tender, thus superior.

2. The larger has more meat and provides a taste contrast.

How can you tell whether a lobster is male or female?

1. The swimmerets under the tail are fringed with hair in the female but hairless and pointed in the male. The tail is broader in the female.

2. If pink roe appears along the tail during cooking, it is female.

Are lobsters poor in nutrition?

No. There is only 0.8 gram of fat per 3 ounces of cooked meat, which is about a quarter as much as found in an equivalent amount of skinless chicken breast.

Why is a wooden peg placed in the hinge of a lobster claw or a rubber band placed around the claws?

1. Mainly to prevent the lobsters in a tank from destroying each other.

2. To protect the human hands that have to handle them.

What is the yield of edible meat from an unshelled lobster?

It varies with size, but a 1-pound lobster will yield 3–4 ounces of cooked meat.

What are the main kinds of lobsters on the American market?

With claws:	From New England or France (Brittany).
Without claws:	From California, Florida, South Africa, Australia. These are also called spiny or rock lobsters and also langouste. They all taste good but are not true lobsters.

Are crayfish (crawfish) a type of lobster?

No, they are a species of freshwater crustacean that look like a cross between a shrimp and a lobster, and in size, between the two. They are sold in United States markets under various names, including South African Lobster Tails or Rock Lobster. They have a green thread along the length of the tail that should be removed.

What is the green material inside a lobster, and is it good to eat?

The green liver is called tomalley. Although there are some who are afraid that it contains small amounts of dioxin, it is prized for eating by many and apparently imparts no harm.

What is the pink material?

The roe, or eggs (called coral), from the female. Edible and is especially used to color and flavor sauces.

Is coral like caviar, eaten raw?

No, cooking changes it from greenish black and firms its structure, making it more edible.

How do you select lobsters?

1. They are best when the shells are fully hardened, in late spring, but are good to eat during other months.
2. Make sure it is still alive, for pathogenic organisms can contaminate the flesh within a few hours of its death.
3. If you have questions as to whether it is alive, pick it up by its back. If the tail doesn't curl under the body, it is dead or practically so.
4. It should smell sweet, without any off-odor.

Do larger lobsters have tougher meat?

Toughness doesn't vary with size.

What should be the concern if lobsters are kept in a market tank?

They are sometimes there for a week or more and diminish in quality of flavor over time.

What should be done with lobsters before cooking?

Soak them in cold water for a couple of hours and they will expel sand and waste.

Seafood

What is the yield of an unshelled lobster?

Four lobsters, 1½ pounds each, yield about 2⅔ cups cooked meat.

What are cooking rules for lobsters?

1. Don't overcook or the meat will end up dry, tough, stringy and shrunken.
2. If to be eaten cold then slightly undercook.

What is the cooking time?

1. After you put a 1-pound lobster in a pot of water, simmer it for only about 6–7 minutes plus 3 minutes for each additional pound.
2. Cooking time when steaming is less critical than when boiling.

How should frozen tails be used?

If you are using frozen tails (from South Africa or Australia, not the true lobster and not as sweet and tender), thaw them overnight in the refrigerator to prevent them from being very tough and dry.

What is necessary when broiling lobsters?

When broiling, baste it often with butter (or flavored butter) to keep the flesh moist and tender.

How should lobsters be steamed?

1. This method is recommended because little of the flavor elements will leach out.
2. Rinse the lobster in cool, running water.
3. Remove the elastic band or peg holding the claws.
4. Put the lobster(s) in the steam pot on their backs.
5. Cover the pot and turn up the heat.
6. Cook 7 minutes at high heat for a ½–1 pound lobster.
7. If large (2 pounds or more) cook 10 minutes.
8. If stacked in the pot more than three or four high then cook 10 minutes.

How should they be prepared for poaching?

1. Poaching yields denser and tenderer meat.
2. Bring to a boil a court-bouillon (a liquid flavored with vegetables, herbs, wine etc.).
3. Rinse the lobster briefly.
4. Remove the elastic band or wooden peg and immerse lobsters in liquid.
5. If necessary, add more liquid to completely cover.

How should they be poached?

1. Have heat at its highest until the liquid is back to a simmer, then reduce the heat to the barest simmer, which means just an occasional small bubble.
2. Cook about 12 minutes.

3. Turn off the heat and let set for 2 minutes more.

4. Remove from the pot and cool slightly before shelling.

How can you prepare and grill a lobster to get a light, smoky flavor?

1. Poach or steam first for about 5 minutes.

2. Cool and shell without breaking up the shell.

3. Cut the meat into large pieces.

4. Marinate briefly with herb butter or rice vinegar, oil and garlic.

5. Lightly oil the outside of the shells with vegetable oil.

6. Pile the meat back inside.

How should they be grilled?

1. Put the lobsters on the far side of the grill (away from the coals).

2. Cover the grill, baste frequently, and let cook until the heat has penetrated to the center of the meat, discerned by putting a small knife blade into the meat, withdrawing it and feel the temperature of the blade.

How can you tell when the lobster is done cooking?

1. Pull its feeler (the stem-like or needle-like protuberance in the head). The feeler will come off easily if cooking is complete.

2. The shell will be red.

What can be done with lobster shells?

1. From the cooked lobster (or shrimp) simmer the shells, covered, with fish stock or white wine and vegetables, such as onions and carrots, and seasonings, such as bay leaf, tarragon and salt, to make a rich-tasting lobster or shrimp bisque.

2. Also, cracked shells can be added in preparation of a lobster sauce to give extra richness. Before serving they must be carefully strained out.

Shrimp

How many species of shrimp are there, and how many are on the American market?

There are 300 species of shrimp reported worldwide but 6 are most common in American markets.

What are the species found in American markets?

1. Gulf White: Most expensive and frequently the best. Wild or farm-raised. Usually grayish-white in color, similar in appearance to Gulf Brown, which are less desirable. Ask to see the box.

2. Gulf Pink: High quality; wild or farm-raised. Shell is usually redder than that of the whites, but may be light brown.

Seafood

3. Gulf Brown: Wild, most likely to taste of iodine. Tend to be reddish brown. Easy to confuse with Whites or Pinks.

4. Ecuadorian or Mexican White: More come from Ecuador than any other country. May be wild or farm-raised.

5. Black Tiger: From Asia, mainly farm-raised. Dark gray with black stripes and red feelers or bluish with yellow feelers. Turn pink when cooked. Inconsistent but frequently quite flavorful and firm.

6. Chinese White: Asian farm-raised with grayish white color, soft, sometimes watery and mild flavored. Usually inexpensive.

What is the difference between prawns and shrimp?

Both are from the same family and the terms are used loosely. In the United States common usage is to use prawns for the larger ones and shrimp for the smaller. There is only one native American prawn variety, and it is found in the southeast part of the country (although it is now cultivated in Hawaii) but not many are on the market. Anything from extra large up might easily be called prawns in the market.

How are shrimp graded?

By size or count.

How must Gulf Brown Shrimp be handled to maintain their color?

They don't maintain their color. They automatically turn pink when cooked.

How are shrimp sizes defined?

Small (50 per pound)

Medium (43–50 per pound)

Medium large (36–42 per pound)

Large (31–35 per pound)

Extra large (26–30 per pound)

Jumbo (21–25 per pound)

Extra jumbo (16–20 per pound)

Colossal (10–15 per pound)

Extra colossal (fewer than 10 per pound)

What are the rules for shrimp grades?

There are few rules governing the sale of shrimp, but the grading is by weight. The terms "small," "medium," "large," "extra large" and "jumbo" are subjective and relative. Small shrimp, i.e., those that are seventy or so to the pound, are often labeled medium.

Are fresh (that is never frozen) shrimp desirable?

If available, fresh are far tastier than the frozen ones, but few really fresh are found on the market.

How can you tell if shrimp have never been frozen and thawed?

While not an absolute indicator, the nonfrozen will be those that still have their heads attached.

How should you select shrimp?

1. First of all, smell them. They should be ocean fresh, not smell fishy or of ammonia. More than a slight iodine odor suggests that iodine was used as a preservative or that the shrimp are not fresh.
2. Frozen are a better buy.
3. The jumbo size (incorrectly called prawns) cost more than the small ones, but the smaller ones are usually more tender and subtly flavored.
4. They should have no black spots or edges (melanosis) on their shells, since that would indicate that the meat has begun to breakdown. Be equally suspicious of those with yellowing shells or those that feel gritty, either of which may indicate the use of sodium bisulfite, a bleaching agent sometimes used to remove melanosis.
5. Thawed shrimp should smell of salt water, be firm and fully fill their shells.
6. They should be firm if thawed and/or cooked.

How can you check for proper labeling?

Either have the purchase weighed or look for indicators such as 16/20 or U-20. The first requires that there be between 16 and 20 shrimp per pound. U-20 requires that there be fewer than 20 per pound.

What considerations should be made in deciding which to buy?

1. The smaller, the less expensive.
2. The smaller are a nuisance to peel, although they tend to be sweeter.
3. They should be firm if thawed and/or cooked.

What is the best all around combination?

The best combination of flavor, value and ease of peeling are those that yield from 15 to 30 per pound.

Is it necessary to devein shrimp?

It is not necessary to devein a shrimp for health's sake, but they do look better deveined. Remember that the intestinal vein is not the black nerve cord than runs down the inside curve but rather the one that runs down the exterior curve. The dark vein, while unsightly, can also have gritty material in it.

How can shrimp be deveined?

1. Hold the shrimp under a slow stream of cold water.
2. Run the tip of an ice pick down the back of the shrimp.
3. This will leave the shrimp clean and whole.

Where is the flavor of shrimp located?

In the shell, and this is then absorbed by the flesh during cooking.

Should they be shelled before cooking?

1. The shell does enhance the flavor if left on during the cooking process. After the shrimp are cooked the shell can then be removed or left on for the diner to do the job. There is a difference in appearance and ease of eating when the shell is left on.
2. When cooked in liquid, such as a sauce or stock, remove the shell first.
3. When grilled or sautéd, cook with the shell on.
4. Unshelled shrimp need to simmer only 3–6 minutes, shelled should simmer 2–5 minutes, depending on their size. They are done when the shells or the shelled flesh starts to turn pink.

How should they be cooked in liquids?

1. Simmer, don't boil them, as the boiling will toughen the flesh, as will overcooking.
2. Or, better yet, bring the water to a boil, take it off the heat, add the shrimp, let stand for 10 minutes or less and then drain.

What is a good procedure to follow to achieve tenderness and a good sauce?

Low-heat braising, which will also prevent garlic (if used) from becoming bitter.

What happens when shrimp are over-cooked?

They become tough and briny.

What is another cause of toughness?

Marinating in too acidic a marinade.

How can you avoid toughness when cooking shrimp?

1. Soak in very cold water for 1–2 minutes.
2. Then place in a deep pot with a small amount of salt.
3. Cover with rapidly boiling water and cover the pot tightly.
4. For large shrimp it will take about 5–7 minutes, for medium sized, about 4 minutes to cook.

How can the flavor of canned shrimp be improved?

Soak the can in iced water for at least one hour before opening.

How can you use shrimp shells?

1. To enrich stock.
2. Pureed with butter and lemon juice for shrimp batter.

What is a good way to defrost frozen, unshelled shrimp?

Soak in brine (a salt solution), which will give good flavor as well as result in less weight loss. Use 2 cups of salt for 2 pounds of shrimp and leave in for about 45 minutes.

What happens if frozen shrimp are defrosted in a brine solution?

1. They will defrost faster than in the refrigerator.
2. They won't lose liquid or flavor.
3. They will gain plumpness and firmness.

How are dried shrimp used?

In cooking, particularly in sauces, to give a delicate flavor.

What should be looked for in dried shrimp?

Chose those with the brightest color (orange/pink). Avoid the grayish ones.

FISH

How long should it take frozen, wrapped fish to defrost in the refrigerator?

About six hours per pound.

What is scrod?

Young cod fish. Sometimes it is used as a name for cod.

What is the difference between flounder and sole?

In the United States and Canada the terms are used interchangeably. Petrale sole is one of the members of the flounder family.

Which are fat fish?

Butterfish, mackerel, pompano, porgy, sablefish, salmon (varies with the variety), sea herring, shad, tuna, whitefish.

Which are moderately fat fish?

Bonito, buffalo fish, carp, sea bass, striped bass, swordfish, trout.

Which are firm-fleshed fish?

Sturgeon, tuna, swordfish.

What is finnan haddie?

The fish (haddock) that has been boned, partially smoked and lightly salted.

What is a quenelle?

An oval ball of pureed fish (can also be meat or vegetables) made with eggs and/or fine crumbs and poached in stock. Usually served with a rich sauce.

What are delicately flavored fish?

Sole, orange roughy, herring, butterfish, sardines, smelt.

Seafood

Which are lean fish?

Angler, bluefish, catfish, cod, flounder, haddock, hake, halibut, ocean perch, orange roughy, porgy, red snapper, rockfish, shark, snapper.

How should a flatfish be gutted?

Cut around the head, pull the head twisting away from the body, and the guts will come out with the head.

What are ways of preserving fish?

Smoking, air-drying, salting, pickling, canning, freezing.

What adjustments should be made in cooking when braising fish (or shellfish)?

1. Use less cooking liquid.
2. Cook for a shorter time at a lower temperature.

What are kippers?

Smoked herring that are a favorite English breakfast specialty, or other fish fillets that are brine cured and cold smoked.

What must be done first when pickling fish?

First brine (salted water) the fish.

Why should only distilled vinegar be used in the pickling liquid?

Because the cider, fruit and flavored vinegars have variable acid (acetic) levels that vary considerably and also may result in an off-taste.

How can you tell if pickled fish being dried are dry enough?

Pinch a thick section, and if your fingers don't leave an impression, the fish can be packed away.

Selection

How good is the Food and Drug Administration's inspection of fish eaten in the United States?

1. Sixty percent of all fish eaten in the United States comes from 116 foreign countries, many with poor sanitation conditions.
2. Only 5% of the fish consumed are actually inspected by the U.S. FDA.
3. The United States has 25,000 fish processing plants: 79,000 fishing ships; fewer than 100 inspectors.
4. Most fresh fish and shellfish are never inspected.

Why is the flesh of a fish delicate compared with meat?

The muscles of mammals and birds are composed of very long fibers in bundles. The connective tissue is about 15% by weight in land animals. Fish muscles consist of rather short fibers separated by large sheets of very thin connective tissue, which is very fragile and easily converted to gelatin. Connective tissue is about 3% by weight. This is why fish meat is so tender and tends to fall apart when cooked.

How should the cooking method influence the selection of fish?

Choose the fat-fleshed fish for baking or broiling and lean types for simmering or steaming.

What is a fish fillet?

A boned piece from either side of the backbone. It may or may not have the skin still attached.

Is the difference in fat content of fish important for other reasons than diet?

Yes. Generally, the fatter the fish, the more flavorful it is, and also vitamins and other nutrients increase with fat content. Of course, the fat fish contain roughly twice the calories as the lean fish.

Does the depth at which the fish swim influence the type of fish?

As a general rule, the deeper in the water the fish lives, the leaner the fish. For example, tuna is a top dweller and fatter; sole and cod are bottom dwellers.

What are the caloric differences among different fish?

For 3.5 ounces of flesh here are some caloric examples:

Salmon, king	222	Carp	115
Salmon, pink	119	Bluefin tuna	145
Shad	170	Catfish	103
Lake trout	168	Halibut	100

What are the safest fish to eat?

Halibut, sole, skip jack and tuna, or commercially raised trout and turbot.

What is considered the highest quality Pacific Ocean fish for eating?

Petrale sole.

Why is fish so nutritious?

1. It is low in fat.
2. Its omega 3 fatty acids have an anticlotting effect and help limit blood triglycerides, a type of fat linked to heart disease.
3. They also help prevent the buildup of artery plugging plaques that block blood vessels leading to the heart.

What fish should you choose if you don't want lots of small bones?

Saltwater has a higher concentration of minerals and therefore higher specific density, thus the fish will have greater buoyancy in saltwater. This buoyancy will allow a saltwater fish to have a heavier bone structure. Therefore, choose ocean fish, as they have fewer and larger bones because of the buoyancy effect of the sea water.

How can canned sardines or salmon be boned?

Don't! Leave the bones in, as they have been softened by the preparation and canning and they are a good source of calcium.

Why is the center cut of fish superior eating to that at the tail end?

The center usually has a higher fat content. Even though the tail end does more exercise and thus develops a more intense flavor, the gain in quantity of flavor doesn't begin to match the loss in flavor quality. The center cuts are more tender and delicious than tail cuts.

Why do river fish usually taste better than lake fish?

Exercise builds flavor into a fish and since a river fish has to swim just to stay stationary, it expends more energy than does a lake fish. Also, a bottom fish that doesn't have to fight against as much of a current will not exercise as much as, for example, a trout in a cold, swiftly moving mountain brook will.

Do fish from cooler waters generally taste better?

Yes, with rare exceptions, such as pompano, the colder their environment, the greater the abundance of plankton at the bottom of the food chain, which gives extra flavor.

Why are farmed fish blander and less flavorful than those harvested from their natural environment?

1. They don't exercise as much. Wild fish, swimming against the currents, are more active and therefore tend to be leaner and firmer.
2. The water farmed fish swim in is usually warmer.
3. The diet of the wild fish is more varied.

What is the quality difference between fresh fish and fresh-frozen fish?

Fresh fish from the sea that are really fresh are wonderful, but in markets they may be anywhere from 1 to 21 days old. Fresh-frozen are frozen on the boat the day they are caught, often within a few hours, and so often they are better quality when we buy them. Since enzymes and bacteria start breaking down fish almost immediately as they are pulled out of the water, they should be frozen/processed as soon as possible when they are brought into the ship.

What are the visual signs to look for when selecting a whole fish?

1. The fish should have all of its scales intact, a sign of proper handling (except swordfish or shark, which have no scales).
2. It should have a bright, reflective skin coloring (something like an aspic).
3. The scales should adhere tightly to the body, be clean and free of slime.
4. If scaled, the skin should be shiny.
5. The eyes should be bright, clear and bulging and look alive rather than dull, cloudy or opaque. The longer the fish has been out of water the more opaque the eyes become.
6. Any exposed flesh should be firm and lustrous, not flabby and dull.

7. Any exposed flesh should cling to a bone.
8. If the whole fish has been gutted, as it should be if it has been dead more than an hour, the stomach cavity should be free of residue.

Do the gills of the fish give a clue to freshness?

Yes! In a properly stored fish the oxygen in the air will help keep the gills bright red for a few hours. Then over-oxygenation gradually changes the hemoglobin from bright red to pink to brownish red and finally to grayish brown. Also because gills are more perishable they will develop off-odors faster, which is an early warning system. Examine the gills, for if the fish is fresh the gills will be a bright red and odor-free.

What if the fish market smells fishy?

Find another one, because the sanitation is probably bad or it has slow turnover.

Are there tactile indicators?

Press the fish with your finger. It should spring back into shape when you remove your finger. Or have the salesperson do it for you.

What does color or appearance of cut fish tell?

1. The longer a fillet or steak has stood, the browner-tinged it becomes.
2. If the cut flesh is opaque rather than translucent, you are probably looking at a fish that has been frozen and thawed.

What does holding a whole fish by the head and tail tell you?

The fresher the fish, the less the sag in the middle for its size.

What is indicated if a whole fish is placed in cold water and it floats?

It has been recently caught.

What should you be looking for when selecting cut fish?

1. Choose a market that cuts its own fillets and steaks.
2. The flesh should have a brilliant, appetizing aspect.
3. Uneven or jagged cutting suggests poor workmanship, dull knives or workers who don't know their trade.
4. Get steaks that are even in thickness throughout so they will cook evenly.
5. As fillets and steaks begin to age, the translucence starts to turn opaque and the outward appearance turns from a bright look to a dull and flat look.
6. Look out for fish that are dripping liquid, for they will lose more when cooked and the flesh will be dry and tasteless.

Which fish are best for grilling?

Best: Those with meaty texture, such as salmon or swordfish.
Next: Fillets that are fleshy and have the skin still on.
Good: Whole, small fish, such as trout, shrimp, scallops.

Preparation

How should fish caught by hobbyists be processed?

The gutting and cleaning should not be deferred to the end of the day if refrigeration, ice or a water pool is not available. It should be done as soon as possible after the fish is taken from the water.

Is it necessary to gut small panfish that are to be cooked whole and then boned and eaten at the table?

No, they are exceptions to the above rule, but they must be kept well chilled until cooked.

What is planking?

Smoke roasting, an American Indian method of cooking meat or fish.

Is the dark flesh that runs the length of some fish, known as the red muscle, safe to eat?

Yes. This red muscle is crucial for long-range swimming and is most pronounced in continuous swimming species, particularly tuna, swordfish and mackerel. Although the red muscle has a higher mineral content and more intense flavor, it is harmless.

What is the dark streak?

Many fish have darker areas, usually a brownish red, which is caused by the pigmentation of the myoglobin (the same protein that produces dark meat in poultry). Myoglobin often turns brown when overexposed to oxygen or heat and thus detracts from appearance.

Which is better, the darker or lighter flesh of a fish?

1. The darker often has a higher fat content and therefore more flavor.
2. The higher proportion of fat shortens storage life.
3. The lighter colored is more delicate.

Since fish have no mechanical mechanism to break up ingested food, how is their food digested?

It is a chemical process that continues even after they are caught and die, so it is important that they be gutted immediately. Otherwise, the digestive juices will continue to act, cutting through the intestinal wall and starting decomposition of the flesh.

Why cook fish if it doesn't require cooking to be tender?

1. Fish has meager connective tissue, the muscle component that makes red meat tough, but the connective tissue of fish is more easily gelatinized by moist heat than is that of meat.
2. If not excessively cooked, the heat coagulates the muscle protein, a chemical process that gives it firmness and a pleasing opaque color.

3. If not done excessively, cooking develops and distributes flavors.
4. Cooking helps destroy any pathogens.
5. Many fish are eaten raw as sushi.

Can fish be prepared with non-heat methods?

Yes, such as marinating in lemon or lime juice, as, for example, in sashimi.

How should the fish be processed to kill larva of parasitic round worms?

Cook to an internal temperature of 140 °F.

Does it make any difference to a cook if the fish is fat or lean?

Very much so.

Why does fat-fleshed fish do better grilled or roasted?

1. Because of its extra oil.
2. Lean-fleshed fish should be cooked in oil or liquid, for grilling or roasting tends to dry out the flesh. They would have to be basted frequently.
3. Lean fish should be coated with butter, oil or bacon when broiled to prevent drying.

How should the rack be prepared for grilling?

The rack should be clean and then greased to prevent sticking. This is especially true for fillets and steaks.

How can small bones be removed?

Use a pair of tweezers or a needle-pointed pliers. Some can be pulled out with fingers, but usually not all.

When should scaling be done?

The taste will be better if scales are removed before cooking.

How can you make the scaling of fish easier?

1. Rub vinegar on the scales.
2. Wet the fish with water.

Which direction should the knife or scaler move when scaling a fish?

Some say from the tail towards the head. Others, just the opposite. I like to start from the tail.

What can be used for scaling?

1. Fish scaler.
2. The handle of a metal kitchen spoon.
3. A small kitchen knife.
4. A metal shoehorn.

Why should scaling be done under running water?

To keep the loosened scales from flying all over.

Why rub lemon juice on fish before cooking?

To enhance flavor and help maintain good color.

Will unboned fish be more flavorful than a fillet (boned)?

Yes, for the bones impart a rich flavor to the surrounding flesh, so bone after cooking for a more tasty dish.

What is the amount of brook trout necessary for a serving?

About 8–10 ounces.

What is the best way to thaw frozen fish?

1. Soaking in milk draws out the frozen taste and provides a fresh-caught flavor.
2. Defrost overnight in the refrigerator.

What does lemon juice in a marinade accomplish?

1. The citric acid of the juice coagulates the protein, thus giving it a cooked texture.
2. The increased acidity acts to inhibit or destroy organisms that may be present.
3. Decreases cooking time.

What will too much acid or too long a marination do?

Overmarinating with the acid will make the flesh fall apart. Orange and grapefruit have lesser levels of citric acid than lemon juice and, if used in place of lemon, can be left in contact longer.

How should fish be prepared for cooking?

1. If it is medium or large size, gut it immediately, before storing, as pathogenic microorganisms can spread from the gastric track into the fish.
2. Since the fish deteriorates quickly, don't store more than a few days in the food compartment of the refrigerator or a month or two in the freezer.
3. If you use frozen fillets or steaks, thaw overnight in the refrigerator, not at room temperature.
4. Remove the gills before cooking, as the whole fish will taste better. This depends on freshness. The gills spoil more quickly, but if not more than a day out of water it is not so important.

How often should fish be turned while cooking?

1. Don't over-handle fish during cooking, because the fish will break apart.
2. Most fish need not be turned when grilling or broiling unless it is quite thick.

When should a steak be skinned, before or after cooking?

After, for it will be much easier to remove then, and it will help keep the flesh together.

Why is fish often cooked with ginger?

Because ginger helps counteract fishy odors and, if not overdone, gives a good flavor.

How should fish be checked for seasoning?

Don't taste until cooking is completed. Parasites may not be dead and infestation has been known to occur from partially cooked fish.

What are tests for doneness?

1. Usually as soon as the translucent flesh turns opaque the protein is sufficiently coagulated.
2. Another test is to probe the thickest part with a fork and if the flesh flakes, it is done.

Why should serving plates be preheated when serving fish?

Because cooked fish cools very quickly.

How can you get rid of fish odor?

1. Rub your hands or cooking utensils with lemon juice.
2. If a pot has a pronounced fish odor, boil a half cup of vinegar in it for a minute or two.
3. Place a small amount of vinegar in the pan before washing.

Baking and Braising

What are recommended temperatures and times for baking fish?

1. Preheat the oven to 450 °F.
2. Bake for 10 minutes per inch of the thickest part.

Can tender foods such as fish and shellfish be braised?

Yes, but less cooking liquid, lower temperature and shorter time are required.

Broiling and Grilling

How should fish fillets be positioned in the oven when broiling them?

1. Make sure that the broiler is thoroughly preheated beforehand.
2. Place on a nonstick pan or cookie sheet that has been sprayed with oil.
3. Place the pan 2" below the heating element.

What is the best thickness for broiling fish steaks?

Steaks are more apt to broil to their optimum if they are approximately 1¼" thick.

Which are the best skillets for cooking fish fillets?

Stainless steel, heavy gauge aluminum, enameled cast iron.

How should fish fillets be turned to complete cooking?

With a wide spatula or two smaller ones.

How should the pan be prepared?

Grease the cooking surface before putting the fillet on it, brushing with a little oil or melted butter before broiling.

When pan frying what kind of coating is best?

A light, filmy coating, as a heavy one will result in a soggy crust.

Should fillets be turned over when broiled?

No, they don't need to be turned, since each fillet is usually thin and will be cooked without turning. A fillet is delicate and the turning is apt to break it apart, particularly if it sticks, even a little, to the hot pan.

What if the fillet varies in thickness?

If a fillet varies in thickness then fold the thin portion under so as to make for equal thickness.

What kind of fish is needed for grilling?

A firm, meaty textured fish such as halibut, salmon, swordfish or tuna.

How should the grill be set?

A really clean grill with medium hot setting.

What are rules for grilling fish?

1. Make sure the grill is very clean.
2. Make sure the grill is very hot before adding the fish.
3. Oil the fish lightly.
4. Let the fish sit on the grill for a couple of minutes before turning or removing.

Why should the grill be very hot when cooking fish fillets?

To keep the fillet from sticking to the grill by melting fat or heating the oil to form a coating on the grill, which keeps the fish from falling apart.

Which is better for grilling fish, gas or electric?

Electric, because of a more even heat.

When grilling fish, which is considered worse: over- or undercooking?

Overcooking, because the fish will dry out and become unappealing and nothing further can be done to save it.

En Papillote
What is en papillote?

Cooking in paper or foil, a way of steaming.

Can fish be cooked en papillote successfully?

Yes, it is a good way, particularly to cook individual portions ready to serve. If seasoning and vegetables are added along with the fish, the whole course can be unwrapped at once.

What fish do not do well en papillote?

Avoid swordfish, shark or tuna, which do better with dry heat.

Which do well?

Salmon, halibut, lean cod (low fat) are best.

Which is the best wrapping material?

Parchment paper, which is grease- and steam-resistant, is better because it cooks faster than foil, but foil will work. The steam from the natural juices of the food does the cooking.

How should foil be handled when baking fish?

Wrinkle the foil first. The fish will brown better and stick less to the foil.

How do you cook in paper?

1. If the fish is very dense, such as lingcod or monkfish, then cut the fish a little thinner.
2. Lightly salt the fish.
3. With lean varieties, such as flatfish, be sure to add a little butter or oil.
4. Bake in a 450 °F oven for 8–10 minutes so the moisture is turned into steam and this will cause the package to puff.

What is the best size for cooking in paper?

½" to ¾" thick, and it should cook in 8 minutes or less.

Should the skin be left on the fillet?

If the skin is left on, make sure it is scaled, but a fillet that is skinned is better for this type of cooking.

Should the head be left on when stuffing a whole fish?

Leave it on and, if desired, removed it just before service.

What can be added to the packet?

1. Shrimp or crabmeat can be added to accent mild-flavored fish.
2. Chopped vegetables.

3. Chopped parsley, minced garlic, minced lemon zest, mushrooms, sliced green olives and capers are some of the seasonings that can be used in addition to salt, pepper or herbs.

4. Cooked rice (white, brown or wild) can be used.

How should the vegetables be prepared?

1. They must be cut into small enough pieces so they will cook in the same short time.

2. Asparagus should be blanched and sliced.

3. Tomatoes will flavor the dish but their juice will result in make a thin sauce.

4. Summer squash may express enough water to dilute the flavor.

How should the covering be handled?

1. Use a large piece of paper so that the edges can be double folded.

2. Fold the edges of the parchment or foil well to enclose the resultant juices.

3. Brush the edges of the parchment paper with oil.

If the paper is properly folded will it make a tight seal?

Not quite, but it will be good enough so that the fish will retain most of the moisture and aroma.

How should it be baked?

1. On a pan with raised edges to contain the juice that will inevitably escape.

2. Bake in a hot oven as quickly as possible.

How should it be handled once cooked?

Serve shortly after removing from the oven, don't let the packages stand. The heat generated will continue to cook the contents for a minute or two.

What are two ways to stuff a fish?

1. Bone the fish by opening along the bag, loosely stuff and close with toothpicks or tie with thread.

2. Take two fillets of equal size and shape. Put the stuffing on one, lay the other on top of the filling and fasten with toothpicks.

Poaching

What is the advantage of poaching fish?

It gives a delicate flavor.

What are rules for poaching?

1. Handle the fish gently.

2. Simmer the cooking fluid, don't boil it, or the flesh may fall apart.

3. Start the fish in cold water so it won't split apart and also so the outside won't be done before the inside is.

4. For a whole fish if you don't have a poacher, wrap the fish in cheesecloth, using the rolled ends as handles for transferring the fish in and out of the pan.

Is it necessary to add wine, lemon juice or other acidic components when poaching fish?

1. Without an acidic counterbalance the alkali present would probably chemically react with the pigment of the flesh and turn it an unattractive yellowish, or off-white hue.

2. If enough acid is added to sink the acid level below a neutral balance, the pigment will become even whiter, but the goal is to maintain color without off-setting the flavor.

Should the skin be removed before poaching?

No, leave it on.

Searing and Sautéing

How should the pan be prepared for searing?

1. Use a heavy, cast iron skillet that heats evenly.

2. Heat the pan before adding the oil so the oil won't be burned. This also means that less oil can be used.

3. Tilt the pan to spread the oil evenly.

How should the fish be seared?

1. Add the seasoned fillets to hot oil and in a few minutes they will have a crisp, golden crust.

2. Turn the fish over and lower the heat to moderate. Cook a short time more, until just cooked through.

What is necessary to get a good coating?

Make sure the oil is hot to start.

Why are fish breaded before searing or frying?

1. To give a different flavor/texture.

2. To protect a soft or delicate fish that would not otherwise stand up to sautéing or frying.

How can fish be evenly breaded?

First dip in flour, shaking off the excess, then dip in liquid and finally in crumbs.

How can you keep fresh fish from sticking to the pan without extra fat or oil?

Sprinkle the bottom of the pan with a little salt.

What caution should be taken when sautéing?

Use a moderate heat setting. Fish tends to be tough if cooked over too high or too low a heat.

Steaming

What are the benefits of steaming fish?

1. Steaming works effectively for both thin and thick pieces, even for whole fish.
2. Since fish pieces can be arranged on a platter before steaming there is no need to turn them during cooking, and thus breaking the delicate flesh into pieces is prevented.
3. It is easy to steam vegetables alongside or on top of the fish.

What fish are not recommended for steaming?

Meaty fish, such as tuna or swordfish, are less suitable for steaming.

How should fillets be prepared for steaming?

1. The rack should be at least an inch above the water.
2. Place fillets on a heat-proof plate that fits easily onto the steamer rack.
3. Fold tail ends of the fillets under so that there is an evenness of thickness.
4. Sprinkle the fish with seasoning.

How should they be steamed?

1. Bring the water in the steamer to a boil, set the plate on the rack and cover lightly.
2. Steam until the center of the thickest piece is opaque, cutting to make sure.
3. Start the fish in cold water so it won't split apart and also so the outside won't be done before the inside.

How long does steaming take?

It takes about ten minutes or less per inch of thickness of the fish at the thickest part.

How long should a whole fish or fillet be steamed if it is to be served cold?

Bring the liquid to a simmering level and steam, covered, a minute or two and then turn off the heat and let it stand until cool.

ANCHOVIES

What are anchovies?

A small member of the herring family.

How can you buy anchovies?

1. In the United States most are canned in oil as fillets, some in brine.
2. Fresh anchovies are rarely available. These small (6″) fish have a green back when fresh that turns darker to almost black as it ages. Some restaurants offer them whole, in which case the fish have been imported from Europe.

How are anchovies used?

Anchovies are excellent in various dishes including Caesar salad, pizza, dipping sauces, spreads, tarts etc.

How should anchovies be stored?

Once the jar/can has been opened, store in the refrigerator in olive oil.

What needs to be done with anchovies packed in brine before using?

Rinse well.

How can anchovy paste be used?

1. Anchovy paste is most often in tubes.
2. Of the paste ½ teaspoon = 2 anchovy fillets.
3. The paste works well to add zest to a fish sauce.

How can the oil from canned anchovies be used?

In marinades, salad dressings, sauces.

CATFISH

How should catfish be cooked?

As skinned fillets.

What is the traditional cooking method for catfish?

Pan-fried, with a cornmeal coating.

FLOUNDER

What are the members of the flounder family?

1. Lemon sole, grey sole, white sole (but not red sole). Only the Dover sole is a real sole.
2. Plaice: sand dabs, dabs.

How are flounders distinguished?

Both eyes are on the same side of the head.

SALMON

What is the difference between wild and farmed salmon?

Wild: More complex in flavor, less homogeneous, a meaty texture.

Farmed: Slightly more fat.

What kind of fish are best for smoking or barbecue?

1. The higher the fat content, the moister the fish remains while being smoked and the juicier and tastier it will be.
2. The richer taste of fat fish balances the smoked flavors the best.
3. Examples of fat fish that are good for smoking are salmon, arctic char, trout, whitefish, tuna and sturgeon.

What is the effect of adding sugar to the curing mixture made for smoking a fish?

1. Sugar has the same water-drawing effect as salt and reduces the saltiness of the smoked fish.
2. 10% sugar gives a mellow taste, 50% sugar gives a sweet taste.

What are the kinds of smoked salmon?

Cold smoked: The fish is not cooked, just smoked to an internal temperature of 85 °F or less.

Cured: A combination of smoking, salting, drying and/or fermenting.

Mild cure: Low salt content.

Hard smoked: Heavily salted, low in moisture, has a long shelf life, intense smoking. Example: jerky.

Lox: A mild cured, salt-brined, salt-cured, smoked salmon, must be refrigerated.

What is gravlaks (also called gravadlaks)?

Swedish cured salmon. The fillet is cured in a mixture of salt, sugar, black pepper, fresh dill and sometimes aquavit, vodka or gin. The fillet is rubbed with the salt mixture, layered in a container, weighted down and chilled for 2–3 days. It is turned periodically during this time.

What is the difference between smoked salmon and lox?

Smoked: Cured (salt and sugar) and then smoked.

Lox: Cured in salt, soaked to get rid of salt, then lightly smoked.

Are all smoked salmons the same?

The fillets, with or without the skin, are smoked. The degree of smoke varies considerably and may be light or heavy to the point of the fish being almost dry (jerky). Some are salt-cured in a brine before smoking.

What should be done before smoking salted salmon?

1. Soak the fish for 15 minutes in water OR at least rinse well to get rid of the excess surface salt.
2. Air-dry the fish 15 minutes or more to form a thin skin, which helps the appearance and slows down the moisture loss as the fish is smoked.

What does a white deposit forming on the surface of salmon when cooking indicate?

The appearance of white albumen tells that the fish is overcooked and/or it was cooked at too high a heat.

Is the gray/brown surface good eating?

Yes, even though visually it is not so attractive. It can be scraped off if desired.

Should salmon fillets be kept on ice?

Fillets should not be allowed to touch the ice, for touching water breaks the texture.

Can whole fish be laid directly on ice?

Yes.

What must first be done to stuff a salmon?

Bone the fish.

SWORDFISH

How should swordfish be selected and handled?

1. The color should be ivory, pink or brown.
2. The dark patch (maroon) is normal.
3. The flesh should be tight.
4. The thicker the steak, the less chance of the fish drying out.
5. The inedible skin can be removed before or after cooking but is much easier after.

How should swordfish steaks be broiled?

Cook steaks that are 1¼″ thick for 6–8 minutes per side as close to the broiler as possible. The center will be slightly pink and the edges flaky.

TUNA

What is most important in choosing quality in tuna steaks?

The shininess is more important than color variation, for a shiny, bright steak is a sign of freshness. A dull appearance indicates that the optimum freshness is past.

What does the color of tuna steaks indicate as to variety?

Yellowfin: The lightest in color, a rosy red.

Bigeye: Dark red.

Bluefin: Deepest red.

Albacore: Pale, white fleshed, this is generally is used for canning.

Does fat content affect color?

The higher the fat content, the lighter the color.

Does the color change with time of year?

In fall, those tuna caught in northern Atlantic waters are high in fat after they migrate from the south and so are lighter in color.

How does the flavor of tuna vary?

It changes with the variety, the age and size of the fish.

How great a variation in size is there in tuna?

From 5 to 1,500 pounds.

What are the grades of canned tuna?

White: From albacore, the best.

Light: From five other species. Nutritious and usually tastes almost as good as the white.

Solid pack: From the loin of the tuna with whole pieces and a few flakes.

Chunk: Chunks of the loin; includes pieces that will have a part of the muscle structure attached.

Grated: Just above a puree.

Tonno tuna: Packed in olive oil.

Flaked: Small pieces left over from processing.

What grade should be chosen for sandwiches?

It doesn't matter which one you choose; the flavor of canned tuna is largely the same.

Does water-packed tuna have a lower fat content than oil-packed?

Water-packed may have no less fat than that in oil, in fact, it may have more. For instance, white albacore tuna of one batch may contain five times more fat than another batch, depending upon the temperature and depth of the water in which the fish is caught. So check the label. Thus, one may have 1 gram of fat, while another may have 5 grams. Oil pack may have 1 gram from the fish plus 2 grams from the oil for a total of 3 grams. Also, higher fat tuna are usually not used for oil-packing.

Does the sodium content vary between water and oil packed tuna?

No, it is the same.

What is the stuff that looks like bits of glass in canned tuna?

It is struvite, a crystalline substance that can form during the canning process and it dissolves in the palm of your hand or with a bit of vinegar. Not much shows up nowadays because the processors add sodium acid pyrophosphate to prevent its formation.

What are other ingredients in canned tuna?

Salt, water, oil up to 18%, hydrolized soy protein or pyrophosphate.

What is the most expensive tuna?

Yellowtail that is used for making Hamachi sushi.

How does tuna rate nutritionally?

A 3 ounce serving has 110 calories, less than 1 gram of fat and 26 grams of protein. It is rich in vitamin B, zinc and selenium.

What are various ways of preparing tuna?

Grilling, broiling, roasting, braising, sautéing.

Can tuna be enjoyed raw?

Most people do not like it raw, but at rare or medium rare the steak is delicious. When well done it is much like the canned version.

How thick should a tuna steak be for grilling?

About 1½" for medium rare.

Which fish is consumed most in the United States?

Tuna, almost 300 million pounds a year. This includes both fresh and canned.

What does "dolphin safe" on the label mean?

The nets used for catching tuna have a shield that prevents, the dolphins from getting caught. The procedure is not 100% effective.

Seafood

CHAPTER TEN

SEASONING AND OILS

What is seasoning?

A process of adding ingredients to food to modify its flavor, which is unique to the cook for a particular food. When adding seasoning, the quality of the food must be taken into consideration as well as the combination of foods it will be served with.

Will foods, such as vegetables, of the same variety, even of the same producer, be the same from one purchase to the next?

They can vary from one day to the next in respect to texture and flavor.

What effect do heat and cold have on the ability to taste flavoring agents?

The perception of saltiness, sweetness and bitterness is the greatest in the range of 60 °F to 100 °F. Below this range, the ability of the palate to discern flavors diminishes, while above that range there can be a distortion of flavor.

What are time restraints in cooking with spices and herbs?

1. Spices become bitter if cooked over high heat for more than a short time. It is not wise to add chili powder or black pepper or like seasoning agents at the beginning of the sautéing process.
2. Don't boil an herb-seasoned dish, just simmer it, as the aromatic oils in the seasonings are volatile and will disappear into the air. Don't add seasonings until 30 minutes or less before the end of the cooking process.

If a dish is to be frozen, when should the seasonings be added?

If you plan to freeze the dish, add all or at least most of the seasoning after you thaw the food. Seasonings lose much of their aromatic and flavoring strength when they are frozen.

How can the flavor of a spice or dried herb be heightened?

Roast the spice in a single layer in a preheated 250 °F oven for 10–15 minutes just before you plan to use it in cooking.

What can be done to enhance a seasoning without heating?

Before adding to soups, stews or sauces, place the herb or spice in the palm of your hand and crush it with the thumb of your other hand. This not only helps release the aromatic oils but also helps to spot and discard unwanted stems.

How are ground spices and herbs measured?

By mesh size (refers to the number of openings in the wire per square inch), with 10 mesh being coarse and sixty mash being finely pounded. Pepper is sold in varying mesh sizes; "coarse" might be from 20–30 mesh.

How can whole (or large pieces of) spices be removed from a dish of liquid?

Add them in a metal tea ball.

What is *nuoc nam*?

This is Asian fish sauce. When opened, store in the refrigerator.

What are other names for *nuoc nam*?

Nuoc nam is the Vietnamese name, *nam pla* is Thai, *petis* is Indonesian, *patis* is Philippine and *tak tray* is Cambodian.

What is anchovy paste?

Pounded anchovies combined with spices and vinegar. Usually sold in tubes.

What is five-spice powder (Chinese Five Spice)?

A mixture of cinnamon, fennel seed, star anise, Szechuan peppercorns and clove in varying proportions according to the producer.

What is filé?

Also known as gumbo filé, it is a fine, starchy powder made from sassafras leaves and acts as a thickener for dishes and, importantly, gives its own flavor. Best known in Creole cuisine. Add after the dish is taken off the heat.

What is the difference between Cajun and Creole cooking?

They both are a combination of southern U.S. and French cuisine, using pork fat and a dark roux as bases. The Creole has Spanish and Caribbean influences and is characterized by spicy seasonings, tomatoes, okra and rice; the Cajun, originating in Louisiana, is characterized by fiery hot seasonings, like cayenne pepper.

What is poultry seasoning?

A mixture of sage, thyme, marjoram, savory etc., which varies from cook to cook and from manufacturer to manufacturer.

Seasoning and Oils

What is gremolata?

A mixture of chopped parsley, grated lemon rind and minced garlic that will spruce up the flavor of cooked vegetables or roasted or braised meat dishes such as osso buco.

How is gremolata best added to the dish?

Half during the braising and half when serving.

What is chutney?

A fruit condiment of vinegar, sugar and spices, of varying texture (smooth to chunky) and flavor (hot to smooth).

What is curry powder?

A combination of dried, ground spices, herbs, seeds. Anywhere from five to fifty different ingredients are used in varying proportions, depending on the degree of hotness desired or particular flavor wanted.

Name some thickeners.

1. Arrow root.
2. Cornstarch.
3. Filé gumbo powder.
4. Gelatin.
5. Flour.
6. Eggs.
7. Fresh bread crumbs (for stews).
8. Tapioca.

MARINATION/MACERATION

What is marination?

A procedure for soaking food in a flavored liquid for flavoring, tenderizing and moisturizing. Meats, poultry, fish and vegetables are marinated in mixtures that are most often acid based.

What is maceration?

Soaking fruit, usually in a sugar syrup, wine or liqueur, usually to soften and sometimes to sweeten and flavor.

What is the basic recipe for a marinade?

Three parts of oil to one part of the acid component, such as vinegar, plus seasoning.

What are the best ways of using marinades?

They are most effective when the surface on which they can act is the largest. For example, a butterflied leg of lamb will marinate better than one containing the bone.

What are marinades that soften meat?

Yogurt: Breaks down the flesh of meat and fish.

Lemon: Softens meat and gives a tangy flavor.

Green papaya: Digests protein.

Tamarind: Tenderizes and seasons.

Vinegar: The acetic acid acts as a softener.

How quickly does a marinade act on fish?

The marinade begins to work in minutes.

What kind of marinades should be used on fish?

White/dry fish: Oil based.

Oily fish: An acidic one, such as citrus, vinegar or wine.

How much marinade should be used so that the meat is flavored, moisturized and tenderized and not overwhelmed?

Mild: About 1 cup for every two pounds of meat, fish or poultry. Totally immerse meat for 2 hours or more in refrigerator.

Strong: Lightly brush on before grilling or roasting.

How long can delicate fish, such as flounder, be marinated?

Delicate fish can withstand 15 minutes and tuna about 30 minutes but no longer, and Chilean sea bass about 1½ hours.

What difference does the skin have on marinating chicken?

1. With the skin on, there seems to be little difference between 2 and 12 hours. Marinate for 24 hours for best results; longer won't bring much further improvement.

2. With skin off, the flavor intensification works in about 3 hours, while a longer time will dry out the meat.

How long should vegetables be marinated?

For vegetables like zucchini, eggplant and mushrooms that absorb like sponges, marinate for 1–2 hours. For others such as asparagus or artichokes that don't absorb well, marination does little.

How can the amount of marinade necessary be minimized?

Seal the food in a plastic bag with the marinade and turn occasionally. This will reduce the amount needed.

Should marinades be reused?

No. When finished simply discard the bag and do not reuse the marinade because the food most likely has enough alkali to neutralize the acid of the marinade.

Can the liquid have any other uses?

While it won't do its original job as a marinade it may be used to flavor a stew.

What should be done if leftover meat marinade is to be reused?

Bring it to a boil to kill any bacteria from the meat it was used on.

What is a dry marinade?

A mixture of crushed herbs, spices and salt that is rubbed onto the surface of meat, fish or poultry prior to cooking.

What is the additional contribution of a dry marinade?

It will give not only flavor, if grilled, but also a seared crust.

SWEET THINGS

Caramel

What is caramel (also known as burnt sugar)?

A thick liquid made by cooking sugar that ranges in color from golden to dark brown. It is also the name for a chewy candy made from sugar, cream and flavorings.

What does "to candy" mean?

To coat by dipping the piece (of fruit, nut, etc.) into a sweet syrup or beaten egg white, then rolled in sugar and dried.

What is the liquid form used for?

For coloring, sweetening and flavoring desserts, sauces, custards and soups.

What is the wet method of making transparent caramel?

1. Combine ⅓ water, ⅔ granulated sugar, such as 2 cups sugar to 1 cup water.
2. Bring to a boil while stirring gently over high heat.
3. While cooking, repeatedly wash down the insides of the saucepan with a clean pastry brush (one that hasn't been used with oil or egg yolk) to minimize the danger of crystallization.
4. When the mixture comes to a boil, add a little corn syrup and continue boiling until the desired color is achieved.

What is the dry method?

1. Combine the sugar with lemon juice, about 1 tablespoon juice per pound of sugar, by rubbing the mixture in your hands to get an even mix. The juice helps to caramelize the sugar and discourages crystals from forming.
2. Cook, stirring continuously.

How is caramel different when made by this dry method?

The dry method produces a slightly cloudy caramel.

Is a cloudy caramel ever desired?

It is all right if an opaque sauce, one to which cream is added, is desired.

What happens if the caramel mixture is removed from heat too soon?

Neither the color nor the flavor will develop correctly.

What happens when it is left on the heat too long?

It will have a bitter taste.

How much time leeway is there?

The difference between too soon and too late can be seconds.

What steps can be taken to prevent the premature crystallization of sugar?

1. Use a copper sugar pot or a heavy bottomed enamel coated pan, both of which are smooth surfaced, preventing any undissolved granules of sugar from being caught on the pan.
2. Be sure that all the sugar is dissolved before the sugar solution boils.
3. Wash down the sides of the pan frequently, once the sugar solution is boiling, with a pastry brush dipped in water.
4. Add an acid, such as cream of tartar, during the boiling process to hasten the inversion of the sugar.

Should the pot for boiling be covered?

Yes, place the lid on the top of the pot so that the condensed steam washes the sides as it drips down.

What is greasing the sugar?

Adding some butter.

What is culling the grain?

Another way of preventing crystallization is to add a little of some other simple syrup, such as corn syrup, which cannot crystallize.

Should the boiling syrup be stirred?

Don't stir the boiling syrup since some of the syrup may be deposited on the sides of the pan and bringing them into the main mixture could start crystallization. Swishing is ok, however.

How can the "after cooking" of caramel be prevented after removing the pan from the burner?

1. Put the pan on ice.
2. If making a large quantity, add butter, cream, liqueur or other ingredients to reduce the temperature.

How can the end point of caramelization be determined?

1. With a candy thermometer.
2. Use a twist of paper to put a drop of the material onto a piece of white paper to check the color.

What happens when hot caramel liquid cools?

It hardens and becomes brittle and cracks easily.

Is the crystallization of sugar ever desirable when making caramel?

Yes; when making fudge or fondant icing, then sugar crystals are necessary for structure.

How can the type of crystallization be controlled?

1. The hotter the syrup, the faster the crystal formation.
2. Add a crystal of desired size to the solution, which then begins a chain reaction in which the syrup uses the seed as a pattern to determine its crystalline structure.

How can the pan used for making caramel be cleaned?

Fill it with water, bring to a boil, stir to loosen and dissolve any remaining caramel, then empty and rinse.

Corn Syrup

What is corn syrup?

A rich syrup composed of simple sugars (glucose and fructose) made by processing cornstarch with enzymes, with color and caramel added.

What are the differences in corn syrup?

Light: Clarified corn syrup, high in the fructose component.
Dark: Caramel flavor and color added, and thus it has a stronger flavor.

Can they be used interchangeably?

Yes, although the color of the item you are making will change, and the flavor will change slightly.

What does corn syrup do?

1. Inhibits the formation of crystals and therefore is particularly good for making jellies and candies.
2. It helps to retain moisture in baked goods.
3. It tends to give a slightly chewy and dense texture.
4. It is less sweet than honey or maple sugar.
5. It can be used as a pancake or waffle syrup and sometimes is maple flavored.

Seasoning and Oils

Honey

How many flowers does a bee have to visit to produce 1 pound of honey?

Two million.

How is honey processed?

When we buy it, it has been heated to 155 °F to destroy sugar-fermenting yeasts, then filtered under pressure to remove grains of pollen and small air bubbles.

What are its basic forms?

Comb: Liquid honey, still in the comb; chewy.

Chunk: With pieces of comb in the liquid.

Liquid: Extracted from the comb.

What are the potential problems of unfiltered honey?

1. It may be cloudy.
2. It may crystallize in storage.

How many varieties of honey are marketed in the United States?

About 300, many of which are only produced on a very small scale.

What should you look for when buying honey?

1. Whether or not honey is labeled "organic" is not important, since bees are sensitive to pesticides and will avoid them.
2. Look for 100% pure, unfiltered, not cooked.
3. Know that honeys vary considerably in taste.

What is creamed honey?

The crystals are finely ground so that the texture is similar to butter.

What are the advantages of honey?

1. While a form of sugar, it does contain a number of trace minerals, which make it more nutritious.
2. It can be used in place of refined sugar, but use less than the sugar called for in the recipe.
3. Some honeys will impart a very delicate flavor of their own.

What are some things to know about using honey in cooking?

1. Honey is sweeter, so use only 90% as much as you would sugar.
2. Since honey is a liquid, adjust the amount of added liquid.
3. One tablespoon has almost as many calories as a tablespoon of sugar.
4. The honey will keep baked goods moister than sugar will.

Is there an easy way to measure honey by volume?

1. Pour some oil into the measuring cup or bowl or spoon and then pour the oil back into the bottle.
2. Measure the honey by pouring it into the now oiled measuring spoon or bowl.
3. The thin oil film will let the honey slip out when poured. This procedure will also work for molasses or corn syrup.

How should honey be stored?

Tightly covered in a warm, dry area, not refrigerated, which will cause it to crystallize or become gray.

What can be done if honey crystallizes?

Heat the container in a pan of warm water. Much commercially sold honey, however, withstands refrigeration quite well, especially if kept in the refrigerator door.

What is extracted honey?

Honey that has been pasteurized to prevent crystallization.

What are some precautions to take when microwaving honey?

1. Remove the lid. When the container has a tight cover it is very likely to explode.
2. If there is a metal band on the container it may create electric sparks (arc), which will damage the oven.

Maple Syrup

What should you look for or avoid when buying maple syrup?

Buy pure syrup, not maple-flavored, because the difference in flavors is significant.

What is "maple flavored" or pancake syrup?

It is mainly corn syrup and rarely contains a single drop of maple.

What is maple cream?

Maple syrup that has been heated to evaporate the water content so that it is thicker than syrup.

What are the grades of maple syrup?

AA or fancy:	Light amber, mild flavor.
A:	Medium amber, mellow.
B:	Dark amber, hearty flavor.
C:	Very dark, molasses-like in taste.

What are the Vermont grades?

The state's grades are based on color, not on thickness.

Fancy:	Light amber.
Medium amber:	Stronger maple flavor.
Dark amber:	Strongest flavor, best for cooking.

What is the reason for paying extra to buy the top two grades?

If you enjoy the full flavor of maple, the AA is light in intensity. In recent years the darker, more amber syrups, which have more flavor, have been given an A designation as have the lighter syrups, and the price is usually the same.

How should maple syrup be served?

At room temperature, for otherwise it will not only prematurely cool the food but some of the maple flavor will be lost.

How should maple syrup be stored, once opened?

When the container is opened transfer what is left to a glass jar and refrigerate. It can be frozen in glass and will thicken but usually will not freeze solid. Let it come to room temperature before using.

Besides a topping for pancakes, waffles and cereals, what else is maple syrup food for?

As a glaze for cooked vegetables such as carrots, or on ham or ribs.

Molasses

What is molasses?

A thick, bittersweet, brown-black liquid made from the refining of sugarcane or sugar beets when the juice from the plant is boiled down to a syrup and the sugar crystals are extracted.

What is the difference between molasses and sorghum?

Both are sweeteners. Molasses comes from the sugarcane or beet, while sorghum from the sorghum (sergo) plant. They can be used similarly, although sorghum has a considerably stronger flavor.

What is sulfured molasses?

This is a by-product of cane sugar production created by the addition of a sulfating agent during the processing to purify and refine the sugar juices. It has a strong flavor and is less sweet than unsulfured.

What is unsulfured molasses?

Made from pure sugarcane juice, resulting in a sweeter, lighter colored syrup and a cleaner, more noticeable sugarcane flavor than sulfered molasses.

Seasoning and Oils

What are the grades of molasses?

Light:	Mild flavored, good for waffles and pumpkin pie, but this depends on the intensity of flavor desired. Removed after the first boiling. Light colored, used as a syrup.
Dark:	Darker in color, thicker in consistency, less sweet than light. Removed after the second boiling. Used as a flavoring.
Blackstrap:	Very thick, dark and slightly bitter, it is rarely used in cooking but is used for making rum or goes into cattle feed. Removed after the third boiling.

Are the grades interchangeable?

Light and dark can be interchanged, but blackstrap cannot.

What is dark molasses used for?

Gingerbread and Boston baked beans are two recipes it is used in.

How can the acidity of molasses be reduced in cooking?

Add 1 teaspoon of baking soda for each cup of molasses used. Mix the soda in with the dry ingredients.

How should molasses be stored?

In a sealed container at room temperature.

What is the weight/volume equivalence?

One pound equals to about 1⅓ cup.

Sugar

What is the difference between beet sugar and cane sugar?

Look at the label, for otherwise you won't be able to tell. They taste and smell the same cooked or uncooked.

Does sugar act as a stimulant?

Just the opposite. In many instances it has a calming effect. A high sugar intake leads to the production of the brain chemical seratonin, which puts you in a peaceful frame of mind.

Is sugar responsible for acne?

No scientific tests have supported this notion.

What is sucrose?

A pure mixture of simple sugars (glucose and fructose) that is sold either granulated or powdered.

What is liquid sugar?

A syrup made with equal volumes of sugar and water, heated to dissolve the sugar.

How does sugar affect the taste of a bitter, salty or sour substance?

Sugar lowers the intensity of taste perception. Use a little sugar to make a bitter coffee less bitter, a salty dish less salty and to counteract the acidity of tomatoes in soup or spaghetti sauce.

What is the nutritional benefit of sugar?

A teaspoon of sugar has 16 calories and nothing more. This is also true for fructose, corn syrup and honey.

What are the markings on the box of confectioner's sugar and what do they mean?

1. The higher the number, the finer the grind. Thus 4-X is not as finely ground as 10-X.
2. If additional strength (firmness) is desired in a frosting then used the coarser one, e.g., 4-X.

What is the difference nutritionally (or otherwise) in the two main sugar substitutes?

Saccharin (Sweet 'n Low, Sweet 10): Has no calories, is not metabolized by the body. Some claim that it has a bitter aftertaste. It is about 300 times sweeter than sugar.

Aspartame (Equal):   Metabolized by the body. About 180 times sweeter than sugar. Persons with the rare genetic disorder (PKU-phenylketonuria) should use it in only limited quantities. It breaks down when heated and so is not suitable for baking. In liquid form it deteriorates with age (in months).

What are the different kinds of white sugars on the market?

Granulated: Table sugar of highly refined white crystals.

Superfine: Finely ground granulated sugar that dissolves quickly and easily without graininess. Used for meringues, sweetening beverages, in finely textured cakes or caramels.

Confectioner's: Granulated sugar ground to a powder and mixed with a small amount of corn starch to keep it from absorbing moisture and becoming lumpy. Used mostly for frostings or sifting over a dessert.

Coarse: Also called pearl or decorating sugar, crystals are about twice the size of granulated. Used for garnishing or decorating.

Powdered: Granulated sugar that is ground to a fine powder.

What is it called if powdered sugar is ground even finer?

Icing sugar, and the grain is almost imperceptible.

What happens when white granulated sugar and water are boiled?

As the liquid begins to evaporate, a syrupy film forms on the sides of the saucepan, which will eventually drip down into the remaining syrup. This will start a chain reaction in which the sugar molecules cling together, forming large crystals which will precipitate.

What is the difference between brown and white sugar?

Brown sugar contains molasses, which is a by-product of refining, and it is the molasses that gives it its distinctive flavor, color and aroma. Dark brown sugar has more molasses added and therefore a richer flavor.

How should brown sugar be stored?

Store the package in a resealable plastic bag or closely sealed glass container to keep fresh after opening. If exposed to air, moisture is lost and the sugar will harden.

How can hardened brown sugar be handled?

1. Place a soft slice of bread in the container, seal tightly and in a few hours the sugar should be soft again.
2. Put in a baking pan along side of an oven-proof cup filled with water. Cover the pan tightly with foil and bake at 200 °F for about 20 minutes.
3. Put a cup in the microwave with a slice of apple and microwave at high power for about 20 seconds. Remove and break it up with a fork. If still hard, microwave in 5-second intervals until softened. Remove the apple and let the sugar cool.

How can you easily sprinkle brown sugar over a dish?

Heat it for 15 minutes in a 250 °F oven, which will dry the sugar and thus allow it to coat evenly when sprinkled. Also works for white sugar.

What is the nutritional difference between refined white sugar, brown sugar, honey and molasses?

Essentially they are all the same, but they are not interchangeable in recipes, for they will give different flavors and often different textures. Blackstrap molasses is rich in iron; honey has flavors from different flowers from which it was collected and is sweeter than sugar; brown sugar has a small amount of molasses in it.

What is Demerara sugar?

Large, coarse golden brown crystals of sugar from Guyana that is partially refined. When slightly more refined and still golden in color but coarse, it is called turbinado.

HERBS

What are herbs?

The seasonings from the leaves of various plants.

How should fresh herbs be selected for purchase?

Choose fresh, clean, aromatic leaves with a bright color that are not wilted or brown.

Can the stems of cilantro, parsley, thyme or rosemary be used?

Yes for parsley and cilantro, no for thyme or rosemary.

If a recipe calls for "½ cup of herbs, finely chopped" is measurement before or after chopping?

Measure, then chop unless the recipe reads "½ cup finely chopped herbs," in which case, chop before measuring.

What are some of the uses of herbs?

Basil:	Tomatoes, soups, salads, pizza, salad dressings.
Bay leaves:	Meats, stews, sauces, soups, pickling.
Chervil:	Eggs, salads, vegetables, soups, fine herbs.
Chives:	Dips, sauces, baked potatoes.
Cilantro:	Salads, guacamole, soups, stews.
Coriander:	Curry, ginger cookies.
Dill weed:	Seafood, salads, butter.
Fennel:	Salads, fish, duck.
Lemon grass:	Soups, sauces, stir fry, Asian dishes.
Marjoram:	Peas, stuffings, soups, salads, fine herbs.
Mint:	Carrots, lamb sauce, pea soup, soft cheeses, cold drinks, vegetables.
Oregano:	Sauces for meats, tomato sauces, vegetables, pizza.
Parsley:	Fish and meat sauces, salads, soups, vegetables, omelettes, fine herbs, sausage, garnishes, almost anything but sweet dishes.
Rosemary:	Lamb, poultry sauces, vegetables, fine herbs.
Sage:	Stuffing, sauces, pork, pizza, fish.
Savory:	Vegetables, dried bean dishes, soup.
Sorrel:	Cold soups, salads, vegetables.
Tarragon:	Chicken, fish sauces, mushrooms, meats, fine herbs.
Thyme:	Chowders, cheese, salads, fish, soup.

What is a bouquet garni?

A bundle of fresh or dried herbs, usually tied in cheesecloth or simply the stems tied together as a bouquet for easy removal. The classic one has fresh parsley, dried thyme and a bay leaf but any combination will do. The herbs can also be put in a metal tea ball.

What are herbes de Provence?

This is a mixture from the south of France of various herbs such as oregano, thyme, rosemary, savory, lavender and fennel seeds. Can be bought as a dried mixture or made up fresh.

How long can you keep dried herbs?

They are at their best within about 3 months from the time the container is opened, but generally the jars should be replaced annually. Mark the date with a piece of tape when the jar is opened. This means that economy-sized packages are really not economical unless you use them a lot.

What changes as dried herbs age?

As they age they lose their volatile oils, so you will need a larger amount of them to achieve the desired level of seasoning.

How can chopped fresh herbs be frozen?

1. Blanch them in lightly salted water, drain and plunge into ice water.
2. Dry, chop and put into a plastic bag with the air pushed out.

How can they be frozen as ice cubes?

1. Put in ice cube trays, add water and freeze.
2. When frozen, put the cubes in a labeled plastic bag.

How should frozen herbs be used?

Add to the dish without thawing, and, in extended cooking, add late in the process.

What must be watched for when using fresh herbs?

Most chefs prefer fresh herbs when it is possible because they taste better but the volatile oils in the fresh are delicate and should not be overcooked. For instance, in long cooking, such as braising, add them later.

What do slightly woody leaves and stems (such as oregano) signify?

They will retain their aroma and flavor better than the more delicate ones such as dill.

How should fresh herbs be stored?

Most cut herbs should be stored unwashed in an airtight plastic container in the refrigerator.

Is this also true for basil?

Basil will keep best if not refrigerated but kept in a cool place, out of the sun, with the stems in water.

How should parsley, mint and dill be stored?

Refrigerate in a covered jar with the stem ends sitting in a 1″ layer of water or wrap the stem ends in a moist paper towel and seal in a plastic bag, then refrigerate.

What should you look for when buying dried herbs by the ounce from large containers?

1. Be sure the store has a rapid turnover. Frequent opening and closing of the jars/containers exposes the supply to repeated doses of air and moisture.

2. Light can also do damage.

3. Don't buy herbs or spices in containers that have cork stoppers since the air can seep though the cork.

How can you check for quality of dried herbs in jars in your pantry?

Sniff! They should have pungency, even though with aging they will have diminished flavor.

Do herbs vary much in intensity?

Yes, they change with the season and also with their freshness.

What can be done with excess fresh herbs?

Make an herb vinaigrette or an herb butter, or dry them for later use.

How should an herbed vinaigrette be made?

Submerge the washed and dried herbs in a plain, good quality vinegar and refrigerate in a jar. When the herbs begin to discolor, discard the herbs and strain the vinegar back into the jar and store in a cool, dark place.

How can an herb butter be made?

Cream the butter (10 parts) and the herbs (1 part). Form into a 1" thick log and freeze.

How should the herbed butter be used?

Slice ⅛" rounds and place them on top of the preparation such as a grilled steak or vegetable dishes. As the butter melts it will flavor the food.

How should herbs be dried?

Heat the herbs on a baking dish in a preheated 200 °F oven until thoroughly dry. Store in sealed containers in a cool, dark place.

How much of the dried herbs should be used if fresh herbs aren't available?

This varies with the age of the dried form and how long their container has been open, but roughly, to get the equivalent of 1 tablespoon of fresh, use 1 teaspoon of dried.

When trying to reduce the salt content from your diet what are some herb and spice replacements for salt?

Allspice:	Lean meats, stews, tomatoes, gravies, applesauce.
Caraway:	Breads, cabbage, noodles.
Chives:	Salads, soups, vegetables.
Dill:	Lamb, chicken, fish, carrots, potatoes.
Mace:	Hot breads, cauliflower, squash.
Nutmeg:	Fruits, pie crust, veal, puddings.
Sage:	Biscuits, green or lima beans, onions.
Turmeric:	Sauces, rice.

What are good herb/meat combinations?

Beef: Basil, thyme, sweet marjoram, summer savory, rosemary.

Veal: Summer savory, rosemary, thyme, basil, tarragon.

Lamb: Mint, summer savory, sweet marjoram, dill, rosemary.

Pork: Sweet marjoram, thyme, sage, chives, basil.

Poultry: Thyme, sage, tarragon, sweet marjoram, chervil, summer savory.

Fish: Chervil, fennel, sage, parsley, dill, sweet marjoram, basil, chives.

When should herbs be added for best flavor?

1. For long cooking add during the last 20–30 minutes.
2. In marinades or salad dressing add at the beginning.

Anise

What is anise?

The leaves of a plant of the parsley family with a distinct licorice flavor. Often considered as a spice.

How is it used?

Anise gives licorice flavor to both sweet and savory dishes and also to various liqueurs and drinks.

Basil

What should you know about basil?

1. It is from the mint family.
2. The fresh and dried are quite different.

Can fresh and dried basil be used interchangeably?

No. For example, you can't make pesto from the dried form.

What should be looked for when buying basil?

They are sold in small bunches of leaves, none of which should be mottled or wilted. It should be aromatic and peppery with a sweet background. The leaves should be soft and shiny.

How should basil be used in a salad?

Fresh leaves can be used as an addition to green salads without blanching or cooking. Basil goes especially well with fresh tomatoes.

How should it be used in cooking?

It should be added toward the end of cooking or it will lose flavor.

How can basil pesto be kept from turning brown?

1. Put lemon juice in the water in which the pasta is boiled.
2. Add lemon juice to the pesto.
3. Add the pesto at the table after the pasta is dished since heat is the culprit.
4. A few leaves of parsley, marjoram or spinach will preserve the intense green of pesto sauce.
5. Keep chilled if not to be used immediately.

How can pesto be varied?

Add spinach, orange peel, arugula, sorrel, mint.

What is opal basil?

A variety of basil that is milder than regular basil and has crinkly purple leaves.

How should a pesto sauce that is too thick be thinned when it is to be served with pasta?

Add a little of the cooking water from the pasta.

Bay Leaves

What should be looked for when buying bay leaves?

1. A bay leaf is at its best when whole and pliable, not broken or brittle.
2. Ignore any with brown specks or a faded hue.
3. They shouldn't be so dry that they crumble when pinched.
4. If possible, choose those with a squat rather than elongated leaf.
5. Sniff the leaves. The good ones have a fresh characteristic aroma.
6. They should be shiny on top and dull on the underside.

What is the flavor of bay leaves?

It is difficult to describe but somewhere in a lemon-nutmeg mixture. It has a slightly woody character.

Are fresh bay leaves better than dried ones?

They are quite different, but fresh ones are rarely found on the market.

What should be watched for when cooking with bay?

The flavor of bay may overwhelm a slow-cooked dish if left in the pot for the entire cooking period. The ideal cooking time is 30 minutes or less.

Why should the leaves be removed before serving?

Always remove the leaves before serving. There are many instances of diners accidently swallowing a sharp-edged leaf. Even though the flavor of the leaf is good and safe to digest, the solid leaf is unwholesome if consumed in more than a small quantity.

Should bay leaves be crumbled before adding?

No, because it will be impossible to remove the pieces.

Capers

What are capers?

They are sun-dried, small, unopened buds of a Mediterranean bush. Although originally from the Mediterranean area they are now grown in California and Florida.

Which are the best capers?

The Petite Nonpareil, originally from Southern France, are considered the best variety and are now grown in the United States. Larger ones, the size of small olives, are grown in Italy and Spain.

How should capers be chosen?

The Petite Nonpareil are usually available pickled in brine in small glass jars. These are sun-dried, small. Unopened flower bulbs are sometimes sold dry. Those pickled should be rinsed in water to remove the salt. For intense caper flavor, choose salt-packed ones, but they also must be rinsed before using.

How are they prepared for market?

1. Brined in salted white vinegar is the most common presentation.
2. The dry salted are usually sold in bulk.

What should be done before using?

The dried should be rinsed in water to remove excess saltiness and then dried, but the brined ones are often used directly from the jar.

How should the jar of capers be handled?

Pour out the liquid and replace it with undiluted, plain white vinegar, which will double or triple the storage life of the capers. After opening, store the jar in the refrigerator.

How can you tell when capers are past their prime?

When they have begun to acquire a brownish tint.

How long can they be kept?

Even with the best of care, after the jar has been opened, they can become mushy after a few months, so replace them on a regular basis.

How can you use capers to their best advantage?

1. Use as a garnish on top of food such as a salad.
2. Smashed or pureed they are good in sauces or eggs.

Celery Flakes

What are celery flakes?

Celery that is chopped and dehydrated.

What is its fresh equivalent?

1 tablespoon = 1 small stalk of fresh celery.

How can it be used?

In soups or stock. If it is for roasts or casseroles, rehydrate it first.

Chervil

What is chervil?

An herb belonging to the parsley family that is often used to replace parsley.

How does it compare to parsley?

It is more delicate and aromatic.

How is chervil used?

Usually in combination with other, stronger herbs or as a salad green.

Cilantro (Chinese parsley, flat leaf parsley, Mexican parsley)

What is cilantro?

The dark green, lacy leaves of the cilantro plant. It has a sharp, tangy, fresh flavor.

How should it be prepared?

Just before using wash, drain and blot dry with paper toweling.

Can the stems be used?

Since they are tender, they can be used along with the leaves.

Coriander

What is coriander?

It is the longest known herb (about 5000 BC). A dried, ripe, spicy fruit of the parsley family that looks like a seed, coriander has a mild aroma with a flavor that is mildly lemony with overtones of sage and caraway.

What is coriander used for?

Both as a seed in making liqueurs or powdered in curries. Goes well with salads, curry, guacamole, soups and stews.

How should coriander be chosen?

Look for bright, even-colored leaves without signs of wilting.

Dill

What is dill?

Another member of the parsley family, it has feathery green leaves and a flavor that is a cross between parsley and anise.

Are fresh and dried dill equivalent?

They are quite different and cannot be used interchangeably.

What is the fresh dill like?

The fresh is assertive and works well with fish (such as salmon) and in salads and sauces. The fresh dill leaves are beautiful as a garnish.

How is dried used?

Dried dill is used in pickling, because of its strong flavor, and in smoking fish.

Lemon Grass (Citronella)

What is lemon grass?

A grass with a lemon-herb flavor. This herb is best when fresh, although often not available so must be used dry. Prominent in Southeast Asian cooking, particularly Thai. Looks somewhat like green onions with serrated leaves.

How should lemon grass be prepared?

Remove the green leaves and any dry, tough, outer leaves. Pound the grass slightly to bruise it and release its aromatic oils.

What does lemon grass blend well with?

Mixes well with ginger and garlic to form the background of much of Asian cooking.

How should lemon grass be used?

Broth: Quarter the white stalk and cut into 2–3″ pieces, but remove it from broth before serving.

Sauté: Cook the stalk, finely chopped, adding it towards the end of the sautéing.

Lemon Zest

What is lemon zest?

The outermost layer of a lemon skin, the yellow part only.

What is it used for?

To flavor food, both cooked and raw. It is not sweet.

Can zest be frozen successfully?

Yes, for several weeks of more.

What fruit gives the best zest?

Organic lemons, because they don't have a wax coating.

Marjoram

What are the forms of marjoram?

It comes in two forms. Sweet is the more common and more delicate, coming from the Mediterranean area. Wild is known as oregano (comes from the Greek meaning "mountain joy"). Most of our supply actually comes from Mexico.

What is the difference between marjoram and oregano?

Oregano is not as sweet but has more pungency and is much stronger.

What should be looked for in marjoram?

It should have a fairly strong aroma and a sweet flavor that can brighten herb mixtures. In taste it is somewhat similar to basil.

How is dried marjoram used?

It has a rather delicate flavor, which goes well with many meats but should be used at the end of cooking.

How is fresh marjoram used?

It goes well with cottage cheese and is used to flavor meats, especially lamb and veal.

Mint

What is mint?

A large family of plants with more than two dozen varieties, of which spearmint and peppermint are the best known. It grows wild and is also cultivated. Peppermint is the strongest and more peppery of the two.

How should mint be chosen?

Select evenly colored leaves without evidence of wilting.

What can fresh mint be used with?

1. It has a special affinity for vegetables such as peas, carrots, eggplants, zucchini and cauliflower.
2. It is also good in fresh salads.
3. It does well with sauteed chicken dishes and also roast lamb.
4. When mixed with other herbs it can be excellent with fish.

5. By itself it is used in making candy.
6. It is excellent as a garnish.
7. It can be paired with basil in making pesto.
8. It softens the bite of peppery dishes.

Why is commercial mint jelly not recommended?
They are usually not very good and mostly over-sweet. When mixed with other herbs it can be excellent with fish. If well-made, excellent on roast lamb.

How should fresh mint be handled?
Since it bruises easily, chop or slice it with a sharp, dry knife.

Oregano

What is the history of oregano?
Oregano was one of the original seasonings and preservatives for beer in Italy, long before hops were introduced. The Romans introduced the herb into Britain, and it was used to season beer in the British Isles. Pillows stuffed with both hops and oregano were claimed to cure insomnia. After the fall of Rome, during the period known as the Dark Ages, trade in oregano and other spices declined. Even today, Birra Perfetto, a beer now brewed in the United States by Pikes Place Brewery, uses a mixture of malted barley, fresh hops, brewers yeast and dried oregano leaves.

How can you tell the nature of oregano?
There are many varieties. The Greek is sweet and strong. Snip off a leaf and taste. The Mexican is less sweet, more pungent and suited for hot, spicy dishes. Works well with cilantro in salsa.

How is oregano used?
It goes well with pizza, in tomato-based preparations and other highly spiced dishes.

Parsley

What is the difference between flat leaf (Italian) and the curly leaf varieties of parsley?
The flat has a cleaner, fresher, stronger flavor and is particularly good for cooking. The curly is more attractive and is excellent as a garnish, but both are good in cooked dishes. They can be used interchangeably.

How should parsley be selected?
It should be bright green without signs of wilting. Sold in bunches.

Should the parsley stems be used?
They are soft and can be used if chopped.

How should parsley be handled for freezing?

1. Wash and dry.
2. Chop in the processor about 20 seconds.
3. Put in a plastic freezer bag and press out the air.
4. Frozen it will keep 5–6 months.
5. If it is used on a dish that won't be cooked further, the parsley will defrost in a few seconds and needs no further cooking.

Does parsley have nutrient value?

It contains vitamins A and C.

What is the caution in eating parsley?

It makes a few people's skin sensitive to sunlight.

Rosemary

What is rosemary?

This member of the mint family has green, needle-shaped leaves and a strong aroma of pine and lemon.

Which is preferred, fresh or dried?

1. Fresh is preferable to dried because it is more aromatic and flavorful.
2. Of the dried, the whole leaf is better than the ground.

When buying rosemary, should large or small stems be chosen?

The larger ones tend to be woody and resinous. The smaller are more tender and work better.

How should dried rosemary be used?

1. Ground rosemary can be added to slow-cooked dishes.
2. The whole leaf is more aromatic.
3. For short-cooked preparations put the ground rosemary in a removable muslin bag, otherwise the leaves will be too hard and unpleasant in the mouth.

With what other seasonings does rosemary work well?

Onions, garlic, lemon. It is often paired with oregano and thyme in Italian recipes.

What foods does rosemary go with?

It is excellent with grilled lamb, chicken, pork and fish.

Can rosemary be used in sweet dishes?

Yes, with a tart lemon sorbet or flavored honey, for example.

What should be done first to use dried rosemary in baking?

Rinse in hot water before mixing it into dough.

How can rosemary be used with kabobs?

Strip off most of the leaves and spear the meat on the rosemary stem. This will result in well-flavored kebabs.

Sage

What do sage leaves look like?

The leaves are gray-green, slender, slightly furry.

What is the culinary timing for the use of sage?

Best to add it about a half hour before the finish of the cooking process.

How long can sage be kept?

It should be kept not longer than 6 months.

Tarragon

What does tarragon taste like?

Somewhat anise-like with an undertone of sage.

How can tarragon be used?

1. Good for chowders, salad dressings.
2. Excellent for savory butters to be used on steaks.
3. Tarragon vinegar is excellent for salads.

Can it be frozen successfully?

Yes, it does freeze very well. Frozen leaves are better than dried ones.

Thyme

Why is thyme called the workhorse herb?

It harmonizes with many cooking ingredients and is compatible with many other seasoning agents, including bay leaf. It is excellent both fresh and crushed/dried but the powdered/dried form quickly loses its aromatics. Very good with poultry, pork, fried chicken. It mixes well with spices such as rosemary and garlic.

What is lemon thyme?

A subvariety of wild thyme, it has a citrus flavor that works well with seafood, baked custards and squash.

What are some of the nonculinary uses of thyme?

1. As a fumigant and an antiseptic since classic times.
2. Extracted thyme oil has been used since the sixteenth century used to make mouth washes and gargles.

Seasoning and Oils

3. As a disinfectant, active against food poisoning salmonella and staphylococcus.
4. Used today in preparations for fungal infections of the skin.
5. An important ingredient in making the liqueur Benedictine.

SPICES

What are spices?

The seasonings from flowers, fruits, seeds and roots of various trees and plants.

What is the history of spices?

Much nonsense has been written about spices. Marco Polo, around AD 1250 , was claimed to be the first to bring spices into Europe, but spices were already used in European cooking when the Polo family, who dealt with spices, took a business trip through Asia. In 2800 BC the ancient Egyptians made use of mint, marjoram, cinnamon and cassia. These were reserved for the Pharaoh, the princes and the priests used them for therapeutic, cosmetic and ritual use. Garlic and onions were the only flavorings of the common people. In the Bible all meat offerings cooked with herbs/spices became the property of the priests. Spices used to be given to bridal couples as a good luck charm.

What is the oldest spice known?

Cinnamon is though to be the oldest of spices. By the Middle Ages it was essential to the culinary arts. Controlling the island of Ceylon, the Dutch were exporting 270 tons per year. When the British took over the island and increased the planting and culturing of the trees their export rose to 1,000 tons per year by around 1850.

In doubling a recipe, should the spices be doubled as well?

No! Taste first to make your judgment. Some recipe writers are not very exact and, in addition, the intensity of flavors varies with the length and method of storage of the spice. Doubling could lead to an over-spiced dish. Use caution and taste as you add. Small recipe amounts are often approximate.

What are the most expensive spices?

In decreasing order: saffron, vanilla, cardamon.

What are some of the uses of the different spices?

Allspice:	Fruit salads, grilled or boiled fish, pickles, candies, poultry.
Anise:	Cookies, pastry, coleslaw, sauerkraut, sausages, creams.
Caraway seed:	Sauerkraut, rye bread, cookies, pork, soups, beef, sweet pickles, dressings, cheese, liqueurs, goose, duck.
Cardamon:	Curries, pea soup, cakes, cookies, jellies, hot dogs.
Celery seeds:	Pot roast, soups, stew, salads, fish, pickling, vegetables.
Chili peppers:	Curry, meat dishes, hot sauces, salsa.

Cinnamon:	Desserts, applesauce, toast, ice cream, dessert sauce, sweet pickles, ketchup, apple butter, spiced fruit.
Cloves:	Ham, desserts, pies, soups, syrups, poached fruit, pickling, barbecuing, beef stew.
Coriander:	Ginger cookies and bread, curry, poultry stuffing, pork.
Cumin:	Curry, cheese, poultry, game, chili dishes, stuffed eggs.
Dill seed:	Cheese, stews, salad dressing, pickles, sauerkraut, sauces.
Fennel seed:	Bread, pork, seafood, sauerkraut, soups, fish, pizza.
Ginger:	Curry, Chinese cooking, desserts, baking, salad dressings, chicken soup, steaks.
Horseradish:	Ground as a meat condiment, with fish balls (gefilte fish), mixed with whipped or sour cream on prime ribs.
Juniper:	Game, stews, goose.
Mace:	Desserts, seafood stews, baked beans, deviled ham, French dressing, Clear soups, fruit cake, donuts, pumpkin pie, pork.
Mustard:	Sauces, deviled eggs, salad dressing, meats, vegetables, glazes.
Nutmeg:	Desserts, apples sauce, cakes, cookies, vegetables, custards.
Paprika:	Stews, sauces, chicken, veal eggs, fish, cheese dishes.
Pepper:	Almost any non-sweet dish.
Poppy seeds:	Breads, cookies, cakes, salads.
Sesame seeds:	Bread, casseroles, toppings for vegetables and soups or ground to make tahini, poultry, baked fish.
Thyme:	Soups, stews, sauces, sausages, chowders.
Turmeric:	Curry, fish, rice, sauces, pickles, poultry.
Vanilla:	Ice cream, chocolate, sweet baked goods.

How should spices be stored?

Heat, light and air help disintegrate them so place in tightly covered glass jars and place in a cool cabinet or in a drawer away from the heat. Properly stored they will keep about two years when ground, about four years whole. Chili peppers and paprika are best kept refrigerated.

Where should spices not be stored?

Never near a microwave or a range. The heat tends to cause a loss of flavor and color.

Which are the two most frequently used spices in the United States?

Pepper and mustard.

Why are cinnamon, pepper and other spices not added until the end when sautéing, deep frying or broiling?

These cooking processes tend to scorch the spices quite quickly and therefore will produce a disagreeable flavor.

Seasoning and Oils

What are the advantages of buying whole spices such as coriander seeds, mustard seeds, cumin seeds and then grinding as needed?

Whole spices keep their potency longer.

When should chili powder and black pepper be added?

It is not wise to add them or like seasoning agents at the beginning of the sautéing process.

Allspice

Where did the name allspice come from?

The taste is a combination of cloves, cinnamon and nutmeg. However, it is a spice unto itself and not a created combination.

What are other names of allspice?

Also known as Jamaica pepper, in the Caribbean as pimiento and in Poland as kulaba.

What is the best allspice to buy?

Buy the whole spice and grind it yourself.

How should it be ground?

Grind only as needed, using a separate grinding mill.

Caraway seeds

What is the origin of these seeds?

These are seeds from a herb of the parsley family. Caraway is most popular in central Europe, including Austria, Germany and Hungary.

What is the culinary contribution of caraway?

It gives a delicate licorice, nutty flavor and adds texture to baked goods.

How can caraway seeds be used?

In cabbage dishes, rye bread, bagels, goose or duck, cream soups and a base for making the liqueur kümmel.

Cardamon

What are the uses of cardamon seeds?

Both the green and black seeds are used. In India, where it is native, both are used. They now also come from the Caribbean. Green is preferred in the Middle East. The black have a slightly smoky quality. The pods keep almost indefinitely, ground seeds keep best refrigerated.

How can cardamon be purchased?

In the pod or ground.

What happens when the cardamon seeds are removed from the pod?

They begin to lose their flavoring oil almost immediately on grinding.

Must the seeds of cardamon be removed from the pod before using?

Not necessarily, although there is very little flavor in the shell, but the pods should be removed and discarded before serving. You can use the seeds alone, which are intensely flavored and are better than the preground. Choose green pods and grind the seeds as necessary.

What are the three types of cardamon pods?

White: Most expensive, used in baked goods.

Green: Medium expensive, for meat and vegetable dishes.

Black: Least expensive, used in place of green, has a smoky flavor.

Cayenne

What is cayenne?

A hot, ground pepper that originated in the Carribean and was spread through the world after being taken to Europe by Columbus.

What is the current product that is on the market?

Nowadays it is a blend of several types of ground, red chili peppers with a tart, smoky, very hot and spicy taste.

Chilies (Chili, Chile)

Why are chilies more popular in the tropics than in temperate zones?

1. They cool the body. The pepper causes the body to sweat. As the heat of the day or a dry breeze evaporates perspiration, the skin cools because as water changes from a liquid to a gas it absorbs a lot of heat calories.
2. They perk appetite. Hot, muggy days can suppress hunger.
3. They add zest to the diet. As lovely as tropical fruits, vegetables and fish are, they tend to be generally blander in flavor.
4. They are a natural preservative and in the tropics, fruits, vegetables and fish suffer from faster spoilage.
5. They can smother the telltale taste and odor of spoilage.
6. They tend, to some degree, to reduce the incidence of diarrhea or other intestinal disorders.

Why are some people less affected by chili peppers than others?

1. Variation in the sensitivity of individuals.
2. The more frequent the exposure, the more tolerance the body develops.

What is the difference between green and red chili peppers?

The color indicates the ripeness of the pepper when it is picked. All varieties are green when young. They lose chlorophyll as they ripen and previously hidden red or yellow or orange colors become visible as the green disappears. The heat takes longer to come on when they are green.

What causes chili peppers to go from mild to firebombs?

The bite comes from capsaicin, which is located in the placenta, the part just under the stem where the seeds attach and down the yellow veined ribs or veins. The seeds are not a source of heat although they may carry capsaicin because they rub up against the hot parts.

What is chili paste?

Pureed, dried and/or fresh chilies mixed with oil and salt into a paste. It may have additional ingredients such as cumin, ginger etc.

What is the difference between commercial chili powder and medium hot, pure chili powder?

1. Commercial chili powder is a mixture of ground hot chili peppers, garlic powder, oregano, cumin and salt. The blend varies with the manufacturer, and, therefore, the pungency will vary.
2. Medium hot, pure chili powder is made only from dried peppers and varies in heat according to the type of chilies used.
3. They cannot be used interchangeably.
4. To keep fresh, store in airtight containers in a cool, dark place, preferably in the freezer.

What is "chili pepper"?

It is made only from dried peppers that have been ground into a powder.

What are chipotle peppers?

Red jalapeño peppers that have been wood smoked and are medium hot.

How should you select and use chili peppers?

1. Buy plump, unshriveled peppers with a brightly hued skin. Reject those with soft spots, cuts or bruises.
2. The less twisted the pepper, the easier to prepare.
3. Generally the smaller, the hotter.

How should they be stored?

Stored in sealed, plastic bags in the vegetable crisper. If you plan to keep more than a couple of days, pierce the bag in several places.

How can the bite be reduced?

To reduce the hotness remove the seeds and membranes before cooking. To further reduce it, parboil them a few minutes.

Will cooking or freezing lessen the bite of chile pepper?

No, only the removal of seeds or veins will really do the job.

What precautions should be taken when using chilies?

1. Certain peppers can burn your skin and especially your eyes.
2. Always wash your knife and chopping block as well as your hands promptly after cutting peppers.
3. Under no circumstances rub your eyes before you have washed your hands well. (Contact lens wearers beware!)
4. If you have mistakenly done so, quickly wash your hands and fingers and flush out your eye(s) with milk or cool water.

How accurate is the grading of hotness, such as the number of Scoville units?

There is considerable variation even among the same varieties, age and color of chili. Although there are measurements of heat/bite, such as Scoville units, they are not absolutely accurate because of these variations.

What are some of the various chili peppers on the market?

Anaheim:	Also called California Chile, bright green or red, about 6″ long. Mild.
Poblano:	Dark green, tapered, thick flesh, about 4″ × 2½″, used in sauces or stuffed. Mild.
New Mexico green (or red):	Medium green in color, about 7″ × 1½″, thick flesh, used for commercial canning, sauces, salsas, a sweet, intense, earthy flavor. Medium hot.
Jalapeño:	Bright green, tapered, about 2″ × 1″, used roasted in sauces or stuffed, hotter than cayenne but the best of the jalapeño leave the bite (in the mouth) sooner. The heat is temperature sensitive, so it should be added towards the end of cooking. Can be hot.
Serrano:	Dark green to bright red, small, tapered, 1–2″ × ½″, used both raw and roasted in marinades. Hotter than jalapeño.
Habenero:	Dark green to bright red, roundish, about ½″ in diameter, used for salsa and marinade. Hottest used by most.
Improved:	Dried for chili powder. The hottest.

What can be done to relieve the burn if chili is too hot in the mouth?

The capsaicin, which causes the heat, is not water soluble so water does not relieve the pain. Milk with its butterfat, ice cream or starches such as rice or potatoes are best.

Will beer or wine cool your mouth?

Just the opposite, for alcohol increases the absorption of capsaicin.

Seasoning and Oils

How can you increase the hotness of commercial chili powder?

Add cayenne pepper.

How can you make your own chili powder?

Blend your own mixture by combining freshly ground: oregano, cumin, cayenne, cloves and allspice. Add finely minced garlic just before using.

What is Tabasco sauce?

This is the trade name for a commercial hot or pepper sauce made on Averey Island, Louisiana. The production is huge, about 75 million bottles per year, 300,000 per day. The plant is located on a salt deposit from which 2 million tons of salt are removed per year and is equal in size to Mt. Everest plus several Rocky Mountain peaks.

How is Tabasco made?

Fresh peppers grown from the original seed are macerated with salt and left to mellow for three years in barrels, then blended with distilled white vinegar, strained and bottled.

Will Tabasco or other bottled chili sauces keep indefinitely?

No. If the color changes from red to brown, replace it because it will have lost most of its fresh, fruity flavor.

Cinnamon

What is cinnamon?

The fine inner bark of wild-growing, tropical evergreen trees. There are two types: Cassia, from a different type of laurel tree has the strong, spicy, sweet flavor and is the one best known in the United States. It also is the one blended with chocolate. Ceylon (true cinnamon) is less sweet, is citrusy and complex and more expensive.

Are cinnamon sticks the best and highest in flavor?

No, the sticks come from the upper branches and are lower in flavor. The ground cinnamon comes from the lower, older bark and is more intense in flavor.

What is cinnamon sugar?

1. Sugar that has had cinnamon sticks buried in it for several weeks but still keeps its white color.
2. Sugar mixed with ground cinnamon; it is colored light brown.

How is cinnamon sugar used?

Both styles are used for seasoning toast or coffee or for decorating baked goods.

What is oil of cinnamon?

Oil pressed from the cinnamon bark that is used in flavoring.

Cloves

What are cloves?

These dried, unopened flower buds of the clove tree have a flavor that is a mixture of lemon, sage and caraway.

How are cloves used?

It is used ground in beef stews and gravies. Whole cloves are used in pickling, as in pickling blends, in baked hams, baked goods and barbecuing. They are also good in the poaching liquid for fruits.

What is the caution in using cloves?

Use sparingly as they are among the strongest of spices.

How should cloves be chosen?

When in doubt about their freshness, crush the head of a clove. The released scent should be pronounced and typical and the texture not unduly brittle.

Coriander

What is coriander?

It is the seed of the plant native to the orient and Mediterranean that produces cilantro and has a light, lemony flavor that combines well with ginger.

How should coriander be used?

It does best with long cooking such as whole roasts or fowl or quicker at high temperatures such as pan-fried dishes.

How is ground coriander used?

It is the traditional part of Scandinavian baked goods and is also used in soups and curries.

Cumin

What is cumin?

It is a dried, caraway-shaped seed native to Egypt from a plant of the parsley family that is available in seed and ground forms.

How is it used?

Cumin is used to season curries, chili powders, salsas, pasta, cole slaw, lentils, chicken, beef, tomatoes.

Curry

What is curry powder?

It is a condiment originally from the cuisine of India, a blend of up to twenty spices and herbs making a mixture that is strong in flavor. Some ingredients are cumin,

Seasoning and Oils

cardamon, coriander seeds, and usually turmeric. Varies in composition from location to location.

What is the best curry powder?

Commercial blends are usually overstretched with relatively inexpensive turmeric. Better make your own blend by mixing cumin, coriander seeds, cayenne, mace, nutmeg and saffron. If you use turmeric, do so sparingly.

What is another reason for making your own blend?

Curry powder loses its bite in a few months.

How can the flavor of individual spices in a curry be brought out?

To make them more intense roast the individual spices in a preheated 350 °F oven for 20 minutes before grinding and blending with the other spices.

Are all curries hot?

Not all of them. Tandoori and maharajah are spicy without being hot, and there are sweet curries, too.

Ginger

What is ginger?

A knobbed, gnarled root of a tropical plant with a sweet, peppery flavor.

How do you choose fresh ginger?

1. Give it a sniff test, for it is only as good as it smells.
2. Avoid if it is cracked, moldy, bruised or shriveled.
3. Look for the smoothest skin.
4. Look for the firmest body.
5. It should break cleanly with a snap.
6. The heavier and the firmer, the better.

What does a wrinkled shoot indicate?

That the root is dry and lower in quality.

What does a blue color in ginger indicate?

That the ginger tube isn't fully ripe but it is still usable.

How can you peel ginger if the recipe calls for fresh ginger root?

Remove a branch from the root, trim off any bumps or bulges with a paring knife or vegetable peeler, then peel off the skin.

Can fresh and dried (powdered) be used interchangeably?

No, although both are good seasonings.

What is the difference between young and mature ginger?

Young: Available in springtime and early summer, has a thin, pale skin that doesn't require peeling, is juicier.

Mature: Available all year around and requires peeling.

What is the use of ginger juice?

When the ginger taste is wanted but the texture is not.

How can ginger juice be extracted?

1. Choose a smooth, shiny, slightly heavy root.
2. Grate the root.
3. Extract the juice in a garlic press or wrap the grated ginger in cheesecloth and twist and press it to extract the juice.
4. Make only as much as needed, for it will keep its fragrance only for a day or two.

What is the yield of juice from ginger root?

Two pounds of root will yield about ¾ cup of juice.

How should peeled root be stored?

Fresh, peeled ginger can be stored for several weeks if submerged in dry sherry in a covered glass jar and refrigerated.

Can unpeeled ginger be frozen?

Yes, and it keeps well for a long time and can be grated easily while still frozen.

How can grated ginger be used?

1. Fine grate works well with stir-fry.
2. It is good for giving flavor to salt-free dishes.

What are the forms in which ginger is used?

Sliced: It is best for flavoring cooking oil, for it doesn't brown as fast as when diced or julienned.

Julienne: Use for stir-fry dishes. Avoid overcooking to prevent loss of texture.

Diced: Diced finely and added with white wine and soy makes a fish or meat sauce.

Grated: Finely grated works well with stir-fry. It mixes with garlic and pepper to make a good dry rub for steaks.

Pickled: When sliced, it is an excellent accompaniment to sushi.

What is ginger oil?

Made by cooking slices in a little peanut oil until the ginger browns and the oil is almost smoking. Remove and discard the ginger before using.

How is the oil used?

Use for dressing pasta or making fish sauce. Good mixed with a little soy sauce.

Why is fish so often cooked with ginger?

It not only flavors fish but helps to counteract fishy odors.

How does crystallized ginger differ from ginger preserved in syrup?

In syrup: Young ginger is cut into pieces, simmered in sugar syrup until it softens and most of the syrup is absorbed. Then it is packed in syrup (which should be discarded).

Crystallized: The ginger is sliced and simmered in sugar syrup and then dried.

Can they be used interchangeably?

Yes.

Horseradish

What is horseradish?

A white root of a plant of the mustard family, a native of eastern Europe, that has strong, sharp flavors and aroma.

How should it be selected?

Look for firm roots without any blemishes or withering.

What is the red horseradish found on the shelves?

It is ground horseradish colored with beet juice which modifies it slightly.

Is pregrated horseradish (in jars) equal to freshly grated?

It varies, for often it is diluted with sour cream or other products. Mainly it is not quite as strong.

What is a caution on using horseradish?

Once grated it quickly loses its exhilarating aromatics, which are essential to offset the natural harsh flavor of the root.

How can horseradish be used?

Serve as a condiment. If added to the cooking or smeared on a roast the cooking heat will destroy much of the enticing aromas.

How can the sharp taste be modified?

A little ground horseradish in sour or whipped cream makes an excellent, not too hot condiment to go with prime ribs. It is delicious mixed with applesauce or with roast pork.

How should the dried powder form be used?

As a dried powder it can be mixed with two parts of water and added as a bite in a horseradish sauce.

Mace

What is mace?

The orange-red outer covering of the nutmeg seed, which is milder and more refined. It turns a bright red after the membrane is removed.

What should be looked for in ground mace?

Sniff it because it becomes rancid rather quickly, particularly when ground.

What is a caution on using mace?

The unground or blade form is more aromatic and flavorful than preground. Add one or more pieces to soups or stews as they cook but remember to discard them before serving.

What can mace accomplish?

A pinch of ground mace added to omelettes or tuna salads lends a new dimension of flavor.

Mustard

What family does it belong to?

The broccoli family.

What are the main styles of prepared mustard?

American (ball park or hot dog):	Made from mild, white/yellow mustard seeds, sugar, vinegar and turmeric, it is a bright yellow with smooth, mild flavors.
Dijon:	Smooth, pale yellow-gray, with a sharp flavor ranging from mild to hot. Some are made with some unground seeds to give a crunchiness.
English:	Made from a mixture of seeds, flour and turmeric, and it is hot.
German:	Spicy, slightly sweet, ranging in color and strength.

Are there new mustards on the market?

Many more, ranging from those flavored with horseradish to those made with beer.

What are the kinds of mustard seeds?

Black:	Most pungent from its essential oils, used commercially for prepared mustards early in the century.
Brown:	Slightly less spicy but hotter than yellow, used for most commercial mustards because the seeds are larger and easily harvested mechanically. The predominant flavor comes from a sulfur compound.
Yellow/white:	Mildest, is the main ingredient in bright yellow mustard. The most common form of mustard on the market.

What are the seeds used for?

Meats, pickling, vegetables and for grinding into a powder.

What is mustard powder?

The seeds are finely ground and the powder used for preparing mustards or directly as a seasoning.

How should a sharp flavor be obtained?

Add mustard in the last minutes of cooking.

Why shouldn't mustard be cooked in aluminum pans?

Mustard and aluminum interact to produce an off-taste.

How should prepared mustard be stored?

Prepared mustard mellows with age when not refrigerated. It will keep very well refrigerated.

What is the effect of heating when preparing mustard?

Using cold water or liquids to mix with the ground seeds develops the flavor, complexity and intensifies the flavor and pungency. Hot liquid will somewhat dissipate the intensity and thus yield a milder product, with more delicate nuances.

How is mustard used in meat glazes?

Mixed with a sweetening agent such as honey, marmalade, maple syrup etc.

Should different mustards be mixed when making glazes or sauces?

Yes, for they provide flavors that can be enticing. Try combining Dijon with whole grain mustard for a salad dressing.

Nutmeg

What is the relationship between nutmeg and mace?

1. Both come from the nutmeg tree, which is native to the Malucca but has spread to Latin America and the West Indies. Both are aromatic and sun or charcoal dried.
2. The nutmeg is the small, brown seed at the heart of the fruit and should be grated fresh for best results. Mace is the outer covering of the seed, and tastes like pungent version of nutmeg.

What is the yield of ground nutmeg from seeds?

One whole nutmeg will yield 2–3 teaspoons of the grated.

How should grated nutmeg be stored?

It should be stored in an air-tight container if ground ahead of time but is best if ground as you need it. It is more delicate in flavor and aroma than mace.

How is nutmeg used?

Cheese dishes, sausages, syrups, cream sauces, hot beverages, quiche.

Paprika

What is paprika?

The plant name is *Capiscum annum*. It originated in the New World and was brought back to Europe by Columbus. It reached Hungary in the sixteenth century. It was always fiery hot until Hungarian millers in the nineteenth century discovered a method to remove the seeds and veins in which the fiery quality lies. Now almost all paprika is sweet and is made from a mild hybrid.

Which paprika is best?

The best comes from Hungary rather than from Spain or California.

What are the grades of paprika?

The Hungarian comes in three grades of hotness: mild (also called sweet), hot and exceptionally hot. Most of what is sold in this country is the mild version and is the preferred choice for flavoring dishes such as chicken paprika.

Does paprika have a constant color?

The color varies from year to year, depending on the growing season.

What is another use for paprika besides being a cooking flavoring?

It can be sprinkled on top of foods for color.

Does paler color mean hotter bite in Hungarian paprika?

Yes, because to increase heat the spicy, lightly colored veins and seeds are ground in with the pepper flesh, producing the lighter color.

Pepper

What is pepper?

A sharp spice from peppercorns. The name is frequently used for chile, cayenne, paprika and even sweet bell peppers.

What are black peppercorns?

The berries left to mature and dry (during which some ferment) so the skin wrinkles and they turn a very dark brown.

Which are the best black peppercorns?

Freshly ground are best and the best of the black is that from India. The top 10% from the largest corns are the Tellicherry, which are the most mature.

How do the white peppercorns differ from the black?

The berries are left on the vine to mature, then picked and soaked and the outer skin is rubbed off, leaving only the pale seed. White pepper is milder and can be used in light-colored sauces because it isn't so visible. It can also be used with grilled meats and potato salads, but it has less flavor, less bite and is more refined than the black.

Are green berries the same?

Green pepper berries are picked when still soft and soaked in brine, vinegar or their own juice. They have a medium to mild flavor and are less sharp than the blacks. Usually sold in cans or jars. The best are packed in brine. They are good whole in pasta.

What is the advantage of green peppercorns?

They are milder than the black and work well to flavor lighter dishes.

How do pink berries differ?

These are not peppercorns and come from a different tree. They have a more delicate flavor and work well with dishes such as crab.

Can black, green and pink berries be used together?

Yes, they can create complex, attractive flavors.

How long do peppercorns last?

The whole peppercorns keep very well so grind them only as needed for the oil fades within months after grinding.

Poppy Seeds

How many poppy seeds are there in a pound?

900,000.

What is the difference between blue and white poppy seeds?

The blue are the most used. The white is used mainly in Asian and Indian cooking. Both add thickening texture and flavor in sauces, and both have a high oil content.

What should you look for in poppy seeds?

Reject seeds that have lost their surface sheen. A dull surface indicates that the oils inside have become rancid.

How should poppy seeds be stored?

In a tightly closed container in the refrigerator to prevent rancidity.

How can they best be used?

For optimum flavor toast poppy seeds before adding to the dish, such as pasta. It is not necessary when you sprinkle them on top of bread dough because the baking process will do the job.

How are the Holland Blue seeds rated as to quality?

Very highly.

Saffron

What is the best saffron?

The best comes from Kasmir in India labeled Magro Cream; the next is Spanish. Avoid Saffron from Mexico even though it is the least expensive for it usually is not saffron. The real saffron are the stigmas (threads) of a purple crocus flower. One acre produces 70,000 crocuses, each of which yields, hand harvested, three threads. It takes 14,000 threads to make one ounce. An acre will yield only one pound of saffron.

Which saffron should be purchased?

Buy the threads rather than crushed. The crushed is easily cheapened by the processor and is generally not very good, often adulterated with turmeric or other spices added. Buy only those containers with red threads, avoiding any with yellow filaments. The crushed form deteriorate rapidly.

How is saffron used?

To use, crush in a mortar or break between your fingers before adding to the cooking pot or soak in a small quantity of the hot cooking liquid for about 4–5 minutes. Then press the saffron with the back of a spoon to release the color and flavor and add the crushed threads and the soaking liquid to the cooking pot. High-quality threads will quickly color the liquid and expand, poor or stale ones will not.

How should saffron threads be stored?

Refrigerated.

Why should the amount of saffron in a dish be limited?

1. An excess of threads can result in bitterness.
2. Unnecessary expense.

How expensive is saffron?

There are quality grades that differ in intensity of flavor, and therefore varying amounts are required to obtain the desired flavored. Prices range from $40 to $70 an ounce or even more, some at $30 a quarter ounce, which would mean $1,920 a pound. It mainly comes from Spain at several hundred dollars a pound. The town of Albacete in central Spain boasts that it is the Saffron Center of the World.

How is saffron used?

Paella, risotto Milanese and baked goods are some of its uses.

Sesame Seeds (benne seeds)

What is the difference between white and black sesame seeds?

White is the most common and is used like poppy seeds in Asian and Indian cuisine. Black are good for seasoning rice and noodle dishes in Japan. Both are good with baked fish or chicken or stir-fried vegetables, cakes, rolls and other baked goods.

What is the caution in using sesame seeds?

They easily turn rancid so smell/taste when grating/grinding so check for wholesomeness.

Should sesame seeds be pretoasted?

Yes, they are better when toasted, but it is not necessary when they are used in baking.

How do you toast sesame seeds?

Use dry heat, such as 350 °F in the oven on a baking sheet or over medium heat in a frying pan, both until golden brown.

How should sesame oil be used?

1. In salads or sautéd foods in small quantities.
2. Add near the end of the cooking, because its aromatics are quite volatile.

What is sesame salt?

A combination of thoroughly ground sesame seeds and salt that is used as a seasoning.

What is tahini?

A thick paste made from ground sesame seeds.

Star Anise (sometimes mistakenly called anise)

What is star anise?

From a small evergreen tree this is a star-shaped (eight point), dried, brown pod of the magnolia family with a pungent, somewhat bitter, licorice flavor, and it is discarded before serving the dish. Not related to anise.

What happens when star anise is crushed?

It loses most of its licorice aroma quality.

How can star anise be used?

1. Whole, as a garnish.
2. Ground, it is a strong flavor when used in cooking.
3. Broken pieces are used in pickling.
4. It is one of the ingredients in Chinese five-spice powder.

How do those from China differ from those from Spain?

Those from China are sweeter and have more licorice flavor than those from Spain.

Turmeric (Indian saffron)

What is turmeric?

It is the root of a plant from the tropics related to ginger.

How is it used?

1. Its spicy, pungent flavor and rich golden color are used as part of curry powder.
2. It gives a golden color to fish, especially to salmon.
3. It is one of the ingredients in Chinese five-spice powder.
4. It is used in making prepared mustard.

Wasabi (Wasabe)

What is wasabi?

The Japanese counterpart to horseradish. A very hot, green seasoning spice. On the American market it is usually sold as a powder, which is used in making a sauce or paste with the addition of a little liquid.

OTHER CONDIMENTS/SEASONINGS

Citrus Zest

What is citrus zest?

The colored outer skin of citrus fruit.

How should fruit be chosen for zesting?

It should be firm, dry, fresh without any wax covering.

How should zest be removed?

Grate: Use a grater with the smallest holes without a plastic cover.
Strip: Use a vegetable peeler and take off the colored part only.

Miso

What is miso?

A fermented, mainly soy bean paste, aged and used as a flavoring base, especially in soups and dips. It is the basis for many Japanese dishes.

Where did miso originate?

In China, more than twenty-five centuries ago.

Why does miso vary in color, flavor and texture?

It depends on the amount of soybeans, salt, rice and/or barley and koji (mold) used and the length of aging.

What is its nutritive value?

Rich in protein and B vitamins.

What are the three basic types?

Barley, rice and soybean based.

How is the light-colored miso (shiromiso) used?

Having less salt, it has a sweeter taste and is good for fish, shellfish and mild sauces.

How should you choose it in the market?

When it is in an air-tight container and refrigerated.

Why does it keep indefinitely in the refrigerator?

Because it has already fermented.

Olives

Do olives lose their flavor with high-cooking temperatures?

No, the flavors are quite stable and heat resistant.

What are the main varieties available?

Kalamata:	From Greece, fruity, long length, dark purple.
Manzanilla:	From California and Spain, green.
Mission:	Black, mild tasting.
Niçoise:	From France, small, dark brown or purple, wrinkled.

What are dry-cured olives?

Packed in salt to remove most of the moisture, a wrinkled fruit results.

How can olives be stuffed for hors d'oeuvres?

Put an almond (salted or smoked) in a pitted olive (green or black).

Salt

What does "below the salt" refer to?

It was an indicator of class difference, for centuries ago only the nobility were allowed to use salt as it was so rare and expensive. Lower-class folks were seated at the end of the table where salt was not served and had to rely only on herbs for seasoning.

What is table salt?

This is what is referred to in most recipes. It is almost pure sodium chloride although sometimes iodine (in the form of potassium iodide) is added to prevent goiter. Free flowing is aided by the addition of agents to prevent clumping, and sometimes dextrose is added as a stabilizer. The crystals are small.

What is kosher salt?

It is manufactured under rabbinical supervision and may or may not have additives.

Why do chefs like kosher salt?

It is easy to grab a pinch and doesn't dissolve on their fingers. Also comes in flake form.

How much kosher salt should be used compared to table salt?

Since it has more water in the crystals and is therefore not so salty (about half), almost twice as much is needed.

How is rock salt different?

It is very coarse and is not for culinary use but rather for melting snow or ice. It is available in hardware stores.

Is sea salt different?

Available either coarse or fine, it comes from sea water allowed to evaporate—the other kinds are mined from the earth. It may have additives. Most sold in the United States is imported. The trace elements of sea salts give special flavors so that the place of origin alters the taste.

What is a simple barometer of a person's salt intake?

Eat a slice of bacon. If it doesn't taste excessively salty, then probably you are eating too much salt. Sodium intake should be no more than 250 mg per day, which is about $\frac{1}{10}$ of a teaspoon. The average American uses about 4,500 mg per day.

Does salt in the diet cause high blood pressure?

No! It does not, although about one-half of the sixty million people who have high blood pressure are salt sensitive. As a result, their pressure rises in response to their salt intake. People who have hypertension should consume less salt.

How does the excess salt influence blood pressure?

A burden is placed on the body's metabolism, causing a possible malfunction. Excess amounts of sodium buildup in the blood stream, whereupon the body retains excess water, thus increasing the blood volume, which causes the heart to work harder, thus leading to an increase in blood pressure.

What can you do to salvage a pot of soup or stew that is too salty?

1. Reboil it with some peeled, quartered raw potatoes, for they will absorb some of the saltiness. The potatoes can be served separately or with the dish you are preparing or thrown out.
2. If feasible, add some tomato base or a little sugar.

Why do many fast food manufacturers use a large quantities of salt?

1. To mask offensive flavor coming from low-quality ingredients.
2. Because Americans are used to a high salt level.

What precaution should be taken when using salt in cooking?

Adding salt at the beginning of a dish can result in excess saltiness, so add near the end of cooking and taste to adjust the seasoning.

Why do cold dishes diminish tasting ability?

Because low temperature diminishes the sensitivity of the taste buds.

What is celery salt?

A mixture of ground celery seeds and fine white salt. The seeds come from a herbaceous plant related to celery.

Why does pickling salt have no anticaking chemicals added?

They would cloud the brine.

Does salt raise the boiling point of water above the 212 degree level?

Yes. Sugar, salt, and other soluble substances will raise the temperature, but only by a tiny amount. Also hard water (containing dissolved mineral salts) will raise the temperature a degree or two.

Soy Sauce

What is the history of soy sauce?

It evolved from *shih*, a fermented grain mixture, which was first used as a preservative and flavoring in China more than 2,500 years ago. *Shih* was introduced into Japan during the seventh century by Buddhist priests who were trying to teach their followers vegetarianism. It was known as *miso-tamari*, a by-product of *miso* (fermented soybean paste). *Tamari* (that which collects) was the name given to the liquid at the top of the *miso* barrels. By 1700, commercial *tamari* breweries were established.

What is the difference between dark, light and "lite" soy sauces?

All soy sauces are made from fermented soybeans and roasted grains such as wheat, barley and rice. The main difference is their salt content and the length of time they ferment.

What is the difference between Japanese and Chinese soy sauce?

Japanese: Made from more wheat and therefore is more mellow, less salty, more versatile.

Chinese: Little wheat, more salty, often has a little molasses added for a slight sweetness. Light: subtle fish; dark: hearty meat dishes.

How is the dark produced and used?

It is fermented longer than light and finished with molasses, which gives it its rich brown color. It is used for stronger-flavored foods like red meats.

What is the application of light soy?

Used for fish, seafood and vegetables or in dipping sauces, it is lighter in color, somewhat milder in flavor, slightly thicker in consistency.

Is "lite" really light?

It has reduced sodium (salt). For instance, Kikkoman Lite has 100 milligrams of sodium in a half teaspoon, which is 40% less than the usual 167 mg. Under the new labeling laws they will not be able to use the term "lite" unless they change the formula, for a factor of 50% less salt is required for a product to be called lite. Incidentally the word "lite" in beer may mean lower in calories.

What are some of the contributions of soy sauce?

1. It has a complex bouquet of flavor and aroma.
2. It adds nuances of taste.
3. It brings out flavor notes of the other ingredients without masking the primary flavors of the dish.
4. Its saltiness adds depth and richness.
5. It is ideal for meat, poultry and seafood marinades.
6. Just a few drops enhances the flavor of scrambled eggs.

What is the difference between soy and tamari?

Soy sauce: Made from equal parts of soybeans and wheat plus water and salt.

Tamari: Made from soybeans, water and salt. It is more intense, complex with a higher concentration of minerals, has a thicker consistency and is darker.

What is the result if soy sauce is made from wheat?

If wheat is used the soy is more subtle though saltier.

What are the three basic categories of soy sauce?

Standard: Deep brown or amber, full bodied, suitable in virtually all Japanese dishes.

Chinese: Densely flavored, quite salty, varies from dark, reddish brown to thin and light. In general the dark is more salty than the light.

Chemical: Thick, almost black, strong with a yeasty aroma, somewhat metallic in flavor, least expensive. This is what is usually given at take-out stands.

How is soy sauce made?

1. Equal amounts of soy beans and wheat are blended.
2. The mixture matures for several days.
3. It is then mixed with salt brine.
4. The fermentation takes place in tanks from 6 months to 2 or more years.
5. Once aged, it is refined and pasteurized.

What is the result of this slow fermentation?

It yields 285 flavor components, including nearly 20 amino acids. These are what allow the soy to boost food flavors without masking them.

What is soy cheese?

A cheese made from soy milk that is lactose and cholesterol-free.

What is hoisin sauce?

A brownish red sauce that is made from soybean paste, garlic, spices, sugar and vinegar that is used in Asian dishes as a flavoring, more often added at the table.

What is oyster sauce?

It is made from boiled oysters, soy sauce, salt and spices and it is from Southern China. It is dark brown and used in stir-frying or as a flavoring at the table.

How should these sauces be kept?

They will keep indefinitely if bottled and refrigerated.

Tofu

What is tofu?

Soybeans that have been cooked, ground and solidified.

What is the nutritive value of tofu?

High in protein, low in saturated fat, and it is easily digestible.

What precaution need be taken when using tofu in cooking?

Cook gently without much stirring, as it is fragile.

What happens when tofu is deep fried?

It becomes sponge-like and then when added to a sauce it absorbs the flavors of the sauce.

What is the difference between firmer and softer varieties?

The softer ones contain more water and expel more water when marinating, diluting the marinade.

Vanilla

What is vanilla?

A whole bean or extract from that bean, which is a seed pod of a climbing orchid.

How should vanilla beans be selected?

The best come from Madagascar, Mexico and Tahiti. The Madagascar are considered the best with Mexican close behind. The Tahitians are especially good with chocolate and fruit. Indonesians are similar to those from Madagascar but less flavorful and not as strong.

Does the size of the bean indicate quality?

The larger the bean the more flavorful. The best are 7–8″ in length. These are more expensive.

What is baker's vanilla?

It is an inexpensive, imitation vanilla.

Can vanilla beans be reused since they are so expensive?

Yes, but they will not be as flavorful. An alternative is to used the bean to make vanilla sugar.

How is vanilla sugar made?

Rinse the bean after its first use, let it dry completely and then add it to a canister of sugar. After 2–3 days the sugar will be subtly flavored, which will keep for a long time. If the dried bean (extracted from the pod) is pounded together with granulated or powdered sugar (works best with powdered), then fine sieved, the flavor in the sugar will be enhanced considerably.

What is the difference between pure vanilla and imitation?

Pure is the bean plus ethyl alcohol. Imitation can be almost any combination of chemicals, usually in an alcohol base, and may contain no vanilla.

What can be substituted if the recipe calls for a vanilla bean?

Use 1–2 teaspoons of vanilla extract for half a bean, but this varies with the strength of the extract.

What does "vanilla flavored" on the label signify?

That there is a mixture of pure and synthetic vanilla.

What happens when vanilla extract is used in cooking?

The heat diminishes its intensity, so for prolonged cooking add it close to the end.

What is double strength vanilla?

Twice as many beans were used in making the extract, the alcohol content remaining the same, that is, single strength.

What is Bourbon vanilla?

A vanilla extract made from beans grown in the Bourbon Islands (in the Indian Ocean, including the island of Madagascar). No bourbon liquor is used.

When should vanilla extract be added to a custard sauce?

After it has been fully cooled so as to prevent the flavoring/alcohol from evaporating, but if the bean has been used it can be put in early in the preparation.

Vinegar

What is balsamic vinegar?

True balsamic (*aceto balsamico tradizionale*) is made by simmering white grape juice for several days to concentrate and caramelize it and then long aged in a succession of barrels made of different woods.

What are the aging requirements?

Vecchio: 12–24 years.

Extra vecchio: a minimum of 25 years.

How does the price vary?

It varies with age and quality. The highest quality ones are very expensive, up to $200 for a small (100-ml) bottle. The best are high in sugar and low in acid. The quality varies with the price.

How can balsamic (lowest grade) be simulated?

Adding a pinch of sugar to wine vinegar will give the character but not the quality.

What is the vinegar made from when the label doesn't specify it?

Almost all vinegar in the United States that has no other designation (there is no modifying adjective such as 'rice') was most likely made from fermented apple cider. The practice in Italy and France is to make it from grape juice.

What is rice vinegar?

A vinegar made from fermented rice. It has mellow sweetness, subtle flavors and is good for peas, cucumbers and other delicate vegetables.

What is the difference between Japanese and Chinese rice vinegar?

Japanese: Neutral, slightly sweet.

Chinese: Sharp, sour, more acidy.

Are fruit vinegars different and good to use?

If raspberry, blueberry, blackberry or other fruits are mentioned on the label, it means that part of the vinegar comes from the named fruit, the rest from wine or cider vinegar or whatever the label says. These can be very good, especially for salad dressings.

How can vinegars be flavored?

Add slightly bruised herbs or fruit, heat the vinegar almost to body temperature, seal the bottle.

What are some of the vinegars on the market?

Distilled white:	Fermented from grain alcohol.
Malt:	Comes from malted barley.
Herb:	Taste has been enhanced with herbs.
Wine:	From fermented grape wine, white or red.
Sherry:	From sherry wine, with a strong nutty flavor that is good on bitey lettuce.

Is the amount of acid the same in all vinegars?

It is not standardized and usually varies with the strength of the base wine. The more structure in the base, the lower the acidity probably will be.

In making a vinaigrette, how should the oil be added?

1. Mix the seasonings together, then beat in the vinegar or lemon juice and finally the oil.
2. When making it in a processor, mix the oil and vinegar and then add the seasonings.

Must a vinaigrette dressing be made with a specific vinegar?

No, not even necessarily with vinegar. Lemon juice can be used.

Would the proportions be the same if lemon juice was substituted for vinegar?

No, for it would be half lemon juice, half oil instead of one-quarter vinegar, three-fourth oil.

What can be done to reduce the tartness of a vinaigrette dressing?

Add a little bit of sugar.

Will an opened container of vinegar spoil?

Since vinegar is very acidic, bacteria grow very poorly in it, or not at all. The vinegar will still deteriorate if exposed to air and/or heat. Keep it capped and store it in a cool, dark, dry place.

If leftover wine is added to vinegar, will a good vinegar ensue?

Only if there is a "mother," or starter, in the base vinegar. There won't be one in any vinegar that has been pasteurized.

What is verjus?

Unfermented grape juice made from almost ripened grapes that are not fully mature and therefore have a high acid level.

What is verjus used for?

This mildly tart juice is used as a vinegar substitute. Made mainly from white grapes but some is now available from red ones. Can create a very good flavor.

How long will verjus keep?

When the bottle is opened what is left will keep for 1–2 weeks in the refrigerator or even months when frozen.

Wine and Beer

Why do wine and beer deteriorate?

The enemy is oxygen from the air, which, once the bottle has been opened, is in contact with the wine or the beer.

What should be done to keep leftover wine from spoiling?

The less space between the wine and the cork or the stopper, the better.

How can this be accomplished?

1. Pour the remaining wine into a smaller bottle so there is little or no air space.
2. Use a wine preservative bottle of nitrogen gas (available at wine shops). This will replace the air (oxygen) with inert nitrogen.
3. Use a special pump to exhaust the air.
4. In addition to any of the above, refrigerate the wine or at the very least keep it cool.

Is the amount of wine to be used in cooking a critical factor?

Yes, it must be limited, or it will dominate the taste of the dish and dilute the desired effect.

Should cooking wine be used?

1. Usually that labeled as cooking wine is of such poor quality that it will harm the taste of the dish rather than enhance it.
2. These cooking wines often have flavoring agents such as salt added, or the alcohol has been boiled off.
3. Fortunately, these cooking wines are less available than previously.

Is an expensive (or high-grade) wine necessary for cooking?

An expensive wine is not necessary, just one that is good enough to drink by itself.

Should it be the same wine as that served with the meal?

It need not be, for the cooking process will change the taste, but it will usually go well.

What else can be done with leftover wine?

Unless it has too much acidity it can be used in marinades. Put it in a smaller bottle, cork and refrigerate to minimize the disintegrating effect of oxygen of the air.

Can wine be substituted for vinegar in salad dressing?

Yes.

Why is wine used so often to deglaze a pan?

To dissolve flavor components that water won't get.

When should wine be added in the cooking process?

1. About a half hour before the dish is finished (braised or stewed dishes) to give the flavor time to integrate.
2. To speed up the process, the wine can be gently warmed before adding.

3. Add sherry or marsala to soups in very small quantities just before serving or else what will be tasted is the wine and not the flavors of the soup.

How much wine should be used in a marinade?

About half wine and half water.

What kind of sherry should be used for cooking?

1. If no sweetness is desired: fino or manzanilla.
2. For fuller flavor with a touch of sweetness: amontillado.
3. For fullest, richest flavor: oloroso.

Are the more expensive sherries needed?

No.

Does adding wine when making a soup or stew mean adding a lot of alcohol?

1. No, as long as if the pot is uncovered during cooking so that almost all of the alcohol evaporates.
2. If sherry is added towards the end of a preparation there will be little alcohol in the dish because one teaspoon of sherry per cup of soup is the maximum that should be added, and less than one-fifth of the sherry is alcohol.

What is another alternative?

Use de-alcoholized wine.

How can beer be used in cooking?

It can be substituted for all the water, wine or stock in many recipes. For example clams can be steamed or sausages braised in it.

What can be done with leftover beer?

Cook with it! It doesn't matter if it is flat because in cooking the effervescence will disappear anyway.

What are the best beers for cooking?

Use full-flavored ones.

How should beers be used when making bread dough?

Make sure the beer is at room temperature, for the cold beer will slow the growth of the yeast.

What is mirin?

A sweet rice wine of the sake family that is used for cooking, such as with sashimi.

What does mirin add to food?

Sweetness with a special flavor of its own.

Why is a slow-cooked coq au vin or stew (made with wine) all right for children to consume?

The alcohol of table wine (10–14% evaporates at 175 °F (versus 212 °F for water). Thus if the pot is uncovered the more alcohol is dissipated but rarely does it disappear completely. There may be, however, some religious scruples against any alcohol. Nevertheless alcohol is found in many products, even though in small quantities.

What alcohol level should be used to flambé a dish?

If the alcohol level is too high (such as 150 proof, or 75%), then there is liable to be an explosion when lit. The best level is that of brandy (80 proof, 40%).

COOKING FATS AND OILS

What is the difference between a fat and an oil?

At 68 °F the fat is solid, the oil is liquid.

What is the role of fat in cooking?

1. Preventing sticking to the pan.
2. Adds its own flavor.
3. Releases fat-soluble flavors.
4. Coats and moistens foods.
5. Contributes to browning, especially for meats.
6. Thickens sauces.
7. Prevents curdling.

Do all fats have the same amount of fat?

Shortening and lard are all fat; butter and margarine are about 80% fat.

What are some lower fat substitutes that can be used?

1. Substitute skim milk for heavy cream in a soup or sauce.
2. Substitute fruit for refined sugar for sweetness.
3. A small amount of whipped cream as a garnish gives the impression of richness more than if more cream was used in the soup.
4. Use grains, vegetables, beans as stuffing instead of fatty meats, substituting all or in part.
5. Stir in pureed fruit, such as apple, banana or pumpkin to replace up to three-quarters of the oil called for in the recipe.
6. Use egg substitute products.
7. Use cocoa powder for chocolate. Add three tablespoons plus sugar for every square of chocolate. This will not work for frostings.

8. In a sauce, replace cream with evaporated skim milk, which has more body and protein than regular skim milk.

9. In soups, replace light or heavy cream with low-fat milk thickened with cornstarch.

10. A dollop of nonfat yogurt instead of sour cream provides a pleasant finish for a soup.

11. In creamy fillings, replace creams with chilled, evaporated skim milk. This works best when mixed with vibrant flavors.

How do cooking fats rank in percentage of saturated fats, from lowest to highest?

Canola, safflower, corn, olive, soybean, peanut, margarine, palm, butter and coconut.

What is the smoke-point?

The temperature at which fats/oils begin to break down and yield a burned flavor and a blue gas.

Why is heating to the smoke point of an oil dangerous?

1. It might catch on fire.
2. It might irritate the eyes.
3. It may make food taste bitter.

Where should a kitchen fire extinguisher be located?

Not too close to the stove, as the fire might keep you from reaching it, but definitely in the kitchen.

Why doesn't water work in putting out a fire of burning oil?

Because the oil will float on the water and continue to burn.

Why do recipes often call for adding some oil when sautéing with butter?

Adding a small amount of oil will raise the smoke point of the butter/fat mixture.

How can hot oil be tested to see if it is still usable?

Drop a small piece of white bread into the pan. If dark specks develop, the oil is deteriorating.

Can fat for deep-frying be reused?

1. Replace about 15–20% of the fat after a daily use.
2. Discard it after five or six uses.

What is the problem with the vegetable oils used by many fast food restaurants for frying?

1. They may contain a high level of coconut and/or palm oil, which are very high in saturated fats.
2. They are not replaced with fresh oil often enough and thus give an off-taste.

What is the displacement method for measuring solid fats?

For example, if you want ¼ cup of butter, fill a cup ¼ full with water and add butter until the liquid measures ½ cup.

What happens when the cooking fat is too hot?

The food is apt to dry and brown on the outside, while remaining uncooked on the inside.

What are various oils that give flavor?

Extra virgin olive oil:	Use in sauces, salads, baking.
Hazelnut oil:	Good in salad dressings, light sautéing.
Walnut oil:	For low heat sauces, dressings, baking.
Almond oil:	For baking.
Toasted sesame oil:	For salad dressing.
Grapeseed oil:	For salad dressings.
Pumpkin seed oil:	For salad dressing, dipping sauces.

Should these oils be used for cooking?

Don't waste these expensive, flavorful oils for frying or sautéing, as they lose their flavors from the heat. Instead use pure olive oil, canola oil, sunflower oil, safflower oil or vegetable oil.

What is cottonseed oil?

An oil obtained from the seed of the cotton plant, which is usually combined with other oils (such as palm) and used for french frying, in margarine and salad dressings.

What is a caution in using nut oils?

They have a strong flavor and should be used in small amounts in salads or to season other oils.

How should toasted/dark sesame oil be used?

It gives a smoky nuttiness if added almost at the end of the cooking, just before serving.

Which cooking oils/fats have the least saturated fat?

Canola 6%, grapeseed 7%, safflower 9%; versus olive 14%, shortening 26%, butter 54%.

Which oils stick to the pan the least?

Vegetable oils, of which safflower is best.

Does olive oil prevent sticking?

No, because it breaks down in high heat.

Which is the best lubricant to prevent sticking?

Nonstick cooking spray that contains lecithin, which makes oil more slippery.

Seasoning and Oils

What is the problem with soy oil for deep frying?

It tends to foam.

What is safflower oil?

Pressed from a plant whose rich, yellow color looks like saffron, it is high in polyunsaturated fats and has a high smoke point.

How should oils be stored?

1. Plain: Well corked, in a cool dark place.
2. Flavored: Refrigerate, or they will lose their flavor.

What happens if fat is kept uncovered between uses?

The oxygen in the air will start breaking it down.

What is walnut oil?

Roasted, shelled walnuts are milled to a paste, then roasted and the oil is pressed out. It has a rich, golden color.

What are some uses for walnut oil?

1. For salad dressings.
2. Sprinkled over white beans, asparagus, green beans.
3. In nut cakes.

What are the attributes of pumpkin seed oil?

Highly flavored, it makes a dipping sauce mixed with mayonnaise and is excellent in salad dressings.

What are the attributes of grapeseed oil?

1. High smoke point (close to 500 °F), so it is good for sautéing.
2. High in vitamin E and omega-6 (linoleic acid)
3. Some give a grape flavor.

What are its negatives?

1. Expensive.
2. Most are very bland in flavor.

What are the functions of cooking fats?

1. Lubrication to keep food particles from sticking to the pan or to each other.
2. Heat transference.
3. Give flavor.
4. Keep texture moist in dry intense heat.

What is the minimum smoke point of an oil to be used for frying?

A smoke point of 375 °F or more is needed.

What are the smoke points or the beginnings of the breakdown of various fats and oils?

Low:	at 300 °F	butter
		margarine
		vegetable shortening
Medium:	400 °F	olive oil
		lard
		coconut oil
High:	above 400 °F	peanut oil
		corn oil
		safflower oil
		canola

What kind of oil should be used when making a fresh (noncooked) sauce for pasta?

A good quality olive oil will do well but not heavily flavored oils (estate bottled) because they may overpower the sauce.

What is virgin olive oil?

The term used to mean a low acid oil (less than 1% acid for extra virgin [sometimes called condiment oil by producers] and less than 2% for virgin) that has not been refined by heat or solvents. No other treatment was allowed except for filtering. The label could also have "cold pressed" on it.

What is the new European standard for olive oil?

The International Olive Oil Council allows only three types: extra virgin, pure and pomace.

What are the different label designations for olive oil?

Extra virgin:	From the first cold pressing without heat from whole unblemished olives. Less than 1% of oleic acid (which gives sharpness).
Pure:	Extracted with heat, has more acid. This acid is chemically treated and a little extra virgin is added for flavor. It might be a blend of refined and ultra virgin.
Pomace:	Rarely seen in the United States. This is heat-processed from previously processed olives.

What does cold press mean?

The temperature during pressing was not raised, the oil might be filtered but has not been heat-refined.

What are the American standards?

There is no U.S. legal definition. With new FDA regulations the phrase "light" is no longer permitted.

What does the term "light" refer to as to quality?

It refers only to color and taste, that it has mostly refined oils and is fairly bland.

What do the various designations of European oil mean as to their origin?

In Europe the source on the label only means the country in which it was bottled, not where the olives were grown, unless the specific estate from which the olives came is given. The best Italian are labeled *produtto e imbottigliato*, which means "produced and bottled by," but if only one of these words are on the label, the olive oil could have come from anywhere, even another country.

Why do some olive oils have sediment and/or cloudiness?

1. Cloudiness results from naturally occurring sediment and/or storage in a cool/cold temperature. Some extra virgin oils are unfiltered and will appear cloudy at room temperature. The sediment is due to very small pieces of olives, which give added flavor and color.
2. Cloudiness can also come from refrigerated storage.

How can cloudiness coming from refrigeration be eliminated?

To clear, pour out the measured amount and let it stand at room temperature for 15–20 minutes.

Will olive oil improve with aging?

No, it is probably at its best soon after first pressed, but the diminution of quality, with good storage, is quite slow.

How can you determine which olive oil is best?

There are a wide range of flavors, depending on variety of tree, how it was pressed and processed etc., but you can either taste it like wine by taking a sip and swishing it around you mouth and tongue, or dip a piece of bread into it and taste. This is the traditional way.

Is the color of the oil a gauge of quality?

Color is not a determinant of quality.

What are factors that should govern choice?

1. Which is best depends on your palate.
2. How you are going to use it.
3. The fruitier (and, incidentally, the more expensive) the less an oil should be used for cooking with high heat, which will often distort the flavors and the oil can become unattractive.
4. The expensive ones are best in sauces or salads or for dribbling on bread.

Why is extra-virgin oil better for a marinade than regular olive oil?

It has more emulsifiers, which penetrate meat and fish better. It is better also than canola oil as a marinade.

CHAPTER ELEVEN

STOCKS, SAUCES AND SOUPS

STOCK (BROTH)

What is stock?

A flavorful liquid made by gently simmering bones and/or vegetables in a liquid to extract their flavor, color, body, aroma and nutritive value.

How is brown stock achieved?

The bones and meat are browned prior to making the stock. Beef bones roasted 20 minutes at 400 °F so that they are browned before the liquid is added will give a deeper hue and fuller flavor.

How powerful should the stock flavor be?

A stock's taste should be definite enough for ready identification but not so strong as to compete with the other ingredients used in the finished dish, such as a cream soup or a braised dish.

What are the types of stock?

White stock, brown stock, fumet, essence, court-bouillon, glace (or glaze), broth and bouillon.

How should stock be cooked?

Simmered only, not boiled, so that the fat will not be difficult to remove.

How is white stock made?

It is mainly from chicken or fish: clear, relatively colorless, made by simmering bones and appropriate aromatics in water to extract the water soluble proteins such as gelatin to provide flavor and body. Delicately flavored.

How long should chicken stock be cooked?

Simmer 3–4 hours.

What is brown stock?

An amber liquid made by first browning the bones and or vegetables and then proceeding as for white stock.

What kind of a pot should be used for making stock?

A tall, narrow pot to slow evaporation because there is reduced surface area.

What is the difference in cooking time in making beef, chicken and fish stocks?

Chicken: Simmer 3 hours.
Beef: Best if bones are browned, cook 4 or more hours.
Fish: 20–30 minutes maximum.

What is good practice in handling stock?

Cool quickly by:
1. Stirring occasionally.
2. Chilling the outside of the pot with running water.
3. Propping the bottom of the pot up, using bricks or measuring cups.
4. Then refrigerating.

How is a fumet made?

A highly flavored stock, generally made with fish bones. Made generally by sweating methods in which the bones and a mirepoix (a mixture of diced carrots, onions and celery) are allowed to cook gently before the liquid is added. It should be cooked for a short time not for hours.

How is an essence different from a fumet?

An essence is the same as a fumet but made with highly aromatic products such as celery and morels, concentrated stock, vanilla or the like.

What is a court-bouillon?

An aromatic vegetable broth that frequently includes wine and/or vinegar.

How is a court-bouillon mainly used?

Used most commonly for poaching, such as for fish.

Is a glace used alone?

A glace (pronounced "gloss") is a stock reduced to a jellylike or syrupy consistency that has a highly concentrated flavor. Used as a sauce base or to bolster other flavors. Most common is *glace de viande*, which is made from brown stock.

What is remouillage?

Made from bones that have already been used for making stock. This second stock is less strong and is usually reduced to make a glace, or it may be used as the liquid for making stock.

What is a broth?

The liquid resulting from simmering meats. Used for a soup such as consommé or for stews.

What is bouillon?

Broth or stock that has been concentrated.

What is the relationship of stock to bouillon?

Ten cups of stock will make 1½ cups of bouillon.

Should the water be cold or warm to start in making stock?

Cold water helps extract flavor because in hot water the starch gels, which slows down flavor extraction.

What are the best bones for making stock?

1. Unless from very young animals, both pork and lamb bones give stock a very pronounced flavor that is not to everyone's liking.
2. Veal bones make a clearer and more delicate stock than do beef bones. They also have a higher gelatin content, which is important in making aspic.

Why are lamb or duck bones not used for making stock?

Because of their very strong flavors, but if the stock is to be used for a lamb or duck dish they can be used.

Why are frozen bones to be used for white stock blanched first?

To remove any impurities that will cloud the stock.

Do the bones from a particular part of the bird or animal influence the stock?

1. For delicate-flavored chicken stock, choose breasts of young birds. For full flavored stock, just the opposite—legs and thighs.
2. The closer the anatomical position of the bone to the nose, tail or foot, the more thickening power it has.

Why should the amount of carrots and peppers used in making chicken stock be limited?

These sweet vegetables can overwhelm the chicken flavor if too much is used.

Can bones salvaged from roasted meats (beef, pork, lamb, poultry) be used for making stock?

They are not ideal for making stock since much of their flavoring capacity has been absorbed by the meat during the cooking process. The best ones are raw bones although salvaged ones from cooked meats will work to some degree.

What is the basis of vegetable stock?

Onions, carrots and celery and then whatever other vegetables are available and desired.

How can beef stock be made very clear?

Mix ground beef and egg white, heat and add to the stock, and then strain.

What should be done with bones for use in making stock?

They should be cracked or sawed into pieces to facilitate the release of their flavoring and of their collagen (a thickening agent).

Why should bones be added to stock while the water is still cold?

A sudden plunge into boiling water will partially or completely seal the bones and thus the tastes, aromas, color, nutrients and thickening agents may not be released into the stock.

How should stock be cooked?

Simmer at a low heat to prevent cloudiness.

What are the three major uses of stock?

1. A base for sauces and soups.
2. A base for stews and braises.
3. A cooking medium for vegetables and grains.

What are the steps in making chicken stock?

1. Rinse the bones, blanching them if they are frozen.
2. Combine the bones and cold water, then lower the heat so it will not boil, just simmer.
3. Simmer for 2 or 3 hours.
4. Skim the surface, as necessary.
5. Add the mirepoix (a mixture of diced carrots, onions and celery) and spices and salt, if used, and simmer another hour, also adding herbs in a bouquet garni (tied together for easy removal at the end).
6. Strain well and cool.

Should the bones be browned?

Generally both bones and vegetables are browned, but this is optional and is not usually done for chicken or fish.

How can stock be clarified?

Add crushed egg shells, egg white, chopped onion or ice cubes to cold stock and cook stirring to a boil. Then simmer 15–30 minutes.

What is a good way to keep stock?

Freeze in small containers or as (ice) cubes.

What should be done with the bones to make fish stock?

1. Use plenty of good bones.
2. They should smell clean and sweet, not fishy.
3. Clean the bones thoroughly.
4. Break the bones into smaller pieces and rinse in cold water.
5. Add cut up vegetables, which are especially good if they have been sweated (lightly sautéd in butter).
6. Cook gently. Cooking time is considerably less than for meat or poultry stocks (maximum about 20–30 minutes).
7. Skim the froth during cooking.

Which are the best bones for fish stock?

Especially use the bones from the head of the fish for they are rich in gelatin and good flavors.

What should be avoided when making fish stock?

1. Overlong cooking, i.e., more than half an hour.
2. Using strong flavored varieties of fish, such as mackerel or herring.
3. Using the fish gills.

What is the scum that surfaces on pots of cooking stock or similar liquids?

These are bubbles of air surrounded by a thin layer of water that is stabilized by dissolved proteins that come from the food being cooked. It has little culinary value and is usually skimmed off because it is aesthetically displeasing and most often doesn't taste good.

How long will stocks keep?

Meat, chicken:	1 week refrigerated, 3 months or more frozen.
Fish:	Best fresh, but about 2 weeks frozen.
Vegetable:	Best fresh, loses flavor when frozen.

Can stock be concentrated (for example to save space) before freezing?

Yes, by about half.

What is a caution when concentrating stock?

Be careful of the salt level, for reducing the volume increases the concentration of the salt.

Stocks, Sauces and Soups

SAUCE

What is a sauce?

It is a liquid seasoning for food and can be made in many ways with many different ingredients. Many basic sauces can be transformed into other sauces by the addition of other ingredients or other treatment in cooking.

What are the particles of meats that adhere to the cooking pan?

The particles are culinary treasures, almost like each particle is a homemade miniature bouillon cube. After pouring off the fat, dissolve these particles over moderate heat in a little water, stock or wine.

What was the origin of sauces?

The first sauces were known as juices and were heavily spiced and thickened with pieces of bread. With all of their spices they seemed designed not to complement the food but to overpower it, to hide spoilage or other imperfections. A recipe from AD 1390 called for shelled oysters to be simmered in wine and their own broth, strained through a cloth, thickened with ground, blanched almonds, flour of rice and flavored with ginger, sugar and mace.

What are the two basic types of different sauces?

Complementary: To enhance the flavor of a prepared dish.

Counterpoint: To give contrast, such as a mustard sauce to pork to balance out over-richness.

What are functions of different sauces?

1. To introduce complementary or counterpoint flavors. Supreme sauce has a deep chicken flavor and a velvety texture and is served with chicken meat to complement its delicate flavor and help intensify its flavor.

2. Sauce Robert is paired with pork to introduce a counterpoint flavor in which the sharpness of the mustard and cornichons (small sour pickle) cuts the meat's richness and introduces a contrast that is pleasing but not startling.

3. A butter-emulsion sauce adds moisture or succulence, particularly with naturally lean foods, such as poultry or fish.

4. A tarragon-flavored sauce adjusts flavors and brings out the mild sweetness of poultry.

What are the functions of a sauté sauce?

1. Capture the flavors of the food that are lost during sautéing.

2. Add flavor to the food being cooked.

3. Add moisture, which is lost during sautéing.

What can a sauce do for a dish that doesn't look exciting?

It adds visual interest when a dish lacks luster or sheen. Lightly coat a sautéd medallion of lamb with a jus líe thickened stock.

What should a sauce accomplish when meat is without texture?

Add texture. Chicken Chasseur can be enhanced with a sauce finished with tomatoes and mushrooms.

What if the meat has a distinct texture?

Use a smooth sauce to contrast with a meat that has a pronounced texture.

Where does the flavor of a sauce come from?

Mainly from the liquid used to make it.

Can a hollandaise sauce be made ahead of time?

While it should be made as close to use as possible, it can be held if:

1. The sauce has enough lemon juice so that the resultant acidity is high enough to prevent bacteria from growing.
2. It can be kept up to an hour if stored over hot water.
3. It can be put in a preheated thermos.
4. It can be refrigerated and then reheated over hot water if the bottom of the pan doesn't touch the water and if it is stirred constantly.

What is a velouté?

A white foundation sauce in which a hot liquid other than milk or cream, such as a broth, has been used.

Are a beurre manié and a roux similar?

Both are flour and butter mixtures used to thicken sauces.

What is a beurre manié?

Equal parts of butter and flour kneaded together thoroughly to form a paste, which is whisked, a little at a time, into an already simmering sauce.

How is a beurre manié used?

The liquid to be thickened is taken off the heat and pea-sized lumps of the beurre manié are added to it. The liquid is brought back to a boil and stirred and cooked until the liquid is thickened. The coating of fat around each fat granule will ensure that the flour can expand without forming lumps.

How does a roux differ?

The word "*roux*" in French means "red." In the eighteenth century roux was cooked long enough to change color.

How does a roux work?

Flour is whisked into a hot fat, such as melted butter or pan drippings, and stirred over low heat until the flour is cooked and the mixture has thickened slightly. At this point, the sauce and the other ingredients are added.

What else can a roux be used for?

1. It is also used as a thickening agent in sauces by separating the individual flour granules. If they were allowed to combine, they would form lumps that are dry inside and surrounded by a water-resistant membrane that would hinder water absorption.
2. This precooking also inactivates the starch-digesting enzymes present in the flour. This requires that the roux must cook at least 3–5 minutes.
3. Another purpose is to begin stretching the molecular structure of the flour granules.

Why is constant stirring essential?

Roux must be stirred frequently to prevent scorching because scorched flour thickens poorly and scorched butter tastes horrible.

Will browning the flour help its thickening power?

The more the flour is browned, the less power it has to thicken, therefore, you will need more flour for a dark brown roux than you will for a pale roux.

What is a béchamel sauce?

A white sauce made from a butter-flour roux to which milk or cream has been infused, plus salt and pepper, and possibly some seasonings such as vegetable juices.

What is critical in making a béchamel sauce?

1. It must be cooked long enough to eliminate the taste of flour.
2. It must be stirred enough to eliminate any lumps so that it is smooth.

What happens if the sauce is cooked too long or too quickly?

The viscosity and stability of the sauce diminishes because the molecular structure of the starch stretches too much and allows the trapped water to escape.

What sauces are good uncooked?

When tomatoes are at their best they can be chopped and mixed with herbs, olives, oils and fine diced soft cheeses (such as mozzarella).

What is a liaison?

A mixture of yolks and cream used to thicken and enrich sauces and soups. After it is mixed it must be tempered by adding some of the hot liquid to it and stirred and then the tempered liaison is added back to the hot liquid so the yolk won't curdle or separate.

Why is a cream sauce better for fettuccine than for spaghetti?

Because the width of the pasta carries the sauce better.

Should you use bread flour for thickening a sauce?

No! Bread flour has a high gluten content, and therefore a sauce made from it tends to get gummy.

What is meant by a "good-tempered" sauce, and name two?

A sauce that can be made in advance and stored in the refrigerator or frozen, such as béchamel and velouté.

What is Worcestershire sauce?

A well-aged mixture of vinegar, molasses, tamarind, shallots, garlic, cloves, onions, chili pepper and anchovies.

What is a coulis?

A puree of vegetables such as red peppers, leeks or broccoli, which is often finished by adding cream or butter.

What is a mirepoix?

A combination of chopped aromatic vegetables (customarily onion, carrot and celery) cooked with salt pork, bacon or ham.

Is meat essential to making a mirepoix?

The addition of the meat is optional.

What is the usual relationship of onion to celery in the mirepoix?

Usually two parts onion to one part of carrot and one part of celery.

How should the vegetables be prepared for making a mirepoix?

Since it is not usually eaten the onion doesn't have to be peeled. For dishes with a short cooking time, the mirepoix should be chopped or sliced finely.

What if the cooking is extended over an hour?

If the cooking time is over an hour then the vegetables can be rough cut.

What is hoisin sauce?

A Chinese sauce made from soybeans and spices. It is thick and brown, sweet and spicy and is added after cooking, usually at the table.

In making a tomato sauce, is the length of time it simmers important?

This used to be the concept, that is the longer the better, but the sauce will lose its best characteristics with overcooking, so the best flavor comes from a brief cooking. Cook it uncovered so that the steaming of the sauce is prevented.

What is a salsa?

The name is Spanish for a sauce. The American (Mexican) usage is mainly for uncooked table sauces used as condiments. Some, however, are simmered briefly. Most are well seasoned.

What are the types of salsas?

Fresca: Fresh.

Verde: Green, made from tomatillos, cilantro, green peppers etc.

Cruda: Not cooked, raw.

Why are the best salsas not canned?

Because the canning heat will reduce their flavor.

What is the recipe for salsa?

There is no single recipe. It can be made of fresh or canned tomatoes, with or without tomatoes, with or without any type of chilies.

What is a tapenade?

Of French origin, it is a thick paste made from ripe olives, anchovies, capers, olive oil, lemon juice and seasonings. Some recipes include other ingredients, like pieces of tuna. Tapenade is served spread on toasts or with crudités, among other possibilities.

GRAVY

What is gravy?

A type of sauce made at the last moment in which the cooking pan is deglazed with water, stock or wine. The liquid is then thickened with flour, cornstarch or arrowroot. The pan drippings are used as part of the liquid. The gravy can be clear or opaque, brown or white.

How can pan gravy for a roast be made?

1. Remove the roast from the pan and tilt the pan to get the fat and juices in one corner.
2. Spoon off and discard most of the fat, leaving the juices.
3. Over medium heat, whisk flour into the juices a tablespoon at a time, until a lightly browned paste is formed.
4. Then gradually whisk in hot stock.
5. Cook slowly until it is thick and bubbly.

How can flour be used in making gravy so that it won't dilute the flavor?

1. Use as little as possible.
2. Dissolve the flour in a little water to make a paste before adding.

What is a method of minimizing the formation of lumps in gravy?

Add a pinch of salt to the flour before mixing it with the liquid.

What can be done to get a richer brown color if gravy doesn't brown properly?

1. Add a small amount of coffee.
2. Separately cook the flour over low heat until the desired darkness is achieved.

Stocks, Sauces and Soups

Egg Sauces

Does milk have to be scalded before using eggs as a thickening agent?

Only if the milk is raw, for once pasteurized there is no need to scald.

Why should unheated raw egg yolks never be added to a hot sauce?

The sudden change in temperature will curdle the yolks and thus prevent them from being evenly distributed throughout the sauce, which is necessary for optimum thickening. So, gradually raise the temperature of the yolks with small amounts of the heated sauce and then the yolks can be safely blended.

What causes the mixture to thicken when using yolks to make a thick sauce, such as hollandaise?

Yolks are 50% water, 34% fats and related substances and 16% protein. The large protein molecules, together with the very large yolk particles (composed of both fat and protein) obstruct the movement of water molecules in the liquid and so the liquid yolk appears thick and viscous. As the sauce is heated, the initially compact yolk proteins, which are long and intricately folded molecules, unfold and tangle with each other and further impede the movement of the water molecules and fat droplets. At this point the sauce is nicely thick.

What happens to the proteins if overheated?

The proteins will bond tightly with each other and the sauce will thin out again.

What is an emulsified sauce?

An emulsion is a stable mixture of two liquids such as oil and water that normally don't mix. The word comes from the Latin for "milk out" and referred originally to the milky fluids that can be pressed from nuts and other plant tissues.

Why does emulsification occur?

Start with the principle that oil and water do not mix, such as in a homemade oil and vinegar salad dressing, which is made by shaking or beating the dressing to disperse the oil throughout the dressing. This breaks the oil into droplets minute enough to temporarily remain suspended. When you stop agitating the liquid, the oil drops start to recombine into drops too large to be suspended and so rise to the top because the oil has a lower specific density than water. An emulsifying agent is added to prevent the separation.

What do emulsifiers do?

Rather than forming a tangled mass of long molecules like starches that hold the water, emulsifiers are fats with droplets that are much more massive and slow moving than the individual molecules of water. They impede the motion of the water, creating a thick, viscous, semisolid consistency. Milk and cream are emulsions of fat dispersed in water, and butter is a water in oil emulsion. They coat the oil and serve as a physical barrier between the droplets, thus reducing the water's surface tension (the pressure of a liquid to reduce the size of its surface), which in turn reduces the ability of water to repulse oil.

Are there other ways to stabilize an emulsion?

Lemon juice or vinegar will help. Commercial manufacturers use monoglycerides, and chefs sometimes use gelatin or starches such as arrowroot but at the possible cost of flavor.

Which is the best-known emulsified sauce?

The best-known is mayonnaise, an emulsion of oil, egg yolks and lemon juice or vinegar. Beurre blanc and sabayon (zabaglione) are also well known.

Can an emulsified sauce be made in a blender or food processor?

Mayonnaise will be okay but slightly inferior, because the blender incorporates less air than beating. Not recommended for hollandaise.

Which is the most celebrated of emulsified sauces?

Hollandaise, which is an emulsion of butter, egg yolk, lemon juice, a little water, salt and cayenne pepper.

How does temperature variation affect the stability of an emulsified sauce?

Temperature extremes will destabilize emulsified sauces. Mayonnaise separates when frozen, as will any sauce with a high fat content. Hollandaise and béarnaise curdle and separate when heated close to 190 °F.

What else will destabilize these sauces?

Excessive agitation, such as overbeating, will destabilize both mayonnaise and hollandaise.

How can the weather affect the making of mayonnaise or hollandaise sauce?

Neither sauce will properly emulsify during a thunderstorm, because such storms are replete with both positive and negative charges that neutralize some of the emulsifying electrical charges of the sauce.

What can be done to save the separated sauce?

1. Add a teaspoon or two of water and whisk vigorously, or
2. Start with a teaspoon or two of water in a fresh bowl and then beat the separated sauce into the water drop by drop at first, and then more rapidly as the sauce reforms.

Will either procedure change the nature of the finished sauce?

With either procedure the reformed sauce will be thinner than the original.

Mayonnaise

What effect does freezing and then thawing the yolks have in making mayonnaise?

This freeze-thaw gives more thickness and this is used in commercial manufacturing so that only one-third of a yolk is needed per cup of mayo.

How can curdling when making mayonnaise be prevented?

1. Dilute the egg yolks with lemon juice (¼ cup per 4 yolks).
2. Add 1 teaspoon sugar per 4 yolks plus ¼ cup water.

Why must oil be added very slowly, in driblets, especially at the beginning?

In order to make very small drops of oil, for the larger ones will rise to the surface and separation will occur.

What are the main criteria for making good, fresh mayonnaise?

1. Use a bland oil such as corn or canola, not olive.
2. Use fresh lemon or lime juice.
3. Add the oil, slowly, a little at a time.

What can be used to flavor or color mayonnaise?

Green:
1. Finely minced herbs such as basil, chives, parsley.
2. Blanched, chopped spinach or watercress.
3. Mashed capers.

Pink:
1. Broiled, peeled, seeded, chopped red bell peppers.
2. Lobster roe.

What effect does salt have in making mayonnaise if added to the yolks before beginning to beat in the oil?

It increases the thickness of the yolk.

What is aïoli?

Garlic mayonnaise, originally from Provence, France.

Hollandaise

What are some of the derivatives or offshoots of hollandaise sauce?

Béarnaise: Which has shallots, tarragon and vinegar.
Bigarade: Combined with the zest and juice of a blood orange.
Choron: Which has tomato.
Maltaise: Which is infused with orange.
Mousseline: Is combined with whipped cream.

Are eggs essential to make hollandaise?

Yes and no. Lecithin, the emulsifying agent in egg yolks, can be substituted. But, as yolks provide some water and a little fat, they enhance stability by increasing viscosity. Most of all they contribute flavor, color and nutrients.

Can hollandaise be made ahead of time?

It can be made a couple of hours before serving, but not if kept warm, and it can easily be overcooked when reheated and thus break or curdle.

What is a good way to keep it warm?

Put it in a prewarmed, small thermos.

Why does an emulsified sauce, such as hollandaise, not separate?

The emulsifying agent coats the oil and, among other actions, gives the oil particles the same electrical charge as the water in the sauce. Then the oil and water repel each other and therefore do not clump together to cause separation.

What can be done if a hollandaise sauce curdles?

Beat a tablespoon of cold water into it.

What can be done if a hollandaise sauce begins to separate?

Add a little boiling water and whisk until smooth.

What is crème anglaise?

Also known as custard sauce. A sauce consisting of egg yolks, sugar, milk or cream and vanilla or other flavorings. Can be served hot or cold with cakes, puddings or fruit.

Thickeners

What is starch?

The name comes from the German *starke,* which means both "starch" and "strength." Chemically it is thousands of glucose sugar molecules strung together into long molecules. Unlike sugar crystals it is not soluble in water at typical ambient temperatures and so it is a way that a plant stores excess energy supplies.

How does starch work?

When starch granules are mixed with cold water, nothing happens and the granules sink to the bottom. When the temperature rises enough, the energy of the starch molecules is sufficient so that there is hydrogen bonding between the starch and the water molecules. The granules then absorb water and swell up.

What happens in the desired range?

The granules suddenly lose all organized structure and become networks of starch and water intermingled. This is called the gelatinization range and can be recognized by the fact that the initially cloudy suspension suddenly becomes more translucent. Then, depending upon the concentration, the mixture begins to thicken. Most sauces are rather dilute and thicken after the mixture begins to clear.

What can be substituted for cornstarch?

For each teaspoon of cornstarch use 2 teaspoons of flour.

What is the ideal temperature range for starch to work?

When the mixture of starch and water heats up to between 175 and 205 °F, well beyond the gelatinization stage, the mixture will reach its greatest thickening.

Is the temperature range the same for all starches?

140–148 °F for wheat flour and 144–158 °F for cornstarch.

What happens to starch-thickened sauces when they cool?

They increase in viscosity as they cool, and this must be taken into consideration. If thickened to the desired thickness on the stove, it is likely that it will become a gummy mess when it cools on the table.

What is a way to judge the thickness of the sauce?

One way to judge thickness is to pour a spoonful into a cool dish and then sample it.

Why minimize the amount of thickener?

The smaller the amount of thickener, the less the dilution of the sauce's flavor.

Why does a starch-thickened sauce become thicker the longer it is stored?

Loss of moisture from evaporation.

What are the main seed starches?

Wheat and corn are the two main types.

What are their characteristics?

They have two general characteristics: a relatively low thickening power and a noticeable cereal taste.

What is the purpose of cooking the flour in butter before adding it to the sauce?

The purpose of making a roux (the cooking of the flour in butter) before adding the liquid is to get rid of this raw cereal flavor.

What are the root starches?

Potato starch, arrowroot, and tapioca are the most common.

What is agar-agar?

It is a mild flavoring agent extracted from red algae. It is used in Asian cooking as a thickener and in baked goods as a stabilizer.

What are its properties?

It has little taste, does not need to be precooked, has more thickening power than root starches and will gelatinize at a lower temperature.

What is agar-agar's special use?

Excellent for last-minute corrections of sauce.

What do you have to look out for in making a starch-thickened sauce?

It will begin to thin if overcooked: maximum time is roughly 5 minutes for regular white flour, 3 minutes for cornstarch, less than 1 minute for arrowroot.

What happens when cornstarch is substituted for flour in a sauce?

It produces a more transparent, glistening sauce than flour.

How does the amount of cornstarch vary from that required for flour?

Cornstarch has about twice the thickening power of flour, so cut the flour requirement in half.

How should cornstarch be prepared for thickening a sauce?

Combine it with a cold liquid, about 2 tablespoon per tablespoon of starch and stir until dissolved and smooth.

What are the disadvantages of cornstarch?

1. It easily forms lumps when mixed with hot liquid.
2. The mixture thickened with cornstarch will start to thin if cooked too long or too hot or stirred too much.

What is the advantage of a wheat flour as a thickener?

It can be cooked at a higher temperature without separating.

What is gelatin?

A protein that, when combined with a warm liquid, will cause the liquid to gel when it cools.

What is commercial gelatin made from?

Pig skins.

In what form is it available?

It comes in sheets or as a powder.

Is there a difference between the two forms?

No, both must be softened with a cold liquid. The leaf has to be squeezed to get rid of the excess moisture. Then they both dissolve in liquid with a small amount of heat.

What should you do before filling a gelatin mold?

Before filling with the gelatin mixture, first dip the mold in cold water.

What are guides to releasing a gelatin mold?

1. When it is set, dip the mold in hot water and shake to loosen it. May have to repeat this hot water dipping.
2. With a serving plate on top turn the mold upside down, and the gelatin will drop onto the plate. It may take another shake.

What is arrowroot?

A starchy product from the arrowroot plant. A white powder that has half again as much thickening power as flour but without a chalky taste. It thickens at a lower temperature than flour but loses that power when over-beaten or over-cooked.

How should flour, cornstarch or arrowroot be added?

They tend to lump if added to hot water, therefore make a slurry (a thin paste) by mixing the thickener in a small bowl with an equal amount of cold water, then gradually warm the slurry with some of the hot cooking liquid. Finally pour the warmed slurry into the pot, stirring constantly.

What happens if a sauce stands too long?

A sauce thickened with a slurry develops a surface skin if the sauce stands for more than a short time, so stir occasionally or place a layer of plastic wrap directly onto the surface.

Where does pectin come from?

Fruits, particularly apples, citrus fruits, cranberries, blueberries.

Preparation of Sauces

How are sauces thickened?

1. By raising the ratio of solids to liquid by adding more solids such as puree of vegetables. The more water-absorbent these food particles are, the thicker the sauce.
2. By concentration through evaporating some of the liquid (which is called reduction).
3. By cooling. There will be an increase in viscosity as the liquid cools, for the water molecules lose their kinetic energy, become less mobile.
4. By adding a thickener.

What else does reduction do besides thickening?

Reduction does more than thicken, it also concentrates the flavor and does not give a floury taste or grainy texture.

What is the clearest and most digestible starch?

Arrowroot.

What happens if an arrowroot-thickened sauce is over-heated?

Its thickening power is hurt by high heat.

What is the advantage of gelatin as a thickener?

Gelatin will dissolve in almost any liquid: water, fruit juices, wine, stock etc.

How can sauces be strained?

Rinse several layers of cheesecloth in hot water and then in cold water to remove any loose fibers. Then drape the cloth over a bowl and pour the sauce in. Close the cloth and twist, holding the cloth at two ends, tightening until all the sauce is in the bowl. This procedure works easiest with two persons.

How can a sauce (or other cooking liquid) be thickened without adding more fat?

1. Add arrowroot: gives the best texture.
2. Add cornstarch: is the most stable.
3. Add potato flour (or instant potatoes), which thickens without boiling.
4. Concentrate the liquid, if feasible, by boiling in an uncovered pot.
5. Add pureed vegetables that were used in making the sauce.

What do purees give besides thickening?

Use potatoes for texture; onions, parsley and celery for flavor; carrots for sweetness (but be careful because carrots can be overdone).

How should cornstarch or arrowroot be added to a sauce?

For either arrowroot or cornstarch make a paste (1 tablespoon per cup of liquid to be thickened) with 2 tablespoons of water, then stir in some of the hot liquid from the pan. Return to the pan and cook 1–2 minutes, stirring until thickened.

How does gelatin act in thickening a sauce?

Gelatin is a protein extracted from animal bones, hooves and connective tissue or from seaweed. It increases the viscosity of a liquid because the moistened gelatin granules swell to approximately ten times their original size, trapping water molecules in the process.

What will the thickened sauce be like?

Gelatin-thickened sauces will be finer textured and will retain their stability under a broader range of temperatures than starch-thickened sauces.

What happens if the wrong amount of gelatin is used?

The firmness of the mixture depends on the ratio of gelatin to liquid, the temperature and the presence of other ingredients in the mixture. Too little gelatin results in a limp product, too much and it bounces.

Can it be reliquified?

Once thickened it can be changed back to a liquid by heating, and this can be done a number of times but not indefinitely because repeated changes partially destroy the thickening ability.

What are some ingredients that will inhibit gelatinization?

1. Sugar.
2. Fresh pineapple will do so also unless simmered for a few minutes before using.

Is this true for canned pineapple?

No. Canned pineapple has had the enzyme that inhibits gelatinization destroyed because it has been heated.

How can sauces be de-fatted?

1. Reduce the heat to low so that the fat will rise to the surface. Add a few drops of cold water. The fat can then be spooned off, or
2. Chill the sauce and lift off the hardened fat.

What are some ways to make low-fat sauces?

1. Use sautéd onion and other vegetables plus Worcestershire sauce and various seasonings such as mustard, vinegar, ketchup, lemon juice or spices for flavor.
2. Gently heat (without boiling) low fat yogurt, tomato sauce, minced basil, grated Parmesan.
3. Mix tahini (sesame paste) with crushed garlic, lemon juice and minced fresh herbs (such as dill or parsley).
4. Puree milk, cottage cheese and lemon juice in a blender.

How much flour should be used for thickening?

Thin:	Decrease the butter and flour to 1 tablespoon each.
Medium thick:	2 tablespoons each of flour and butter per cup of liquid.
Thick:	3 tablespoons each.
Extra thick:	Such as for coating food for deep frying, use 4 tablespoons each.

What happens if more is used?

Too much produces a gooey mess that is not usable.

What is the main result of adding butter?

It intensifies the flavor. The amount determines how rich the sauce will be.

What can be added to hide a burned flour taste in a sauce?

Try adding a teaspoon of peanut butter, which shouldn't alter the taste.

What is a meat glaze (glace de viande)?

1. A concentrated, gelatinous paste made from brown stock that has been reduced slowly to about one-tenth of its original volume.
2. It is mainly made from veal but can also be made from poultry, fish or beef stock.

How should it be added?

Add to a sauce in small amounts to enhance the flavor.

What is a demi-glace?

It is a basic sauce, highly flavored and glossy. The name means "half-glaze."

How is a demi-glace made?

1. The onions from the mirepoix are browned in hot oil, then the rest of the vegetables are added and browned.
2. Tomato puree is added and sautéd lightly until caramelized.
3. This mixture is thickened with a brown roux and heated thoroughly, at which point the brown stock is incorporated.
4. Simmer for 2–3 hours, skimming the surface as necessary.
5. Finally it is strained and cooled. It can then be stored, if desired.

How is the quality of a demi-glace evaluated?

1. It should have a rich, full flavor.
2. Because it is based on brown veal stock its flavor should be that of veal. The aromatics, mirepoix and tomatoes should not overpower the main flavor.
3. It should have a deep brown color.
4. When properly simmered, skimmed and reduced, it should be translucent and highly glossy.
5. It should have considerable body, but never feel gluey or overly tacky in the mouth.
6. It is at correct consistency when it evenly coats the back of a spoon.
7. The initial roasting of bones, trimmings and mirepoix should give it a pleasant roasted or caramel aroma that is readily discernible when the sauce is heated.

How can you prevent a skin from forming?

To prevent a skin from forming, use a thin layer of clarified butter on the surface to protect it from contact with air.

What happens if you use other solid ingredients such as cheese?

The solids lower the proportion of the water content, and the sauce becomes thicker.

What are the influences of other sauce ingredients on the thickening?

Salt:	It has little effect unless in large quantities.
Acid:	Wine or vinegar cause the starch granules to gelatinize and disintegrate at lower temperatures and make the sauce less viscous. Gentler cooking will compensate to some degree.
Herbs and spices:	These have little effect.
Protein:	Flour is about 10% protein by weight, and it is mostly insoluble. Flours with a high gluten content slightly increase viscosity.
Fats:	Do not have much effect on the starch.

What does the fat accomplish?

It increases "mouth feel," contributing to smoothness and moistness. When used in a roux, it prevents starch from clumping and so is a safeguard against a lumpy sauce.

Can good tomato sauce be made with canned tomatoes?

Yes, and canned plum tomatoes work best.

What must be done if canned tomatoes are used in making a sauce?

Puree or press the tomatoes through a strainer to eliminate any chunky pieces.

Why should some (about ¼) of beaten whites first be folded into a thick and heavy sauce instead of all the whites at once?

To loosen the heavy mixture so that the rest of the whites can be gently folded in without breaking down the whipped character.

How can a lumpy sauce be salvaged?

1. Use the blender or food processor.
2. Press it through a fine sieve with a wooden spoon.

When should vanilla extract be added to a custard sauce?

Only after it has fully cooled to prevent the flavoring/alcohol from evaporating.

If a vanilla bean is to be used, when can it be added?

The bean can be put in early in the preparation.

Can wine be used in making sauces?

Wine has been used in cooking since Greek and Roman times. A Roman sauce consisted of oil mixed with wine and brine, then boiled with herbs and saffron to make a double sauce. The Byzantines were lavish with spices, adding pepper, cloves, cinnamon and others.

What does wine do to the sauce?

Wine, besides adding flavor, has glycerine that helps to bind sauces, its nutritional virtues help with the cooking and digestion, its good flavor allows the cook to go easy on salt, its tannin (especially when using red wine) helps stimulate digestion and, also after being cooked, it has a little alcohol that stimulates the tastebuds.

SOUPS

What is your favorite soup recipe?

It contains whatever is in the refrigerator (vegetables, stock etc.) and the pantry (barley, rice, potatoes etc.). In other words, there is no set recipe for soups, they can be varied almost without limit.

How can fat be removed from soups or stews?

1. Refrigerate overnight so that the fat congeals on top and can be lifted off easily.
2. If the soup must be served just after preparation, then skim the fat off with a shallow ladle or skimmer.

3. Drop a few ice cubes into the liquid and stir. The fat will cling to the cubes. Remove the cubes after a few seconds.

4. Wrap ice cubes in a piece of cheese cloth or paper toweling and skim over the top. The oil will adhere to the cloth or toweling.

5. Place a few lettuce leaves or several sheets of paper toweling on the surface. The fat will cling to them.

6. Clear soups may be blotted with strips of unwaxed brown paper by floating the strips on the surface and then carefully lifting them off.

What happens if a soup boils rapidly?

The fat will emulsify with the stock and thus be difficult to remove, resulting in a greasy, cloudy product.

Why should leftover potatoes not be used for making soup?

The soup will be cloudy.

In making soup, should you ensure that the vegetables used are fresh and crisp?

No, the soft ones that are no longer young, but not rotten, will result in rich flavor and consistency.

How can a soup be stretched?

1. Add a pasta, rice, barley or beans.
2. Add stock.

How should pasta for soup be cooked?

Separately so it won't overcook and become mushy.

What is a bisque?

A thick and creamy soup made usually from shellfish and thickened with a vegetable puree, rice or a roux.

What fish are not good for soup?

Oily fish such as salmon or swordfish.

How can excess saltiness of a soup be handled?

1. Gently cook it some more with a peeled, halved potato(es) and then remove the potato.
2. Add a can of peeled tomatoes.
3. Add a small amount of brown sugar.

Which soups require more seasoning, hot or cold?

Cold.

Should soups be reheated?

1. Reheat only the amount necessary for serving.
2. Clear soups should be brought just up to a boil. Check seasoning, consistency and garnishes before serving.
3. Thick soups, especially creams, purees and bisques, should be reheated very gently. A thin layer of water or stock should be put in a heavy gauge pot before adding the soup. Start at low heat, stirring frequently, until it softens slightly. Then check seasoning and consistency.

What are characteristics expected in a cream soup?

1. Thickening with heavy cream.
2. Velvety, smooth texture.
3. Strained.
4. May have a garnish of diced meat or vegetables or croutons.

How does a pureed soup differ from a cream soup?

Purees are thicker and somewhat coarser in texture although basically smooth.

How can curdling be prevented when making soup with buttermilk?

Add the buttermilk after the soup has been cooked.

What is the advantage of oven roasting soup components?

The sugars in the ingredients are caramelized.

When preparing tomato soup should the soup be added to the milk or the milk to the soup?

Pour the soup into the milk to prevent curdling.

How can cheese rinds be used in making soups?

Add the rinds, especially from Parmesan, but remove them before serving.

How can leftover vegetables and tough stems be used?

Pureed.

What can be substituted for meat in a soup?

A little soy (tofu or tempeh) and oil.

How many clams are needed for New England clam chowder?

There is no standard way to measure, since it will vary by the variety and sex of the clams. In addition there is no sizing standard in the industry. By weight it will be about 7 pounds for a chowder for six.

Are potatoes good for thickening New England clam chowder?

No, they really don't break down and remain mushy in the soup.

What potatoes are best for the chowder?

Boiled red.

Should milk or cream be used to get a creamy chowder?

So much milk is needed that the clam flavor would be lost, so cream is best.

What is the difference between minestrone (Italian) and pot-au-feu (French)?

Minestrone: A soup of good strong stock, vegetables, pasta and sometimes meat.

Pot-au-feu: A soup containing meat and vegetables, slow simmered for a long time. It can be served as a soup or as a main course or the liquid used as a stock.

What is hoppin' John?

The Southern term for soup made from black-eyed peas and saltpork and spices.

What is a madrilène?

A consommé flavored with fresh tomato juice.

How can color be added to a white soup?

Parsley, red or green bell peppers, thin sliced cucumbers, mushrooms and asparagus tips can all be added as garnishes.

What is a chowder?

A milk-based soup with seafood and/or vegetables, such as clam chowder or corn chowder.

What can you do to a too-thick soup that must be reheated?

If too thick then water or an appropriately flavored stock can be added. Recheck the seasoning just before serving.

What if the soup is too thin?

1. A small amount of diluted cornstarch or arrowroot may be added. The soup should be at a simmer or slow boil when the thickener is added and should be stirred continuously and should continue simmering for 2–3 minutes.
2. Pureed potatoes or other vegetables can be added.

How can soups be thickened?

1. With a roux, cornstarch etc., but if a roux is used that is insufficiently cooked it will make the soup gluey.
2. With a puree of cooked rice or other grains.
3. With vegetable purees.

4. With grated corn kernels.

5. With cooked grains, such as barley or rice.

What can be done with oxtail meat left over from making soup?

1. Remove it from the bone, shred it and put back into the soup.

2. Make it into dumplings by grinding together with bread, egg, cheese, parsley, onions etc.

3. Grind for a meat loaf or a hamburger.

Why must soup made from pieces of bones be carefully strained?

Small, sharp pieces could be swallowed unknowingly and pierce the throat or intestinal tract. The best way is to use a fine strainer.

What kind of turtle should be used in mock turtle soup?

None, it is made with a calf's head.

How can consommé be clarified?

Heat gently with egg white and then strain.

What are good additions to consommé?

1. Diced or julienne vegetables.

2. Beans or lentils.

3. Pasta.

4. Grains, such as barley or wild rice.

5. Small seafood, such as slices of fish or small shrimp.

6. Edible flowers.

What is gumbo?

A thick stew or soup made with okra and onions. It was often thickened with filé powder.

How can a cold soup's flavor be strengthened, since cold decreases the ability of the palate to taste?

1. Increase the seasoning.

2. Cook the vegetables used in a rich stock instead of in water.

Why use wine in making soup?

The alcohol dissolves the fat and other compounds and results in great depth of flavor.

CHAPTER TWELVE

VEGETABLES

What is the history of the words "fruit" and "vegetable"?

Both words came originally from Latin. At first "fruit" meant any plant used as food but gradually it came to mean the edible layer surrounding the seeds. "Vegetable" made its first appearance in the eighteenth century meaning plant foods eaten along with meat or other parts of the meal; originally it meant simply a plant as opposed to an animal or inanimate object. There are other definitions that are in common usage in our language, such as "This job is a plum," "That's a peach of a dress," "That show was pure corn."

What is the botanical definition of a fruit?

A fruit is the ovary of a plant, that is, the section of the plant that houses the seeds.

What foods are commonly known as vegetables but are actually fruits?

Tomatoes, eggplants, cucumbers, okra, peppers, pumpkins and squash are fruits according to the scientific definition.

How does the U.S. Department of Agriculture make the distinction?

If you usually eat it as part of the meal's main course, it's a vegetable. The food is a fruit if you normally enjoy it as a dessert or as a between meal snack. Therefore, to the government (at least to one department), tomatoes, eggplants, cucumbers and pumpkins are vegetables. This latter definition was upheld by the Supreme Court, which made a decision because of questions about import duties.

Which vegetables don't have to ripen completely on the vine?

Asparagus, head lettuce, broccoli.

What are the general results of different cooking techniques in cooking vegetables?

Boiled: Tender, moist.

Baked: Fluffy, dry, mealy.

Stir-fry: Crisp texture, good color.

Should vegetables be kept in cold water prior to cooking?

No, for it will leach out flavor and nutrients and also cause sogginess.

What can be done with over-salted vegetables?

Place them in a sieve or colander and pour boiling water over them and drain. If still too salty, gently stir in a little (2–3 tablespoons) of cream.

How can vegetables be reheated?

1. In simmering water or stock.
2. Microwave.
3. Sauté.

How young are baby vegetables?

There are no set limits, and some are not young but rather are hybrids selected because they grown small.

What is a duxelles?

A mixture of minced mushrooms, onions, shallots, and herbs cooked slowly in butter. It is used to flavor soups and sauces and sometimes as a garnish or stuffing.

NUTRITION

Why do raw, unprocessed fruits and vegetables tend to deteriorate so rapidly?

1. Attacks by microorganisms.
2. Enzymatic action.
3. The decomposition process generates heat, which accelerates the rate of microbial and enzymatic damage, and the resultant moisture loss withers the food.
4. If not chilled quickly by the producers they will go downhill.

Why are fruits and vegetables, like apples and cucumbers, sometimes coated with wax?

1. Wax seals in the moisture and therefore extends the life of the item.
2. Retention of moisture minimizes weight loss and therefore there is more to sell.
3. Gives an attractive sheen to the product.

Is wax beneficial for the consumer?

This is strictly for the benefit of the food industry. Wax is safe to eat according to the industry but it can give an off-flavor. It is next to impossible to wash it all off and get rid of foreign substances like pesticides.

Which fruits are most often waxed?

Apples, oranges, cucumbers, grapefruit, bell peppers, pears, cantaloupes, plums and yams are the ones most often coated.

Are raw vegetables more nutritious than cooked ones?

1. No minerals are destroyed by cooking.
2. Cooking triggers some loss of B and C vitamins.
3. Raw foods contain some enzymes thought to be disease-preventing, but these enzymes rarely survive the acid environment of the stomach, and their disease-preventing qualities have not been proved.

How can leached minerals and vitamins be salvaged?

Recycling the cooking liquid can salvage leached minerals and vitamins.

What are some ways to improve the nutritional value of a recipe without decreasing the attractiveness of the dish?

1. Reduce or eliminate the amount of fat such as trimming off the fat from a roast or other pieces of meat.
2. Use a different cooking technique (such as steaming instead of pan frying).
3. Avoid long cooking times. Cook just to the point of doneness. This can save a lot of nutrients.
4. Serve a vegetable or bean puree over a grilled fish instead of a butter sauce.
5. Use egg whites rather than whole eggs where possible. Sometimes eliminate yolks or reduce their number.
6. Use nonstick pans to minimize or eliminate fat.
7. Sauce can be further thickened with cornstarch or flour that has been dissolved in a little water or the addition of a pureed vegetable.
8. Use a sprinkling of grated Parmesan cheese instead of salt.

Which have more vitamins, canned or fresh vegetables?

Contrary to expectations, it is the canned ones, because they are processed more quickly after picking, while fresh produce loses vitamins and other nutrients as it ages.

Which are more nutritious, canned or frozen foods?

Frozen, because the heat of the canning process destroys vitamins.

What foods are good sources of calcium?

Dark green vegetables, milk, cheese, oranges and navy beans.

What are good sources of magnesium?

Leafy greens, nuts, beans, whole grains, bananas, tofu.

What are foods least likely to contain pesticide residual?

Brussels sprouts, corn, cabbage, green peas, sweet potatoes, cauliflower, avocados.

Which are most likely to have pesticide residue?

Mexican carrots, American cherries, apples, pears, raspberries, nectarines, strawberries.

Where does most food contamination come from?

According to the Centers for Disease Control in Atlanta, 77% of food-borne outbreaks are due to improper handling, less than 5% from an unsafe original source.

Are fresh vegetables or frozen vegetables the most nutritious?

Frozen are just as nutritious. Fresh ones often sit around for days before being sold and/or eaten and thus decrease in nutritive value. Even the heat of canning doesn't destroy many nutrients.

What is the definition of organic?

Grown without any harmful pesticides, herbicides, fertilizers. There is no national standard but under the Federal Organic Food Products Act (1990) there must be a third-party verification of growing methods, soil and water testing and strict record keeping. The certification must be repeated on a regular basis. The land must be free of all synthetic compound materials for a minimum of three years.

What are transitional food products?

The product may be sold as transitional after the first year of converting a farm to organic.

Is there a difference in nutritional value of a transitional product?

There is no difference in nutritional value, although they usually are more healthy because of what they don't contain, that is, certain chemicals.

Are organic vegetables better than nonorganic ones?

Pro: Organic vegetables have no pesticides or other harmful chemicals and probably arrive at the market fresher.

Con: Organic are more expensive and more difficult to find.

Do organic vegetables or fruits taste better?

It is hard to tell the difference in flavor, and there is no scientific evidence to confirm it. Because they are often picked when riper and handled more carefully, it would seem that they are better. I buy them whenever they are available, but not just for taste.

Are organic vegetables more healthful?

The amount of pesticides or other chemicals in nonorganic ones is minimal, but there is a slight difference.

How can one get nicotine without smoking?

Cauliflower, eggplants, tomatoes and potatoes contain enough nicotine to confuse urine tests for nicotine. A third of a pound of potatoes or half a pound of ripe tomatoes provide the amount of nicotine a nonsmoker would absorb during three hours in a room with a low level of tobacco smoke, according to a report in the *New England Journal of Medicine.*

Vegetables

What can be done to decrease the nicotine content?

Cooking any of the vegetables in water decreases the nicotine content.

Will a strict vegetarian diet cause an iron deficiency?

No. A survey of 6,500 Chinese who eat little meat did not show any iron deficiency. It is true that meat fanciers are right when they praise red meat, dark fowl, fish, etc. as sources of heme iron (nonprotein iron-containing pigment that is a component part of hemoglobin and myoglobin). However, vitamin C from leafy vegetables, dry beans and peas, dried fruit, breads etc. makes nonheme iron more available to our bodies.

What are some of the edible flowers?

Honeysuckle, rose, scented geraniums, lavender, calendula, chive, dill, chervil, fennel, nasturtium, daisy, dandelion.

How can they be used?

In salads, to flavor butter, flavoring oils, as decorations, flavoring sugar.

In order to get the best results of strong flavored greens such as kale or mustard greens, which is a better way to precook: blanching or boiling?

Blanching, for the smaller amount of water results in less dilution of flavor.

What is hydroponic growing of vegetables?

Growing them in nutritionally enriched water instead of in the soil.

What are the pros and cons of hydroponic farming?

Pro: Produce is available all year round and easy to clean.

Con: Fruits and vegetables have a less-pronounced flavor.

What are ways to protect the nutritive elements of vegetables?

1. Don't cut them up until ready to use, for exposure to oxygen saps the nutrients.
2. Avoid boiling, rather use steaming or microwaving, because the boiling leaches the nutrients into the cooking liquid.
3. Use quick cooking, such as stir-fry, for extended exposure to heat destroys the nutrients.

Do vegetables contain dangerous chemicals?

Only potentially. The danger levels depend both on quantity ingested and individual sensitivity.

What are the potentially dangerous chemicals found naturally in vegetables?

Solanine: This is associated with arthritis pain: green potatoes, tomatoes, red and green peppers, eggplant.

Thioglucoside: May adversely affect the thyroid gland: cabbage, turnips, kale, rutabaga, watercress. However, this is destroyed by cooking.

Psoralens:	This causes cancer in laboratory animals: parsnips. Peeling and cooking gets rid of it.
Beta carotene:	It may interfere with menstruation: carrots, squash and broccoli are high in carotene. Women with menstruation problems should refrain from eating too much of these.
Oxalic acid:	Interferes with calcium absorption: spinach, rhubarb, coco (chocolate) and excess should be avoided as you approach middle age.

SELECTION

What are the grades of canned, frozen and dried vegetables and fruits?

U.S. Grade A	Fancy
B	Choice or extra standard
C	Standard

How are grades of fresh vegetables and fruits established?

Grades are determined by color, size, shape, maturity and number of defects or blemishes.

Are young vegetables, such as cucumbers, eggplants, zucchini and others, better than the large, more mature ones, or vice versa?

Most fruits and vegetables reach their first stage of maturity before they have completed their growth. If harvested at this point then they are more tender. Later the cell walls begin to thicken and the woody cellular substance, lignin, which cannot be softened by cooking, becomes more abundant. Fully mature ones also have more seeds.

Which size vegetables are usually available?

Despite the superiority of the young ones, the larger ones are usually stocked in the stores, because there is more profit in them. On a pound-per-pound basis it costs less to grow the big ones because of labor savings.

How do most shoppers base their quality judgments?

Most American shoppers equate large size with quality.

STORAGE

What produce should not be stored in the refrigerator?

Potatoes, dry onions, bananas.

Do plant cells continue to live at lower temperatures, such as when refrigerated?

Yes, but their biochemical activity is slowed. This is also true for the spoilage microbes, which grow less rapidly and need air and a low water content (humidity). However, those fruits native to tropical or subtropical climates do not do well in the cold. The skin of the banana turns black; avocados darken and fail to soften below 45 °F.

How should vegetables be machine-dried?

1. Choose only ripe, most perfect ones.
2. Rinse and dry.
3. Halve small ones, slice larger ones.
4. Set apart in drying rack so that pieces don't touch. Place in dry area. The warmer it is, the faster they dry.
5. Dry until crisp if they are to be powdered, chewy if to be eaten as such.

PREPARATION

Should vegetables such as artichokes, string beans, zucchini, spinach and carrots be soaked, as recommended in some Italian cookbooks, to remove the harsh mineral flavors imparted by rich soil?

No! Vitamins B and C are water soluble and will be leached into the water. To maximize vitamin retention, skip soaking and cook by steaming or microwaving.

What are exceptions to the need for soaking?

Two exceptions and only if very dirty, otherwise a quick rinse is sufficient:

1. To prevent discoloration, place artichokes in acidulated water until ready to cook.
2. Tubers, such as potatoes, may be briefly soaked in several changes of water to remove excess starch.

How should vegetables be washed?

1. Never soak them in water, as they will become soft and mushy.
2. Rinse them in cold running water and then blot dry with paper toweling.
3. Alternatively wipe them with a damp paper towel dipped in lemon water (for example, to maintain the whiteness of a mushroom).

How long should vegetables be marinated?

It takes time, so try to plan 24 hours ahead or overnight.

What is the advantage of adding salt to the vegetable washing water?

It will draw out insects and also help to remove sand.

Why should cylindrical vegetables, such as carrots or cucumbers, be cut on the diagonal when stir frying?

1. The pieces look more attractive.
2. There is more surface area for quick cooking.
3. There is more surface area for the sauce to flavor.

How can wilted (uncooked) vegetables be revived?

Freshen them (to a degree) by soaking for an hour in cold water together with the juice of a lemon.

COLOR

Why do some vegetables often turn a drab olive color when cooked?

The acidity of lemon juice, wine or vinegar protects color for avocados, cauliflower or potatoes but doesn't do that for green vegetables. So don't use them for cooking green vegetables. Acid, coupled with heat, are the villains. In combination they denature the chlorophyll, the pigment that gives green fruits and vegetables their color.

How can they be kept from discoloring?

1. If the sauce or seasoning is acidic, dress just before serving and serve immediately.
2. Avoid acidic vinaigrettes.
3. When possible, such as in a salad, use raw vegetables.

What is the purpose of plunging vegetables in boiling water for a moment and then putting them in cold water?

To stop further reaction and thus keep the color bright and the taste essentially raw.

How does baking soda help maintain color?

Baking soda helps to maintain the vivid green because it is an alkali and neutralizes the discoloring acid.

What is the reason this procedure is strongly discouraged by some?

Adding baking soda, while used by some, is strongly discouraged because it also destroys vitamins (particularly C and thiamin) and also because it softens the hemicellulose of the vegetable's cells, resulting in a mushy texture.

What are some other ways the color of vegetables can be saved from discoloring when cooked?

1. Avoid subjecting green vegetables to acid such as lemon juice or vinegar (as in a vinaigrette).
2. Cook green vegetables in a large amount of salted water, uncovered, which allows the acid to evaporate, and the large amount of water will dilute the acid.
3. Microwave or steam the veggies.
4. Blanch the vegetables before cooking, which will leach out some or most of the acid in them. Boil briefly, drain and rinse in cold water, then finish cooking in fresh water.
5. Don't cook vegetables in cast-iron skillets or in tin-lined pans.
6. Keep the cooking time below seven minutes. Don't overcook the vegetable, as this will cause the color to change.
7. Add a small amount of milk to the cooking water.
8. Cut large pieces into smaller ones, so that they will cook faster.

How can red vegetables, such as beets, be prevented from turning blue?

1. Make sure that the acid level is maintained. Red vegetables will turn blue when the acid level drops, i.e., when they become more alkaline.
2. Add a little lemon juice or vinegar when cooking.
3. Add buttermilk or sour cream, both of which are acidic.
4. Don't overcook.

Why does lemon juice prevent discoloration when added to sliced or peeled avocados or potatoes?

The discoloration is largely caused by oxidation, and the ascorbic acid of the lemon juice slows down the oxidative process.

What is another technique?

Another technique is to cook the food, because heat inactivates the enzymes in the food that would otherwise bring about discoloring in the presence of oxygen.

What does blanching do for vegetables?

1. Makes the skin easy to remove.
2. Eliminates or minimizes strong odors and flavors.
3. Sets the color, especially when the vegetable is to be served cold.
4. It is the first step for later cooking procedures.

COOKING

Which is more important in determining whether a vegetable has been overcooked: color or texture change?

With green vegetables, such as broccoli, it is the color, while for white and/or orange, such as cauliflower or carrots, it is texture.

Does the acidity of the cooking liquid affect the cooking time of vegetables?

Yes: Acid slows down the cooking action. Therefore, beans cooked in a casserole that is made with tomatoes require 10–20% more cooking time than nonacidic baked beans.

What does alkali do to cooking time?

Alkali has the opposite effect, it shortens cooking time.

What does "sweat the vegetables" mean in a recipe?

Slice or diced vegetables are cooked in a very small amount of water or stock over a low heat to soften and develop flavor. Don't cook to develop color, just to soften, stirring occasionally. This is not a quick cooking procedure.

Should vegetables be cooked in chicken stock?

Most have a better flavor when cooked in chicken stock.

Can beef stock be used?

It can be used for some strong vegetables such as carrots or turnips. For others beef stock often will overpower the vegetable.

Blanching and Parboiling

What is blanching?

Immersion of food in boiling water for a brief time.

What is the purpose of blanching?

1. Set the color and flavor of fruits and vegetables before freezing.
2. Facilitate peeling of peaches, plums, tomatoes, onions etc.
3. Rid bacon of excess fat and salt.
4. Firm tissues such as brains and sweetbreads.
5. Soften vegetables without cooking them completely.

What is scalding?

To bring the liquid temperature to just below boiling, with tiny bubbles appearing around the edges.

What is parboiling?

This is partial cooking in boiling water or stock. Have ready a pot of rapidly boiling liquid and a bowl of iced water. Cook the food, particularly dense vegetables such as carrots, for a short time in the boiling water and then cool quickly in the iced water to stop the cooking process.

What is the difference between blanching and parboiling?

Parboiling is similar to blanching, and sometimes the terms are used interchangeably whereby food is partially boiled until nearly tender and then cooked through by other means. It is used for vegetables that need to cook for a longer time. Example: potatoes cooked with a roast.

Blanching is the same process but for a shorter time. It can be done either to loosen skins or set color.

Should summer vegetables, such as carrots, be handled the same way as winter ones, such as broccoli and brussels sprouts?

Spring and summer: Raw or use a quick blanch.

Fall and winter: Slow cooking, braise or roast.

Roasting and Broiling

How should vegetables like eggplant, carrots or dinner squash be broiled?

Slice not too thin, brush with oil and broil watching carefully to prevent overcooking.

How can root vegetables be roasted in less time?

Thinly slice them, toss in a little oil, spread on a lined bakery sheet and roast at 450 °F for 20–25 minutes and they should require less roasting time.

What is the difficulty in grilling vegetable brochettes?

Different sizes and odd shapes make timing difficult.

What can be done to overcome this?

1. Use only one kind of vegetable on each skewer.
2. Use medium heat.
3. Cut large vegetables into uniformly sized pieces.

How should vegetables be tested for doneness when roasting in the oven?

Poke with the tip of a pointed knife. They should be tender but not falling apart.

Which vegetables do well when baked?

Potatoes, carrots, beets, squash, turnips, sweet potatoes.

What is the effect of a little sugar in the vegetable cooking water?

It will bring out the flavor.

What is caramelization of vegetables?

The browning of the sugar in the vegetables.

When is this important?

Particularly for those with a high sugar content, such as onions or carrots.

Why should a pat of butter be added to cooking water of greens?

It will prevent the water from boiling over, without your having to constantly stir.

Why should water used for boiling vegetables be boiled for at least two minutes before putting the vegetables in it?

This will cause the water to lose a large percentage of its oxygen. It is the oxygen that causes the vitamin C content to be reduced.

Can glazing be done in advance preparation?

No. Glazing should be done just before the end of cooking so that the appearance will be bright.

Can all vegetables be roasted satisfactorily?

No. Leafy ones just wilt. Brussels sprouts, broccoli, cauliflower and cabbages of various kinds can become bitter.

How can root vegetables, such as rutabaga, turnips etc., be made more attractive?

Puree like mashed potatoes and season with herbs or spices.

What are some vegetables that can be stuffed?

Artichokes, eggplant, mushrooms, tomatoes, peppers, squash.

What are some things that can be used as stuffing?

Chopped vegetables, cooked pasta, orzo, barley, rice, mushrooms, cheese, caramelized onions, prosciutto, fresh bread crumbs, tomatoes.

Vegetable Stock

What are the cautions about the use of vegetables in making a stock?

1. Don't use beets unless you want a red stock.
2. Use only a limited quantity of asparagus unless you want a green stock.
3. Use strong-flavored vegetables such as brussels sprouts or broccoli only in moderation.
4. Roast the vegetables in the oven before making the stock if you want a brown, hearty stock.

How can you ensure a clear vegetable stock?

1. Skim off the foam that rises to the surface from time to time.
2. Strain the finished stock after skimming and let it cool to room temperature.
3. If you are going to freeze the stock, make sure that it has cooled to room temperature before putting it in the freezer.

How can a measured amount of stock be unfrozen for cooking?

Premeasure the stock before freezing, such as in 1- or 2-cup amounts, and label the containers.

ARTICHOKES

Where do artichokes comes from, and when are they on the market?

Almost all come from California, mainly from Monterey County along the Pacific Coast. The peak harvest is March and April but they are available throughout the year.

What should govern the selection of artichokes?

1. Pick compact, tightly packed, heavy chokes with green-looking leaves, which will indicate that they have not lost their moisture from the field.
2. The leaves should look plump and not shriveled. When bent back they should snap back, not tear. They should squeak when squeezed.
3. Avoid artichokes with leaves that are separated, for that shows that they are old, tough and bitter.
4. Look for freshly cut stems.

5. Avoid brown stems and leaves that have more than a slight brown discoloration. A little brown indicates some frostbite, which will enhance a nutty flavor.

6. Avoid any with signs of mold.

7. Choose the heaviest. Size is not related to quality.

8. Choose uniformly sized chokes when cooking more than one at a time.

What does the size of the artichoke indicate?

It indicates where the chokes were on the stalk. The larger ones are at the top. Very young ones are also small.

How can an artichoke be kept from turning brown from cooking?

1. Use stainless steel cutting tools.

2. Rub the cut surfaces with a sliced lemon.

What do purple tips on an artichoke indicate?

Purple tips indicate too much exposure to sunlight or too great maturity.

How many should you buy for a dinner?

Plan one choke per person.

How should baby artichokes be stored?

1. Sprinkle with a little water and place in a plastic bag.

2. Put in the coldest part of the refrigerator.

3. Will keep up to a week.

Which is the better way to cook artichoke, steaming or boiling?

Steaming, but even better is braising in some stock.

What is a caution in cooking artichokes?

They are easy to overcook.

What is the easiest way to cook artichokes?

1. Trim the bottom of the stem, slice off the top quarter of the leaves.

2. Steam either in a steamer or pressure cooker.

3. Sprinkling with salt is optional but recommended.

How can you test for doneness?

Pull off a leaf and taste.

How can a sweeter flavor and better color be achieved?

Add a small amount of sugar and salt.

How should baby chokes be cooked?

Baby chokes are best grilled or braised. Trim well. Cut in half and remove fuzz. Braise with a little water, oil, herbs. Season with lemon juice and salt.

Vegetables

What preparations should be made for cooking artichokes that will also prevent blackening?

1. Do not use aluminum or cast-iron pots. Use stainless, Teflon-lined or enamel pots, or the chokes will turn a dull gray-green.
2. They tend to darken quickly in air when trimmed.
3. Halve two lemons, squeeze the juice from three of the halves into a large pot of cold water.
4. Peel the outer leaves, snapping them off at the base until reaching the pale golden leaves.
5. Slice off the green top.
6. Rub the chokes with the remaining lemon half.
7. Trim the base where the leaves were snapped off of any remaining fibrous green parts and rub the area with the lemon half.
8. Trim off the bottom ¼″ of the stem and pare away any tough outer skin and then rub it with the lemon half.
9. Remove the fuzzy part of the choke.
10. Drop into lemon water.
11. Place a thin slice of lemon over the trimmed top, then tie it on with a piece of string to hold it in place while cooking. This is optional.

Are artichokes fattening?

A 12-ounce choke has only 25 calories and no fat.

What can be done with the artichoke cooking water?

1. Use it as soup stock.
2. Thicken it with trimmed leaves and stalks (pureed).
3. If too lemony, counter with milk, cream or sour cream.

How can artichokes be prepared for stuffing?

1. Remove and discard the coarse outer leaves.
2. Cut away the coarsest part of the stem.
3. Place in cool, acidulated (lemon juice or vinegar) water to prevent discoloration.
4. Drain and blanch in boiling water (with lemon juice, salt and seasoning) about 5 minutes until tender but not soft.
5. Remove the bottom leaves and scoop out the tender heart with a small spoon.

Can the removed artichoke stems and leaves be used?

Yes, by running them through a food mill. The puree can be combined with mashed potatoes and piped into the choke as a stuffing.

How should stuffed chokes be cooked?

Broil until the filling and chokes are thoroughly warm, about 5 minutes.

ASPARAGUS

What should you look for when selecting asparagus?

1. If the bud cluster at the tip isn't compact, it is over the hill. The buds should be tightly closed.
2. Ideally the exterior should be green from tip to the bottom of the stalk, unless it is white asparagus.
3. It should not be stringy or crooked. The stem should be firm.
4. It was harvested too long ago if the cut base is woody or dried out. Should appear freshly cut.
5. A purple-white stalk at the bottom is ok if not more than 2–3". Cut it off, however.
6. The stalk should be semi-rigid, firm and not limp.
7. Straight stalks are preferable to curved ones.
8. Green asparagus should have a bright hue without a yellow tinge.
9. Stalks that are flat or angular are usually tough.

What is important in selecting for uniform cooking?

That the asparagus have the same diameter.

How are asparagus classified commercially?

Pencil-sized, standard and jumbo. All can be equally tender.

What is the nutritional value of asparagus?

Low in sodium and calories, no fat or cholesterol, good in fiber.

Is thinness of the asparagus stalk an indication of age?

The thinner ones are not necessarily younger.

How can asparagus be kept fresh?

1. Asparagus begins to lose its sweet character when harvested so use a quickly as possible but to be kept the best stand in a tall vase with the stalk end in 2–3" of water.
2. Put the container in a cool room or add a few ice cubes if the room is warm.
3. Refrigerate wrapped in damp paper towels and placed in a plastic bag.

Should asparagus be salted before cooking?

Add 1 tablespoon of salt to the cooking water when the water is boiling.

How should asparagus be cooked?

1. Since the bottom of the stalk is tougher the best way is to have the stalk vertical in boiling, salted water. The tops will cook from the steam.

2. Easiest way to handle is to tie the bunch together.

3. Have the pot covered so that the steam will cook the tops.

4. Another way is to wrap them in parchment paper.

5. They do well in a microwave oven, laid flat in a pan with only the water left over from rinsing them and covered with plastic wrap.

How can asparagus be prevented from overcooking?

Watch carefully, remove from cooking water when just tender, drain and immediately plunge into ice water. Serve cool in a salad or reheat as needed.

When steaming asparagus, what can be done if your pot isn't tall enough?

Trim the stalks so that they are of even length. Tie them into a bunch with a white string. Put the bunch into the pot with about 3" of water, use another pot as the cover.

Should asparagus be peeled before cooking?

The stalk is more tender if peeled but there is not agreement among cooks as to whether it is necessary. They will cook faster peeled. The fresher the spear the less need to peel. I rarely find it necessary to do so. Peel only if the stalks are old and tough, or if you want a more elegant, formal presentation.

Can asparagus be roasted?

Yes. Snap off the tough end, place in a roasting pan, single layered, mix with a little olive oil, salt and pepper. Roast at 450 °F for about 10 minutes or until tender. Drizzle a little balsamic vinegar over them.

Where does white asparagus come from?

It is asparagus harvested before the spear emerges from the ground (usually the plants are mounded up to block exposure to light). The chlorophyll that gives it its green color only develops when exposed to light. The white form is particularly favored in Europe but is gathering popularity in the United States.

How are white asparagus different from the green?

They tend to be slightly more fibrous than the green and are therefore frequently better when peeled and may have a slight bitterness but are still delicious. Available mainly in May and June but are occasionally available in winter months.

How do purple spears differ?

They are a little sweeter than the green ones but they turn green when cooked.

How do you get rid of the woody base of the asparagus spear?

Hold the spear about half way down the stalk. With the other hand hold the base between your thumb and index finger about 1" or so up. Bend the stalk until it snaps. Or feel the stalk and use a small, sharp paring knife and, trying the stalk from the base as you work upwards until the knife can make an easy cut.

Vegetables

What should you do with the asparagus ends that you cut off?

1. Throw them away.
2. Use for making asparagus soup.
3. Use as one of the vegetables for stock.
4. Freeze them until needed for stock.

How should a can of asparagus be opened?

Turn it upside down and open from the bottom to avoid breaking the tips.

When should canned asparagus be used since their delicate flavor has been diminished in the canning process?

1. When fresh asparagus are out of season.
2. They need no further cooking, that is, for immediate use.
3. They work well in salads.

AVOCADO (ALLIGATOR PEAR)

What are the characteristics of the Hass variety of avocado?

1. A creamy texture and rich flavor.
2. Oval shaped, available year round.
3. Medium sized.
4. A rough skin that darkens as it ages.
5. Peels easily.

How are Fuerte avocados different?

1. Medium sized.
2. Available late fall to spring.
3. A smooth, green skin.

How are the Florida avocado varieties different?

1. Available July to February.
2. Larger than California varieties.
3. Not as creamy because they are lower in fat.
4. Lighter in consistency.

What is the nutritive value of avocados?

They are sodium-free but high in potassium, vitamin E and folate.

Is an avocado or a raw coconut higher in fat?

They are equal; both about 85% from fat.

Are avocados rich in saturated fat?

A medium avocado has 30 grams of fat, of which about 5 grams are saturated.

What should you look for when selecting avocados?

1. They should be heavy for their size.
2. Just beginning to soften.
3. Without dark or bruised marks or sunken areas.
4. Most avocados on the market require several days of softening at home, so plan ahead.
5. If buying for immediate use, choose those with an exciting fragrance and that feel slightly soft.

What does a really soft one indicate?

A really soft one will be past its prime, but a wood-hard one won't ripen properly.

How can you feel for ripeness?

It is ripe when it gives slightly to finger pressure.

How can you hasten ripening?

Keep at room temperature in a pierced paper bag. It will ripen even faster if you put an apple in the bag, because the apple gives off ethylene, which is an avocado-ripening gas.

How can you retard oxidation of a cut avocado?

1. Use stainless steel to cut it.
2. Leftover puree or pieces will not brown as readily if you store the avocado pit with them, so cut off from the pit only as much as you need.
3. Coat the pieces with lemon or lime juice and then store them covered with plastic.
4. If the avocado pit is left in a guacamole dip it will keep the dip from turning black.
5. Spreading a little butter over the cut surface will help.

If an avocado cut in half turns brown, should it be discarded?

No, just scrape off the brown part.

How can browning of guacamole be prevented?

Place plastic on the surface to seal off exposure to oxygen.

BEANS, DRIED—see chapter on GRAINS, BEANS AND PASTA

BEANS, GREEN

What should be looked for in selecting green beans?

1. Solid green color.
2. No scars or discoloration. The skin should be unblemished.

3. Take slender, smooth, slightly velvety pods without bumps.
4. The bean should break easily, with a crisp snap.

How does size affect cooking time?

The younger, smaller, more immature pods are more tender and need only a brief steaming.

What do the bumps indicate?

The bumps are from bulging seeds and indicate overage and toughness.

What is the advantage of roasting green beans over steaming or sautéing?

The flavor and texture will be enhanced.

What is the difference between string beans and snap beans?

String beans have been bred to eliminate the "string" and now are called "snap beans." If you get some beans with a string, snap off the stem and pull the string down along the bean and discard.

How can green beans be best kept?

1. Refrigerate.
2. Don't soak in water.

Should green beans be sliced lengthwise?

1. The French style, the very narrow, long beans, do not need it.
2. The larger wider beans may be cooked without cutting, but slicing them with a bean slicer can cut down cooking time and yield a very tender, crisp and delightful treat in very short cooking time.

BEETS

Should you choose small or large beets?

1. Don't select the large ones as they are not as tender or as flavorful and are often woody. There is little difference in flavor or texture between small and medium ones.
2. Fresh tops mean fresh beets.
3. Choose firm, smooth beets with deep color and a slender main root.
4. Canned beets are barely discernible in taste from those cooked fresh.

How do golden beets differ from red ones?

These newcomers on the market are similar to red ones but somewhat sweeter. Frequently sold very small, about thumb sized. The red beet is a relative of the sugar beet.

What are beetroots?

The British name for beets.

What are good procedures for preparing beets?

1. Don't throw away the greens from young beets, for they can be cooked like spinach.
2. Cut the greens off as soon as possible, because they draw out nutrients and moisture.
3. Scrub the beets carefully, for if you rupture their thin skins they will stain. If you must use very large beets then quarter them.
4. Don't peel beforehand.
5. Never cut the stem closer than 1″ from the bulb, because it will bleed into the cooking water.

Are beet greens usable?

They are attractive. Cook quickly by steaming or sautéing with butter and a little lemon juice.

How should beets be cooked?

1. A pressure cooker is a good, quick way of cooking.
2. They can be boiled or steamed.

Can beets and greens be cooked together?

No, cook separately to prevent discoloration.

How should beets be boiled?

1. Remove the tops, stems and greens.
2. Simmer 15–20 minutes or until tender.
3. Drain and rub off the skin under cold running water.

How should beets be baked?

1. Wrap in foil with the stem end slightly exposed.
2. Bake in a preheated 400 °F oven until very tender.
3. Rinse under cold running water and rub off the skin.
4. Trim the stem end.

What will steaming accomplish?

Steam them to minimize bleeding and to concentrate flavor.

How should they be steamed?

In acidic water (lemon juice or vinegar) for 30–45 minutes until they are easily pierced with a thin knife.

What does the acid accomplish?

It keeps the color the best.

Is roasting a good method for beets?

Roasting works similar to steaming but not quite as well. Wrap them in foil after oiling the skin.

How can beets be peeled?

After cooking, peel by cradling the beet in a paper towel in your hand, then peel off the skin with thumb and forefinger.

What are two other ways?

1. Briefly deep fry.
2. Peel with a swivel peeler.

How can cooked/peeled beets be used?

1. Warm as a vegetable with the entrée.
2. Grated or diced in a salad or in salsa.

Should beets be baked or boiled for a salad?

This is optional, but baking gives a more intense flavor.

Can they be used raw in salads?

They can be used in salad if finely grated.

How should beets be added to a salad?

Add at the end of the salad making, so other ingredients won't be stained.

Why shouldn't you slice beets on a wooden board?

Slice on a nonporous surface rather than on a wooden cutting board, for the juice will badly stain the wood.

BELL PEPPERS (SWEET PEPPERS)

How should bell peppers be selected?

1. Choose richly colored, red, green, orange or chocolate-colored shiny, smooth-skinned peppers with fresh-looking stems.
2. Avoid limp, shriveled ones or any with soft spots.

What does the color indicate?

1. Green (bell) peppers are the most popular although they are the ones not fully ripened.

2. The red ones are simply green peppers that are vine ripened. They also have more vitamin C and are sweeter and have a mellower flavor than the green.

3. The yellow ones are the riper stage of a different variety of green peppers and are the sweetest and least acidic of the peppers.

How can peppers be served?

1. All colors are excellent as crudités.

2. They can be eaten raw or cooked.

What does the appearance of the bell peppers indicate?

1. Very shiny peppers usually have been wax coated to preserve them. The wax itself is harmless but it may contain pesticides.

How can peppers be prepared?

1. Wash, drain and cut in half vertically.

2. Remove the seeds, the core and any internal membranes.

3. The top may be cut off, and, if this is done, remove seeds and cores before stuffing and baking.

How should bell peppers be handled for stuffing and baking?

1. Cut in half crosswise.

2. Coat the outside of the pepper with vegetable oil so it will retain its color.

3. Place in a buttered muffin tin to retain its shape.

How are they peeled?

1. To skin, roast them whole or halved or steam in a paper bag, or char the skin in the oven or over direct flame.

2. After roasting, place them in a plastic bag and let sit for 10 minutes. Then, under running water, rub off the skin and black particles. Then halve and seed.

What does roasting peppers accomplish?

It brings out the flavor and makes peeling easy.

BOK CHOY (CHINESE WHITE CABBAGE, PAK CHOY)

How should bok choy be chosen?

Look for white, firm stalks and unblemished, crisp, green leaves.

Which is the best selection?

Baby bok choy; the smaller leaves and stems are tenderer and have a more delicate flavor.

How can bok choy be treated to minimize wilting when cooked?

Plunge it into hot water, remove quickly and drain immediately.

How can it be used?

Use raw or lightly sautéd in a stir-fry. It does best with some seasoning such as garlic and/or ginger.

BROCCOLI

What should you look for when buying broccoli?

1. The bud clusters should be bright-hued and tightly packed. If tiny flowers are emerging from the buds, it is past its prime.
2. The stems should be smooth, slender and pliable. Woody stems indicate that the broccoli is too old or the harvested broccoli has been stored too long.
3. Choose crisp, uniformly green or purple heads with tight clusters. Avoid all that are yellowing or have a stale odor.

When are the best available?

The best broccoli specimens are not found during hot weather.

Why shouldn't the outer leaves be trimmed?

Unless the outer leaves are yellow or blemished they should be kept, because it is in these leaves that most of the nutrients are located.

What are the best ways for preparing broccoli?

1. Remove the stalks, slice them into ½" discs and begin steaming or simmering them about 5 minutes before adding the florets.
2. Alternatively, marinate the discs in an herb, olive oil and vinegar mixture and serve as a raw snack.
3. One way to cook the whole broccoli is to stand it, stem and all, upright in 1" of rapidly boiling water. Cover the pot, reduce the heat slightly and cook 12–15 minutes, depending on size.

What are the best ways to cook broccoli florets?

Steaming or microwaving.

What kind of sauce should be used with broccoli?

It should be strongly flavored.

Is broccoli good to eat raw?

Yes. Use small, raw florets and sliced (trimmed) stems as crudités.

How should broccoli be prepared for a salad?

1. Cut into spears and steam until just tender.

2. Rinse immediately under running, cold water.

3. Wrap well and refrigerate.

What can be done to accentuate the broccoli flavor in a broccoli and cheese sauce?

Use the broccoli cooking water instead of milk.

How should broccoli be steamed?

1. Slice or cut into 1½-inch pieces.

2. Peel tough stems.

3. Steam the stems 2–3 minutes.

4. Add the florets and steam a short time, about 5 minutes.

5. Drain and serve.

What can be done with thick stems?

Trim and slice them thinly and cook with the florets.

How can broccoli be cooked ahead?

Steam, and chill in cold water to stop the cooking, drain and refrigerate. Reheat to serve.

Why does broccoli turn an unattractive gray when blanched and then sautéd with oil, garlic and lemon juice?

Chlorophyll, the green pigment, is highly susceptible to both heat and acid. Add the lemon juice or other acid only after the vegetable has cooled slightly, as the chlorophyll doesn't degrade at lower temperatures. Cooking the vegetable in abundant water will allow the acid to escape as steam, but excess water promotes loss of some nutrients, such as C and B vitamins. Don't steam more than a couple of minutes or microwave at maximum power, or color and nutrients will be destroyed.

What are the nutrients in broccoli?

Vitamins A, B and C.

How do broccoli sprouts compare to alfalfa sprouts?

They are sharper, more peppery.

BROCCOLI RAAB (RABE, RABI)

What is broccoli raab?

It is a winter vegetable. Looks somewhat similar to broccoli. Its small sprouts and indented leaves have a pungent bitter taste. Stems are thinner than broccoli and should be moist, crisp and snap if broken.

Can the stems be used?

Discard the bottom 2–3", which are usually woody.

Does the rest of the stem need peeling?

If the bottom is discarded then it is not necessary, but cutting them into small (1″) pieces helps.

How should broccoli raab be prepared?

Parboil for 4–5 minutes and then sauté.

BRUSSELS SPROUTS

What should you look for when buying brussels sprouts?

1. Select the smallest you can find, for they will be the tenderest and sweetest.
2. They look like miniature cabbages.
3. Buy at their peak period—fall and winter.
4. Avoid those whose leaves are dull-hued, are tinged with yellow, loosely packed, wilted or are marred with insect holes or nibbles.
5. Open packaged sprouts and look at the bottom layer, because bottom layers are usually not as good as those showing on top.
6. If you can buy them on the stem they will probably be firmer, fresher and keep longer. In any case use them as soon as possible.

How much should you buy per serving?

About four ounces.

What happens to sprouts when they age?

Don't keep (uncooked) any longer than necessary, for the longer they age in the refrigerator or out, the stronger their flavor becomes.

How should brussels sprouts be prepared?

1. Remove any leaf that does not cling tightly, as they tend to be tough. Trim the stems.
2. They will cook quicker and more evenly if you cut their stem ends with a deep X pattern.

Is it necessary to cut an X in all sprouts?

While the X will allow steam to penetrate the stem better, it is not necessary with smaller sprouts.

How do you cook sprouts?

Steaming is the best method of cooking, about 10 minutes. If you add 1 teaspoon of mustard seeds to the water, the vegetable will be infused with a tangy mustard flavor.

How can you check for doneness?

To test for doneness try piercing the stem end with fork tines. If it can be penetrated without undue pressure it is done. If there is no resistance it has been overcooked.

Another test is to check the color of the outer leaves. The sprouts are done when the leaves turn a vivid green. If you overcook they will turn a drab olive brown, become mushy, lose there desired crisp tenderness and also develop a strong, unpleasant smell.

How else can they be cooked?

Whole or chopped and sautéd.

CABBAGE

What are the four main cabbages found on the market?

Green:	Also called Scotch White. Round with smooth, tight leaves. Good raw in coleslaw or cooked in soups or stuffed.
Red:	A purple-red in color, with a peppery flavor.
Savoy:	Mellow when cooked, deep veined leaves. Good stuffed or braised.
Peking (Napa Cabbage):	Mild, sweet, like broccoli in taste. More delicate in taste and texture than green.

Why does red cabbage turn bluish purple when cooked?

The main pigment in red cabbage is anthrocyanin (same coloring agent as in grapes). Acid turns it red, alkali a bluish purple. Cabbage has a high acid content, but when cooked for more than a brief period much of the acid escapes into the air with the steam. Add some tart apple or a little vinegar or lemon juice to the cooking water to preserve the red color.

What does the hardness of the water do?

The harder the water (that is, the more alkali) the more the discoloration.

How do you choose a head of cabbage?

1. If the head is exceptionally white for its variety it is over-mature and not worth buying.
2. It should be heavy for its size.
3. It should also be firm and compact for its variety.
4. Smell it, newly harvested cabbages have a fresher more inviting smell.
5. Smell the core for sweetness.
6. Avoid any with worm holes.
7. Green and red cabbage should have tight leaves with good color.

What does a cabbage with a puffy head tell you?

It has been stored too long.

What are the different cabbages best for?

Green cabbages are best for cooking, white ones are good for cole slaw or sauerkraut but also good cooked.

Do white or red cabbages have a greater food value?

The nutritive value depends more on the conditions under which the cabbage has been stored, the length of storage time or how it has been cooked, not on the color.

How do you cook cabbage?

1. Discard a few of the outer leaves.
2. Core.
3. Cabbage cooks very quickly. It requires only a few minutes shredded. If over-cooked it will give off an unwelcome odor.

How should cabbage be boiled?

Best if not boiled, for boiling will cause wilting. Best stir-fried, braised or steamed.

What can be done to keep a cabbage wedge from breaking apart?

Skewer it first with one or two toothpicks.

How can gassiness from eating cabbage be minimized?

To reduce gassiness, parboil the cabbage for 4–5 minutes, discard the water, rinse and finish cooking in fresh water.

How should cabbage be prepared for salads?

For salads a brief blanching is excellent, but this is not absolutely necessary and definitely not needed for braised dishes.

How should you prepare cabbage leaves for stuffing?

1. To remove each leaf without tearing, first remove most of the core of the whole cabbage with a sharp knife.
2. Then submerge the head in boiling water, turn off the heat and let it stand in the pot for a couple of minutes.
3. Remove and drain. The slightly softened leaves should come off with ease.

What can be done to help crisp the cabbage for slaw?

Immerse in iced water for an hour or so, then drain, blot dry and slice.

What is sauerkraut?

It is a dish made by shredding cabbage and then fermenting it, often with spices. Generally used as a condiment. Although generally thought to be a German dish, it is Chinese in origin.

Which is better, fresh or canned sauerkraut?

Fresh, because it is milder. Canned is often too salty and needs to be soaked in cold fresh water, then drained and dried before use.

CALABAZA

What is calabaza?

A squash of Caribbean origin that is shaped like a pumpkin. It is of varying size and color, ranging from red-orange to green. Generally similar to winter squash.

How can calabaza be prepared?

Baked, steamed or simmered, much like you would a butternut squash.

CARROTS

What gives carrots and other yellow-orange fruits and vegetables their color?

Carotene, a valuable nutrient, and provitamin A, which the human body converts to vitamin A.

How do you judge carrots?

1. The freshest will have their green tops on.
2. Examine the stem end. If you see a green stock, the carrots have been recently harvested, if not, they might have been warehoused for weeks or months.
3. Avoid unusually long or thick ones, those with cracks or those that have a green tinge, which comes from excessive exposure to sun rays.
4. Choose the ones with a bright, healthy glow rather than those with a dull appearance or those that are limp or bend under a light pressure.
5. Reject those with rootlets growing out of their sides. This indicates that they are too old or have been stored too long.
6. They should have a smooth surface and be bright in color.
7. Avoid flabby, shriveled ones or ones with a rough exterior.

What should be done when you take them home?

As soon as possible after you buy them remove the carrot tops, because they draw out the internal juices.

How does size affect use?

The smaller ones are best for eating raw, the larger are good for cooking and slicing.

Should carrot and celery sticks be soaked in ice water?

Yes. If they are less than fresh they may have lost some of their crispness. Soaking in ice water returns some of this crispness, because the food cells regain some of their lost water through osmosis. The individual cells swell, press against one another, making the entire structure more rigid and therefore crisper. The lower temperature helps.

Should fresh carrots be soaked?

If they are fresh, then soaking will have no benefit. They will lose a little of their freshness because of water buildup between the walls of already plump cells.

Why should carrots not be soaked for long periods or scrubbed?

They will lose natural sugar, all the B, C and D vitamins and all minerals except calcium.

What happens when carrots are sliced before cooking?

Whole: The carrots retain about 90% of their vitamin C and most of their minerals.

Sliced: They lose almost all the vitamin C and niacin content.

What are storage or preparation hints for carrots?

1. They can be stored up to a week in a sealed plastic bag in the vegetable crisper.
2. Never store them with apples, because apples produce ethylene gas, which makes them bitter. Keep them away from other fruits and vegetables due to possible ethylene gas problems.
3. Keep refrigerated.
4. Don't store in water as this will drain off vitamin A.
5. Cut off the tops before storing or they will become limp and dry.

How should carrots be prepared for a stew?

Sauté them in butter or olive oil before adding to a stew. The temperature caramelizes the carrot sugar, giving them a new flavor dimension.

Do carrots have to be peeled?

1. Depends largely on their age and use. Peel fully mature ones, as what you lose in nutrients you gain in flavor. Baby and young carrots don't need to be peeled.
2. Another reason to peel is for appearance, so if, for instance, they are to be pureed or stewed in a dark sauce they need not be peeled.

What can be used to glaze carrots?

Honey works well.

CAULIFLOWER

What are the types of cauliflower?

White is the main one, but there are also green and purple varieties, which are also very good. The green variety is less dense.

What should you look for in buying cauliflower?

1. The curds of white cauliflower, the most common variety, should be evenly hued, void of discoloration and be quite white.
2. The leaves should be vivid green, not browned or withered.

What should be avoided?

1. Avoid frozen cauliflower, for freezing hurts both nutrients and flavor.
2. Avoid those with a speckled surface, which is a sign of insect injury, mold or rot.
3. Smell the head carefully; there should not be any bad odors.
4. Don't buy those already cut into florets. They are apt to be old.

Is the size of the cauliflower head important to quality?

The size of the head is not important to quality, so the best buy can be the largest head.

How should cauliflower be stored?

It is perishable, so store it in a sealed, perforated plastic bag in the refrigerator crisper and use within a day or two, keeping it as cold as possible.

How should it be prepared?

1. Prior to cooking, soak the head down for 30 minutes in salted, acidulated water to remove grit and insects.
2. The stems do best when peeled. The stems can be cooked sliced, chopped, raw in salads or as crudités.

How should cauliflower be prepared?

1. Marinated overnight in a vinaigrette sauce, it is excellent served cold.
2. Best methods of cooking are steaming or stir-frying or eating raw as crudités.
3. If you steam or cook it whole, hollow out the stem first.
4. When cooking keep it bright and white by adding 1 teaspoon of lemon juice or ½ teaspoon vinegar to the cooking water, but if the cooking water is particularly hard even this may not help.
5. Taste for doneness by piercing with a knife point.

What happens if you overcook cauliflower?

It will become mushy, the odor will be offensive and the food value diminished.

What can be done with overcooked cauliflower?

Puree it, blend in butter and season with salt and pepper.

How can cauliflower be made more attractive in appearance?

When serving, jazz up the appearance with a sprinkle of chopped parsley or with hollandaise sauce.

What does salt do to cauliflower?

Salt toughens cauliflower as it cooks, therefore don't salt until after cooking.

Is cauliflower good raw?

It is good raw as crudités, especially with a dip.

What is the effect of cooking on its nutritive value?

Lightly cooking will break down the high fiber content, and this will free the nutrients that are stored in the raw product and make them more available. Overcooking diminishes nutritive value.

CELERIAC (CELERY ROOT, CELERY KNOB)

What is celeriac?

It is a branch celery that is cultivated for its root.

How should celeriac be selected?

1. Choose relatively small, firm ones with the least number of knobs and rootlets.
2. Avoid those with soft spots.

How should celeriac be used raw?

1. Peeled, raw and cut fine in julienne strips, grated or shredded. It is excellent in salads with a sharp dressing.
2. When served raw, it should be marinated with the dressing for several hours to tenderize and mellow.
3. It goes best with other strong flavors such as beets, carrots, smoked meats, anchovies, onions.
4. Soaking in acidic water (use lemon juice) prevents discoloration.

How can celeriac be used cooked?

1. When peeled and sliced it cooks in about 15 minutes.
2. It is an excellent addition to mashed potatoes when pureed.
3. It goes well with meats when braised.
4. Don't overcook it, as it goes from firm to mushy.
5. It should be peeled for all cooking procedures.
6. Mashed like mashed potatoes.
7. As a stuffing for poultry.

What are its nutrients?

Small amounts of vitamin B, some calcium and iron.

CELERY

How do you select celery?

1. It should be stiff and crisp.
2. Color is not a governing factor.

What are the best ways of using celery, and how should you handle it?

Use the tougher outer stalks for cooking, the tender inner ones for eating raw and the leaves for flavoring stock and stews or in a tomato aspic.

What preparation steps are recommended for celery?

1. Since farm dirt readily lodges between the stalks always scrub the separated stalks well with a vegetable brush.
2. To refresh a slightly limp stalk stand it stem side down in a jar of ice water for an hour or two with a slice or two of raw potato.
3. The celery leaves are excellent garnishes in salads and soups.

Should celery be peeled (strings removed)?

Peeling will make the larger branches less stringy and more attractive to eat raw.

How can celery be peeled?

Make a cut halfway through the stalk, bend, pull apart and pull the strings down the length, or trim with a vegetable peeler.

How should celery be stored?

1. Soak in cold water with some lemon juice before refrigerating to prevent it from turning brown.
2. For no more than a week. If stored in the vegetable bin of the refrigerator for more than a week, it will begin to lose flavor and become flabby.

How long must celery be cooked to soften the fibrous strings?

They don't really soften, so when present it is best to peel them before cooking.

CHARD (SWISS CHARD)

Is chard really a beet?

Yes, it is a type of beet, but it is grown for its leaves and can be substituted for spinach if the chard is young.

How should chard be selected?

1. Choose crisp bundles with white, unblemished stems and large, dark green leaves.
2. The stems are considered by many to be its best-tasting part.

How should chard be prepared?

Wash well before cooking.

How is chard cooked?

The green leaves are used in the cuisines of Italy, Southern France, Turkey and Lebanon and are considered sweet, mild and tender. They are slightly cooked and then, chopped or left whole and served with a dressing added.

Are the chard stalks edible?

If blanched, then baked golden brown with a topping of a little butter and grated cheese, they are both edible and attractive.

CHIVES

How should chives, that special member of the onion family, be chosen?

Look for uniform green color without discoloration, browning or wilting.

How should chives be stored?

1. Wrapped in a paper towel in a plastic bag and refrigerate.
2. The best way to freeze, after washing and drying, is to cut them up and put them in an air-tight plastic bag.

How should chives be prepared?

1. Because the bulb is so little, the green stalks are all that are used.
2. The long, slim stems are excellent for decorating.
3. Chives lose their flavor quickly. Once dried, they have little flavor left and are usually not worth buying.
4. They are susceptible to heat, so add after the cooking is finished or at the very end of the cooking process.
5. They are easily cut with scissors.

How are chives used?

1. They give a special flavor when mixed with cream cheese or bland dips.
2. They add flavor to mashed potatoes.

What are garlic chives?

Also known as Chinese chives. A perennial herb with long, fat leaves and garlic taste. Can be sprinkled onto soups or salads or stir-fried or used as an alternative to plain chives or scallions.

What can be used if fresh chives are not available?

1. Dried chives (not recommended).

2. Scallions (green onions) chopped very fine.

3. Freeze dried chives.

What happens if chives are added to a dish early in the cooking?

The chives will develop a slightly sour and harsh taste.

CORN

What is the grain with the lowest nutritional value?

Corn.

Is there a nutritional difference between white and yellow corn?

Yellow corn has more vitamin A than white corn.

How should you inspect corn for purchase?

1. Buy for immediate consumption, as the flavor declines within days after harvest. The sugar converts to starch, and the corn flavor and sweetness diminish. If you grow your own, have the pot boiling before going out to pick it, to retain flavor. However, new strains of corn coming onto the market hold their sweetness longer.

2. Look for vivid green husks that snugly encase the kernels. They should not be yellowed, wilted, moist or dry.

3. The exposed threads should remind you of silk. If they have started to brown or dry, the ear has been around too long.

4. The stem end, cut surface, should be relatively soft and moist. A woody texture indicates long or improper storage.

5. It should smell garden fresh.

6. Peel back part of the husk. The rows should be parallel, not crooked or crowded. The area near the tip should not have missing or stunted kernels. Each kernel should be plump and springy when pressed with your finger. If you cut into one, the liquid that comes out should be milky, not watery.

Which corn on the market should be avoided?

If possible, don't buy prehusked corn, for they lose quality quickly.

Is corn edible without cooking?

Very fresh, recently picked ears can be enjoyed raw.

How can the silky strands of the ear be removed?

Two ways to remove the silk are to rub the ear with a slightly moistened paper towel or to rub it with your hand under running water.

How should corn on the cob be cooked?

1. Don't overcook, as that will toughen the corn.
2. The fresher the corn, the quicker it will cook. In a generous amount of water, fresh corn will take about 3 minutes, an older ear will take 10 minutes.
3. Cover the cooking pot to trap the steam, which will cook any of the corn protruding out of the water.

What should be added to the cooking water?

1. The kernels will toughen if you add salt to the water. Table salt is not pure sodium chloride but contains traces of other substances such as calcium, which toughens the skins of the kernels. This is also true for peas and lima beans. This is not as important as it was in decades gone by, because today's commercial salt is purer than it was, but let your guests salt their own ears, if desired.
2. Add a little milk and sugar to the cooking water for better taste.

Can corn be microwaved?

To microwave corn, remove the silk, wash the cobs but don't dry them and loosely wrap in waxed paper. The amount of time will vary with the power of the oven and the number of ears being cooked together.

Can corn be cooked without removing the husks?

This results in steaming instead of boiling, which is good. It will also retain the heat until serving but is somewhat messy at the table. Cook in the microwave with the husks on and when finished dehusk and take the corn silk off with a paper towel.

What does steaming the ears with the husks still on achieve?

The corn will be sweeter.

How much corn should you plan per serving?

This will vary, of course, with what else is being served, how hungry your guests are and how big the ears are, but one to two ears per person is usually adequate. The cobs can also be broken in two and then the serving can be one and a half, or the serving can be one with half-ears available on a platter for those who want more.

How does removing the kernels alter the amount needed?

You will need approximately twice as much.

Which is higher quality, white or yellow corn?

The white generally is more tender and flavored more subtly; yellow more robust and fuller flavored. The white usually comes on the market in the first part of the season. Both are wonderful foods, so enjoy them both. New strains are coming into the market, so that it is difficult to generalize. In recent years white corn has been available during the whole season.

How else can kernels be used?
Corn off the cob fits well into many dishes, such as pasta, salads, souffles, casseroles and puddings.

How can kernels be removed from corncobs?
Slice down one side of an ear with a sharp knife, slicing as close to the ear as possible. Then rotate the ear and repeat until all rows are done.

How should corn on the cob be handled to get the "milk" or juice?
1. Score the kernels with a knife.
2. Slice the kernels off the cob.
3. Scrape the cob.

What are other ways of taking the kernels off?
1. One of the best instruments for taking the kernels off is a metal shoe horn.
2. The corn can be grated off for souffles, fritters, puddings and other delicate dishes. Use a large-holed vegetable grater. Then with the back of a knife scrape off remaining pulp but do not scrape too hard or the hulls will also be pulled off. This gives a smoothly textured, hull-free puree.

What is succotash?
Cooked corn kernels and lima beans.

What can be salvaged after taking the kernels off?
1. Any corn pulp remaining can be scraped off and used for other dishes such as salsa.
2. The cob can be added to stock to give a corn flavor.

How can corn on the cob be grilled with the husk intact?
1. Pull back the husk but don't remove it completely.
2. Remove the silk.
3. Replace the husks and tie the ends with twine.
4. Soak the ears in cold water for 30 minutes to prevent the husks from burning.
5. Remove from the water and drain.
6. Grill over glowing coals, turning 3 times, for about 15 minutes.

What is a way of adding additional flavor?
Put herb butter on the cobs before tying the husks.

How can corn be stored?

If it is necessary to keep a couple of days, cut off a small piece from the stalk end, leave the hull on, store vertically in a pot, stem down with an inch of water.

CUCUMBERS

What is the difference between regular cucumbers and the English variety (hothouse cucumbers)?

The common variety has many seeds, while the English are dark green are seedless or the seeds are very small.

What should be looked for in selecting cucumbers?

1. They should be long and slender, with a good green color, firm and smooth.
2. Take only firm ones that are well shaped.
3. Large, yellow ones tend to be pithy, so choose younger, smoother ones, which are not as bitter, have a thinner skin and fewer and smaller seeds. The seeds of older cukes are often bitter.
4. Old cukes look shriveled and spongy.

How should cucumbers be stored?

1. Refrigerate upon purchase.
2. Keep away from fruits while in storage, as many fruits' surfaces contain ethylene gas to enhance their ripening and looks, but this causes the cukes to harden.

What is the easiest way to seed cucumbers?

Cut the cuke in half lengthwise and scrape out the center seeds with a small spoon or the handle of a vegetable peeler.

How can you tell if a cucumber has been waxed?

Lightly scrape the skin with your fingernail or knife. If a string come off, it is wax. If it has been waxed, peel the cuke or scrub it.

How should you prepare cucumbers for a salad?

1. Peel the entire cuke or scrub well with a brush under hot, soapy water, as most cukes are waxed for market.
2. Slice in half lengthwise.
3. Scoop out the seeds and surrounding gelatinous material from each half.
4. Place the seeded cuke, open side down and slice into thin half-moon shaped rings.
5. They may be sliced whole after peeling or scalloped and then put into a salad.

How can cucumbers be prepared for salad and maintain their crunchiness?

1. Salt the slices as for seasoning.
2. Place in a colander under a sealed plastic bag filled with water.
3. Let the weight press out liquid for an hour or so.

What are ways to cook cucumbers?

1. Sautéing or roasting but not boiling or slow stewing.
2. Seeded and stuffed with sauteed diced mushrooms and wrapped in bacon and then baked.

DAIKON (WINTER RADISH, ASIAN RADISH)

What is daikon?

A large radish from Asia that is similar to jicama. It has a slightly sharp or bitter taste that is a good contrast to rich foods.

How should daikon be chosen?

1. Although these members of the radish family grow large, choose the smaller specimens available.
2. The root should feel firm, solid and heavy for its size.
3. The skin should be without cracks and free of blemishes, somewhat shiny and opalescent.
4. Avoid the very large ones, which tend to be fibrous.

How should daikon be prepared?

1. Peel and slice or cut into strips for crudités.
2. Shred it as a garnish with a Japanese dish, with fried food or raw in a salad.
3. Shredded or julienned, it is good in salads or salsas and in stir-fries.
4. The leaves are peppery and can be stir-fried with other greens.

DANDELION GREENS

How should dandelion greens be selected?

Best when very young, because they become more bitter with age.

Why are dandelion greens added to salads?

They give a bite and a slight bitter undertone. Usually used uncooked, and they give a special flavor to a salad mix.

Vegetables

EGGPLANTS

Have eggplants always been popular?

No, they were once known as "mad apples," because it was thought that they caused insanity or death. They have been used in China since 600 BC.

What are the two main kinds of eggplants?

The large, rounded European (also called Western) ones, with a shiny black skin, which are the most common in our markets, and the elongated, white to purple Asian.

What is the Italian variety?

Also known as "baby eggplant," it is a small version of the European, but with a thinner skin and not-so-tough flesh.

What are other types of eggplants?

In addition there are small, often rounded ones that vary with the variety from a pale green to a bright orange. The Western has a somewhat bitter taste and is best when pickled or used in curries. The Thai eggplant is bell shaped, small, green striped, bitter but good pickled. The white eggplant is oval, sweet, firm.

What do the number of seeds indicate?

The fewer seeds, the sweeter the eggplant, the more, the older the eggplant.

How should you select eggplant?

1. The larger the eggplant for its variety, the more bitter it will taste and the tougher its peel will be. Its ratio of seeds to edible flesh will be higher. So buy the *smallest* in the bin, unless you need large slices for a recipe.
2. They should be firm, not shriveled, free from abrasion and soft spots and heavy for their size. The skin should be shiny, not dull. The flesh should be springy, giving slightly to finger pressure.
3. Soft ones are usually bitter.

How can you tell the difference between a male and a female eggplant and why bother?

Male: These are rounder, smoother at the blossom end. They have fewer seeds, but they are often bitter.

Female: They are more oval, and the blossom end is usually deeply indented. They tend to have more bitter seeds.

How should eggplants be stored?

Keep in a cool place in a plastic bag, but not too cool; they begin to deteriorate below 50 °F.

How long can they be kept?

Do not store any longer than necessary, because they are highly perishable.

How should you prepare eggplant?

Mature eggplants should be peeled, but baby ones are best left unpeeled unless they have been waxed.

Why cook immediately after peeling or cutting?

The exposed flesh discolors rapidly because of oxidation. To prevent this, start cooking as soon as you have cut it. If there is an unavoidable delay, promptly coat the surfaces with lemon juice or submerge the pieces in acidulated water.

How should eggplant be purged?

Either by salting or with high heat.

How are the white eggplants different?

The thick skin of the white eggplant is usually discarded, but opinion is divided; some like it, most do not.

Why do eggplants absorb so much oil?

Because they have inner air pockets, they can absorb several times their weight in oil, even when breaded. This increases fat and breaks down texture.

How should eggplants be oiled?

Brush the oil on lightly.

How should eggplant be cooked?

Bake or microwave. Frying requires special skill to achieve good results.

What is the effect of salting?

Chefs argue about this. It probably helps when frying, for this will prevent the absorption of too much fat and reduces bitterness and moisture content.

1. Salt draws water out of the cells by creating such a high concentration of dissolved ions outside the cell walls that the water inside is drawn out.
2. Salting alone is not enough. The flesh must be firmly pressed between sheets of paper towels to extrude the juice and compact the flesh.
3. To do a good job the salting should be done for at least 1½ hours, better for 2 hours or even 3 before frying.
4. But be sure to rinse off the salt and blot dry with toweling before cooking.

Why does cooked eggplant sometimes taste bitter?

Like many other vegetables, bitterness comes with age. It is sweetest just after it is picked, before the sugars convert to starch.

Vegetables

Will salting eliminate bitterness?

Salting will not eliminate bitterness if the eggplant is bitter to start with.

Which eggplants are better for stir-frying?

The long, thin Chinese variety, sliced, because they cook quickly.

How should they be cooked?

1. It is excellent sliced, baked or broiled, usually lightly coated with oil, melted butter, soy sauce or a mixture of them.
2. With a dish requiring extended cooking, add the eggplant in the last 5–10 minutes.

How should eggplants not be cooked?

1. Don't overcook such as in a stew, because they will become waterlogged.
2. They also absorb oil and butter like mad, so cook them in only the minimum of fat or oil or without any.

What is eggplant caviar?

Steamed and pureed eggplant seasoned with garlic, lemon and olive oil.

ENDIVE (BELGIAN ENDIVE, FRENCH ENDIVE)

What is endive?

This is the sprouted shoots of chicory roots, which are not put in soil, but rather sprout in three or four weeks in cold storage in a dark environment to prevent greening.

How should it be selected?

1. Look for heads with long, thin yellow-white leaves and few green leaves.
2. The leaves should be tight, about 5–6 inches long and have no brown edges.

What is the difference between yellow and red leaved endive?

No essential difference, but browned ones are to be avoided.

What does a greenish cast of the leaves indicate?

The greener the cast, the more bitter the leaves.

What is the concern when purchasing endive?

Because they are expensive, they may have been on the produce shelf for many days before you purchase them.

How long will endive keep?

It will keep in the refrigerator wrapped in tissue or plastic wrap for 4–7 days or longer. It needs to be refrigerated.

Does endive need to be soaked or rinsed?

Since the leaves are clean they need only a slight rinse in cold water after removing the core with a paring knife. Dry before using.

How should endive not be handled?

1. Exposure to light will cause the leaves to turn green.
2. Prolonged soaking will increase bitterness.

How should endive be used?

1. They are excellent in salads by themselves.
2. They marry well in salads with oranges or grapefruit or mango.
3. Vinaigrette made with fruit vinegar, e.g., raspberry-flavored, is excellent with endive.
4. They can be cooked, braised, sautéd or baked.

How can they be cooked whole?

Tie with a string, brown in butter and then simmer briefly in a little chicken stock.

FENNEL

Are fennel and sweet anise the same?

Although the two names are commonly used interchangeably in markets, sweet anise is an incorrect synonym for fennel, which is sweeter and more delicate than sweet anise. Fennel gives a slight, subtle licorice flavor.

How should fennel be selected?

Choose fennel bulbs that are firm, plump, white to pale green, with a stalk attached. They should be heavy for their size and free from blemishes.

What can you do with fennel without cooking?

1. I like this refreshing tuber best in salads or as crudités.
2. The fine, thread-like greens can be used to flavor salads, or they are lovely as a plate decoration or garnish.
3. It can be used as an appetizer with thinly sliced smoked salmon or prosciutto seasoned with pepper or fennel seeds.

How can fennel be used cooked?

1. It can be braised, added to stews or mixed with other vegetables, such as tomatoes or eggplant.
2. Roasted or baked with sautéd sausage.

How can the flavor be enhanced when cooking?

Add some fennel seeds.

What must be done to prepare fennel?

The core is usually tough, but it can easily be removed with a short bladed, sharp paring knife.

How can fennel be made into a salad?

1. Remove the core and most of the threads, slice thinly and dress with a vinaigrette.
2. Orange slices, freshly grated ginger root or pieces of mango will add color and zest.

If the fennel is not young and fresh, how can the flavor be intensified?

Add a teaspoon or two of Pernod.

GARLIC

What is garlic?

A member of the lily family and closely related to onions. While there are some three hundred varieties known, only three are commercially grown in California, where most American garlic comes from. The bulb is subdivided into about nine cloves. It is originally from Iran.

What are pointers for buying garlic?

1. Heads of garlic cloves sold loose in a bin are usually much fresher than those in small paper boxes.
2. In no case should you choose boxes with the garlic cloves separated, as they will often be over the hill.
3. Squeeze the head. It should feel firm, not shriveled. Soft spots indicate internal decay.
4. Lift the garlic. It should be heavy for its size. Lightness indicates dehydration and/or internal decay.
5. Rub it gently. It is probably past its prime if the papery outer layers crinkle and fall off readily.

What is the difference between white-skinned garlic and the purple-red ones?

The white is the stronger in flavor.

Why should garlic powder or garlic salt be avoided?

If possible use fresh because of the diminished garlic quality or a bitterness in the powder or salt.

What is the minced yield of a clove of garlic?

For an average sized clove, about a ½ teaspoon.

What is the advantage of large cloves?

They require less peeling time than small ones on an ounce-per-ounce basis.

Vegetables

Which garlic is strongest in flavor?

The strongest flavored are the small, white-skinned variety. Next are the violet-skinned ones. The oversized elephant variety is the mildest.

How can garlic be handled so that it is sweet and creamy?

1. Slice about ½" from the head so that the tips are exposed.
2. Poach in milk and then give a quick rinse before roasting.

How is garlic best stored?

1. In a cool, dark, well-ventilated space.
2. If refrigerated, place in a tightly sealed plastic bag to prevent premature decay and giving off and/or absorbing odors.
3. It can be kept peeled in the refrigerator, if completely covered with olive oil.
4. It can be kept unpeeled in a hanging wire container for months, although it will lose some of its weight as it dries.
5. To save preparation time, peel garlic as soon as you bring it home. Place the whole, peeled cloves in a jar, cover with oil and refrigerate. Use as needed. Should keep fresh at least a couple of weeks, as long as they have not been sliced, chopped or minced.

How can minced garlic be kept from spoiling and yet be easily available?

Form it into a log shape, wrap tightly in plastic and freeze. Then slice off as needed.

Can grated garlic be frozen?

Not well, for it tends to become mushy in texture and not as good in flavor.

Why shouldn't garlic be stored in the refrigerator?

Refrigeration promotes rot.

Is there a difference between garlic that is squashed and that which is just sliced?

If squashed (as with the flat of a knife or by a hammer) the juice is released to give a very pronounced garlic flavor. However, the oils in the juice turn rancid rather quickly, especially if heated. It will then turn bitter and lose its better cooking effect. The longer the cooking time, the large the pieces of garlic should be (such as sliced broadly).

What happens when herbs and garlic are chopped together?

The garlic clings to the herbs rather than to the knife.

Should cloves be peeled first when using a garlic press?

They can be, but the crusher will be easier to clean with the skin left on the cloves.

How should garlic products in oil be kept?

1. Make or buy in small batches, for they do not keep safely very long.
2. Always store in the refrigerator.

What are good ways to peel garlic?

1. Blanch in boiling water for about 10 seconds.
2. Crush the clove with the flat of a knife or a small hammer and then strip off the skin.

Is the green stalk sometimes found in the middle of a clove harmful?

It can be bitter, but if the garlic is sautéd or roasted, it need not be removed.

How should cloves be chopped?

The garlic will stick less to the chopping knife blade if you sprinkle salt on the garlic, but be sure to reduce the quantity of salt called for in the recipe. This also means that the sprinkled salt will absorb the garlic flavor that normally would be lost on the chopping board.

What are five ways to roast garlic and still retain flavor but avoid mushiness?

Poach:	Loosen the papery outside by rolling back and forth on a cutting surface. Rub away the loose skin. Cut about ½" from the tip so that most of the interior is exposed. Place the heads cut-side-down in a medium saucepan. Add milk (1 cup per 4 heads) and poach over low heat. Drain and rinse under cold running water.
Bake:	Place 1 head in the center of an 8" aluminum foil square. Drizzle ½ teaspoon oil or melted butter over it. Then gather up the edges and twist shut. Roast the heads in a small baking dish at 350 °F for about 1–2 hours, or until tender. Let cool, remove from foil and squeeze out the softened garlic.
Microwave:	Place oiled heads on a microwave-safe dish and microwave on high power for 1–2 minutes, or until soft.
Roast:	Preheat the oven to 400 °F. Slice the unpeeled head in half horizontally. Place on a sheet of foil, cut-side-up. Drizzle olive oil over it and then wrap each half in foil, cutting vents in the foil to let the steam escape. Bake 45 minutes, or until tender.
Garlic roaster:	Use a garlic roaster and follow its instructions.

How can roasted garlic be used?

Spread on crackers as a canapé or add to a salsa.

How can you minimize the garlic odor on the cutting board?

If the recipe calls for both garlic and parsley, chop the garlic first. Then chop the parsley. The chlorophyll in the parsley will neutralize much of the garlic scent. If that doesn't do the job, rub the board with lemon juice.

How can garlic flavor be kept from being excessive?

Put garlic flakes into a tea ball and immerse in the cooking soup or stew. Taste periodically while cooking until the desired flavor level is reached.

How long can you sauté garlic?

Garlic scorches and becomes bitter if you add it to the sauté pan at the same time you add onions. It cannot be sautéd for more than a minute or so. Thirty seconds is probably the limit if the oil is very hot. The cloves should be chopped. The oil should be hot but not too hot.

What causes garlic in a tomato sauce to taste bitter?

When strong garlic flavor is desired cook the garlic in oil until it just turns golden. If it gets too brown it indicates that it has become bitey and bitter.

Should the green shoots of garlic be used?

No, as they are usually quite bitter. Trim and discard them.

JERUSALEM ARTICHOKES (SUNCHOKES)

What are Jerusalem artichokes?

This member of the squash family is called *topinambour* in French. A better name is "sunchokes," for they are not artichokes but the tuber of a type of sunflower.

When are they best?

In fall and through the winter.

What is the nutritional advantage of Jerusalem artichokes?

High in iron content.

What is the nutritional disadvantage of Jerusalem artichokes?

They have indigestible carbohydrates like beans that can cause flatulence.

How should they be chosen?

Choose ones that are sprout-free, smoothly skinned and firm to the touch.

Why shouldn't Jerusalem artichokes be cooked in an aluminum pot?

To avoid blackening.

What happens if Jerusalem artichokes are overcooked?

Overcooking will toughen them.

How should they be prepared for cooking?

Scrub them well to get rid of deeply lodged dirt.

How should Jerusalem artichokes be used?

1. The skin is edible and nutritious.
2. Eat them raw in salads or as crudités. They are good marinated.
3. Roasted or boiled, mashed or pureed in soups.

4. Treat them as pureed sweet potatoes.
5. They can be mashed into balls and fried.
6. Deep fried when sliced paper thin.

How can they be used like potatoes?

Slice, boil 15 minutes, drain, then bake for 15 minutes, turning once so that they are browned on both sides.

JICAMA (MEXICAN POTATO)

What is jicama?

This root vegetable is indigenous to Mexico and resembles a large, brown turnip.

How should jicama be selected?

1. The dull, dark beige skin should be thin and able to be pulled off with a sharp knife. The darker, rougher skinned ones tend to be tougher and drier.
2. The jicama should have a cream-colored flesh that is crisp.

How should jicama be stored?

It can be stored in a cool, dry place for several weeks.

How can it be used?

1. Both cooked and raw.
2. Peeled and sliced as crudités.
3. Julienned or grated into salads.
4. In a stir-fry.
5. Thinly sliced in sandwiches.

Should jicama be peeled?

Yes, both the brown outer skin and the white fiber just underneath should be peeled off.

How can a jicama slaw or salad be made without excess moisture?

After shredding, place it in a clean towel and twist until dry.

How can it be used cooked?

Cook only for 1–3 minutes, depending upon the thinness of the cut.

KALE

What is kale?

It is a member of the cabbage family.

What is the color of kale?

It ranges from pale green to deep green, from white to purplish, depending on the variety.

How should it be chosen?

Choose crisp, rich-colored leaves, avoiding any limp leaves or any that are yellowing.

What cautions should be taken when using kale?

1. Discard the ropey ends.
2. Remove the stringy stalks.
3. Steam the leaves or shred and put them in soup.

What is the nutritional advantage of kale over spinach?

The human body absorbs only about 2% of the iron in spinach. Kale does not interfere with the body's absorption, so while kale has less iron, more is absorbed. It also has about two and a half times more vitamin C than spinach.

KOHLRABI (TURNIP CABBAGE, CABBAGE TURNIP)

How is kohlrabi selected?

1. Buy the smallest (about 3" in diameter), with vivid green young stalks bearing apple-green or purple leaves protruding from the bulb.
2. Choose ones with thin skins that are free of cuts or soft spots.

What is its flavor?

A blend between turnip and cabbage.

How should kohlrabi be used?

1. Eat raw or steamed.
2. It works well with dill.
3. Large bulbs should be peeled before eating.

Are the leaves edible?

They can be steamed or sautéd.

Can kohlrabi be eaten raw?

Young (small) ones that are sliced paper-thin work well in salads.

LEEKS

What should you look for in buying leeks?

1. Leeks range from two feet tall to babies that look like green onions.
2. Immature leeks are the most tender and delicate tasting. When older they have a fibrous texture and assertive flavors. Signs of overage include a thick stem and a relatively large bulb (a protruding ring) just above the rootlets.

3. The leaves should not be flabby, yellow-tinged, withered, or have lost their bright green hue or have bulbous root ends.
4. The white stem should be long for the size of the leek and should not be marred or discolored.
5. Choose ones that are less than 1½″ in diameter, are firm, have a straight base, are crisp, and have dark green leaves.
6. Buy uniformly sized ones for evenness in cooking.

What time of year are they at their best?

The best time for leeks is early in spring, before they become woody.

How should leeks be stored?

Refrigerate and they will last about a week.

Can leeks be eaten raw?

Yes. The tiny shoots are very good in salads when raw. In fact, leeks are easier to digest than onions.

How should leeks be prepared for cooking?

1. Trim off the rootlets, leaving just enough to hold the layers together.
2. Cut off the leaves just above where the light green turns dark green.

How should they be cleaned?

1. Soak in cold water to loosen any dirt and then rinse in lukewarm water, pulling the layers apart or clean well under running water.
2. When large, slit in half lengthwise and soak in cold water for 10–30 minutes. Then give a quick rinse in running cold water and drain.

How should leeks be cooked?

1. Boil, drain and chill for use in a salad.
2. Brown in the broiler with a cheese or cheese sauce cover.
3. Steam, stir-fry or grill.
4. Slice and sauté.

What is another way to use leek?

Combine with potatoes in a soup.

LETTUCES

What should be looked for in selecting lettuce?

1. It should be crisp and free of blemishes.
2. It should smell clean and fresh.

3. Avoid those with wilted leaves or bug holes.
4. The greener the leaves, the higher the vitamin and mineral content.

How does iceberg lettuce rate in quality?
1. It is the variety that is most used.
2. Its leaves don't hold dressing well.
3. It is the lowest in nutritive value and is low in vitamins A and C.
4. While the least expensive, I believe it has the least flavor.

Why should washed lettuce be dried?
So that the dressing will cling to the leaves and won't become diluted.

What are some of the greens besides iceberg lettuce used in salads?

Amaranth: (Also known as Chinese spinach) many subvarieties, slightly notched green leaves.

Anise: Dark green with a licorice flavor.

Arugula: Sweet, small, notched leaves. Also known as rocket. It resembles radish tops. It has a delicately peppery, mustard-like flavor and when used raw in salads, gives a spicy, roasted flavor. Large leaves may be cooked. Best when young. Mixed with other greens, they should be a small part of the salad, with the aim of adding zest.

Chervil: (Also called French parsley) sweet aromatic herb with a very faint anise-like character. Fernlike foliage.

Chicory: (Also called curly leaf Endive or frisée) many different varieties with large, curly edged leaves. Slightly bitter, but a 5-second blanching will soften the bitterness.

Escarole: Similar to chicory but with broad, flat leaves. Best blanched 5 seconds in boiling water to tenderize. Slight bitterness.

Radicchio: A member of the chicory family with an attractive, slightly bitter taste. Its red color brightens salads. Good by itself in salads or sautéd lightly and added to pasta.

Romaine: (Also known as cos) firm, long leaves. Large long heads, white at the bottom of leaves and tend to be green at the tip and also green in the outer leaves. Crisp texture, good flavor.

Spinach: Choose the flat leaf, instead of the curly leaved, because it has thinner leaves and thus is more tender. Baby spinach is even better. Buy in bunches, not in bags.

What is mesclun?
A mix of salad greens typically including chervil, dandelions, chicory etc.

How should greens be prepared for salad?

1. Wash well by submerging in cold water to eliminate sandy grit.
2. Handle gently or small cracks will occur.
3. Dry well.

What does orange or lemon zest accomplish in a salad dressing?

Yields a fresh citrus flavor without discoloring vegetables as would an acidic dressing.

How should dressing be tasted?

Rather than using a spoon, dip a piece of lettuce in the dressing, then taste the combination.

Why should a vinaigrette not be added to a salad until just before serving?

Because the lettuce will wilt.

How much dressing should be added to a salad?

Less than you think you want, because more can be added but excess is difficult to remove.

What is an easy way to dress a salad without using a bowl?

Put washed and dried greens in a large plastic bag, pour dressing on top of the greens, close the top of the bag, shake and then discard the emptied bag.

How should salad greens be stored?

If possible don't store them. If you must, however:

1. Refrigerate unwashed in a plastic bag after removing bruised, wilted, or browned leaves.
2. If it is necessary to wash them ahead of time, then spin dry (not too hard) or dry with toweling or layer between paper toweling, put in a well-sealed plastic bag and refrigerate in the crisper drawer.
3. Don't add the dressing in advance.

Should lettuce leaves be torn or cut?

There is disagreement whether lettuce leaves should be torn or cut. Both sides win. If you use a knife, make sure it is stainless steel.

Can browned lettuce leaves be used?

Not very well in salads, but if not slimy they will be satisfactory when sautéd.

How should salad greens be transported for a picnic?

Wrap in a moist towel and add the dressing at the picnic when ready to serve.

LIMA BEANS (BUTTER BEANS)

How should lima beans be selected and handled?

1. Pods should be dark green and bright in color, not dried out or spotted.
2. Choose the plump and tender ones.
3. When shelled they should appear green or greenish white.

How should lima beans be handled after being shelled?

1. They are very perishable and should be used as soon as possible.
2. A small amount of baking soda may be added to the cooking water to help retain color. This is a debated exception to the general rule of not using baking soda for this purpose.

MUSHROOMS

What are mushrooms?

A primitive plant, a fungus, that lacks chlorophyll (the green pigment that captures energy from sunlight and stores it as sugar molecules). Some live on dead leaves or other organic material, some have a parasitic or symbiotic relationship with plants and/or trees. They have a natural flavor enhancer (glutamic acid) that strengthens the flavor of other ingredients with which they are cooked.

How do mushrooms rate on the nutritional scale?

Low in calories and cholesterol-free.

How should mushrooms be washed?

Traditionally they are not washed because they absorb water, but since they are about 90% water, washing doesn't increase their water content appreciably. If they are washed in cold water this should be done just before using.

How can flavor, appearance and nutrients be best maintained?

1. Don't peel.
2. Sprinkle with lemon juice.
3. Keep wrapped when marinating.

How should dried mushrooms be soaked?

Add hot water for about half an hour and then squeeze out the moisture.

Can they be soaked longer in advance?

Yes, most do well with a day or two of soaking.

What is the ratio of dried to fresh mushrooms?

After soaking, one ounce of dried mushrooms is the equivalent of about one pound of fresh. The amount varies slightly with the particular mushroom.

Which is the most expensive and most highly esteemed mushroom?

Porcini, which sells for as much as $30 a pound or even more.

What is the background of porcini?

In the old days, because of their strong nutty taste, porcini canceled the taste of poison, so some Romans who wanted to get rid of an enemy served them. They were also believed to remove blemishes and freckles. Bohemian lumberjacks believed that they prevented cancer.

Where do porcini come from?

Most come from France and Italy. Lesser amounts from Spain, Poland, Chile and northwestern United States.

What is the problem with U.S. porcini?

They often are worm-infested and frequently have hollow stems.

Are they available dried?

In dried form they are marketed as porcini, cep, or cepes, the French name.

How should dried porcini be selected?

1. Choose large pieces rather than small ones.
2. Look for uniform color, not too dark.
3. Avoid those with tiny holes.
4. Smell for a pleasant aroma.
5. Select those with the least percentage of stems.

What are button mushrooms?

The most common, commercially grown white mushrooms.

What is the caution in cooking button mushrooms?

Don't overcook them.

What are shitake mushrooms?

They look like the white button types, except they are light brown in color and have a meaty texture.

How should they be chosen?

Choose those that are firm, fleshy and have large caps and small stems.

How are shitakes used?

1. Good baked or grilled or in stews.
2. Good for soups, sauces, stir-fry.

Do they have nutritional benefits?

They have been a mainstay of Chinese medicine, and Japanese research indicates that they help process cholesterol and help protect against hepatitis B and cancer.

Are shitake mushrooms available dried?

Yes. They can be freshened by soaking in warm water for half an hour or more.

What are enokis (also known as golden needles or snow puffs)?

The top looks like a light-colored bunch of stems with tiny caps on them.

How are they used?

Mild in flavor, good raw in salads or sandwiches or cooked in a stir-fry or consommé. Don't overcook.

Which are the chanterelles?

Golden with inverted caps with rolled edges. These are the wild mushrooms most often found in stores. Vary from fruity to nutty in aroma and flavor. Have intense flavor.

How should they be used?

Good grilled or lightly sautéd. They should be dry sautéd, for with oil or butter they often come out slimy.

What are morels?

Mushrooms with an almost peanut shell appearance, with a darker skin and light colored ridges. Vary in size from small to the size of an apple. Their ridged surfaces and hollow stems require careful washing.

What should be looked for when selecting morels?

They should be heavy for their size, without shriveling, plump, firm though spongy.

How should they be prepared?

Good sautéd or simmered in pilaf, noodles or pastas. The hollow stems can be stuffed.

What are portobellos?

These are the big button-shaped mushrooms, growing to almost a foot in diameter.

How are they used?

Both cap and stems are edible. Beef-like in flavor when grilled. Can be added to soups or braised dishes. Mainly grown in America despite their Italian name.

What should be looked for in portobello mushrooms?

1. Look for rounded, not flattened, caps that are firm.
2. Check for gills that are clean, not bruised or soft, not mashed.
3. Use the best quality for grilling, the older ones and stems for sauces and stews.

How are they prepared?

Excellent for pasta sauce or a ragout with bacon, tomatoes and Parmesan cheese or broiled or baked.

How do you select mushrooms?

1. Hand select rather than buy packaged mushrooms. Those loose ones are often more expensive but they are usually of higher quality and less likely to have been sprayed with sodium bisulfite as a preservative.
2. The standard whole white mushroom is no longer in prime condition when the rim of the cap separates from the stem, showing the gills.
3. The surface can be white or slightly brown-flecked, but not excessively so, nor should there be bruises or soft spots.
4. Select ones with relatively short stems because the cap is more tender and decorative.
5. Select equal-sized ones for evenness of cooking. They will also have uniform look when sliced.
6. If buying packaged mushrooms, check the label for the preservative sodium bisulfite, which changes the flavor and to which some people are sensitive.
7. They should have a rich, earthy aroma.

How should mushrooms be stored?

Don't store in a closed container or a sealed bag, as they need a generous supply of cool, moist air to stay fresh. One way is to put them in a paper bag or wrap them loosely with slightly damp paper towels and put the package in the crisper.

What is the best way to freeze them?

Slice, sauté in butter, then freeze in a plastic bag with the air squeezed out.

What happens when they are cut?

The cut surface darkens quickly, so prepare at the last minute or coat the exposed surfaces with lemon juice or other acidic liquids.

How can the flavor be enhanced?

Mushrooms will be more flavorful and have better texture if sautéd in butter before adding to a stew or braised dish.

What is the caution in seasoning mushrooms?

They can be overwhelmed by the seasoning so that the varietal special flavors will be lost.

How should they be sautéd?

1. Sauté, not steam sauté. Steam sauté will take place if there are too many mushrooms in the pan so that the trapped steam cannot escape into the air or if they have been soaked in water.
2. When sautéing, add a teaspoon of lemon juice to each ¼ pound of butter to keep them white and firm.
3. To cook with a minimum of oil/fat, cook first without any fat until the liquid extruded evaporates and then add a reduced amount of cooking fat.

How can a large quantity of mushrooms be washed?

1. Plunge the caps into a bath of 2 quarts of water with ½ cup of vinegar and one quarter cup of salt.
2. Briefly swirl the caps to dislodge the dirt.
3. Lift the caps out and drain.

Are raw mushrooms edible?

Yes, and good tasting. When chopped and mixed with mayonnaise, blended with cream cheese or other binders, they make a good canapé spread. They are also good in salads.

How are dried mushrooms selected?

1. Avoid any bags of broken caps or caps with dust on them.
2. The darker the mushroom, the stronger the flavor.

How should dried mushrooms be used?

After rinsing well, soak in warm water just to cover, until moistened and soft. Use minimal liquid.

Can the soaking liquid be used in other dishes?

The soaking liquid will be full of flavor and good for sauces.

How should mushroom caps be prepared for stuffing?

1. Carefully pull off the stems.
2. Scoop out excess flesh on the underside with a small teaspoon or a melon baller to get more room for additional stuffing.
3. The stem and the removed flesh can be used in the stuffing.

OKRA

How should okra be selected?

1. The pods should be relatively firm and small (less than 4″ long are best), with tops that bend easily.
2. They should be bright and free from spots and mold.
3. Avoid stringy, dry or flabby ones, which might be woody.

How should it be stored?

Don't buy more than for a few days storage. Refrigerate them dry in a paper bag.

How should okra be prepared?

1. Wash and dry before cooking.
2. If of miniature size, cut off the stems or protrusions.
3. If large and are to be cooked whole, shave off the cap but be careful not to open the capsule and expose the seeds.
4. If slicing is specified, then cut off the whole top and slice.
5. If the skin is fuzzy, rub the unwashed pod with a towel.

ONIONS

Why is the onion family so widely used in cooking?

Onions, scallions, shallots, leeks and others do more than add flavor. The volatile oils irritate your eyes and your taste buds and olfactory cells. This is a plus if kept in bounds, because if the taste buds and olfactory cells are slightly teased you are better able to taste and smell the food, but there is no advantage to tearing eyes, which are just acting defensively to expel the irritant.

Some onions are very strong. Is there a way to soften the bite?

1. Slice the onions, soak them in cold water and chill for a few hours or overnight, depending on the onion's pungency. Then drain and pat dry.
2. Blanch sliced or diced ones in boiling water for a moment only and then rinse in cold water. Drain the slices and pat dry.

What should you look for in buying onions?

1. If possible don't buy dehydrated or frozen onions.
2. The white skinned ones are less sweet but have a more definite flavor that stands up better to cooking.
3. The yellow skinned ones cost less and are especially good for soups, stews and fried onion rings.
4. Look for heavy onions for their size, onions that are similar sized and are not sprouting and those that are unblemished and without a green tint.

What irritates the eyes when working with onions?

Their sulfur content. The sweet ones have a lower sulfur level.

What are the two main types of onions?

Mild flavored: Bermuda type: flat, white or yellow.

                    Spanish type: oval, white, yellow or brown

Strong flavored: Smaller: white, yellow or red.

Why are some onions sweeter than others?

They have a higher water and sugar content and a lower level sulfuric compounds. Sweetness depends on the type of onion, the climate and the soil they were grown in. Accepted standard for a sweet onion is at least 6% sugar, and it sometimes reaches over 10%, depending on the particular growing season. Their water content is higher than regular onions, which further dilutes the sulfur.

What are the sweet onions now available?

Oso:	From Andes Mountains, South American: late December through March. Expensive. Sugar content varies with the harvest. In 1996 it was more than 12%.
Vidalia:	Georgia, late April–late June.
Walla Walla:	Washington, mid-April–early June.
Texas 1015 or 1015 Supersweet:	Texas, mid-April–mid-June.
Maui:	Hawaii, mid-February–late November. The most expensive.
Sweet imperial:	California, mid-April to early June.
Italian red:	California, mid-April to early June.

How can you tell whether an onion is a sweet one?

1. Sweet onions have a thinner, lighter colored skin.
2. Tend to be most fragile.
3. Usually are designated in the store by signs.
4. Are much more expensive, ranging from $0.79 a pound to about $5 for the Maui.

How is the taste of a sweet onion different?

1. It tastes sweet and is milder in flavor.
2. Has very little sharpness.
3. Has a subtle, fruity flavor.
4. Produces very little or no tearing.

How should sweet onions be stored?

Differently from regular onions. They should be refrigerated in a brown paper bag.

Can sweet onions be used to make onion rings?

The rings from them are wonderful.

How can onions be handled when peeling or cutting to minimize tearing?

1. Put the onions in the freezer for 20–30 minutes before cutting.
2. Refrigerate for a couple of hours before slicing.

Vegetables

3. Wear safety goggles.
4. The sharper the knife, the cleaner the cut, and, thus, the faster the job is done. Also the amount of juice will be reduced by using a sharp knife.
5. Turn the exhaust fan on to high and chop under it.
6. Hold a couple of wooden matchsticks between your teeth (tips outside).
7. Chew gum while slicing.
8. Cut off the root last.
9. Peel under cold water, which will prevent the volatile oils from rising.

Is there an easy way to peel pearl onions?

1. Drop them into boiling water, bring the water back to boil, and boil for 1–2 minutes.
2. Transfer to a colander and run cold water over them to stop the cooking.
3. Trim the root ends, keeping the base intact.
4. Squeeze the onion gently from its skin.

How can you cook onions?

1. Don't sauté at too high a temperature or too long.
2. A little lemon juice, vinegar or cream of tartar will help keep them from turning yellow.

How can onions be caramelized?

Sauté them slowly until soft and then increase the heat to moderate and add a little sugar (less than a teaspoon).

What should be done with the peeled skins?

Don't throw the paper-like skin into the garbage disposal or it might clog; instead throw them in a wastebasket.

How can onion juice be obtained?

1. Skin the onion, cut it into pieces, puree in the food processor and strain off the juice.
2. Cut the onion in half horizontally and extract the juice, using a lemon squeezer.

Why are onions cooked in butter more flavorful than those cooked in water?

The butter not only contributes its own distinctive flavor, but its fat content (about 80%) captures the desirable onion essence that would otherwise partially dissipate into the air.

Can onions be chopped in advance?

Not long, only for an hour or two. Refrigerated perhaps for three or four hours but unless they are in glass containers filled with water and tightly sealed (not with plastic) the sulfurous odor will contaminate other foods.

Why does French onion soup sometimes turn blue or blue-gray?

Red onions have a pigment that turns the soup alkaline, which causes the blueness.

What can be done to prevent this discoloration?

It can be overcome or prevented by adding an oxidative agent, such as lemon juice or wine.

Why does the inside of a whole onion sometimes pop out when boiled?

The force that pushes it out is pent-up steam. To avoid, pierce the onion a couple of times with a thin skewer or make a ¼" X-shaped incision into the root end. In any case simmer, because boiling increases the chance of pop-out, because the bulb bounces around in the pot.

What causes boiled white onions to turn yellow?

The whiteness of these (also true for cauliflower) is due to the pigment flavone. When flavone is subjected to prolonged heat, a brownish-yellow tint develops.

What are some countermeasures to yellowing?

1. Don't overcook.
2. Buy young, fresh onions in good condition.
3. If your cooking water is hard, try adding a touch of lemon juice or cream of tartar to help neutralize the alkalinity. The more added, the whiter, but don't add so much that the flavor of the whitener becomes obvious.

How can onions be hollowed for stuffing?

1. Cut a slice about a ½" from the top.
2. Parboil the onion about 20 minutes and drain.
3. Scoop out the center with a small spoon.
4. Leave about a half inch shell.

Why is it essential to add the garlic near the end of the sautéing process when sautéing both onions and garlic?

If you sauté the garlic as long as the onion, you will burn the garlic. If you shorten the cooking time too much, the onions will be raw, unsweet, too strong in flavor.

PARSLEY—see chapter on SEASONING AND OILS

PARSNIPS

What should you look for in parsnips?

1. This sweet root is best in cooler months of the year.
2. Color should be beige to brown.

3. Avoid pitted ones.
4. Choose uniformly sized ones, if possible, that are firm and straight.
5. Avoid tops that show sprouting seed stalks.

Which should be selected for cooking whole?

Choose parsnips the size of small walnuts and uniform in size. They can be cooked and served whole and are delicious.

How should parsnips be prepared?

1. They are not very attractive raw.
2. They need not be peeled before boiling, steaming etc., for once cooked the peel comes off easily. The exception to this is when they are cut into pieces for salads and pizzas.
3. The finish point is when the center is tender and creamy.

What is the best way to serve cooked parsnips?

Puree them.

How should they be flavored?

Since they are quite sugary, they should be counterbalanced with salty, smoky or bitter flavors, such as anchovy, ham or bitey leaf greens.

How should parsnips be handled in the microwave?

They do not do well in the microwave.

PEAS

What should one look for when buying peas?

1. The pods should be small, firm yet flexible, vivid green. Avoid pale or shriveled pods.
2. Choose cold pods, because when warm their sugar turns to starch.
3. The peas inside should be fresh and reasonably uniform. They should be glossy, crunchy, not starchy, but sweet to the taste.

How can the quality of shelled peas be checked?

When in doubt about the quality of shelled peas, cover them with water in a bowl. Discard those that float.

How should peas be prepared?

Shell just before using, for peas begin to convert from sugar to starch when they are picked, and shelling just accelerates this process.

Must they be shelled before cooking?

No. They can be cooked in the shell.

How should they be cooked?

1. If cooking them with acidic ingredients, such as lemon juice or tomatoes, leave them uncovered, or they will develop an unwanted, olive-drab color, especially if they are even slightly overcooked.
2. The sweetness of peas begins to diminish after they are picked, so often a little added sugar is an advantage.

How many peas will a pound of peas in the pod yield?

About one cup. Plan about a half pound of unshelled peas per serving.

What can be done with pea pods after shelling them?

Use for making soup stock, especially chicken or vegetable stock.

What are sugar peas (also called sugar snap peas)?

Sugar peas are plumper, almost translucent. They are a cross between the English pea and the snow pea.

How are sugar snap peas best prepared?

Blanch first, then put them in a bowl of cold water to limit further softening, then cook as desired.

What are snow peas?

Snow peas (also called Chinese pea pods) are peas that don't mature and are chosen for their pods which are thin, flat and crisp.

How can sugar peas be used?

1. Eat them raw after removing the stem.
2. Cook very briefly, for just a minute or so, in hot oil with constant stirring.
3. Stir-fry.
4. Quickly cook them in hot stock, not much more than a blanching.

PICKLES

What is pickling?

Preservation in vinegar that is highly spiced or in seasoned brine.

Are pickles always sour?

They can be sweet, sour, spicy, hot, dill-flavored or with other flavorings.

What is pickle relish?

Chopped pickles, sometimes with seasonings.

What is the best vinegar for pickling?

While any vinegar with enough acidic acid (4–6% in most commercial ones) will work, distilled white vinegar is good, because it won't compete with the flavor of the vegetable or fruit being pickled.

How long does it take for pickled food to develop its full flavor?

At least six weeks.

What vegetables can be pickled?

Cucumbers, cabbage, onions, beets, green peppers, radishes and also fruits and nuts.

When selecting pickles out of a barrel, which should be chosen?

Look for ones that look fresh and green, not pale or grey.

How are sweet pickles made?

First brined, then drained and packed in a mixture of sugar syrup and vinegar.

What should be done to pickles before pickling?

Cut off ¼″ from each end of the pickle because the end has an enzyme that may cause the pickle to soften.

Why should iodized salt not be used for pickling?

Because it creates a film.

How can bitterness be minimized with cucumbers to be pickled?

Soak in salted water, drain, rinse in cold, running water.

What can be done with pickle juice?

Use it in dressing coleslaw, especially from sweet pickles.

POTATOES

What is the history of potatoes?

Potatoes grew wild in South America and even as far north as Colorado. Only the South American Indians knew what to do with them. They were cultivated as early as 750 BC by Andean Incas in Peru and Ecuador and the northern part of Chile. Spanish conquerors took them back to Europe, and from Spain they spread throughout Europe. They appeared in Ireland and England about 1580, but were thought to have come from Virginia. One legend says that when the Spanish Armada was defeated, several Spanish ships foundered on the western coast of Ireland, and the potatoes came from these ships, which had them for use as regular food.

How did the Europeans react to the new vegetable?

Europeans mistrusted them at first because:

1. Any vegetable grown from a tuber, not from seed, couldn't be good.
2. The Scots denounced them because they were not mentioned in the Bible.
3. The French thought they caused leprosy.
4. The Spaniards called them "edible stones."
5. The Germans fed them only to livestock.
6. In the late seventeenth century, the Irish accepted the potato wholeheartedly and made it their most important crop.
7. In North America about 1769, when the Irish settlers came to Londonderry, New Hampshire, potatoes were accepted. Before that they were used for fodder or as food only for slaves.

What are some other uses for potatoes other than eating?

1. Clean silverware: Wash the silver in the water in which peeled potatoes have been cooked.
2. Clean window panes and mirrors: Cut a large potato in half and rub the cut side on the panes. When the potato gets dirty, cut off a slice and continue. Rinse with clear water.
3. Rest tired eyes: Grate a potato and squeeze out the liquid with a towel. Soak compresses in the liquid and gently put over eyes for 15 minutes.

How are fabricated potato products, such as Pringles, made?

From dehydrated potatoes.

What is bubble and squeak?

An English fried dish of equal parts of mashed potatoes and chopped, cooked cabbage.

What is the advantage of cooking potatoes with the skin still on?

They will retain more of their nutrients.

Nutrition
What is the nutritional value of potatoes?

A 6-ounce potato yields: 110 calories (The same amount of rice or pasta yields 400 calories).

23 grams of carbohydrates.

3 grams of protein.

0 fat or cholesterol.

Practically all the vitamins except A.

What does processing or cooking the potatoes do to the nutritional content?

Processing or cooking the potato and/or reheating it a few hours later will reduce the vitamin content.

How can the nutrients of potatoes be best preserved when cooked?

1. Cook with the skins on, then remove the skins, if desired, before serving.
2. Skins, even though they may taste good particularly when baked, are potentially dangerous. A number of toxins and pesticide residues may be left even after washing and cooking. There are few nutrients (except for some fiber) in the skin, mostly they are found just under the skin.

Are potatoes dangerous when they develop green sprouts?

Yes. The green tubers or spots should not be eaten and they should be cut off and discarded and the skin peeled.

How are potatoes classified and chosen for each recipe?

Mainly by their starch content.

Which are the high-starch potatoes?

Russets: best baked, mashed, deep fried, or used for potato-based dough. Tend to crumble in water when boiled, cook dry and mealy.

Which are medium starch?

Yukon gold, Eastern, yellow Finns: best mashed, steamed or in soups or stews. Moister than russets and need less butter to moisten.

Which have the lowest starch?

Small reds, ruby crescents, red boiling, blue caribe: Good for steaming, barbecueing, roasting whole, especially salads and gratins. Cook moist, light and waxy.

Selection

What makes new potatoes different?

They are harvested before the starch is fully developed, are still immature and therefore contain the lightest starch of all. They have thinner skins and more moisture.

How should new potatoes be chosen?

Select hard ones with almost translucent skins. Use promptly, as they are not good keepers.

Some potatoes seem to work well with all types of cooking. Which are they?

Yukon gold, yellow finns, kennebecs.

How should potatoes be selected?

1. Choose those that are firm and blemish-free.
2. Select similarly sized ones.

3. Avoid those with soft spots, cracks, sprouts or a green tinge.

4. Sniff for any off- or negative odors (as opposed to an earthy smell).

How can you tell if a potato is high in starch?

1. If you don't know the variety, the ones with a rough, dull skin are high in starch.

2. If you slice it raw and it looks grainy, then it is heavy in starch.

3. The less starchy ones tend to have a glossy exterior and when sliced raw are less grainy and look smooth.

Should you buy or use green-tinged potatoes?

No! Green surface color/blemishes are caused by overexposure to light. The tainted areas will taste bitter and contain some level of a toxic alkaloid, solanine — not enough to kill, but it can make you sick. Potato sprouts contain solanine so discard these too.

Should potatoes be peeled before cooking?

No, for with their skin on they will be more flavorful, hold their shape better and absorb less water.

Yes, for dishes such as gratin. Put the peeled ones in water with a little lemon juice or vinegar to prevent browning but don't keep them submerged too long or they will absorb too much moisture.

How are fried potatoes in the Spanish cuisine different?

They are boiled first before being cooked in fat.

Storage

How should potatoes be stored?

1. Keep in a dark well-ventilated place at 45–50 °F.

2. Put in a brown paper bag, not plastic, because otherwise they will start to sweat and mold.

3. They will keep 7–10 days, sometimes longer.

4. If kept longer or exposed to light for any length of time or to very cold or fairly warm temperature, they will start to sprout and/or turn green.

5. Potatoes produce chlorophyll, which gives the green coloration and serves as an indicator of aging, but at the same time it produces a toxic alkaloid, which is not destroyed by cooking.

How can peeled, sliced potatoes be kept from discoloring?

Keep them covered with cold water with a little lemon juice or vinegar and refrigerate.

Why not store a raw, whole potato in the refrigerator?

The cold environment encourages the conversion of too much of the starch into sugar. If you want sweet potatoes, then buy sweet potatoes. However, the sugar will revert back to starch if left at room temperature for several days.

Why shouldn't you store potatoes and onions together?

They both emit gases that have negative effects on the flavor of the other and also speed up the rotting process.

How can old potatoes be salvaged?

A small amount of sugar in the cooking water. This will help bring back some of the lost flavor.

How can potatoes be prevented from sprouting when in storage?

Store in a brown paper bag at room temperature. For even better results, put an apple in the bag.

What do brown areas on sliced potatoes mean?

The vitamin C has been destroyed.

Frying, Sautéing

What is the procedure for getting the best french fries?

1. Let the cut potatoes stand in cold water for about an hour before frying.
2. Drain and dry thoroughly before cooking.
3. Sprinkle with flour to get a good golden color.
4. Fry twice: fry just a few minutes and drain off the grease. The second time fry until golden brown. The second fry can be considerably later.

What is the British name for french fries?

Chips.

What is the purpose of double-frying french fries (or chicken)?

1. It allows the body of the potato to cook before the exterior is sealed off by the formation of a crust.
2. It reduces the time necessary to prepare the potatoes for serving. The second frying will take only a minute or so, and this means the bulk of the work can be done ahead of time.
3. They come out lighter this way.

What can be done to prepare french fries other than by double-frying?

Blanch in boiling water. This is not recommended, because the water will evaporate when deep frying and lower the temperature of the oil.

Why don't potatoes need a coating when french fried?

Because they are 20% starch, which expands in the hot oil, making the potatoes less dense, and they then cook internally at the same rate as the surface.

At what temperature should potatoes be french fried?

At first fry 325 °F, second fry 375 °F.

What happens if the oil is too hot?

The fries will brown before they are cooked through.

What causes french fries to absorb too much oil and be greasy?

When the oil is not hot enough.

Why are russet baking potatoes desired for deep frying?

Because of their low moisture content they are less apt to splatter the oil or to absorb grease.

What is the purpose of coating (flour or batter) in deep frying?

1. It acts as a barrier between vegetables and/or meat and the fat.
2. Gives flavor.
3. Gives a contrast in texture.

What are the different sizes of french fries?

Classic: 4″ long, ¼″ wide
Shoestring: 3″ long, skinny
Matchstick: 1½″ long, ¼″ wide

What are safety precautions to take when deep frying potatoes?

1. Dry the potatoes well to prevent spattering of the oil by the water.
2. Never use water to extinguish a grease fire, for it will just spread the fire.
3. Keep the lid to the pot at hand to smother the flame, if necessary.

What are things to watch out for in the oil for deep frying?

1. The oil must be tasteless.
2. The oil or shortening must heat to 300 °F without breaking down, olive oil is not a good choice, for it won't withstand high temperatures.

What should be done if you keep the oil for reuse?

1. Strain the oil after each use through cheesecloth or paper toweling.
2. Refrigerate the oil to preserve it.

How many times can the oil be reused?

1. Discard the oil after five or six uses, for it develops fatty acids that will result in bad flavors.

2. Use the oil for potatoes only, which will prevent the transfer of flavors from one product to another.

Why shouldn't expensive green olive oil be used for frying potatoes?

1. It will give a bitter taste.
2. It doesn't withstand high-enough temperatures.

How can low-fat, crunchy potato chips be made?

1. Cut the peeled potato in half crosswise.
2. Cut into paper thin slices.
3. Put the slices on an oiled cookie sheet.
4. Brush the top of the slices with corn oil.
5. Bake at 450 °F about 10 minutes, or until golden brown.
6. Place in a brown paper bag with a small amount of salt and shake.

How are potato bird's nests made?

1. Peel and then grate potatoes into matchstick size.
2. Layer the inside of a white ladle with the shredded potatoes and place a smaller wired ladle over it. Clamp the two together.
3. Plunge the ladles into 300 °F oil.
4. Fry for about 5 minutes, or until golden brown.
5. Remove from oil, drain, salt and keep warm until all are done.

How are potato pancakes made?

1. Grate raw potatoes coarsely.
2. Squeeze out all possible liquid. This is critical for a good crust.
3. Mix with egg or egg substitute, salt and pepper and a little flour.
4. Fry to a good brown on both sides so that they are crisp and lacy. The patties should be small, about 3″ in diameter and about ½″ thick.

How can discoloration be prevented if the potato pancake batter is not used immediately?

A little lemon juice will keep the potatoes from darkening.

How can the pancakes be given additional flavors?

1. To get additional flavor, mix the batter with grated, squeeze-dried onion or mashed garlic, or both.
2. Other ingredients, such as chopped bacon, toasted pine nuts and sautéd diced vegetables, can be incorporated.

Why should only small amounts of potatoes be cooked in a sauté pan at a time?

Too large an amount will trap steam, causing potatoes to lose structure and/or flavor.

Why flour between layers of potatoes when making scalloped potatoes (American) and not with the parallel European dish, pommes de terre dauphins?

American baking potatoes are moister than the European varieties, and the flour is necessary to soak up the liquid on the surface of the slices. If this is not done with the American varieties, the dish will be gooey.

Roasting

What are the best potatoes for roasting?

All-purpose, such as red, California white rose, Yukon gold or yellow Finnish. Those with low starch. The best are new potatoes.

How can sticking to the pan be avoided when roasting potatoes?

1. Oil both the pan and the potatoes lightly before roasting.
2. Roast in a preheated oven at 450 °F.
3. Periodically during the roasting period scrape the potatoes loose from the pan.
4. Then shake the pan and keep the potatoes in an even layer.

How can a moist interior be achieved?

Cover them during part of the roasting time.

Baking

How should potatoes be baked?

1. To ensure a fluffy inside, choose the right potato, i.e., one with a high starch content (russet, Idaho, yellow Finn, Yukon gold).
2. Choose potatoes of the same size (about a half pound) so that they will cook evenly.
3. Bake at 425 °F for about 1 hour.

Should potatoes be pierced for baking?

1. They will have better texture, be mealy rather than soggy.
2. The trapped steam won't explode the potato.
3. If not pierced before, then do it immediately after baking to release the steam.
4. If you run a large nail or spike through a potato it will shorten the baking time but will allow too much steam to escape, negatively affecting the texture. Some steam needs to get out, however, to prevent possible explosion. So pierce the skin 1″ deep or so in several places with the tine of a fork before putting it into the oven.

How can potato baking time be shortened?

1. Oil the skin before baking.
2. Boil in salted water for about 10 minutes or microwave until just beginning to soften before placing in a very hot oven.

Why are baked potatoes fluffy?

Because they are high in starch and the starch cells, when heated, separate from one another.

What does an aluminum foil covering do to a potato when baking?

Produces more of a steamed than a baked potato, because the foil traps the heat. So don't use it if you want the best flavor and texture. If you do use it, then after the first half of the baking time uncover the potatoes so that the skin will dry and crisp during the rest of the baking.

Should you rub the skin with butter or oil before baking a potato?

Yes, if you want to eat the skin with more flavor, shorten the baking time and/or prevent cracking.

Why are Idaho or other mature potatoes better than new potatoes for baking or frying?

Mature potatoes are drier, starchier and mealier, so they will become fluffier and lighter-textured when baked.

What is a good way to bake potatoes in a microwave?

1. Choose equally sized potatoes.
2. Puncture with a fork and bake at high power for 7 minutes (depends on power of microwave).
3. Then wrap the potato in aluminum foil, shiny side inside, and leave at room temperature for 10 minutes more.

Mashing

What is the role of starch in making mashed potatoes?

Since potatoes are mainly starch and water, and the starch is in the form of granules in the starch cells, then the higher the starch content, the fuller the cells. In high-starch potatoes, the cells are completely full. The space between the cells is mainly water. The full cells are most likely to maintain their integrity and stay separate and thus give a fluffy, full-textured product.

Which potatoes are best?

Select flaky, high-starch ones, such as Idaho or Yukon gold, for they have the highest starch content, have similar texture and are fluffier when cooked. The yellow-fleshed Yukon gold has a rich flavor. Don't use low-starch, waxy reds or California whites, as they don't absorb cream or butter well.

How do you make the best mashed potatoes?

1. Wash and drain the potatoes before adding to boiling water. There is disagreement as whether to peel the potatoes; I personally like mine mashed without the peel. Some fiber will be lost by peeling, but few vitamins, and without the peel the appearance is more attractive.

2. Add 1 tablespoon of salt to the boiling water.

3. Cook until fork tender.

4. Drain the potatoes the moment they finish cooking.

5. Then carefully shake the potatoes in the pot over low heat to dry the surface and get rid of any excess moisture.

6. Make sure they are dry. They are properly dried when no steam rises. The low water content will allow them to absorb milk, cream and/or butter without becoming gummy or watery.

7. Add a little hot (not boiling) milk when mashing. A little baking soda (about a teaspoonful) when mashing helps.

8. Then beat vigorously, as that will help produce a light and creamy product.

9. Add cold butter in small amounts, waiting for the prior butter to be incorporated before adding the next, stirring constantly.

10. Combine with the milk gradually.

How can they be kept warm?

1. Once they are mashed, don't cover the pot or bowl, for otherwise the trapped steam will give a soggy consistency.

2. Cover with a clean dish towel, which will absorb excess moisture and keep the heat in.

Why not use cold milk?

Combine mashed potatoes with warm milk only, because cold milk or cream lowers the temperature and makes them gummy.

What will happen if the milk is boiling hot?

Boiling milk tends to make the potatoes sticky.

What happens if you over-mash the potatoes?

If you over-mash the potatoes you rupture the cell walls, allowing starch granules to escape and cause gumminess. Use the medium disc of a food mill or a potato ricer to get a smooth puree.

What can be done if mashed potatoes have been over-cooked?

Carefully fold in stiffly whipped egg white(s) and then bake in a hot oven.

Is a blender or processor good for mashing?

A food processor or blender should not be used, as the high speed brings out too much starch, resulting in a gooey dish.

Can they be made ahead of time?

Yes, let them cool, then cover with plastic and refrigerate up to about 5–6 hours. Reheat in the microwave, adding milk or broth (not water) if necessary.

What is a good tool for mashing?

A potato masher in which the cooked potatoes are forced through a sieve-like cup.

Should potatoes for mashing be peeled before or after cooking?

After. If peeled or cut before being put into boiling water to cook, the potatoes will gain too much weight due to absorption of water, and the result will be a more watery mush of the mash.

What are some variations on mashed potatoes?

1. Equal parts of potato and cooked vegetables, such as chopped spinach.
2. Grated cheese, about 1 cup per 2 pounds of potatoes. If the cheese is strong, such as Gorganzola, then use about a ½ lb per 2 pounds of potatoes.
3. Flavor with mashed, roasted garlic.

What is the difference between colcannon, kilkenny and rumbledethump?

All are potatoes mashed with kale. Colcannon is the Irish name, kilkenny is the Scottish name and rumbledethump is Welsh.

How can low-fat mashed potatoes be made?

Boil the potatoes in salted water until fork tender, mash with fat-free sour cream, salt and pepper and sprinkle with sliced green onions.

What is a way to make mashed potatoes less caloric and still have them tasty?

Instead of milk, cream or butter, use some of the water that they have been boiled in.

Should mashed potatoes be mixed with other pureed vegetables?

Equal parts of potato and the other vegetable will work well.

Potato Salad

Why are new potatoes better than Idaho or other mature baking potatoes for making potato salad?

1. New potatoes have more moisture and a lower starch content than bakers and thus absorb less cooking water.
2. They need less mayonnaise or vinaigrette dressing and are less likely to break when the salad is mixed.
3. Because the dressing is not so thoroughly absorbed, the flavor of the potato, which is more delicate, won't be overpowered.
4. Since less sauce is needed, it means fewer calories.

What are ways of getting color into potato salad?

1. Use a mixture of different types of potatoes, such as Peruvian blue, Finnish yellow.
2. Add vegetables such as red onions, red or yellow peppers, broccoli florets.

Why should the potatoes be peeled, cut and seasoned while still hot?

Hot potatoes will absorb flavors easily, cold ones won't.

What are the best potatoes for making salad?

Low-starch ones, such as new potatoes or red bliss.

How should potatoes for salad be boiled?

In salted water.

Should potatoes be skinned before boiling for salad?

No. Skinning potatoes offers no advantage in flavor but usually results in loss of texture.

Should the skin be left on after cooking when making potato salad?

1. Optional, if using thin-skinned new or red-skinned potatoes.
2. If they are to be peeled, peel when they are still warm; it will be easier.

Is the microwave a good method for cooking potatoes for potato salad?

Only if using a potato like a Yukon gold.

PUMPKINS

Are mini-pumpkins edible?

Yes. These members of the squash family have flesh that is sweet and velvety.

Can they be roasted whole?

Yes.

How can pumpkins be roasted?

1. Puncture each with a fork.
2. Put on a baking sheet in the middle of a preheated 350 °F oven until tender.

How can they be used?

1. They make convenient single-serving side dishes.
2. They make a fine edible serving dish. When baked, fill with soup.
3. Roast, seed and then fill with a rice pilaf, risotto or soup.
4. To keep their shape, don't over-bake if it is to be used as a container for a filling.

Can canned pumpkin be used for making good pies?

Yes, pumpkin is one of the best of the canned vegetables.

How should pumpkins be selected?

1. The young are sweeter than the old and need less sugar, i.e., the smaller rather than the bigger, which are more fibrous.
2. Choose brightly colored pumpkins that are heavy for their size and have rinds that are free of blemishes.

How can whole pumpkins be used in cooking?

1. Select either pumpkins small enough for individual servings or one small enough to fit into the oven but not too heavy to carry to the table.
2. Cut off the top and scrape the solid pumpkin clean.
3. Bake until the pumpkin is tender but don't overcook.

How can pumpkins be baked?

1. If they are small enough to put in the oven, then bake at 400 °F until tender.
2. Cut into wedges and season with brown sugar and spices and bake at 400 °F for about 45 minutes.
3. Peel and dice and bake with other vegetables.

Can the baked pumpkin be frozen?

It will collapse if frozen.

Are very large pumpkins better than smaller?

No, usually just the opposite.

RHUBARB

How should rhubarb be selected?

Field-grown: A cherry red stalk and coarse green leaves. They have more flavor but also tough, fibrous strings that need to be removed.

Hothouse-grown: Light pink stalks and tiny yellow green leaves.

How are the new varieties in the market different?

New varieties on the market, such as Cherry Red, Chipman and Valentine, are deeper in hue and retain color better when cooked and are also sweeter.

What are the cautions about rhubarb?

1. It can be very sour and overpower other flavors.
2. If cooked with too much heat, it can break down and be watery.
3. It can lose its attractive color and turn gray.

How should it be selected?

1. It resembles a celery stalk with a pink/red color and should have no browned edges.
2. Discard the leaves, as they can be poisonous (oxalic acid).

How can rhubarb be tested for freshness?

Snap the base of the stalk, there should be a slight resistance, and the leaves should be fresh, not wilted.

Should rhubarb be peeled?

Only if they have stringy fibers.

How should it be prepared for cooking?

Soak pieces for 20–25 minutes in cold water.

How is rhubarb used?

1. It is almost always served cooked.
2. It can be stewed, chopped into cake batter or pies or relish.

Why should it be sweetened?

It is usually quite sour and needs sweetness (sugar or honey) to bring out its attractive quality.

RUTABAGA (SWEDES, YELLOW TURNIPS, SWEDISH TURNIPS)

What are rutabagas?

Members of the cabbage family but a root vegetable that looks like a turnip. They are pale yellow both in skin and flesh.

How should they be chosen?

Select heavy ones that are firm with a smooth surface.

How are rutabagas used?

Much like turnips.

SALSIFY

What is salsify?

A root vegetable resembling parsnips, though smaller, that is a member of the chicory family. Also called the oyster plant because it has some resemblance in taste to oysters.

How should salsify be cooked?

1. Boiled, mashed, mixed with eggs, flour, salt and butter to make into patties that are fried in butter.
2. Boil and serve with butter and seasoning or with a cream sauce.
3. Use in soups.

SCALLIONS (GREEN ONIONS)

What are scallions?

This variety of the onion family is milder than young onions, and, while either can be used in recipes, the regular onion will be stronger in flavor.

How should they be selected?

1. Choose those with crisp, firm tops, a deep green color and a white base that is firm.
2. The best are those about ½″ in diameter.

How should scallions be stored?

Refrigerate unwashed in a plastic bag.

How should they be prepared?

Trim off and discard the rootlets.

How can scallions be used?

1. They can be used raw or briefly cooked.
2. Snips (by scissors or by knife on a cutting board) are excellent in salads.
3. They do not react well to heat, so add to a cooked dish when it is almost finished or after it has been taken from the heat.
4. The green stalks can be substituted for chives.

How many scallions are required if a recipe calls for 1 cup chopped?

About 9–10.

SHALLOTS

What are shallots?

A native of Central Asia now grown in the United States, especially in New Jersey and New York. The taste is a mild cross between onion and garlic. They come in a head with cloves, somewhat similar in form to garlic.

How should they be selected?

1. The skins should be unblemished, snugly encasing the firm, plump body.
2. Avoid those wrinkled or sprouted.
3. The smaller varieties tend to have the most intense flavor, although the larger ones are easier to peel.

How should they be sautéd?

Never sauté for more than a minute or two because they scorch easily. So sauté quickly over low heat and with care.

How should they be cooked to add to potato salad?

1. Snips can be added without cooking.
2. Simmer slowly in red wine vinegar and add when warm.

SOYBEANS

Why are soybeans nutritionally good?

They are rich in vitamin B, calcium, omega-3 fatty acids and all eight essential amino acids.

What is soy milk?

It is pressed from ground, cooked beans.

What happens if soy milk curdles?

Tofu is formed.

SPINACH

What are the advantages of spinach in recipes?

1. Available year-round, although best in the cooler months.
2. Good raw or cooked.
3. Excellent for getting green color in a dish.
4. Cooks quicker than kale, Swiss chard etc.

What should be avoided in selecting spinach?

Avoid bunches with wilted, yellowing or darkened leaves.

What is the best way to use steamed spinach?

1. Discard the stems.
2. Lightly squeeze it to get rid of excess moisture that will otherwise flow into the other food on the plate.

Which is more nutritious, raw or cooked spinach?

The cellular walls of the spinach are rather hard and as a result many of the nutrients and vitamins of the spinach pass through your digestive tract imprisoned within these cells. Cooking breaks down the cellular walls and allows the nutrients to escape and thus be absorbed.

What is the nutritive value of spinach?

It has iron and vitamins A and C, folate and beta carotene.

What spinach makes the best salad?

Flat leaf sold in bunches are more tender, moist and lettuce-like.

What is the best cleaning method for washing spinach?

Since most spinach is grown on sandy soils, residual sand has to be removed. Place in a large pot of warm, not hot, water and shake gently. Keep repeating the process until no sand shows on the bottom of the pot.

What is an easy way to blanch spinach?

Put the leaves in a colander, rinse well, then pour boiling water over the spinach and let it drain into the sink.

SPROUTS

What are sprouts?

Small, tender shoots sent out by cracked seeds, peas, beans.

What are some of the kinds of sprouts?

The most common in Chinese cooking are from mung beans, but they also come from sunflower seeds, garbanzos, green peas, wheat berries, clover etc. The most common on the market are bean sprouts.

What are alfalfa sprouts?

Germinated alfalfa seeds, which form white and green sprouts used for sandwiches and salads.

How should sprouts be selected?

Since they are extremely perishable they should be crisp, fresh, smell clean, and not be discolored or sticky.

How should they be used?

1. They are excellent raw in salads.
2. If used in cooking, such as stir-frying, add at the very end, preferably when the fry is off the heat and they will be warmed by the sauce.

Vegetables

Are sprouts nutritious?

1. They are low in calories, essentially fat-free.
2. Some, such as from beans or lentils, have vitamin C and B vitamins.

SQUASH

How should summer squash be selected?

1. The shell should be smooth and glossy but with a soft rind.
2. The smaller are tastier.

How should they be stored?

Refrigerate and use within 5–6 days.

How can the blossoms be used?

Eaten raw in salads, deep-fried or used as wrappers for various fillings.

How are the winter squash different?

They have a hard, firm rind that protects and is often not edible.

How should squash be selected?

1. They should be free of mold or blemishes and be deep in color.
2. Choose only if firm and heavy for its size with the rind free of cuts or soft spots.
3. They come in various colors, shapes and sizes.

How should they be cooked?

1. Bake, boil, simmer, steam or microwave.
2. Peel after it is cooked.

How should squash be pureed?

Cut in half, scoop out the seeds, bake until tender, then scoop out the softened flesh.

What is a precaution to take when baking a squash whole?

Pierce it several times so that it won't explode.

What are seasonings that go well with squash?

Thyme, oregano, sage, dill, cloves, basil and especially ginger.

What are the main winter squashes?

Acorn:	Serve with brown sugar and butter.
Butternut:	In soups or pureed for stuffed pasta.
Hubbard:	Less sweet, use baked in soups and purees.

Vegetables

What is acorn squash?

A small, dark green acorn-shaped squash with deep ridges.

What is spaghetti squash? (Also noodle squash)

A winter (and autumn) squash that, when cooked, separates into strands that are spaghetti-like.

What does it taste like?

Sweet-flavored with a crunchy bite.

How should spaghetti squash be cooked?

Boiled:	Pierce the shell several times and cook 30–50 minutes. It is done when easily pierced. Cut it in half and scrape the flesh out with a fork.
Baked:	Heat about two hours at 350 °F.
Steamed:	Put the halves in 2–3 inches of water and steam until tender.
Microwave:	Cook halves about 7–8 minutes a side or a little longer.

What are the nutrients of spaghetti squash?

An 8-ounce serving has 75 calories and is a good source of complex carbohydrates.

What are the nutrients found in squash?

A good source of beta-carotene, fiber and potassium. They are also low in calories.

SWEET POTATOES/YAMS

What are sweet potatoes?

The sweet potato is a true root of a member of the morning glory family and despite a resemblance to the yam is entirely unrelated to it. It is native to Central America but may have spread to Polynesia before the arrival of Columbus who brought it to Europe on his first voyage. By the end of the century it was established in China and the Philippines. It is now cultivated in most subtropical areas and is noted for its 3–6% sugar content, which increases with warm temperatures.

How do the nutrients compare to white potatoes?

It has more calories, minerals and vitamin A, but less protein than does a white potato.

What is a yam?

The yam is the tuber of a plant related to the grasses and lilies. Among the earliest of flowering plants it had spread across the continents before they separated. It may have been cultivated 10,000 years ago. Apparently it had evolved separately in Asia, Africa and America and may have been cultivated as early as 8000 BC in Asia. But what are called yams in the United States are actually a variety of sweet potato. True yams have a higher sugar content and can be found in Mexico or in Latin American markets.

What kind of sweet potatoes should be chosen?

Dry: White- to yellow-fleshed are only slightly sweet with a high starch content; tend to be somewhat mealy.

Moist: Orange to red-orange of varying shades with a higher sugar content that is more easily caramelized.

How should sweet potatoes be selected and stored?

1. The skin should be uniformly colored. Do not purchase if they have white areas or are damaged as this indicates decay.
2. Avoid those with skin abrasions or soft spots.
3. The ones with a deeper orange or red skins (for example the garnet) are sweeter and have a less mealy texture.
4. The smaller ones are less fibrous so select either small or medium sized ones.

How should sweet potatoes be stored?

1. Store in a cool, dry place but do not refrigerate, as the cold temperature will cause the starch to change to sugar and change the cooking quality.
2. Don't wash them until ready to use.
3. Don't store in a plastic bag, rather use a perforated paper bag.
5. Keep in a dark, well-ventilated place.

What advance preparation do they need?

Scrub well for baking.

How should sweet potatoes be boiled?

Boil until tender although the skins are less attractive this way.

Are they good microwaved?

Microwaving will cook them, but the skin doesn't soften and the sugar doesn't carmelize, so they tend to be soggy.

How should sweet potatoes be baked?

1. They generally take less time to cook than do regular potatoes.
2. At 400 °F, on the center rack of the oven, coated *lightly* with vegetable or olive oil (not butter), *not* wrapped in foil but on a baking sheet lined with foil.
3. Pierce to allow steam to escape and thus prevent explosion.

How can boiled sweet potatoes be peeled easily?

1. Don't peel before cooking.
2. When tender take from the boiling water and immerse immediately in very cold water to stop further cooking. Peels come off easily.

How can a sweet potato salad be made?

1. Boil potatoes slowly in their skins, dropping them one at a time into boiling water.
2. They are done when a fork will easily penetrate to the center.
3. Drain, peel, cool and cut into the desired size and shapes and add the dressing.

What happens when sweet potatoes are overcooked?

They will fall apart.

SWISS CHARD—see CHARD

TOMATILLO

What are tomatillos?

While actually a fruit, they resemble small green tomatoes and when fully ripened turn yellow.

How are they used?

They are best when still green and are used raw or cooked in salsas.

TOMATOES

What is the story of tomatoes?

The tomato first grew wild as small berries in the Andes of South America. From there it developed in Mexico and the conquistadors brought it to Europe. It was regarded, at first, as a poison in America because of its relation to deadly nightshade. Now they are a central part of our cuisine, and each man, woman and child consumes about 80 pounds each year. There are almost 3,000 different varieties known. In California the season runs from June through November, and the farms produce more than 10 million tons per year.

Why do most of the mass-marketed tomatoes have lesser flavor and texture than home-grown?

1. The flavor of these tomatoes is relatively bland and the texture cottony because commercial growers harvest them with days of handling and shipping in mind. Tomatoes are still green when picked, immature. This is done because the green unripe tomatoes are less fragile, less perishable and better shippers.
2. They are red when they reach the store because they have been gassed with ethylene. If they had been left on the vine to ripen naturally they would have generated their own ethylene gas.
3. When plant geneticists developed these new strains of plants, their priority was tomatoes that would travel and store well, not flavor.
4. Many stores carry vine-ripened tomatoes, which are better-tasting but much more expensive.

Vegetables

How can whole tomatoes be preserved by freezing?

Just wash them and remove the stem end.

What can be done to ripen partially ripe or green tomatoes?

Let them finish their ripening process in a paper bag. This prevents the ethylene gas from the tomato from dissipating, instead concentrates it. Be sure to pierce the bag with a half dozen holes or so, well distributed, for in order to stay sound tomatoes need to take in oxygen and give off carbon dioxide.

How can green tomatoes be used?

1. Use in stir-fry.
2. Slice, dust with cornmeal and fry in a skillet with olive oil and clarified butter.
3. Slow roast.
4. Use in salsa.
5. Use in salads.

Are yellow tomatoes different?

They have lower acidity than red tomatoes, thus a milder flavor. They can be used like red tomatoes but are best eaten raw.

What can be done to improve the taste of out-of-season tomatoes?

Liven their taste with a little vinegar and sugar and/or other seasonings. Fresh plum tomatoes are often the best tasting out of the regular season.

How should tomatoes be refrigerated?

They shouldn't, because they are more flavorful when kept at 50 °F and less tasty when stored chilled.

What is the yield of tomatoes when pureed?

3 large tomatoes = 2 pounds = 3 cups puree.

What is the equivalent of fresh to canned tomatoes?

1½ cups chopped, fresh = 1 cup canned
2 pounds fresh = 3 cups or 28 ounces canned in juice.

What should you look for in selecting tomatoes?

1. The best are vine-ripened varieties, even though these are usually more expensive.
2. Sniff first for a fragrant scent. If they are fresh and flavorful they should emit an enticing, earthy, tomato aroma.
3. Color may be deceiving, since they are sometimes artificially reddened.
4. If they are to be used for cooking they can be soft and almost overripe.
5. Tomatoes continue to ripen after picking if kept above 55 °F. Below that temperature the color may deepen but the flavor doesn't.
6. To serve raw or to freeze make sure they aren't overly juicy and have no mushy spots.

How should tomatoes be handled after purchase?

1. If slightly under ripe, store in a pierced paper bag at room temperature for a day or two but when ripe use immediately or refrigerate.
2. They store better if placed stem down.
3. Never try to ripen in direct sunlight as they will lose most of their vitamins.
4. If the tomatoes haven't turned their final color, put them in indirect sunlight OR put in a paper bag (with holes) so that the gas emitted will help ripen them and check decay.
5. Store in baskets or bowls in which there is plenty of ventilation, and keep out of the refrigerator, for chilling dulls the flavor.
6. Refrigerate to prevent rotting of soft tomatoes but take them out long enough before using so that they return to room temperature.

How should tomatoes be prepared?

1. Store-bought tomatoes should be washed gently but thoroughly with a vegetable brush or nylon scouring pad to help get rid of any possible chemical coating.
2. When cooking whole or quartered tomatoes in a sauce, soup or stew, either peel ahead of time or strain afterward, for otherwise the diner will be eating shriveled, unchewable skins. You don't have to peel them for cooking purposes if they will be fine chopped first, since the pieces of skin will be so small.
3. Slice with a serrated knife (e.g., a bread knife) to avoid tearing the skin.

How should tomatoes be prepared for sauces?

Drop into rapidly boiling water, immediately remove with a slotted spoon and put into iced water. Then pull away the skin, cut in half and squeeze out the seeds and coarsely chop.

How can they be peeled?

1. To peel them, put them in a pot of boiling water for 15–60 seconds, depending on their size and then immediately submerge them in cold water. The skins will come off easily if the tomatoes are reasonably ripe.
2. Pierce with a fork and hold over a direct flame (gas) until the skin shrivels.

How should tomatoes be cut for salads?

Cut them in wedges instead of slices if you want to minimize the amount of juice that coats the lettuce leaves and thus dilutes the dressing.

How should they be cooked?

Don't cook tomatoes in untreated aluminum or cast-iron pots, since the acid of the tomato reacts with the metal and gives the tomato a brownish tinge and adversely affects the flavor.

Should a raw tomato sauce be refrigerated before using?

No, set aside at room temperature, for it will lose its flavor if chilled.

What are the advantages of plum tomatoes?

1. Out of season they are probably the best tasting on the market.
2. They have less juice and therefore a sauce made from them won't be so watery.
3. They taste good.
4. The canned ones are very good.

How should sun-dried tomatoes be reconstituted?

If dry: Cover with boiling water, let stand 15 minutes and drain.

In oil: Drain and use.

With what foods do oven-dried tomatoes go?

In salads or tossed with pasta.

How should they be stored?

In oil and refrigerated. Will keep several months.

How can you give flavor to old or bland tomatoes?

Blanch and season with dill or other herbs.

TURNIPS

What should be looked for in selecting turnips?

1. Avoid darkening, softness or sponginess at the stem.
2. Choose small to medium sized ones, which are sweeter.

Why are young turnips more attractive?

The flesh becomes coarse and stronger as it ages.

How should they be prepared?

Handle them much like a potato.

What can be done to make turnips taste better?

They mix well when pureed and are more attractive with mashed potatoes or carrots or applesauce.

Can turnip greens be used?

1. Discard the stems, for they give a harsh taste.
2. They can be used interchangeably with beet greens or Swiss chard.
3. If tough, first blanch them before cooking.

Why should the cooking water of turnips never be salted?

It removes the sweetness of the turnips.

How should turnip greens be selected?

Pick those without any yellowing, rather look for bright green.

How should they be cooked?

1. Softly, gently.
2. They do well Spanish style with oil, garlic and chorizo.
3. They can be added to potato or bean soups.

WATER CHESTNUTS

What are water chestnuts?

An edible tuber, chestnut shaped, mahogany colored, but not a member of the chestnut family.

How are they used?

Lightly boiled or simmered, then chopped and added to other dishes to give a crunchy texture and a slightly sweet flavor.

What is chestnut powder?

Also called chestnut flour, it is used as a thickener or a coating (dredge) before frying.

How should they be stored?

After being washed and dried, they can be stored several days in a plastic bag in the refrigerator.

WATERCRESS

What is watercress?

It is a member of the mustard family that has a strong, peppery flavor and small, tender leaves. It was originally from Asia Minor and the Mediterranean region. It grows wild by streams.

What should be watched out for when buying?

Avoid bunches with wilted or yellow leaves.

What is the nutritive value of watercress?

It is high in calcium and vitamins A and C.

Can it be used raw?

After removing the tough stems, it can be used raw in salads and sandwiches to give a peppery taste.

How should watercress be stored?

After being washed and dried, it can be stored several days in a plastic bag in the refrigerator.

Can it be cooked?

Cooked in soups or stir-fried or sautéd with meats or alone as a side dish.

When a recipe calls for a bunch of watercress how much should it weigh?

About 7 ounces.

YAMS—see SWEET POTATOES

ZUCCHINI (COURGETTE)

How do you select zucchinis?

1. The most tender and delicately flavored are the small, young ones. Use the larger ones for pureeing or cutting into long, fine noodles or for stuffing.
2. Reject them if their skins are cut, coarse, bruised or dull. The zucchini should not be waxed.
3. If it has lost its firmness, it is past its prime.

How should raw zucchini be used?

For salads, raw and not peeled, diced or thinly sliced.

How should they be cooked?

1. They are good steamers but poor for simmering.
2. They bake well if kept moist.
3. They bake well halved, with the center scooped out and then filled with a somewhat moist filling such as with a crumb/cheese/oil mixture.
4. To minimize a watery consistency, cook quickly with a high heat.
5. When batter-fried, salt before cooking.
6. Small ones can be roasted whole when tossed with a little oil.
7. When cut into long noodle shapes, quickly blanch, drain and toss with a dressing or mix with pasta.

Do they combine well with other foods?

Their mild flavor allows them to be used with both subtle and intense flavorings.

What should be done with the yellow zucchini flowers?

They are edible by themselves when sautéd or lightly battered and fried.

What can be done with overcooked zucchini?

Puree it to make a soup or bread.

CHAPTER THIRTEEN

UTENSILS

MISCELLANEOUS KITCHEN TOOLS

Why is the small instant thermometer better than a traditional one (that is kept in the roast during the entire time in the oven) better for checking temperature of roasting meat?

1. An instant thermometer is more accurate.
2. It makes a smaller hole in the meat and therefore less juice escapes.
3. The small, instant thermometer allows you to check in various places.

How does a vacuum bottle, like a Thermos, know whether to keep a liquid hot or cold, and how does it do it?

It doesn't know, it just maintains isolation. Heat travels in the direction of the colder region, whether away from hot point or toward a cold one. It travels by conduction (direct contact) or convection (motion, currents) or radiation. The vacuum bottle blocks these three paths by glass liners to reduce conduction, a near vacuum space to reduce convection and its silver inner lining to reduce radiation.

How can cleaning a cheese grater be made easier?

1. Lightly spray the grater with nonstick oil before using.
2. Rub a raw potato over it before washing.
3. Use a pastry brush or toothbrush to remove citrus zest or other material grated.

How can large ice cubes be made?

Use cardboard milk cartons for the mold.

What can a simple blender do as well or better than a food processor?

Shredding, slicing, grating, chopping, grinding nuts, making bread crumbs, handling small amounts.

What is a blender best for?

Making pesto, frozen drinks, crushing or breaking ice, making very smooth soups.

How can apples or stuffed peppers keep their shape when baked?

Use a well-greased muffin tin.

What is the difference between Japanese and Chinese chopsticks?

Japanese have pointed ends, Chinese blunt ones.

How should measuring cups be selected?

1. Buy heavy gauge material—metal, glass or plastic.
2. They should have easy-to-read markings for accuracy of measurement.
3. For dry ingredients the top measurement should be at the top so any excess can be smoothed off with a knife blade in order to get greater accuracy.

What is a baker's peel?

A flat wooden or metal paddle for removing bread or pizza from the oven.

What can be substituted for a pastry bag?

Use a plastic sandwich bag, cut off a small piece of one corner and insert a metal decorating tip.

How can the life of a rubber spatula be extended?

1. Don't put it in the dishwasher drying cycle.
2. If the edge becomes ragged, trim it with a scissors.

Which is the best timer?

One that fits on your belt, so that you won't miss the alarm sounding.

What is a zester?

A stainless steel tool with notched edges that cut ¼″ strips from the rinds of oranges or lemons.

If a zester is not available what can be used?

A fruit peeler and then cut or mince the strips.

How can kebobs be kept from spinning on the skewer?

Use a two-prong steel skewer with thin, double blades.

How can a funnel be improvised?

1. Cut a corner off of a plastic bag.
2. Make a funnel out of a double thickness of aluminum foil.

CUTTING BOARDS

How should wood cutting boards be selected and handled?

1. Make sure the wood is fine grained.
2. Before using the first time, rub in a light coat of nontoxic mineral oil.
3. Always have a separate board for meat.

How should a wood board be cleaned?

1. Clean by washing with soapy water, rinsing quickly, then wiping dry with toweling.
2. Don't soak it or run it through the dishwasher.
3. If used for cutting meat occasionally scour it with a paste of baking soda and water.

How should a wooden board be stored?

Vertically.

How should a plastic board be cleaned?

1. Clean it after each use with soap and water, rinsing, then drying with toweling.
2. Periodically put it in the dish washer, vertically, and let it go through the complete cycle.

How should a plastic cutting board be stored?

It, too, should be stored vertically.

What can be done if the plastic surface loses its smoothness, i.e., becomes chipped or badly cut?

Discard it, for the breaks in the surface become good nesting places for food poisoning bacteria.

Does the cutting surface affect a knife's sharpness?

The harder the surface, the more quickly a knife dulls. Hard surfaces include metal, marble, granite, tile, china and most countertops.

What is the advantage and disadvantage of a wooden cutting surface?

The softest cutting surface, and therefore the most desirable, is wood. Though softwood does less harm to the knife, it doesn't last as long and is more absorbent of juices etc., so hardwood is mostly used and is better.

What is the advantage of polyethylene boards?

These boards work quite well, except for the molded ones, which often deliberately do not have a smooth surface, don't clean as easily and can become unsanitary.

What should be avoided in storing a board?

Avoid nicking the hard surface such as when inserting or withdrawing the board from it its storage area.

WHIPS (WHISKS)

What is most important in selecting a wire whip?

That the handle fits your hand. A handle of the right size allows for a strong, easy grip.

What is the best size for a whip?

They come in many shapes and sizes. The 8″ and 10″ whips are most popular. The bigger the job, the more wires there should be.

What is the best number of wires to get sufficient aeration?

To achieve more air whipped into the mixture, ten wires should be the minimum for most jobs. The more wires, the more air enclosed.

Which is the best shape for whipping egg whites?

The balloon shape is best.

Why should the point of the whip be narrow?

The point should be narrow enough to reach into any corners of the pan or bowl.

Should the wires be strong or very flexible?

1. Flexible and thin are best for beating air into light batters.
2. Strong are best for heavy batters.

STRAINERS

What is the difference between a colander and a strainer?

Both strain, but the colander has larger holes and also has legs so that it will stand up by itself. A strainer must be hand-held or set over a pan.

What is a colander best for?

It is best for cleaning or draining larger pieces of food.

What is the best shape for a strainer?

Conical, because it is easier to press juices out from the solids as they drop to the bottom.

What should be used to press out juices through a strainer?

A cone-shaped wooden rod works very well with a funnel-shaped strainer. In any case, use a wooden instrument, such as spoon, instead of a metal one to press the food.

Why should a sieve be washed promptly?

Because when food particles dry they are difficult to dislodge from the holes.

ROLLING PINS

What is the American rolling pin?

It is cylindrical and has a metal dowel running through the center with handles on either end. About 10″ to 15″ (exclusive of handles). Best for heavy bread dough since the ball bearings and handles allow extra pressure to be exerted.

Which are the French style pins?

They are 18″ to 20″ long without handles. Simply a round piece of hardwood. Gives a good feel of the dough being rolled, since your hands are directly on the barrel.

What is the tapered French style?

In the French style, also without handles, but narrower at the ends than in the middle. Good for lighter, more delicate dough.

What is the advantage of the French pin?

It helps prevent the pastry dough from being too thin at the edges.

How can the tapered pin be used for pie crust?

By anchoring at one end with one hand it can be useful for round pastries, such as pie crust.

What is the Scandinavian pin?

It is an American-style pin with handles, but the surface is notched with indentations to make Swedish flatbread.

When a pin is not available what can be used in an emergency?

A wine bottle.

STOVES AND OVENS

Which are better, gas or electric ranges and ovens?

Ideally, in my experience, a gas stove top and an electric oven, but there are some who favor gas ovens.

What are the advantages of gas stove tops?

1. They respond to temperature adjustments more quickly.
2. They can be set to more different temperatures.
3. If something starts to boil, it takes only a moment to turn down the heat, but an electric coil will take several minutes to cool down.
4. Gas can be a lot hotter, more focused, than the electric.

What is the advantage of an electric top?

1. The stove may be better in maintaining a consistent very low heat.
2. Some electric tops are easier to clean.

What is the best lineup of burners?

In line, that is, four side-by-side across without back burners.

What are the advantages of electric ovens?

1. They maintain a more constant temperature.
2. They are more accurate, especially at low temperature settings.
3. Electric can be self-cleaning.
4. Electric heats the kitchen less.

What are things to check when selecting an oven?

Capacity, cleaning facility, timing devices, convection, strong doors (when open) for resting pans.

What are the disadvantages of electric ovens?

1. Electric usually requires more maintenance.
2. They are shorter-lived than gas ovens.

What are the disadvantages of gas ovens?

1. Many gas ovens, unless turned on full blast, fluctuate by 25 degrees or more.
2. Some have distorted readings, even at their hottest.

What is a convection oven?

It has a blower or fan that increases the circulation of the hot air molecules.

Is a convection oven better than a traditional one?

1. It is a boon when roasting meat or poultry or baking bread and pastry.
2. The temperature is more uniform throughout the oven, meaning more even cooking and browning especially the underside of the item being cooked.
3. The required cooking temperature is lower, baking temperatures about 50 degrees lower.
4. Baking time can usually be reduced almost a third.
5. Most meats won't require basting.
6. Energy savings are often realized.
7. Pan placement is not such a sensitive issue, since the hot air is constantly moved about.
8. Requires minimal preheating.

What are the cautions to be taken with a convection oven?

1. Unless you are used to the faster cooking time that comes with this oven, over-baking/cooking might occur the first few times that you use it.
2. They can harden and crack crusts before the inside of the bread loaf is cooked through.

Why is self-cleaning not completely possible in a gas oven?

It takes a temperature of 1,000 °F to disintegrate clinging grease into fine particles. Gas ovens do not reach this temperature.

Should you buy a restaurant-style oven/stove for your home?

Not unless you have sufficient ventilation (because they generate considerable heat and fumes, which may scorch wood walls and shelves) and a sufficient energy source (they demand more).

What is best for home use?

Commercial quality that is designed for home use.

Why is it important to have a clean oven?

Because small pieces of residue can start smoking at high temperatures and set off the smoke alarm.

What are the advantages of a restaurant stove/oven?

1. Both baking and cooking will be faster.
2. Stir-frying can be done more efficiently.

What are the disadvantages?

1. The amount or level of heating is more than you are used to and so the danger of burning food is high unless close attention is paid.
2. Often the gas supply in a home is insufficient to obtain the benefits that should come.
3. Many home kitchens don't have adequate heat/smoke removal.

What are the types of hoods?

1. One sucks air out of the kitchen to the exterior.
2. The other only filters and recycles the air and is therefore less efficient.

What should be the size of a hood?

It should cover both the front and rear burners and be big enough to extend over the edges of the stove at least 3″.

What height above the stove should the hood be?

No more than 20″ above the burners or it becomes less effective.

Which is the better hood filter: a baffle or wire mesh filter?

Baffles, for they are less likely to become clogged.

What should be the shape of the exhaust ducts?

Round.

How long does it take to preheat an oven?

About twenty minutes, but this varies. The older the stove, usually the longer it takes to preheat.

How reliable are oven settings?

Many give false readings by as much as 25 degrees or even as much as 75 degrees, which is enough to cause trouble. Test the oven at least twice a year (or more often) with a reliable thermometer.

What will happen if the oven reading is off and the temperature is too low?

For example, a pie dough baked in a cooler than required oven will not form steam quickly enough for flaky expansion, and the proteins might not set soon enough so that the texture will not be at its best.

What should be done if the readings are off?

The dials in some oven gauges can be adjusted, but for those that can't you will have to make a mental adjustment. Thus, if the oven is producing a temperature that is 25 degrees too high, the setting must be 25 degrees lower.

What should you keep in mind when using an oven?

1. Preheat long enough to reach the desired temperature.
2. Never overload the oven, because you will achieve poor results.

What should be kept in mind when baking?

When two racks, one over another, are filled with pans of cakes or cookies, often neither bakes well. The lower rack ones are usually too brown on the bottom and uneven on top. Those on the upper rack are too dark on top and often half-baked on the bottom.

Where should pans be placed in the oven?

1. Most cakes, cookies and puff pastries bake best on the second rack from the bottom.
2. Put filled tarts on the lowest rack, because they need more intense heat from underneath to help bake through properly.
3. Put unfilled pastry shells and tartlets on the second rack, so that the heat is even all around.

How should the top rack be used?

The top rack is best when the tops of tarts or other pastry need a last-minute browning or when broiling meat or fish.

What will happen if food is placed on the top rack?

This can result in a browned top and an uncooked bottom.

Is this true for a convection oven?

Convection ovens minimize this problem.

What should be looked out for when using a convection oven?

Foods brown quickly, so they to be may needed, cover but covered casseroles are not affected.

What time adjustment should be made when using a convection oven?

Temperature setting: 25 degrees less.

Timing: 1–2 minutes less for short cooking (15 minutes or less)

                       5 minutes less for 30 minutes of cooking.

What are factors that influence baking time?

1. Accuracy of the temperature setting.
2. If a range of time is given in a recipe, always check for doneness when the shortest time given has elapsed.
3. Both the size of a pan and the material it is made from influence baking time.
4. If the recipe is doubled or halved, the baking time must be adjusted.
5. Extremes of weather conditions, i.e., hot or cold, can affect the ingredients and therefore the required baking time.

Is the toothpick test always accurate?

Toothpick tests are useful but not for every cake. Over-baked cakes always produce clean toothpicks.

What adjustments need to be made when baking at high altitudes?

Temperature: Over 3,500' altitude, increase the temperature setting 25 degrees.

Flour: Continue adding 1 tablespoon of flour for each 1,500' above 3,500'. Thus at 5,000' add 2 tablespoons.

Leavening: If 1 teaspoon is required at sea level, then

               $\frac{2}{3}$ teaspoon at 3,500'

               $\frac{1}{2}$ teaspoon at 5,000'

               $\frac{1}{3}$ teaspoon at 6,500'

               $\frac{1}{4}$ teaspoon above 6,500'

What effect does using glass dishes or Corningware in the oven have on temperature demand?

Because glass conducts heat so well, the temperature setting can be reduced 25 degrees.

MICROWAVING

How does a microwave work?

Electromagnetic waves produced are scattered by a fan-like reflector. These waves penetrate the food and cause the water and other liquid molecules to vibrate and bounce against each other. These collisions create friction, which, as a by-product, produce the heat that cooks or warms the food. The plate holding the food is not heated by these electrical waves because it is solid and its molecules do not become agitated. If it gets hot it is because heat is transferred from the cooking food.

What are the advantages of microwaving?

1. Speed. Food cooks in almost a quarter of the time, because the food cooks from within.
2. Cost, requires one-fourth the power.
3. Baked goods rise higher.
4. No heat or odors are given off to the kitchen.
5. Utensils are easy to clean.
6. Makes cooking without fat easier.
7. There is less loss of nutrients.
8. Preserves flavors.
9. Makes reheating a cooked dish easier.

What are the disadvantages of microwaving?

1. Baked goods don't brown as well, or not at all.
2. Meats tend to have a mushy center.
3. Can't use metal pots or dishes, because of the possibility of arcing (electric spark) when the pot is close to the wall. Also they reflect the electromagnetic waves and thus cause uneven cooking.
4. Frozen foods take a long time to cook because the water molecules are frozen solid and the microwaves don't agitate them, but frozen foods can be defrosted in the microwave.
5. Foods must be chopped evenly in order to get an even cooking.
6. Foods, with skins, like sausages and baked potatoes will explode if the skin is not pierced.
7. Flans and tarts cooked *with* filling in them tend to become soggy.
8. Squid will toughen.

Utensils

What is the advantage of a turntable?

More even heating.

How should food be placed in the microwave oven?

If cooking several pieces, place them on the plate with the narrow point of the food towards the middle.

What are some things that microwaving is good for?

1. Melting chocolate and crystallized sugar.
2. Defrosting breads, buns, bagels.
3. Heating maple syrup or softening clumped brown sugar.
4. Softening cream cheese or butter.
5. Cooking bacon, particularly with a ridged bacon dish that will give very crisp slices.
6. Cooking polenta and some vegetables such as asparagus or corn on the cob that has been rinsed in water with the husk still on.

Are racks to stack one dish above another worthwhile?

The results will be uneven and the cooking will take longer.

What governs cooking time?

1. The wattage of the oven: the higher the power, the less time.
2. The amount of food being cooked: the more food the more time.
3. The thicker the food, the longer time.

Can applesauce be made in the microwave?

Yes, cover with plastic and cook the apples until very soft.

Which foods should not be cooked by microwaving?

1. Pastry.
2. Soufflés, meringues.
3. Gratins, where a browned top is critical.
4. Broiled, grilled meat or fowl.
5. Fried foods.
6. Eggs in their shells.
7. Food with a high water content.
8. Foods with irregular shapes, such as poultry legs.
9. Baked goods where browning is necessary.

What should you look for in buying dishes for microwaving?

1. Labeled "suitable for microwaving."
2. No metal rim.

3. Straight sides for even cooking and stirring.

4. Casseroles with lids for dishes that require stirring.

How can you tell if a container is safe for microwaving?

Place the container next to a half-full cup of water and use full power for 1 minute.

If the container gets hot, don't use it.

If the container is warm, it is ok for warming.

If the container is cold, it is ok for general use.

What containers should not be used?

1. Metal reflects microwaves back against the magnetron (wave source) and can damage the oven and cause sparking.

2. Any dishes with silver or gold decorations.

3. Wood stands that might split.

4. Plastic containers that might melt because of heat transference.

Is timing the same from one microwave oven to another?

No! They vary considerably. Some have no settings for different power strengths. Some can be set to higher powers than other.

What are safety precautions in using a microwave?

1. Have holes in the lid or plastic covering so steam won't burn you when uncovering the container.

2. Remove the container with a pot holder.

3. Use microwave safe cookware, such as glass, ceramic glass, paper towels, waxed paper.

What happens when poultry is cooked at highest power?

It will be dry and stringy. Microwave ovens work better for poultry at medium-to-low power.

How should whole potatoes be baked?

1. Pierce both top and bottom ends to release the steam produced.

2. Make sure the potatoes are 1" apart from each other.

3. Put them on paper toweling to absorb moisture.

4. Don't cover or wrap in foil.

What can be done to make microwaved potatoes even better?

The results will be even more attractive if the potatoes are finished for 10 or 15 minutes in a hot oven.

What are some guidelines for microwaving?

1. Vegetables that are very fresh, and therefore have a high water content, will cook faster than older ones that have lost much of their moisture.

Utensils

2. Cheese, such as Gruyère, tends to become rubbery, so it should be added near the end of the cooking.

3. The colder the food, the longer the cooking time required. Starting with the food at room temperature is best.

4. Seasoning and spices become more pronounced.

5. Foods with irregular shapes should be turned midway in cooking.

6. Foods have to be covered unless the moisture content is reduced, such as frozen spinach.

7. Cooking continues after the power is off, so allow for this in timing.

8. Don't place food to be cooked directly on the bottom of the microwave, rather put it on a plate or other container or wrap it in waxed paper or plastic.

Is much time gained in cooking pasta or rice in the microwave?

Very little, not worth the bother and, additionally, there is the possibility of it boiling over.

What is a good use for the microwave with pasta or rice?

It is very good for reheating such dishes.

Do microwaves work at different speeds on different foods?

Fats and sugars absorb microwave energy more efficiently than do water and other liquids. Thus foods with high sugar or fat content will cook faster. The microwave is, therefore, good for softening such items as cream cheeses, butter, brown sugar (that has hardened) but heats water no faster than the stove top.

What penetration into food do microwaves have?

Microwaves penetrate food up to about 1–1½″ thick, so if the food is thicker, be prepared to turn it over midway in the cooking.

How will the amount of food affect the timing?

The greater the mass of food, the longer it will take to cook. If the recipe is doubled, then probably the time required will be half again more.

Is there an advantage to boning meat before microwaving?

Yes, with the bone out the cooking will be more regular.

What are special considerations in cooking lamb?

1. Since it is high in fat, lamb lends itself to microwaving.

2. Avoid irregular pieces such as shoulder or leg.

3. Bone the meat.

4. Use a meat thermometer to achieve a rare piece of meat.

What must be done to achieve a 'rare' finish?

It must be watched carefully, checked frequently and turned.

Utensils

How should food be arranged on a dish?

1. If cooking a small amount of small pieces, it doesn't matter. Just heat for about half the expected cooking time, stir and then finish cooking.
2. If there are pieces such as legs of chicken that don't lend themselves to stirring, then put the larger parts on the outer perimeter.
3. If there are thick pieces, such as chops, then turn them over halfway through.
4. If feasible, put the food in a ring with the center open (like a donut shape) with the thickest portions pointed to the outside so the cooking time will be shorter and the cooking more even.

What precaution should be taken when microwaving with the food covered with paper toweling to prevent spattering?

Only use toweling without any printed design as the printing ink might be transferred to the food.

Should the food be covered with plastic wrap?

Yes, especially with delicate foods, to promote more even defrosting, to help retain nutrients and to keep the heating time to a minimum and thus retain the flavor at its best.

Won't the accumulation of steam, if covered with plastic, be undesirable?

1. While the accumulation of steam is desirable for some foods, too much is not, so make a small vent at one corner so some part of the steam can escape.
2. Don't use a covering for whole, unpeeled potatoes.

What happens if the microwave is empty when the power is turned on?

The mechanism may be damaged.

What is necessary for popping corn?

1. Do not try if the oven capacity is less than 500 watts.
2. The kernels should be fresh, i.e., not dried out.
3. Do not use any oil or butter.
4. Put a small quantity in a small brown bag and gently fold over the top. The bag will help to absorb the moisture that would toughen the popped corn.

KNIVES

Which kind of knives are the most dangerous?

Dull ones.

Utensils

Why are they more dangerous?

1. People tend to be more careful with sharp knives.
2. The duller the knife, the more apt it is to slip while cutting, because it requires more downward pressure.
3. Sharp knives are easier to work with and do the job quickly.
4. Sharp knives make clean cuts, thin slices.

What are safety precautions when working with knives?

1. Always warn fellow workers when carrying a knife.
2. Always carry a knife with the pointed end down and the blade side away from you.
3. Always place a knife on the work counter so the entire tool rests on the surface and no part extends beyond the edge. If it does then it may be knocked off by someone passing by.
4. Never place a knife where it can't be seen, such as in a pile with other utensils or in a sink covered with water.
5. Always dry blades from the back spine to the cutting edge.

How should knives be transferred from on person to another?

Lay the knife on a counter so that the other person can pick it up.

Will a first-class, well-made, properly stored knife need resharpening?

It will require routine maintenance, but the better the knife, the longer it will retain its cutting ability.

Why choose a heavy blade (for its type)?

Less force is necessary for cutting, and also the side of the blade can be used for crushing herbs or spices.

How long should a good kitchen knife last?

A lifetime.

How often does a good knife need sharpening?

Rarely if the blade is regularly maintained on a sharpening (or butchers) steel.

What happens if a blade is allowed to oxidize?

The oxidation contributes to dullness.

What is the worst way to sharpen a knife?

The worst way is one of the coarse grinding wheels or belts used by key makers or peddlers. Repeated sharpening on these will wear away the blade in a few years. Almost as bad are the small, rotating disk cylinder types that attach to a kitchen door or cabinet or are hand-held. They devour the metal and also tend to scratch the blade and throw it out of alignment.

What is the best way to sharpen a knife?

The best is the butcher's (or sharpening) steel, which dresses, not sharpens, the blade. Dress before and after each time you use the knife and frequently during a larger job. You can pull the blade toward or away from you. Use one side of the steel for one side of the blade, the opposite side for the other side.

How can the sharpness of a blade be tested?

Hold a piece of paper in front of you and make a downward slice. The blade is sharp if the cut is smooth and the paper doesn't crumble.

How does the shape of the butcher steel affect the job?

Round: Most used, easiest to store in a knife block.

Oval: Has more contact with the blade.

Flat: Greatest contact with blade, needs fewer passes.

What are the kinds of sharpening steel?

Regular cut, fine cut, polished.

What is the difference in effect of the cut?

Polished: Does no sharpening, only realigns the edge.

Fine: Does a little sharpening.

Regular: Does a little more sharpening.

How can you tell the type of a sharpening steel?

Look for the grit number. The large the number, the smaller and finer the grit, but often they are only classified as coarse or fine.

What angle should the blade be to the sharpening steel?

15–20 degrees.

What are the main considerations in using a sharpening steel?

1. Stroke the whole length of the blade.
2. Use the right angle and keep it constant.
3. Use a light touch.

What should be done if the knife is too dull for the butcher's steel?

1. Use a whetstone (a block of exceptionally hard silicon carbide or carborundum).
2. Place the stone on a flat, stable surface and make sure there is plenty of lubricating oil.
3. Draw the knife across the stone at the same 20-degree angle that you would use with the butcher's steel. Do this several times on both sides of the blade.

4. Work across the coarser grit, then finish with the finer grit. Good stones are often coarse on one side and smooth on the other. Repeat the process five or six times until the blade is sharp. A final touch on the butcher's steel is recommended.

5. Use a good electric sharpener.

Are electric sharpeners recommended?

Those that have multiple sharpening and buffering wheels with different levels of coarseness, such as Chef's Choice, work very well.

What is a good procedure for keeping a whetstone in good condition?

While oil can be added during the sharpening process, prior to sharpening, lightly coating the whetstone with oil is recommended.

What is the purpose of putting a coating of oil or water onto the sharpening stone in honing a knife?

The liquid is there to keep the metal particles from the blade from clogging the pores of the stone, and thus glazing it.

How should a serrated knife be honed?

Sharpening the serrations correctly is very difficult and needs be done only by experts. However, Chef's Choice Select 120 now has a method for serrated blade sharpening. There are thin serrated knife sharpeners on the market.

What is the bolster of a knife?

The collar or shank at the point where the blade meets the handle.

What is the tang of a knife?

The part projecting from the blade that extends into the handle.

What are two wise rules when buying/using kitchen knives?

1. Buy quality carbon steel or high-carbon stainless.
2. Keep them well-honed.

What is a forged blade?

A single piece of steel is heated until it is soft and then shaped by a mechanical hammer. Tends to be a heavy, relatively thick blade with a bolster to add strength where the blade meets the handle. Also has a guard, often a full tang that helps provide weight and balance. The blade is then tempered by repeated heating and cooling to achieve the desired hardness and flexibility.

What is the disadvantage of a plain, stainless steel knife?

Although stainless steel will stay sharp for an extended time it gradually loses its edge and the blade is virtually impossible to resharpen.

What is a stamped knife?

A blade stamped from a single sheet of steel. Relatively light in weight.

What is sintering?

The blade, bolster and tang are forged separately and then welded together. Hinckels Company manufacturers claim this allows them to use the best kind of steel for each part.

How should a knife blade be heated?

It should not be heated, because exposure to high heat will cause permanent damage.

How many different knives should a cook have?

A good starter set would be six, with emphasis on quality, not quantity.

1. A 3″ to 4″ (blade length) paring knife.
2. A 6″ utility knife.
3. An 8″ serrated slicing knife.
4. A 10″ chef's knife for slicing and chopping.
5. A 10″ nonserrated slicing knife for carving.
6. A 10″ butcher's steel for honing.

Of these six, which are the most important?

1, 3, 4 and 6 but cooks eventually increase their collection in order to do specific jobs better.

What is the difference between a slicer and a carver?

Only the length of the blade: a carver is 8″ or less, a slicer 10″ or more.

What should you look for when buying a kitchen knife?

1. Carbon steel or high-stainless.
2. A quality manufacturer.
3. The tang (the part of the metal enclosed in the handle) should run the full length of the handle and be well secured by at least three rivets or some other method.
4. The handle should be easy to grasp and feel comfortable in your hand. Try the grip to see how it fits your hand. It should feel like an extension of your hand. Make sure the bulge in the handle put there by the manufacturer fits the way you like to hold the knife.
5. The handle should be a poor conductor of heat, such as hardwood or modern plastic, but be careful of plastic hilts as they be made of cheap material that won't hold up.
6. It is the right style for what you want to do.
7. Make sure the knife is free from defects or flaws.
8. There are no gaps between the blade and the handle that are left open or filled with putty or plastic.

Which are better, wood or plastic handles?

Both are good materials.

How can you test for balance of a knife?

Pinch the blade at its base (next to the handle) and lift up. It should be balanced and not tilt up or down.

How do carbon steel and stainless knives differ?

Both have blades of steel, which is an alloy mainly of iron mixed with carbon and a smaller amount of other elements. The critical difference is that the carbon steel has a higher carbon content, while the stainless has more chromium and often some nickel.

What are the pros and cons of carbon steel?

Carbon steel will take a sharper edge but dulls faster and can discolor, rust and pit more easily. It is more brittle and can break under stress.

What are the pros and cons of stainless?

It is more difficult to give it a good edge, but once achieved will hold it longer.

What is high carbon stainless steel?

It is halfway between the two, a relatively new development. Won't discolor or rust as easily and takes a keener edge than regular stainless but not as keen as carbon steel. I find that I automatically used my high carbon knives more often since I automatically and frequently use my butcher's steel.

What are two ways to clean a discolored carbon steel blade?

1. With scouring powder on half a lemon.
2. Sprinkle salt on the end of a cork and scrub the blade with the cork.

What are the pluses and minuses of a tapered blade?

The taper gradually decreases in width and thickness, producing a hefty, very strong, resilient blade. The weight of the blade makes it easier to cut through food. Forged knives, the most expensive, are typically taper-ground.

What is a flat ground blade?

Flat ground blades have the same thickness from top to cutting edge. This is the cheapest to produce but is not necessarily low quality.

How should a knife and fork be used to turn a piece of meat?

Use tongs instead so that no holes are made, which would allow the juice to escape.

What are the two types of Chinese cleavers?

Meat and vegetable.

How can the meat cleaver be used?

The heavy blade is good for chopping chicken bones, flattening meat, chopping meat and can also be used on vegetables if your hand is strong.

What is the vegetable cleaver best for?

The delicate, sharp edge is similar to a chef's knife and is good to cut julienne, slicing and mincing.

What are the different weights of Chinese cleavers?

Heavy:	For chopping meat bones.
Medium:	For slicing and chopping poultry bones.
Light:	For carving boned meats, slicing, cutting vegetables.

What is the advantage of a hollow ground blade?

Can be very sharp, because the cutting edge is quite thin, but the hollowed out area can be weak and vulnerable to breakage.

What is the function of a slicing knife?

The slicing knife is relatively thin so that the friction and food crushing is minimal as the knife slides through the food. The thinner edge allows the carver to make narrower and more uniform slices, because the blade stays reasonably parallel to the face of the cut.

How does a chef's knife differ?

The chef's knife (also called a French knife) is broader on the top of its cross section, and its extra weight gives more power to help chop through firm food. It is also used for slicing.

How should a knife be cleaned?

1. Wipe the handle and the blade with a soapy sponge or dishrag.
2. Rinse, and dry with a soft towel.

How should a knife not be cleaned?

1. Don't put it into a filled sink or full pot, as you might grab the sharp blade by mistake.
2. Don't put the knife in the dishwasher, as the blade can become nicked as it is jostled about. Also the high heat can affect the tempering or split the handle.
3. Don't soak it, for that may harm a wooden handle.

How should knives be stored?

1. In a wooden knife rack.
2. On a magnetic bar.
3. In a partitioned drawer.

What is a mezzaluna?

The word means "half moon" in Italian and is a chopper with one, two or three parallel crescent-shaped blades. It is used to chop vegetables and herbs, because its design allows for an, easy, rhythmic, side-to-side chopping motion.

Ceramic Cutlery

What is ceramic cutlery?

Knife blades made from zirconium oxide or an advanced engineered ceramic known as Zirconia.

How hard is the blade?

This ceramic measures in hardness just below that of a diamond. On the hardness scale units are measured in "Mohs," the higher the number, the harder the material. Stainless steel is 5–6, zirconia 8.2, diamonds 10.

What are the advantages of ceramic knives?

1. Don't rust, stain or corrode.
2. Sharpness lasts a long time.
3. Cut and slice well.
4. Don't impart metallic taste or smell.
5. Easy to clean.

What are their disadvantages?

1. Have no flexibility so that they cannot be used for prying.
2. Cannot be used on meat with bones or they might break.
3. Should not be used on hard surfaces such as tile, only on hardwood or plastic board.
4. The blade cannot be realigned or sharpened on a sharpening stone.
5. A butcher's steel cannot be used for maintenance.

What is their basic use?

Slicing. Avoid chopping or prying.

How should they be cleaned?

With soap and liquid dish detergent. A mild cleanser can be used if any stain remains after regular washing.

How should they not be cleaned?

In the dishwasher.

How long will sharpness last on the blade?

From three months to three years on average.

Must they be thrown away when they dull?

No, they can be sent to Kyocera Company (800-537-0294), who will sharpen it on a commercial diamond sharpener.

What is a ceramic stick?

It looks like a small-sized butcher's stone, about 4" long, with a wooden or plastic handle, but it cannot be used on ceramic knives.

How should a ceramic stick be used?

The knife blade is held steady, and the stick is moved over the blade from the heel to the tip. The blade is then turned over and the action is repeated on the other side, or the stick may be alternated from one side to the other.

POTS, PANS AND BOWLS

What are characteristics of good cookware?

1. Heavy-gauge metal so heat will spread evenly.
2. Good conductivity so the outer perimeter should be at the same temperature as the inside.
3. The metal should be permanently chemically inert.
4. It should have stay-cool handles that are oven safe.

What is indicated if you find you must cook most dishes at high temperature?

Your pots are not conducting heat very well.

Why should baking tins be lightweight?

Lighter and medium-weight tins transmit heat evenly and quicker.

Which are better mixing bowls?

Stainless:
1. Convenient because they conduct heat and cold.
2. They are lightweight.
3. Virtually indestructible.

Glass:
1. Useful for whipping cream etc., because their extra weight prevents the bowl from moving around.
2. They are microwave and oven safe.

Why should a complete set be purchased when buying a bowl?

With nesting, storage space is saved.

Why is fast heat distribution necessary for a stove top pan?

Unless the heat can spread quickly through the entire bottom, hot and cold spots will develop directly over where the flame or electric coil comes in contact with the pan.

Why are hot spots a problem?

1. Hot spots scorch food, unless you lower the heat, which can result in insufficient heat to cook other portions of the food.
2. Hot spots are not so important when there is a generous amount of liquid in the pan.

What pan materials conduct heat the fastest?

Silver, copper, tin, aluminum.

What are the slowest?

Glass, porcelain, earthenware, pottery.

What are slow conductors good for?

These are good for servingware, since they give up heat so slowly that they will keep the food warm.

What are the medium conductors?

Cast iron, carbon (or rolled) steel, the sheet metal used to fashion woks and crepe pans, and at the low end of middle is stainless steel.

Does the thickness of the steel make a difference?

The thicker the gauge, the more uniformly a pot heats food and holds the heat better when food is added to a heated pan such as a searing piece of meat. Thinner pans also warp over time.

How can you test a pan for hot spots?

Pour a uniform layer of 4–5 tablespoons of sugar mixed with a couple of tablespoons of water into the pan, then turn the heat to low to medium and wait for the mixture to start to caramelize. If it caramelizes evenly there are no hot spots.

What can be done if a pot to be put into the oven does not have a lid?

Cut a piece of parchment paper slightly smaller than the top and put it onto the food. Then cover the top with foil. Not as good as a metal top, but is second best.

What are elements to look for when buying pots and pans?

1. Choose heavy-gauge material to prevent warping, denting and hot spots, so as to get even heating.
2. Select handles that are secure, sturdy and oven proof.
3. Favor a pan that feels right for your hand.
4. Select a pan that responds to heat quickly for sautéing or quick cooking.
5. Make sure the sides will heat quickly if the pan has high sides.
6. Make sure the lining is not reactive to acidic foods such as fruit, wine etc.
7. Use nonstick pans if reducing fat is an issue.

How should you handle a pan with stainless steel handles?

1. The handle will heat, so that it must be handled with a mitt or glove.
2. Choose a pan with a handle that narrows at one point, which will minimize heat transference from the pan to the part of the handle that will be held.

Why should a roasting pan have sides no higher than 2–3"?

So the steam will not be retained.

What type of pan should be chosen for large quantities?

For large amounts of food, such as soups that will stay on the stove for a long time, choose a heavy stockpot with a good cover.

What is a nonreactive pot?

One that is not sensitive to acids in foods or liquids.

What are cast iron pans recommended for?

Cast-iron pans are good for searing chops and steaks. You must keep the pan well seasoned.

How should you clean a pot with a residue of sugar/caramel?

First, soak it with cold water, not hot.

Why should a sauté pan have low sides?

With high sides, steam can be trapped and the food will be steamed instead of sautéd. This will also happen if the pan is covered.

Aluminum

What are the advantages of aluminum pans?

1. Low cost.
2. Low toxic effect.
3. Heat conductivity is second only to copper.
4. Lightweight and thus easily handled.

What are the problems with aluminum?

1. Because unanodized (not mixed with small amounts of magnesium and sometimes copper) it develops a thin oxide layer that is reactive to food molecules (acids, alkalis, hydrogen sulfide), which may discolor very light-colored foods.
2. It seems to intensify sulfurous odor of cabbages, broccoli and related vegetables, especially if they are overcooked.
3. Aluminum pots warp easily when subjected to abrupt changes in temperature and dent easily, especially if thin gauged.

Why does an aluminum pan stain some foods?

When an unlined aluminum pot is used to cook high alkali foods, such as potatoes, or the medium is hard water, or the pot has been washed with a high alkali cleaner, the metal's surface will stain. Then, when it is used to cook tomato sauce or other highly acidic ingredients such as onions, wine, lemon juice, the acid chemically removes some of the stain from the pot and it is transferred to the food. Not a health threat but it will not be good for aesthetics or taste.

What are the advantages of multi-ply bottomed pans?

1. The middle aluminum layer (between two stainless steel) cannot become discolored because it is completely enclosed.
2. The upper stainless steel layer won't develop hot spots by the time the heat reaches it because the heat has been diffused by the aluminum layer, which is an excellent conductor of heat.
3. Since the entire exposed surface is stainless it has an attractive finish and is easier to clean.
4. The ply structure decreases the possibility of warping.

Does the use of aluminum cookware cause Alzheimer's disease?

No one actually knows what causes this disease that impairs memory, thinking and behavior, but most scientists do not believe that aluminum is the cause.

Copper

What are the pluses of copper pots?

1. Very even heat distribution throughout the base and lower sides of the pan.
2. The copper distributes heat very quickly.
3. Unlined copper utensils are excellent for cooking sugar and whipped egg whites.
4. Beating egg whites in an unlined copper bowl results in an electrostatic charge that builds up between the metal whisk or beater and the copper. This charge allows the whites to incorporate more air, thereby making for a fluffier, more stable mass. The copper also helps to stabilize the puffiness so that adding cream of tartar to help stabilize is not usually necessary.

What are the negatives?

1. Copper utensils are very expensive.
2. If the copper becomes mottled with a black carbon deposit, the heat distribution is greatly impaired and hot spots develop.
3. Unlined copper will react with acid (tomatoes, vinegar, wine) and form a toxic compound.
4. The melting point of tin in tin-lined copper pots is quite low, about 450 °F, so these pots must be carefully used only with low cooking temperatures.

What is the upkeep of these pots?

They must periodically be relined with tin (tinned), because once the tin begins to wear away, too much of the copper is leaching into the foods and can be noxious. A few scratches won't be dangerous if you avoid dishes high in acid that chemically hasten the release of copper and its oxides.

Some come from the manufacturer with a protective lacquer coating. What must be done?

The coating must be removed before use. Submerge the pot in a solution of baking soda (¼ cup to 1 gallon hot water) and simmer gently for about a half hour. Then peel off the lacquer and wash and dry the pot.

What are the pluses of tin-lined copper cookware?

1. The tin doesn't affect flavor.
2. Tin is an excellent liner for copper pans and thus allows the cook to take advantage of the fast, even cooking of copper.
3. It prevents the copper from producing toxins in reaction with some foods.

What are the problems with the tin-lined?

1. Because tin has a low melting point (400 °F), it is not hard enough to use for making pans.
2. Even when used as a liner it will blister, wrinkle or melt if overheated.
3. It can easily be damaged by metal utensils.

What are the best ways to use tin-lined copper pans?

1. Cook over low to medium heat.
2. Never expose the pan to heat unless there is food in the pan with some liquid covering the pan's bottom surface.
3. Use only soap and water to clean, not an abrasive powder.
4. For stubborn food particles stuck to the pan, soak and then scrub gently with a plastic bristle brush.

How should copper pans be cleaned?

To clean copper use a mixture of one part vinegar or lemon juice and one part salt. Then rub the solution gently over the surface and rinse.

Even with proper care will the tin last?

Even with proper and careful care, the tin will wear off over time and should be re-tinned when the exposed copper reaches the size of a quarter or more.

Cast Iron

Why should you use cast-iron cookware?

1. It browns food well.
2. Food cooks evenly.
3. It is widely available.
4. It is inexpensive.
5. It develops a nonstick layer over the years, because of its porosity.

6. It lasts practically forever, is practically indestructible.

7. It retains heat well.

What happens to food cooked in cast iron?

Some foods cooked in cast iron contain more iron, up to double their original iron content.

Why shouldn't you use them?

1. They are heavy.

2. They are not good for highly acidic foods.

3. It takes time for the nonstick finish to develop, i.e., for the pan to become well seasoned.

4. They are slower to heat to cooking temperature.

5. They will rust if not dried after washing.

What happens when cast iron or a carbon-steel pot is seasoned?

The unseasoned surfaces are rather porous and have microscopic jagged edges. Rubbing the surface with oil and heating it 30–60 minutes and then cooling it to room temperature results in the oil filling the cavities. The baked oil becomes entrenched and, as well, rounds the sharp edges.

What are the benefits of seasoning these pots?

There are two benefits: the surface develops a nonstick quality, and the oil coating protects against rusting that would give the food an off-flavor.

How should the new cast iron be seasoned?

1. Melt some shortening in it.

2. With a soft cloth wipe the pot/pan and lid inside and out.

3. Cook a couple of hours in a 350 °F oven upside down with a drip pan underneath. Every half hour rewipe the pan with shortening to make a thin coating.

4. Let it cool in the oven.

5. Use the utensil a half dozen times with bacon, popcorn or something with fat.

6. After each of these uses don't wash, just drain off the residue, lightly rinse with scalding water and wipe dry.

7. Then the utensil can be used for stews, soups or other liquid dishes.

Once a pan has been seasoned can it be washed with soap?

It's all right to wash the pan briefly with a little soapy water if it is then thoroughly dried.

Why do pans sometimes become deseasoned?

1. Scratches, such as from a metal spatula.

2. Rust, which needs to be scoured with soap or detergent, which in turn removes the oil and calls for reseasoning.

Utensils

What happens if the damage is slight?

The pan will automatically reseason itself the next time it is used for frying.

What happens if the damage is severe?

1. It will require seasoning from scratch.
2. If rust has developed deep inside the pores of the interior surface, dump the pan into the trash bin.

What should be done to maintain the finish?

1. Remove the food immediately after cooking.
2. While still hot, rinse the pan with hot water and, if necessary, scrub with a stiff brush or rub a spoonful of salt on the interior.
3. If the food has stuck badly, fill with water and boil on the stove and then scrub with a stiff brush.
4. A good procedure is to add a little oil after drying, then wipe the excess off with a paper towel.

What shouldn't you do?

1. Don't use a wire brush or a steel pad.
2. Don't air dry, rather use a soft cloth.
3. Even better is to put the pan on a warm burner for a few minutes.
4. Don't store it with the lid on, for any residual moisture can cause rusting.
5. Don't used acidic foods unless the pan is very well seasoned.

What can you do if rust develops?

Rusted pans can be saved by remove the rust with steel wool and then reseasoning.

What is a platt pan?

A Swedish pan of heavy, cast iron with 7–9 shallow depressions into which batter is poured for frying Swedish pancakes.

What else can a platt pan be used for?

To make crumpets, English muffins, round fried eggs, silver dollar pancakes.

NONSTICK

What is nonstick cookware?

Cookware that does not react chemically with food, impart an off-taste and/or dull its color. Examples: glass, stainless steel, porcelain, hard anodized products like Calphalon.

Which are reactive pans?

Those that react with the food when in contact more than fifteen minutes. Examples: cast iron, aluminum.

What are the advantages of nonstick coatings?

1. Able to restrict fat usage.
2. Wash easily.
3. Good for sautéing, frying eggs etc.
4. The surface is much harder than stainless steel.

What is lost with the nonstick?

1. Loses some of the flavor normally derived from butter or fats.
2. Will discolor with misuse or time.
3. Many of the coatings are too thin and result in uneven heat distribution.
4. When the pan heats to close to 500 °F and is empty, the coating will start to boil off.

How do Teflon, Calphalon, Silverstone and similar nonstick surfaces work?

Teflon is a solid, slippery, chemically inert plastic (polytetrafluoroethylene) that is baked on the surface. Calphalon, anodyzed aluminum and Silverstone are similar but last longer. The best of these pans do not require oil or butter to keep food from sticking, but a light coat will enhance the cooking process, giving pancakes, sautéd meats and the like a golden color and a crisp texture. They are really low-stick rather than nonstick.

How should these pans be stacked in storage?

With paper toweling in between them.

Porcelain/Enamel

What are the drawbacks of porcelain/enamel pans?

1. Limited nonstick quality.
2. Difficult to clean charred food off the scorched pans.

Why can a quick temperature change shatter glass?

Glass has a natural brittleness and poor conductivity. It has low heat flow efficiency. When something hot is poured onto a cold glass bottom and it expands while the upper part hasn't yet expanded, cracking can ensue. Treated glass, such as Pyrex, is less vulnerable but it has its limitations. Corningware is even less susceptible to cracking.

With glass/porcelain/pottery what is the best procedure?

It is best to preheat the vessel with hot tap water before placing it a hot oven.

How can spots be removed from enamel pots?

Mix bleach with water and boil until the spots are gone.

Stainless

Why doesn't stainless steel rust?

When iron is exposed to air, it quickly oxidizes and forms a loose powder of ferric oxide. This is why pure iron is not found in nature. When chromium is mixed with iron in making stainless steel (in the molten state or as a coating), the chromium oxide forms a thick protective coating.

How can water spots be removed from stainless steel?

Put alcohol or white vinegar on a cloth and rub the spot.

Clay Pots

What is the advantage of clay pot cooking?

It is excellent for oven baking delicate foods, such as fish, where, by keeping them moist, it will help prevent them from overcooking in the intense oven heat.

What is the value of first soaking a clay pot in water?

When the pot is submerged in cold water for fifteen minutes, it will absorb water, which will then be released as it heats in the oven. This creates a steaming effect in the food.

Can you start the cooking process with the pot first on a stove burner and then bake it?

No, direct heat will probably cause the pot to crack.

How can you clean a clay pot with burned food stuck on it?

1. Scrub it with a nylon pad (never use stainless steel) with a little liquid soap.
2. Let the pot sit overnight with hot water and baking soda.
3. If necessary, fill with water, add baking soda and bake an hour at 400 °F.

What is the advantage of stoneware?

The glaze has been fired at a very high temperature so that the piece is durable, chip resistant and both dishwasher and oven safe.

Should clay pots be cleaned in a dishwasher?

No, because the clay is porous and can retain a soap residue.

What is the advantage of stoneware?

The glaze has been fired at a very high temperature so that the piece is durable, chip resistant and so is both dishwasher and oven safe.

PRESSURE COOKER

Why is a pressure cooker faster?

When the cooker is over high heat and the pressure builds, then temperature will be at about 250 °F instead of 212 °F of boiling water.

What is the advantage of this quick cooking?

1. The high pressure and super-heated steam tenderizes fibers and quickly mingles flavors.
2. Fewer nutrients are lost because the cooking is so fast.
3. The nutrients that are lost in steam condense back into the food rather than escaping into the air.
4. Less fat is required.
5. When making risotto it doesn't have to be stirred.

How full should the pressure cooker be filled?

Not more than ⅔ full for soups and high liquid dishes, ½ full for beans and grains, ¾ full for other foods, so that there is room for the steam pressure to build.

How does the size of the cooker influence cooking time?

While a larger pot takes longer to heat, the cooking time, measured from the time when the indicator reaches its proper point, is the same. Use a timer to avoid overcooking.

What is the difference between using the cooker on an electric versus a gas stove?

If the pressure is allowed to come down naturally, let the cooker sit on the turned-off burner if it is gas, but move to a cool burner or off the stove if it is electric, for it takes time for the electric coil to cool.

What is an important thing to check when cleaning the cooker?

See that the vent is not clogged.

What should be looked for when buying a pressure cooker?

1. A 6-quart size is probably the most all around useful, but a larger one (8–10-quart) is good for making larger quantities of soup or stocks.
2. Choose a cooker with a stainless steel bottom but made with aluminum or copper layers in order to get the best heat distribution.

How is pressure released?

It depends upon the cooker. Either cool it under running water for jiggle tops or, on the newer and more expensive models, they have a quick action release.

Utensils

ELECTRIC COOKER

What should be looked for in a deep-fryer?

1. Heat-proof handles.
2. A good frying basket that rotates.
3. At least a four-cup capacity and a volume large enough to prevent overflowing.

What is the key to how a rice cooker works?

When the rice is almost cooked, the cooker will automatically reduce the heat so that the rice will steam.

What is another use for a rice cooker?

It is good for reheating cooked rice.

FREEZER STORAGE

How should the freezer compartment be set?

At 0 °F or below.

How should casseroles be prepared for freezing?

1. Cook for a shorter time than normal.
2. Cool quickly to stop cooking.
3. Make sure it is packed as solidly as possible, the less air space the better.

What are some freezing tips?

1. Check the temperature of the freezer with a freezer thermometer.
2. Slightly undercook food before freezing, for when reheated it will cook further.
3. Freeze food in small portions, so that it will freeze quickly and be easier to defrost and reheat. Home refrigerators are not designed to have the capability of rapidly cooling foods in large containers or bulk.
4. Wrap food tightly or use heavy-duty freezer bags, squeezing the air out before sealing shut.
5. Remember that water expands as it freezes. Food with a high liquid content such as soup or stews will expand about 10%, so leave room at the top of the container.
6. To pre-cool before freezing, use water baths, shallow pans or a combination of procedures to get more rapid cooling.
7. Don't cover wire shelves in a freezer with foil or other material to get a "neat" look, because this reduces the free flow of the chilled air.

How should plastic wrap be used in freezing?

1. Place plastic wrap directly on the food surface to protect it against the dry freezer air.
2. If using plastic, use two layers, or one layer of plastic and an outer layer of foil.

How should foods to be frozen be stacked in the freezer?

Allow for circulation of chilled air around the containers. Don't tightly stack them in the freezer or refrigerator until cooled or frozen.

Should the freezer be fully filled?

1. Don't overfill. For the freezer to run the most efficiently it should be about ¾ full.
2. Don't overcrowd any part of the freezer compartment so air circulation is blocked.
3. Don't add too much fresh food all at once.
4. Put new additions in back and use food on a "first in, first out basis" (FIFO).

Is freezer burn dangerous?

Since the burn occurs from oxygen it will be safe to eat, but it will probably be dry and not taste very good.

How should frozen food be defrosted?

1. Put fruits and vegetables in the refrigerator overnight. Defrost carefully in the refrigerator or in a microwave.
2. Meats, poultry and fish can be defrosted in the refrigerator, but it can take several days.
3. In a hurry for meats and poultry? Put the bag in a pot of cold water for 3–4 hours.
4. Breads, cakes and other baked goods defrost well at room temperature, and they won't dry if in a plastic bag or covered with plastic.

Should you combine bell peppers and broccoli together in one plastic freezer bag?

No. Don't put two foods with unlike moisture contents together.

FOOD WRAPS

What are the goals of food wrapping materials?

1. Prevent the passage of moisture in or out.
2. Keep food fresh.
3. Keep food from emitting or absorbing foreign odors.
4. Keep food from drying out.
5. Keep food from becoming soggy or sticky.
6. Resist tears.
7. Keep the food from air (oxygen) contact.

Why wrap foods in lettuce leaves, corn husks or other coverings when moist-cooking?

Unlike dry heat, which seals the surface of the food, moist heat does not create a seal, and therefore a certain amount of flavor is transferred into the cooking liquid. To minimize this loss is the reason for sealing.

Why is aluminum foil a good wrap?

1. It molds tightly around the product.
2. It acts well as a tent, e.g., for a turkey.
3. It is a good barrier to moisture and odors.

What are its disadvantages?

1. It punctures easily, but the thicker the foil, the more resistant.
2. The thicker the foil, the more expensive.

How is parchment paper used?

1. To line baking pans and sheets to prevent sticking.
2. To make for easy removal.
3. For cooking en papillote.

Why is parchment paper better than waxed paper in lining a baking pan?

Pro: 1. It is paraffinned on both sides and is moisture proof and grease proof.
      2. Stays even when wet.
      3. Is good for candy, greasy foods.

Con: It is expensive.

Why is plastic wrap good?

1. It is easy to use since it clings to itself, the food or containers.
2. You can see what has been wrapped.
3. The best ones resist odors as well as foil does.

What are its negatives?

1. Some brands don't cling well to plastic or stainless steel.
2. When used in a microwave it must be above the food to keep the moisture in, especially with fatty or sugary foods.
3. In high temperatures some brands will melt.

Why use freezer paper?

1. It is strong.
2. It comes in very wide sheets.
3. It is resistant to moisture, more than plastic or foil.
4. It is easy to label, simply by writing on it.

What are its minuses?

1. Odor protection is only average.
2. It won't stay folded against itself and therefore has to be taped, for it works well only when tightly closed.

How is rice paper made?

Rice flour, water and salt are rolled paper thin and dried.

What is a way of using rice paper ?

Wrapped around fish fillets and pan fried until crisp will yield a moist, steam filled fish.

How else can it be used?

1. Wrapping cold foods.
2. Steaming, sautéing, deep frying and in spring rolls.

Are plastic containers good for freezing?

Yes, because:

1. They provide good protection from moisture and odors.
2. Some can be heated in the microwave.
3. They are reusable.

What are their drawbacks?

1. They can retain odors from previously stored food.
2. They are often difficult to clean.
3. Food stored in them can suffer freezer burn or become rancid if the air space is too large.
4. Many are not microwave safe, and can discolor, bubble, or melt with the heat of the food.

How should plastic storage bags be used?

1. Put food into bags and then into the refrigerator or freezer as promptly as possible.
2. Store vegetables unwashed and uncut if possible; if washed, drain thoroughly before bagging.
3. Fill the bags at least half full; if necessary, use a smaller size of bag to achieve this.

When should aluminum foil not be used?

1. Do not store high-acid foods, such as orange sections or leftover veal, under aluminum foil. Acid reacts chemically with the metal, giving food an off-flavor. If you have used it and the foil has a white discoloration, damage to the veal has already occurred.

2. Placing foil tightly over a roasting turkey or chicken helps keep the meat from drying out in the oven but can also make the meat mushy, because it will cause steaming, not roasting. To prevent the bird from drying out, baste it more frequently. Foil on a turkey breast for a short period to prevent overbrowning is fine, though.

3. Never put aluminum in the microwave.

How can plastic wrap be prevented from sticking to itself?

Store it in the refrigerator.

What are edible wraps?

Materials that enclose other foods and become part of the dish, such as phyllo, puff pastry, tortillas, rice paper, bread dough, crepes, pasta sheets, lasagne noodles, and won ton wrappers.

What can be used for wrapping corn (as for tamales)?

Best are corn husks, either dried or green. Banana leaves will work but will give a somewhat grassy flavor.

What should be done to store food in edible wraps?

When refrigerated or frozen, they often need to be protected with plastic or foil wrap.

LABELS AND DEFINITIONS

Are nutritional declarations on the labels of commercial products accurate?

Only the national brand labels were found to be consistently accurate, not the locally distributed ones or even regionally distributed ones, according to the St. Luke–Roosevelt Hospital Obesity Research Center in New York.

What leeway is allowed in label declarations?

The Food and Drug Administration allows a variation of 20% in an "accurate" label, to allow for the natural variation in foods.

What do the terms "diet" and "dietetic" mean on a label?

They *may* be lower in calories, carbohydrates, fats, sodium or sugar. Read the label to determine what has changed, including what may have been added as compensation.

What do the following terms mean?

Low Fat:	Dairy products with this classification may contain between 0.45% and 2% fat by weight.
Extra Lean:	Usually pertains to meat or poultry, which must contain no more than 5% fat by weight to qualify.
Lean:	Usually refers to meat or poultry, which must contain no more than 10% fat by weight.

Leaner:	Usually refers to meat or poultry, which must contain at least 2.5% less fat than a standard cut.
Sugar-Free:	A food that contains no refined sugar (sucrose) but may contain honey, corn syrup, sorbitol, or fructose, which are simply other forms of sugar and equally high in calories.
Fat-Free:	A food may have up to 0.49 grams of fat per serving and still be called "fat-free."

What is the difference between "expiration date" and "pull date" or "sell-by date"?

Expiration:	The last date that the food should be consumed.
Pull or sell-by:	The last date the food should be on the store shelf.

What does the letter "K" on packaged foods mean?

It stands for "kosher," indicating that the food was produced under the supervision of a rabbi. However, in most states the "K" logo is not protected by law, so there is no guarantee that the product's preparation really was supervised.

What about the letters "KD"?

They stand for "kosher dairy product."

Is there a better indication that a product is kosher?

The letter "U" in a circle indicates that the food has been certified kosher by the Union of Orthodox Jewish Congregations, under supervision of an individual rabbi or a regional certifying agent.

What does the word "pareve" on a kosher product indicate?

The food can be used with either meat or dairy products.

What is meant by the term "organic"?

"Organic" foods are those grown without toxic pesticides, fertilizers, herbicides or growth regulators. In 1990, the Organic Foods Production Act required certified "organic" producers to get third-party verification of their growing methods, to include inspection, soil and water testing, and strict record keeping. Certification is to be repeated on a regular basis. The land must be free of all synthetic material for a period of at least 3 years prior to certification, during which time it is inspected annually. In May 1998, the U.S. Department of Agriculture added additional restrictions: Organic plants could not be genetically engineered or irradiated.

What is meant by the claim that a product is "transitional"?

After one year of compliance with organic standards, a food in the process of certification may be sold as "transitional."

What is "FIFO"?

It stands for "first in, first out." This is the procedure that should be followed in home larders to prevent spoilage or deterioration of quality for all food products, fresh, canned or dried: use the older products first.

INDEX

curdling, 99–100; Hollandaise sauce, 406; mayonnaise, 404; pineapple and, 166; soup, 415; soy milk, 496

currants, 153; soaking, 9

curry, 365–66

curry powder, 335, 365–66

custard, 42–44, 132–33; frozen, 103; in pie, 56; vanilla in, 381

cutlets: chicken, 285–86; pounding, 249

cutting boards, 509; for beets, 439; for garlic, 463; safety information, 281

dabs, 328

daikon, 456

dairy products, 83–113

dandelion greens, 456

dates, 153

daube, 239

deep fryer, 538

deep frying, 235–36

deer, 270–71

deglazing, 227; roasts, 243; wine and, 384

demerara sugar, 345

demi-glaze, 411–12

deveining, shrimp, 311

deviled eggs, 123

Devonshire cream, 98

diet, definition of, 542

Dijon mustard, 369

dill, 348–49, 353

dill seed, 359

dill weed, 346

dirty rice, 201

dishes: glass, 516; for microwave, 518

diver scallops, 303

docking, 7

dolphin-safe tuna, 331

donuts, 44

double frying, 485

dough, 3; cleaning up, 24; over-kneading, 14, 24; over-mixing, 10; pasta, 216; rising, 10, 19, 28

dough relaxer, 28

Dover sole, 328

drawn butter, 85–86

dressing, 276–77; salad, 469. See also stuffing

dried beans, 186–90

dried fruits: in batter, 9; in bread dough, 26; storage of, 143

dried herbs, 334; rosemary, 356; storage of, 347

dried mushrooms, 471, 474

dried shrimp, 313

dried tomatoes: oven, 504; sun, 217, 504

dried vegetables, 425

drop biscuits, 20

dry ingredients, measurement of, 2

dry rub, 234

duck, 275, 277, 287–90

dumplings, 22

Dungeness crabs, 304–5

Dutch cocoa, 67

duxelle, 420

Earl Grey tea, 77

edible wraps, 542

egg(s), 115–40; in angel food cake, 37; Benedict, 124; cooking, 121–40; in custard, 43; deviled, 123; fried, 127; functions of, 115–16; halving, 2; hard-cooked, 122–23; measurement of, 1–2, 120; nutrition and health safety, 116–18; omelettes, 124–27; in pie meringue, 57; poached, 123–24; sauces, 402–6; scrambled, 124–25; selection of, 118–20; separation of, 7, 117; soft-cooked, 123–24; storage of, 120–21; temperature of, 8

eggnog, 116

egg pasta, 213

eggplant, 457–59; caviar, 459

egg roll wrappers, 221

egg wash, 28, 116; for pastry, 49

egg whites: beating, 127–32; in omelettes, 124; in sauce, 413; in soufflé, 136–37; stages of, 129; uses of, 120; whisk for, 510

egg yolks: and beating egg whites, 128–29; in bread dough, 26; in ice cream, 107; in mayonnaise, 404; in sauce, 403; uses of, 120

electric cookers, 538

electric stoves and ovens, 511–12; with pressure cooker, 537; stir-frying on, 238

Emmenthaler cheese, 92

emulsified sauce, 403–4

enamel cookware, 535–36

endive, 459–60

English Breakfast tea, 77

English cucumbers, 455

English mustard, 369
enokis, 472
en papillote, 6, 234; fish, 323–25
entrails, 226, 256–59
escarole, 468–69
espresso, 73–74
essence, 394
European oysters, 302
evaporated milk, 110–11
expiration date, 543
extra lean, definition of, 543

fallow deer, 270
farina, 184–85, 195
farmer cheese, 91
fat(s), 386–91; in avocado, 436; for barding, 233; for browning, 247; in cake, 34; in chicken, 280–81; in corn, 192; in fish, 313; functions of, 3, 389; in ground beef, 253; in lamb, 261; in meat, 223; in nuts, 173; versus oils, 386; in omelettes, 125; in pastry, 47–48; in pie, 52; in poultry, 275; and sauce, 412; in tuna, 331; in veal, 259; in venison, 271
fat free, definition of, 543
fell, 226, 262
fennel, 346, 460–61
fennel seed, 359
feta cheese, 95
fiber, in bread, 22
field peas, 211
FIFO, 539, 544
figs, 153–54
filberts, 177–78
filé, 184, 334
fillets, fish, 315, 322, 326
finnan haddie, 313
fire extinguisher, 387
firm cheeses, 92
first in, first out, 539, 544
fish, 313–31; ginger and, 368; grilling, 235; herbs for, 349; marinades for, 336; for soup, 414; velveting, 274–75
fish stock, 397
five spice powder, 334
flambé, 386; crepes, 135
flan, 44, 99, 134
flank steak, 250
flat-ground blade, 525

flat leaf parsley. *See* cilantro
flatus, 186, 445
flavored butters, 87–88
Florida avocado, 435
flounder, 313, 328
flour(s), 12–17; bleached versus unbleached, 17; measurement of, 16; in pastry, 47; and potatoes, 488; in puff pastry, 57; for sauces, 400, 408, 411; in sourdough starter, 27; for stew meat, 241
flowers, edible, 423; zucchini, 506
focaccia, 29
foie gras, 276
folding, 129–30
Fontina, 92–93
food processor, 508
food wraps, 539–42
fool, 142–43
forcemeat, 225
forged blade, 523
frangipane, 8
free-range poultry, 279–80
freezer paper, 541
freezing, 538–39; bacon, 267; breads, 30–31; cakes, 34; cheese, 96; chicken broth, 287; coffee beans, 73; cranberries, 152; eggs, 121; ginger, 367; grapes, 155; herbs, 347; meat, 224; meats, 228; mushrooms, 473; pancakes, 47; parsley, 356; pork, 263; pretzels, 60; pumpkins, 493; scallops, 303; seasonings and, 334; stock, 397; tomatoes, 502; vegetables, 421–22; whipped cream, 102
French cheeses, 89
French endive, 459–60
french fries, 485–88
French ice cream, 103
French knife, 526
French meringue, 131
French onion soup, 478
French roast, 74
French rolling pin, 511
fresh cheese, 91
fricassee, 277
fried eggs, 127
frittata, 126–27
frosting, chocolate, 70
frozen desserts, 103–8
frozen yogurt, 104, 112

hand-whipping, 7
hanger steak, 251
hard cheese, 92
hard-cooked eggs, 122–23
hard wheat, 14
hash, 256
Hass avocado, 435
hazelnuts, 177–78; oil, 388
head cheese, 94
heart, 256, 258
heart disease: eggs and, 116; shellfish and, 295
heavy cream, 98; versus whipped cream, 102
herb(s), 345–58
herbal tea, 77–78
herbed butter, 87, 348
herbed vinaigrette, 348
herbes de Provence, 347
high altitude cookery, 19, 515–16
hoisin sauce, 379, 401
Hollandaise sauce, 399, 404–6
hollow-ground blade, 526
hominy, 194
homogenized milk, 109–10
honey, 340–41; in biscuits, 21; in bread dough, 26
honeydew melons, 156
hoods, 513–14
hoppin' John, 416
horseradish, 359, 368
hot dogs, safety information, 227
hot house lamb, 261
hot spots, 528–29
hubbard squash, 498
hummus, 195
hydroponic farming, 423

iceberg lettuce, 468
ice-box cookies, 41
ice cream, 103, 105–6; almond, 175; for topping pie, 55
ice cream cakes, 36
ice cubes, large, 507
iced coffee, 77
iced tea, 79
icing sugar, 344
Indian saffron. See turmeric
instant foods: coffee, 75; polenta, 193; rice, 204; yeast, 17–18
instant quick frozen (IQF) fish, 296

iron, 423, 466
Israeli couscous, 194
Italian eggplant, 457
Italian meringue, 57, 131
Italian red onions, 476
Italian roast, 74

Jalapeno chili peppers, 363
Jamaica pepper. See allspice
Japanese soy sauce, 378
Japonica rice, 200
Jasmine rice, 200
Jasmine tea, 77
jerky, 226
Jerusalem artichokes, 464–65
jicama, 465
Jinenjo soba noodles, 220
juicing: lemons, 157–58; onions, 477
juniper, 359

Kalamata olives, 375
kale, 465–66, 491
kasha, 190
kidney, 256–58
kilkenny, 491
king crabs, 304
kippers, 314
kiwis, 156
knives, 520–28; ceramic, 527–28
Kobe beef, 229
kohlrabi, 466
kosher foods: chicken, 279; labeling, 543; meat, 229, 248; poultry, 273
kosher salt, 376
kumquats, 141, 156

labels, 542–44
lamb, 260–63; chops, 260–62; cuts for stew, 241; herbs for, 349; microwaving, 519
lard, 4; leaf, 264; in pie crust, 52–53
larding, 233
lasagne, 218
latte, milk for, 112
lattice top, for pie, 56
leaf lard, 264
lean, definition of, 543
lean dough, 3
leaner, definition of, 543
leavener, 6

potatoes, 490; scalding, 23–24, 109; and soup, 415; in soup, 416; unpasteurized, 43, 89

milk chocolate, 66; chopping, 70

milk fat, 108

milk-fed lamb, 261

milk products: in bread dough, 26; in pastry, 48

millet, 197; in pilaf, 203

mincemeat, 226

mincing, meat versus vegetables, 227

Minestrone, 416

mint, 346, 348, 354–55

mint jelly, 355

mirepoix, 394, 396, 401

mirin, 385

miso, 209–10, 375–76

Mission olives, 375

mixing, cake, 32

mocha, 70

mock turtle soup, 417

molasses, 342–43; in biscuits, 21; in gingerbread, 40

mold(s): on bread, 31; on cheese, 96; gelatin, 408

mole, 70

Monterey Jack cheese, 93

morels, 472

Mousseline sauce, 405

muffins, 45–46

mugwort soba noodles, 220

mung bean sticks, 221

Muscovy duck, 287

mushrooms, 470–74; for pizza, 59

muskmelons, 143

mussels, 299–301

mustard, 359, 369–70

mustard powder, 370

mustard seeds, 369–70

mutton, 261

Naam Pla, 334

Napa cabbage, 444

natto, 209

nectarines, 160

net, 223

New England clam chowder, 415–16

New Mexico chili peppers, 363

new potatoes, 483

New York steak, 251

New Zealand lamb, 261

Niçoise olives, 375

nicotine, in vegetables, 422–23

non-alkalized cocoa, 65

nonfat dry milk, 111; in ice cream, 106

nonreactive pots, 530, 534–35

nonstick cookware, 534–35

noodles, 216, 220–21; in stir-fry, 239

noodle squash, 499

Nuoc Nam, 334

nut(s), 172–81; in batter, 9; on cake, 36

nutmeg, 349, 359, 370

nut oils, 388

nutrition information: for fish, 315; potatoes, 482–83; vegetables, 420–24

oatmeal: in bread, 25; cookies, 41

oats, 198

octopus, 298–99

offal, 252

oil(s), 386–91; almond, 388; anchovy, 327; in bread, 23; of cinnamon, 364; in cookies, 40; for deep frying, 235, 486–87; and eggplant, 458; versus fats, 386; garlic in, 462; ginger, 367–68; measurement of, 3; olive, 50, 238, 388, 390–91, 487; for pasta cooking, 217; peanut, 179; in peanut butter, 179; and rice, 205; sesame, 374, 388; soy, 210, 388; for stir-frying, 238; vegetable, 4–5

okra, 474–75

olive oil, 238, 390–91; extra virgin, 388, 391; with phyllo dough, 50; and potatoes, 487; virgin, 390

olives, 376

Olympia oysters, 302

omelettes, 124–27; soufflé, 140

onion(s), 475–78; and garlic, 478; green, 495; juice, 477; in mirepoix, 401; rings, 476; sweet, 476

oolong, 77

opal basil, 350

orange(s), 142, 160–62; juice, 161

Orange Pekoe tea, 77

oregano, 346–47, 354–55

organic, definition of, 422, 543

organ meats, 226, 256–59

oso onions, 476

rinds: cheese, 96, 415; of ham, 269
ripened cheese, 90
rising: dough, 10, 19; in overn, 28
risotto, 206–7
river fish, 316
roaster, 279
roasting, 242–46; asparagus, 434; beets, 439;
    chicken, 283–85; coffee, 74; duck,
    288–89; fish, 318; garlic, 463; goose,
    290–91; meatloaf, 255; nuts, 173; pan
    for, 530; potatoes, 488; pot roasting,
    246–47; poultry, 274–75; pumpkins,
    492; and soup, 415; turkey, 291;
    vegetables, 428–30
Robusta coffee beans, 72
Rock Cornish game hens, 278
rock salt, 376
roe, lobster, 307
rolling pins, 511
rolls, 21; glaze for, 10
romaine, 468
root starches, 407
rosemary, 346, 356–57
roux, 399–400, 407
rumbledethump, 491
russet potatoes, 486
rutabaga, 494
rye, 208–9
rye bread, 25
rye flour, 15

saccharin, 344
safety information: for chicken, 281–82; chili
    peppers, 363; for deep-frying potatoes,
    486; for eggs, 116–18; fire
    extinguishers, 387; for knives, 521; for
    meats, 227–29; for microwave cookery,
    518; for poultry, 273; for steak tartare,
    253; for stuffing, 276
safflower oil, 387
saffron, 333, 373; Indian. *See* turmeric
sage, 346, 349, 357
saki, 200
salad: broccoli, 441–42; cabbage, 445;
    chicken/turkey, 275; cucumber, 455–56;
    dandelion greens, 456; fennel, 461;
    jicama, 465; lettuce, 468; pasta, 219;
    potato, 491–92, 496; spinach, 497; sweet
    potato, 501; tomatoes, 503

salmon, 316, 323, 328–29
salmonella contamination, in eggs, 116–17
salsa, 401–2
salsify, 494–95
salt, 376–78; and asparagus, 433; in baking, 8;
    in bread dough, 26; and cauliflower,
    449; and chicken, 283; correcting for,
    377, 414, 420; and dried beans, 188–89;
    and eggplant, 458–59; functions of, 5; in
    ice cream, 105; in lite soy sauce, 378; in
    mayonnaise, 405; in pastry, 48–49; for
    pickling, 481; and rice, 205; and
    roasting, 246; and sauce, 412; sesame,
    374; for steak, 250
salted butter, 83, 87
Salzburger nockerl, 140
sand dabs, 328
sandwiches, 22; grilled cheese, in bulk, 98
sardines, 316
satsuma, 142
sauce(s), 398–402; Asian fish, 295, 334;
    barbecue, 286; for broccoli, 441; for
    duck, 287; egg, 402–6; functions of,
    398; good-tempered, 401; for pasta, 216,
    218, 390; preparation of, 409–13; in
    stew, 241–42
sauerkraut, 445
sausage: lamb, 263; pork, 265–66
sautéing, 234, 236–37; brains, 259; chicken,
    286; fish, 325–26; garlic, 464; lemon
    grass, 353; millet, 197; mushrooms, 474;
    pan for, 530; potatoes, 485–88; sauce,
    398; shallots, 496; shellfish, 297
savory, 346
Savoy cabbage, 444
scalding, 23–24, 109; and egg sauces, 402;
    vegetables, 428
scale, 2
scaling, fish, 318–19
scallions, 495
scalloped potatoes, 488
scallops, 303–4
Scandinavian rolling pin, 511
scones, 21
Scotch barley, 185
scrambled eggs, 124–25
scrod, 313
seafood, 295–331
searing: fish, 325–26; meat, 233; steak, 250–51

Index

stable foams, 129

stainless steel: cookware, 536; knives, 523, 525

stamped knife, 523

star anise, 374

starch, 406–7; in potatoes, 483–84

steak, 249–52; cubed, 226; fish, 321; swordfish, 330; tuna, 331

steak tartare, 253

steam, in baking bread, 29

steamed rice, 205

steaming: asparagus, 434; beets, 439; broccoli, 442; brussels sprouts, 443; corn, 453; crabs, 305; fish, 326–27; lobster, 308; seafood, 296–97; spinach, 496

stew, multiplying recipes for, 227

stewers, 279

stewing, 241–42; chicken, 280

stick noodles, 220–21

sticky rice, 200, 206

stiff peak, definition of, 129

stir-frying, 237239; eggplant, 459; vegetables, 420; velveted foods, 275

stock, 393–97; brown, 393–94; chicken, 286–87, 394, 396; clarifying, 397; definition of, 393; fish, 397; lemon grass in, 353; vegetable, 430; white, 393

stone crabs, 304

stone-ground flour, 14

stoneware, 536–37

storage: apples, 147; artichokes, 431; bacon, 266; bivalves, 299; breads, 30–31; brown sugar, 345; butter, 84, 87; cakes, 36; carrots, 447; celery, 450; cheeses, 95–97; chestnut powder, 505; chicken, 281; chili peppers, 362; chocolate, 69; coffee beans, 73; cooked legumes, 185; cookies, 41–42; corn, 455; crabs, 304; crème fraiche, 99; cucumbers, 455; dried herbs, 347; duck, 288; eggplant, 457–58; eggs, 120–21; flours, 16–17; fruits, 143; garlic, 462; grapes, 155; herbs, 347–48; honey, 341; ice cream, 106–7; jicama, 465; knives, 526; mushrooms, 473; mussels, 301; nuts, 173; oils, 389; okra, 475; pies, 56; poppy seeds, 372; potatoes, 484–85; poultry, 274; rice, 201; saffron, 373; salad greens, 469; spices, 359; stock, 397; sweet onions, 476; sweet potatoes, 500;

tea, 78; tomatoes, 502–3; turkey, 291; vegetables, 424–25; vinegar, 383; whipped cream, 102–3; white chocolate, 72; wine and beer, 383–84; yeast, 18. *See also* freezing

stoves, 511–16

strainers, 510–11

straining, sauces, 410

strawberries, 170–71

string beans, 437

strip steak, 251

stuffed pasta, 216, 218–19

stuffing: artichokes, 432; bell peppers, 440; cabbage leaves, 445; chicken, 283; for Cornish hens, 278; duck, 288; fish, 324–25; goose, 291; lamb, 262; mushroom caps, 474; olives, 375; onions, 478; poultry, 275–77; salmon, 329; turkey, 291; vegetables, 430

substitutions, 8; barley, 185; bread crumbs, 255; buttermilk, 88; butter types, 87; cocoa/chocolate, 65, 69; coconut, 41; cornstarch, 406; cream, 100; eggs, 116, 131; fats, 386–87; lids, 529; pastry bag, 8, 508; postum, 75; ricotta cheese, 94; rolling pin, 511; salt, 348–49; sour cream, 100; sugar, 344; sun-dried tomatoes, 217; whipped cream, 103; yogurt, 112; zester, 508

succotash, 454

sucrose, 343

sugar, 343–45; in angel food cake, 36; in biscuits, 21; in bread, 25; burnt, 337–39; cinnamon, 364; in egg whites, 130; functions of, 6; and gluten formation, 13; greasing, 338; in ice cream, 106; measurement of, 1; and salmon, 328; vanilla, 381; for whipped cream, 102; and yeast dough, 19, 24

sugar free, definition of, 543

sugar (snap) peas, 480

sugar syrup, for fruits, 146

sulfured molasses, 342

summer coating, 71

summer fat, 86

summer squash, 498

sunchokes, 464–65

sun-dried tomatoes, 217, 504

sushi, 318, 331

sweating, vegetables, 427
swedes, 494
Swedish turnips, 494
sweetbreads, 256–57
sweet imperial onions, 476
sweet onions, 476
sweet pizza, 59
sweet potatoes, 499–501
sweets, 337–45
Swiss chard, 450–51
swordfish, 323, 326, 329–30
syrup(s): boiling, 344–45; corn, 339–40; ginger
    in, 368; liquid sugar, 343; maple,
    341–42; pancake, 341; sugar, 146

Tabasco sauce, 364
tahini, 374, 411
Tak Tray, 334
tamari, 210, 378
tamarind, as marinade, 336
tang, of knife, 523
tangeloes, 142, 171
tangerines, 142, 171–72
tapenade, 402
tapered blade, 525
tapioca, 184, 407
tarragon, 346, 357
tarts, 58–59
tea, 77–79; bags, 78–79; caddy, 78; caffeine in,
    81; pots, 78–79
Teflon, 535
Teleme cheese, 93
tempeh, 211
temperature, 2; for baking, 8; for creaming, 7;
    of custard, 42; for deer, 271; and flavor,
    333; for french fries, 486; and glass,
    535; for hamburgers, 253; of
    ingredients, 7–8; for lamb, 262; of meat,
    228; pans and, 516; for pork, 263; for
    puff pastry, 57; for quiche, 58; for
    roasting, 243; of steak, 249; for stuffing,
    277; and thickening, 406
tempering, chocolate, 68–69
tenderizing: chicken, 283; meat, 230–32
terrine, 225
Texas onions, 476
thawing, 539; breads, 30; cheese, 96; chicken,
    281–82; fish, 313, 319; goose, 290; meat,
    228; shrimp, 312–13; vegetable stock, 430

theobromine, 62–63
thermometers, 507
thermos, 507
thickeners, 241–42, 335, 406–10, 412; for egg
    sauces, 402–3; for soup, 416–17
thioglucoside, 423
3-2-1 dough, 53
thyme, 346, 357–59
timbales, 42
timers, 508; pop-up, 293
toasting: cornmeal, 193; sesame seeds, 374
tofu, 210–11, 380, 496
tomalley, 307
tomatillo, 501
tomato(es), 501–4; and beans, 187; and meat
    cooking, 233; and roasting, 243
tomato sauce, 401, 413, 503; garlic in, 464;
    uncooked, 400
tomato soup, 415
tongue, pickled, 257
toothpick test, 515
tortillas, 60, 184; corn, 193
transitional food products, 422, 543
transparent noodles, 221
tripe, 226, 257
triticale, 211
trout, brook, 319
trussing, chicken, 282
tryptophan, 111
tuna, 323, 326, 330–31
turbinado sugar, 345
turkey, 291–93
Turkish coffee, 75
turmeric, 349, 359, 374–75
turnip(s), 504–5; yellow (Swedish), 494
turnip cabbage, 466
turnip greens, 504–5
turntable, 517
tying, roast, 244

udon noodles, 220
ugli fruit, 142
univalves, 297
unleavened bread, 6
unpasteurized milk: in cheese, 89; in custard,
    43
unripened cheese, 90
utensils, 507–44
utility knife, 524

vacuum bottles, 507
Valencia rice, 203
vanilla, 333, 359, 380–81; in sauce, 413
vanilla sugar, 381
variety meats, 226, 256–59
veal, 259–60; cuts for stew, 241; herbs for, 349; osso bucco, 248
vegetable(s), 419–506; color of, 426–27; en papillote, 324; marinades for, 336; with pork, 264; in soup, 414; stir-frying, 237, 239; stock, 430
vegetable cleaver, 526
vegetable oil, 4–5; for poultry, 274
vegetable shortening: for creaming, 7; in pie crust, 53
vegetable stock, 396
vegetarian diet, 423
velouté, 399
velveting, 274–75
venison, 270–71
verjus, 383
Vidalia onions, 476
vinaigrette, 383; herbed, 348
vinegar, 381–83; and fish, 314, 321; as marinade, 336; for pickling, 481
volume, measuring by, 1

Walla Walla onions, 476
walnut(s), 180–81; oil, 388–89
wasabi (wasabe), 375
water, 5; boiling, 224, 377, 429; in bread dough, 26; and coating chocolate, 67; for coffee, 73; and dried beans, 189; in grunt, 7; in ham, 268; in meat, 226; in sourdough starter, 27; for stock, 395; for tea, 78
water bath, for cheesecake, 38
water chestnuts, 181, 505
watercress, 505–6
water ice, 104
watermelons, 172
wax: on cucumbers, 455; on produce, 420–21
weather: and emulsified sauces, 404; and white chocolate, 71; and yeast doughs, 19
weight(s): in baking pie crust, 55; measuring by, 1–2
Welsh rabbit (rarebit), 98

wheat: cracked, 191; flour, 14, 407–8; tortillas, 60
wheat berries, 183, 211
whipped butter, 84
whipped cream, 101–3
whipping, 7
whipping cream, pasteurized versus unpasteurized, 102
whips, 510
whisks, 510
white asparagus, 434
white chocolate, 71–72
white eggplant, 458
white flour, 47. See also flour(s)
white pekin duck, 287
white pepper, 371
White Rock hens, 278
white sole, 328
white stock, 393
whole wheat flour, 15–16
wild duck, 288–89
wild pecan rice, 200
wild rice, 212
wilted vegetables, 425
wine, 383–86; with clams, 300; and fish, 325; with goat cheese, 89; in risotto, 207; in sauce, 413; in soup, 417; in stew, 242
winter nels pears, 164
winter radish, 456
wok, 237–38
wood, for smoking meat, 233
Worcester sauce, 401

yams, 499–501
yearling lamb, 260
yeast, 6, 17–19; active dry, 6
yellowfin tuna, 330
yellow tomatoes, 502
yellow turnips, 494
yogurt, 112–13; frozen, 104, 112; as marinade, 336
yogurt cheese, 113

zest: citrus, 142, 375; lemon, 158, 353–54; in salad, 469
zester, 508
zucchini, 506; and pasta, 220